Setting the Record Straight

COLIN SYMES

◆

Setting the Record Straight

A MATERIAL HISTORY OF
CLASSICAL RECORDING

◆

WESLEYAN UNIVERSITY PRESS
Middletown, Connecticut

Published by Wesleyan University Press, Middletown, CT 06459
© 2004 by Colin Symes
Printed in the United States of America
5 4 3 2 1

Library of Congress Cataloging-in-Publication Data

Symes, Colin, 1945–
Setting the record straight : a material history of classical recording / Colin Symes.
    p. cm. — (music/culture)
Includes bibliographical references and index.
ISBN 0–8195–6721–3 (cloth : alk. paper)
    1. Sound recordings—History. 2. Sound—Recording and reproducing—History.
I. Title.
ML3790.S97 2004
781.49'09—dc22   2004017354

The author would like to thank the following for permission to reproduce
copyright material:

Windels Marx Lane & Mittendorf, the executors of Igor Stravinsky's estate, for the quotation
    from Igor Stravinsky's *Chronicle of My Life* (1936).
Surhkamp-Verlag and Dudley Steynor, the executor of Basil Creighton's estate, for quotation
    from Hermann Hesse's *Steppenwolf* (1965).
James Jolly and Haymarket Publications for quotation from Alec Robertson's "Editorial" in
    The Gramophone (1956).
Cambridge University Press for quotation from Gerald Genette's *Paratexts* (1997).
    Permission obtained by Cambridge University Press.
Bill Hamilton as the Literary Executor of the Estate of the Late Sonia Brownell Orwell,
    Martin Secker & Warburg Ltd. for George Orwell's "Boys' Weeklies" in *Inside the Whale
    and Other Essays* (Copyright © George Orwell 1933 and Harcourt Brace Jovanovich).
Extract from "Unpacking My Library" in *Illuminations* by Walter Benjamin published by
    Pimlico. Used by permission of The Random House Group Limited. Copyright © 1955
    by Suhrkamp Verlag, Frankfurt a.M., English translation by Harry Zohn copyright ©
    1968 and renewed 1996 by Harcourt, Inc., reprinted by permission of Harcourt, Inc.
"What Will Become of the Phonograph" reproduced by permission of *The Spectator*.

FOR CLAIRE O'CONOR

The other source of music in my life

Contents

◆

Figures and Tables

◆

Figures

Tables

Preface

Books demand much of their authors and those that endure the authors' company. This one is no exception. It is a fruit of long hours of labor that has required manifold sacrifices on the part of those closest and dearest to me, at home and at work, who have been polite and patient enough to endure convoluted explanations about this book and the state of its progress. I would take this opportunity to thank them for their patience and forbearance.

My biggest thank you, though, must to go to the libraries, from the very large to the very small, that have played an invaluable role in the preparation of this book. It would be meanspirited of me not to acknowledge that without their collections and the assistance of the librarians who manage them, this book could not have been contemplated, let alone undertaken and completed. In scrolling and thumbing (some still have card indexes) through their catalogues, I have made many unexpected discoveries, often by serendipity, that invaluable friend of scholars, such as accidentally flipping a page to reveal a textual jewel that a more methodical, electronically assisted, search had failed to uncover.

My own local library, the Rockdale Municipal—in one of Sydney's more-out-of-the-way suburbs—has a special music collection that includes a treasure trove of gramophone literature. It has been the site of many fortuitous finds. Equally helpful were the State Library of New South Wales, which by dint of its position as an outpost of the British Empire acquired much early "literature" on the gramophone, and ScreenSound—Australia's media archive—located in Canberra. I would like to thank the librarians of these institutions. I would also like to thank the librarians at the various academic institutions with whom I have been associated over the years and who have satisfied my numerous requests for interlibrary loans, including the librarians at the Queensland University of Technology (QUT), the University of

Technology, Sydney (UTS), and Macquarie University, also in Sydney. I would also like to thank the librarians at the British Library, who granted me access to the materials held in the British Sound Archive. I would like to thank UTS, which helped partially fund a visit to the United Kingdom to conduct research at the British Library.

Another thank you must go to those record dealers in various parts of the world, including London, Paris, Florence, and Singapore, but particularly in Brisbane, Canberra, and Sydney, who have paid host to my phonographic "field work" and tolerated my note taking in their busy shops with stoic good humor.

On a more personal note, I would like to thank my current Head of School at Macquarie University, Pamela Coutts, who was kind enough to reduce my teaching load, and those colleagues of mine who endured the effects of this reduction, particularly my immediate colleagues Deborah Youdell, now at the University of Cambridge, and David Saltmarsh. I would also like to acknowledge the patience and indulgence of many colleagues, particularly at UTS, who were kind enough to hear me out when I spoke about this book's contents, and those at QUT who read early drafts of its chapters.

I would also like to acknowledge my "family" who bore the brunt of my "setting the record straight"; to Claire, the book's dedicatee, in particular, for encouraging me to persevere when an unanticipated change in academic positions seemed to put the book out of my reach, for providing me with the loving environment that spurred its writing, and for generally helping me to get the book to its finished state; and to Alexis and Tom, for tolerating a new member of their family and his raucous music with an amiable indifference. I would like to extend an apology to my mother, Edna Margaret Symes, who on a flying visit to Sydney in the days leading up to the book's completion could not be given the generous hospitality that her visits ordinarily evince.

I would also like to acknowledge the assistance of my friend Tony Deguara, who applied his considerable graphic and computer skills to preparing the illustrations and helping to turn seemingly recalcitrant images into ones that now look better than they did in their original state. I would like to thank the record labels and publishers who assisted me in obtaining permission to reproduce these illustrations.

I would also like to thank the readers of the initial version of *Setting the Record Straight* for their helpful comments and important suggestions as to how some of my arguments might be better framed and made clearer to my potential readers. Finally, I thank all of those at Wesleyan University Press who have been involved in seeing this project through, particularly to Leonora Gibson, Jessica Stevens, and Nils Nadeau, whose editing eliminated much "blithe redundancy," resulting in a much "happier" text.

I would also like to thank my prospective readers and apologize for any scholarly inadequacies in advance. The record culture, I have discovered, is an endlessly complex one whose richness this book can only appreciate in a very modest and superficial way. I hope that my example will inspire others to explore the world that I have only begun to analyze.

Finally, might I crave from my readers one more indulgence; as befits a book that deals with parerga as they pertain to recorded music I would point out that that some of the "action" of this book takes place in its own "parerga," its endnotes. In addition to accommodating further references and more "exemplary" aspects of the "thick description" that is the phonographic culture, the notes also hold another narrative, one that forms a counterpoint to the main contents of the book. Much of the content of this counterpoint is speculative and provides a further round of ideas and reflections impossible to hold within the book's linear argument. I hope that my readers will be patient with this counterpoint and accept it for what it is: an acknowledgment of the fact that there are many more sides to the record than those few about which I have written.

Setting the Record Straight

CHAPTER ONE

Playing by the Book
Toward a Textual Theory of the Phonograph

In Books lies the *soul* of the whole of Past Time; the articulate audible voice of the
Past when the body and material substance of it has altogether vanished like a dream.
—Thomas Carlyle, *Hero as Man of Letters,* 7

By the end of the nineteenth century two revolutions, one in light, the other
in sound, had occurred that transformed the entire nature of art and culture.
Their legacy lives on, albeit in considerably more complex forms of technology, and continues with each new dramatic development to infect every
niche of modern life, improving the medium of access to myriad cultural
forms. It is hard not to be overwhelmed by the significance of technology
that can conserve critical aspects of experience and transport them across
generations of time and to every part of the planet with ease and alacrity. The
facsimile culture that this technology helped generate, which began with the
camera and was followed by the phonograph, is significant on a number of
counts: first, it enabled the most ephemeral parts of experience to be preserved; second, it allowed them to be replicated almost without end; and
third, it enabled a range of cultural forms—and recordings of classical music
are cases in point[1]—to be privatized and embodied. Moreover, as the technology involved has undergone progressive refinements, it has led to forms
of reproduction whose verisimilitude competes favorably with, and in some
instances surpasses, that of the original. This has provoked a range of questions to do with the nature of original art in relation to its various forms of
reproduction, and with exactly what qualities of the original works of art, if
any, transcend reproduction (Banfield 1984; Benjamin 1970a; Genette 1999;
Gracyk 1997; Mattick 1993; Rössing 1984; Struthers 1987). In spite of these
questions, the existence of mechanically and digitally reproduced forms of
art has nevertheless added to the envelope of ordinary experience, providing

opportunities to access the most "sacred" forms of culture without the need for their immediate proximity. The new technologies of communication and reproduction, among which the phonograph is one of the most significant, have played an important role in decentering culture, rendering its core elements accessible from a distance and enabling the periphery to act, as never before, on the artistic center.

More broadly, though, phonographic culture has contributed to the gradual electrification of society and, as national grids were established in the 1920s, has benefited from that electrification. Indeed, it is sometimes hard to separate the evolution of the phonograph from developments occurring in cognate areas of technology, such as semiconductors and plastics, that the phonograph then appropriated, just as it appropriated other cultural technologies, such as printing. Too often, examinations focusing on the electrical conditioning of contemporary society have concentrated on its bells-and-whistles effects and have overlooked the way these effects have profoundly reordered and reshaped society, creating new types of social encounter and transforming access to fundamental cultural forms such as music (Marvin 1988; Thompson, J. 1995). Furthermore, very few analyses and histories of music (save those dealing with its popular varieties) consider the impact of the phonograph, and where they do, the discussion is mostly perfunctory. This reflects an ongoing legacy, one at the very heart of music, that has on the one hand disparaged mechanized music, and on the other has restricted the ambit of musical analysis to matters of composition and performance. This has resulted in a generalized eschewal of important sociological phenomena that relate to the material practice and political economy of music, and to the complex social networks that collectively make music possible (Attali 1985; Becker 1984; Chanan 1994; Zolberg 1990). The phonographic industry is one of these phenomena, and its significance in transforming the cultural conditions of classical music cannot be underestimated.

It is hard to imagine what the world was like prior to the advent of the phonograph and the dramatic impact that it had on those experiencing its sounds for the first time. Whenever and wherever the phonograph was demonstrated in public, it attracted, in spite of the "smudged" quality of its output, huge audiences that were hypnotized by its capacity to preserve and retrieve sounds that would have ordinarily "evaporated." Many listeners, including some very eminent ones, found its ability to transgress the laws of ordinary experience disarming.[2] From relatively primitive beginnings the phonograph has transformed the entire topography of sound and the conditions of listening (Hennion 2001; Morton 2000: 171; Schafer 1980: 89). It has also reshaped the dimensions of domestic space, adding walls of sound to home interiors. Notwithstanding these transformations, from which it is hard to escape, the cultural significance of the phonograph has generally been overshadowed by the more "sensational" forms of mass communication that followed in its wake, such as film and television (Eisenstein 1980: 11; Gronow 1983: 53; Kenney 1999: xii; LeMahieu 1988: 82). Questions about the impact of the phonograph on contemporary culture have not received the critical attention they deserve. Indeed, in studies of mass communication the phonograph hardly figures at all. The record of recording is "relatively thin" (Kahn 1999: 5), which is ironic; of all the various forms of mass media, recording is by far the most dominant in terms of its presence and profile. There is hardly an avenue of life that has not been the object of recording, or a place where recording devices have not been deployed (Morton 2000).

Yet it is the domain of music itself that has been most transformed by the advent of recording (Biocca 1988: 4). Although Edison was slow to appreciate the musical potential of the phonograph and was adamant that its future lay in the office, it was as a device for delivering music that the general public eventually adopted the phonograph. This was contrary to the desires of not only its inventor but also the musical elites, who feared that the phonograph threatened the aesthetic and moral conditions of music. Again, from the vantage point of the present, when there is hardly a musical tradition that is not represented on record, it is hard to imagine the nature of a culture where the main vehicles of musical dissemination were embodied ones, performers and musicians in specified environments such as concert halls.

Recording radically changed the "geography" and the "history" of music, liberating it from the here and now and utterly transforming its "tense," its spacing and timing. It enabled music to be heard in private, with its social scaffolding removed; a "Symphony of a Thousand" could be heard by one, and a nocturne could be heard in the morning (Eisenberg 1988: 24), all at the behest of the listener, who also had more discretion (unlike the radio listener) over that to which they listened. Moreover, as the repertoire of recorded music was extended, it became possible to hear music that was rarely (or never before) performed in public. For whatever else it has engendered in the way of cultural transformation, recording has increased the diversity and availability of music and created audiences for music that was (literally) unheard of before 1877 (Hamm 1975: 262). That was the year that Thomas Alva Edison's strip of tinfoil produced an echo, almost inaudible due to its scratchiness, of the words of the nursery rhyme "Mary Had a Little Lamb," a telling phrase, given that for a long time Edison's invention was regarded as more toy than musical instrument. But this most innocent of echoes has produced in the intervening one hundred and thirty years a culture in which music is as much on tap as water or electricity. In fact, recording's impact on the culture of music is analogous to the impact of printing on the written word. Edison is, in many respects, the Gutenberg of sound. But the analogy extends further, for the narrative structures of the modern book provided precursors for those of the record.

The Printing Press and the Development of the Narrative Architecture of the Book

It has been argued that the printing press irrevocably changed Western culture, transforming everything from the nature of epistemological enquiry to the ways individuals managed their quotidian lives (Eisenstein 1980; Febvre and Martin 1997; Luke 1989; Olson 1994; Ong 1982; Steinberg 1974). More importantly, it brought a new unity to the many facets of Renaissance humanism, which in the latter part of the fifteenth century was dispersed throughout Europe. It also led to the establishment of a new cultural industry centered on the print shop, which became a magnet of intellectual life, attracting and galvanizing the energies of scholars who helped oversee the production of their texts in conjunction with the artisans of print. The exigencies of book production helped to standardize orthography and grammatical practice across the major European languages. They also led to the adoption of more readable typographies such as Roman, that were easier to cast as movable type than the then-dominant font, Gothic. In general, then, the printing press led to dramatic improvements in the "flow of information" and the development of standardized forms of textual representation that could be replicated almost without end with levels of accuracy that had been unknown in the scribal era. In fact, the printing press created increased respect for the integrity of the text and led to techniques of editing which helped to eradicate linguistic "aberration." The printing press also acted as a vehicle for the dissemination of vernacular expression and helped to stimulate traditions of national literature, even leading to the revival of minority languages that challenged culturally more dominant ones. This occurred in the more polyglot regions of Europe such as the Balkans; though German remained the hegemonic language there, the advent of printing helped counter it and encouraged a renaissance of literary expression in ethnic languages (Steinberg 1974: 122).

These changes, of course, took centuries, and many arose from the contingencies of book manufacture and distribution. For several decades after Gutenberg's invention, the book continued to be influenced by the illuminated manuscript, which represented the model for its layout. The book's contemporary format took several generations to evolve. Such taken-for-granted features of the modern book as pagination and title pages are cases in point. The latter emerged because the book's first page, exposed and prone to soiling, was left blank. Much of the information relating to a book's provenance, now occupying the front cover, was consigned to its latter pages, to its "post-text" regions where indexes and appendices now appear. It was not until the middle of the sixteenth century that printers settled upon the practice of using the first page to locate this information, along with the book's title and author (Febvre and Martin 1997: 84).

At more or less the same time, and in response to the public demand that they be more portable, the dimensions of books were reduced. By the end of the sixteenth century, the demand for books and the need for mechanisms to monitor their circulation led to book catalogs and bibliographies—texts for accessing texts. Book fairs in the European centers of publishing also began to be held with increasing regularity, another sign that book consciousness was in its ascendancy. The fairs reflected the emergence of a cultural infrastructure dedicated to managing and administering the economy of the book and navigating its many manifestations. This new book consciousness also extended to the material realm and led to new methods of housing and storing books—to placing them on shelves, in an upright position, with their spines "outward bound" and in order (Petroski 1999: 125). These now commonplace bookish habits had to be invented and took time to develop before being assimilated by book users.

Most importantly, however, the invention of the printing press represented an archetypal form of mass production that saw the ascendancy of an aesthetic economy in which the phenomenon of repetition was the dominant principle. This meant that a philosophical treatise could be reproduced in the absence of its author almost without limits, and that the place of its composition and conceptualization were not necessarily the same as its site of replication and distribution (Olson 1994; Ong 1982). Moreover, the advent of the printed word led to the emergence of a "documentary reality" that has become one of the bedrocks of modern society, fundamental to its governance and regulation (Smith, D. 1999). Print has meant that the actions of individuals are increasingly mediated and negotiated through documents; everything from the acquisition of basic citizenship rights to complex cultural practices such as those associated with listening to music have been partly created and mobilized by documents of various types. In this respect, documents help to produce behaviors, granting authority and legitimacy to certain practices, while discouraging and repressing others.

Discs and Discourses:
Administering Phonograph Populations

Discourses are more than just "strings of words"; they are powerful engines of meaning underlying so-called "regimes of truth." French theorist Michel

Foucault was the architect of this sense of discourse, and he thought that they helped frame our views of culture and human beings, and our notions of right and wrong, truth and untruth, and normality and aberrancy. Discourses are the mental flows governing the various conducts of society, the bodies of knowledge that enable us to think about and engage with our important cultural practices (Foucault 1972; 1974). Although the principle conduit of discourses is language, they can also take a pictorial form. Images, such as Jeremy Bentham's panopticon, which conveys the idea of modern power and self-surveillance (Foucault 1979), are also important discourse vehicles.

From the outset, we need to recognize that discourses are part of the realities of which they speak and help to produce the populations associated with them. Changes surrounding sexual conduct exemplify this force of discourse. According to Foucault, scientific studies of sexuality in the nineteenth century brought many sexual practices out of the closet and categorized some as "pathological." Prior to the nineteenth century, they had remained undiagnosed, unseen parts of sexual repertoire; they were not regarded as egregious acts requiring treatment and intervention. Scientific discourses of sexuality brought these practices under control, made them objects of medical and psychological scrutiny, and in effect, constituent elements of "regimes of truth." This had the effect of pushing them beyond the bounds of normality and containing their practice there. But the act of discourse was also enabling: it provided the scope to generate counter-discourses, challenging the dominant regimes of sexual truth (Foucault 1980).

Discourse, in this respect, helped to create a language for speaking and thinking about the phonograph that drew on existing cultural vocabularies and ideas. Its architects were a group of gramophone "intellectuals" who came to prominence during the 1920s and challenged prevailing ideas about mechanized music. They insisted that the phonograph was an authentic musical instrument warranting cultural accreditation. Their discourses were improvised around existing belief systems about music and were articulated in magazines, advertising, and books—in the documentary reality, that is, associated with the phonograph. This reality told and sold the "truth" about the phonograph, and it was set forth in words *and* pictures that crystallized the power of the disc. It is an integral part of the culture of the phonograph, and it neither stands apart from nor rises above the phonograph—it is as much a part of its "physicality" as its actual machinery.

These discourses reveal that the phonograph was an object of considerable contestation, that a cultural war raged around the legitimacy of mechanized music, and that many people questioned the phonograph's authenticity as a vehicle of music, whose conditions it effectually destabilized. Even those who did not doubt its status in this regard held that phonographic music needed regulation lest its influence become unmanageable. A particular fear pertained to the corrupting power of popular music, specifically jazz, which the phonograph had assisted in disseminating and whose popularity, many feared, would threaten the moral force of classical music. Arguably, classical musicians used the phonograph to consolidate the rift that had emerged in the nineteenth century between popular and serious music, drawing attention to the potential of the latter to form a superior and ethical self while demonizing the former as ephemeral and morally hazardous, a marginal and threatening other. Above all, though, the phonograph challenged the authority of music in its live state and offered an alternative kind of access to music that was private rather than public.

These discourses helped to mobilize support for the phonograph, but in classical music circles, at least, as will be argued in chapter 2, they never threw over the idea that the concert was the ultimate articulation of music and that the phonograph should defer to it. Modes of representing classical music on disc that have abandoned this concert benchmark have tended, with rare exceptions, to be marginalized. In this context, the concert discourse fulfills a "keystone" function. That is, it is a discourse upon which other discourses rest, and without which other supporting discourses cannot stand. Keystone discourses thus hold together particular regimes of truth. In the case of classical recording, the concert discourse governs not just the representation of classical music on record but also the way it is evaluated and reviewed. It thus outlaws certain forms of phonographic representation and provides a clear benchmark for distinguishing good recordings from bad ones. In a context where other attitudes to recording have certainly been espoused, the keystone discourse is critical in positioning listeners' reactions to recordings, determining their phonographic attitudes by creating a sense of rightness for certain acoustic representations and wrongness for others. It also serves to generate correlative micropractices associated with listening to records that, in effect, support the keystone but are meaningless on their own.

The history of the phonograph, then, is not merely the history of a machine; it is the history of an *idea,* or more precisely the history of many ideas that came into being around its advent. The history of reproduced sound is housed not just in its machinery but in magazines and books where the rules and grammar of contemporary recording are articulated. In these magazines and books we can also discern populations being "worked upon," having their minds changed or made up about recording. This highlights the degree to which cultural practices—including those associated with the phonograph—are social constructions. They are not Kantian phenomena transcending their contexts but rather arbitrary realizations that are fed and legitimated by social forces linked to cultural power. That is why the industry

why not just thinking? Why manipulation?

of texts—much of it taking the form of the throwaway literature of advertising, trademarks, brochures, and slogans—associated with recording is so significant: it provides traces and inscriptions of a culture at war with itself, in this case, over the legitimacy of the phonograph. It serves to make sense of a medium of musical presentation that was wholly new, and that rendered existing understandings and vocabularies inadequate. None of the processes involved are easy to chronicle; their history jumps back and forth and marshals many cultural forms: graphic arts, advertising, novels and short stories, and so on. The complex algebra involved invokes many factors, owing as much to the forces of the market as to the power of certain groups of cultural voices to enlist literary mechanisms, to promote their various phonographic causes.

The sense of discourse adopted in this book, then, is an elastic one, owing much to the aforementioned idea of discourse as a political and epistemological force in the formation of the contemporary subject. Discourses are part of a framework for knowing phenomena, their various objects, and the knowledge appertaining to them, and for providing regimes of truth for their articulation, for meaningful exchanges to be conducted about them. But there is a political sense of discourse that recognizes that cultural meanings are arbitrary and the objects of struggle, as one cultural group seeks to enforce its values over others. One can see this in the gendered nature of the record culture, particularly in the domestic sphere, where it is, by and large, men's business. The impression emerges in the gramophone literature that women are unhappy about the colonization of the home by sound equipment—both physically and audibly—and need appeasing that its colonization was a limited one.

Moreover, in a consumer democracy, individuals cannot be forced to invest in recordings and the equipment on which to play them, but they can, through discourses, be persuaded that it might be in their social interest to do so, on the grounds that owning discs offers manifold moral and aesthetic dividends. The aggregate effect of these discourse maneuvers associated with the phonograph helped create a community of interest across the globe, a constituency of specialized phonographic subjects: record producers, cover designers, reviewers, performers, journalists, listeners, collectors, and hobbyists. Indeed, the remarkably quick manifestation of the record industry across the globe meant that the take-up of the phonograph was, by and large, similar in the United Kingdom, United States, and Australia.

Discourses are communicated much in the way infectious diseases are, almost without a community's awareness. They are then free to mutate, evolving into new species of practice, extending their reach, sometimes fissuring into even more specialized communities of interest. They are conveyed by the aforementioned circulatory system of magazines, books, and advertising, where the main characteristics of phonographic thought are "graphically" represented and reproduced, and where the epistemological "truths" appertaining to the phonograph are adjusted in the light of new auditory imperatives. From this circulation of texts, readers are conditioned to accept the normality of technological change in the recording industry. For unlike the book, which has remained a relatively static medium of information technology, the phonograph has undergone at least five main phases of development: acoustic (1877–1926), electric (1926–1948), long-playing (1948–1958), stereo (1958–1983), and digital (1983–). The political economy of the recording industry is thus predicated on periodically staging its own extinction, thus requiring its participants to invest in new equipment and new types of disc every quarter century or so and to accept that the logic of this is compelling and necessary.

Furthermore, that music (as well other sounds) could be present without the presence of musicians and could be reperformed almost without end represented a profound shift in auditory metaphysics for which there were no obvious precedents. Thus, the invention of the phonograph required a series of secondary inventions, more rhetorical than material, that would accommodate the ramifications of this new metaphysics. Among other matters, for example, ways of listening to, using, and representing sound on the phonograph all had to be invented and then reinvented as each new development in the technology of sound was confronted. Discourses—and the texts that enact them—provide that "invention" in its traditional rhetorical sense of re-making and reconstructing meaning (Said 2000: 14).

For the discourses of the phonograph deal typically with what records to acquire and how to optimize their auditory potential, and they are manifest in the phonograph's textual supplements. The sheer versatility and convenience of the bibliographic form—books and magazines—and its capacity for annotation are marks in its favor, and it therefore continues to remain the principal vehicle through which the phonographic community propels its discourses. But these same bibliographic forms are extremely dispersed. To combat this, the central ideas associated with the phonograph have also come to be expressed in aphoristic forms that speak on behalf of this dispersed multitude of documents. They crystallize a particular theme of phonographic philosophy. One prominent figure in the industry, one performer, one label, one quotation, or one manner of recording comes to epitomize a particular discourse that then reverberates across the record community. Thus discourses have helped to produce various phonographic populations—popular, rock, classical, audiophile and so on—and equip them, so to speak, with relevant habits, patterns of listening, and musical enthusiasms.

And although the vast majority of the population never reads the many "literary" extensions of the record, enough of their contents flows off the page into the ether of quotidian life that individuals, even ones who confess no interest in recording whatsoever, through processes of cultural osmosis, absorb the proper vocabularies and practices, as well as enough of the etiquette of auditory conduct, to play and purchase records. They do this just as assuredly as they as have absorbed the practices associated with other facets of mediated culture, such as the home computer.

Raising the Voices of the Dead: The Archetypal Metaphor of the Phonograph

The prehistory of the phonograph is an extensive one, existing "on paper" centuries prior to its material existence. Legends abound across the world, telling of contrivances that had the capacity to capture musical performances and disperse them through the environment without the need for human intervention. Such "legendary" anticipations of the phonograph, for example, appear in Rabelais's satirical account of Renaissance humanism.[3] Arguably, these prepare the ground for the phonograph and create imperatives for the phonograph's eventual incarnation, as did the mechanized nature of musical production. A musical instrument, after all, is only a mechanism for synthesizing sounds, but it is one, unlike the phonograph, that depends on the physical execution of musicians for the realization of its musical powers. However, many mechanical devices and automata—early essays in robotics—did exist that could produce music of their own accord without the need for human intervention; player pianos, for example (Chavez 1937: 44). Indeed, until player pianos were overtaken by the radio and phonograph in the late 1920s, they put up fierce competition for the phonograph, and one model even possessed a phonographic facility (Bowes 1972: 179; Moogk 1975: 110).

Arguably, the advent of musical notation itself was a critical point in the development of a technology of musical disembodiment (Taylor 2001: 3). It also enabled "musical information" to transcend its corporeal expression and live beyond the circumstances of its performance, in effect existing in another state, as an "exosomatic" form (Young 1988). Notation was, after all, a means of preserving music by placing it in a state of suspended animation; prior to the advent of musical notation, the only way music was ever reperformed or re-executed was as an echo. Notation and ultimately the phonograph provided that echo with a memory, one that gave music lasting power by preventing its immediate extinction. For as Young also notes, exosomatic devices—writing is the classic example—are anti-amnesic; that is, they are memorizing technologies that translate neurological information into material form, circumventing the processes of deterioration and distortion that are associated with memory. Furthermore, music's eventual existence as an exosomatic form allowed it to be investigated and analyzed.

The forces that led to the development of the phonograph stemmed from beyond musical circles. In France they were catalyzed by the revolution in visual representation generated by the invention of the camera, which provoked interest in developing an "acoustic Daguerreotype" able to fix sounds in the way that the camera had fixed images. In fact, Edouard-Léon Scott de Mandeville produced such a machine in 1855; his "phonautograph" was able to inscribe the vibrations of the human voice and provide a visual record of their pattern. Importantly, Scott anticipated an era when future generations would be able to listen to the inscriptions produced by such "voice writers" (Flichy 1995: 60). Another of his compatriots—the French were prominent players in the phonograph's history (Bernard 1951: 12)—almost produced such a writer: in April 1877, the poet and scientist Charles Cros deposited with the Académie des Sciences—some eight months prior to Edison lodging his own patent—the "charte fondamental de la machine parlante." It seems that only poverty and the paucity of laboratory resources, which Edison had in abundance, prevented Cros from realizing his "charte" (Cros 1951: 17).[4]

Edison's own foray into the physics of sound preservation was an off-shoot of his experiments into developing a high-speed telegraph relay system.[5] One of these experiments had utilized a strip of paper, a stylus, and a Morse-code key to produce a signal sounding akin to a human voice (Ford 1962a: 221; Millard 1995: 24), which suggested to Edison the possibility of re-versing the process: through speaking into a diaphragm connected to a stylus that could inscribe the sound of the voice onto a malleable surface as a series of indentations, it might be possible to replay the voice and thereby transcend the processes of sound extinction. This experiment proved a success for Edison and meant that the audible present could be preserved and represented, moreover, at any time or place in the future. In familiarizing the public with these transporting effects of the phonograph, early enthusiasts often invoked the idea of an auditory immortality. The first communication published on the phonograph suggested that it would allow the "familiar voices" of the dead to be heard "long after" they had "turned to dust" (Johnson 1877).

Curiously, Edison, in spite of his sanguine feelings about its future, let his stake in the phonograph lie dormant for a decade and turned instead to the pursuit of electric light.[6] He allowed others—much to his subsequent cha-grin—to evince the cause of the phonograph. It was the improvements to the phonograph by others, principally Chichester Bell and Charles Tainter, who built a machine they called a "Graphophone" that used wax as a recording medium, that revived Edison's interest in the phonograph. He then developed the "Perfected Phonograph," which prompted a set of written reflections on the phonograph as well (Edison 1888). Though he paid heed to its musical potential, he mostly discussed the phonograph as an all-purpose language machine, one able to redress the inherent fallibilities of writing, its inability, for example, to represent the nuances of speech. The phonograph could offer an "unimpeachable" account of language just as the photograph had offered unimpeachable images of the world, and it would give, he hoped, greater moral and legal authority to the spoken word (Edison 1888: 649), leading to a more "phonocentric" culture. Above all, he hoped, the ease and immediacy with which messages could be committed to the phonograph might make it the principal mode of communication, eventually superseding even writing.

Thus the revolution of the phonograph immediately produced a culture of the absent-present that disrupted the existing parameters of time and space, altering their significance in the metaphysical equations of everyday life. The remote could be rendered close, the present preserved, and the past resurrected *ad nauseam*. Indeed, the capacity of the phonograph to perform miracles that defy the laws of time and space has become commonplace and has resulted in such musical miracles—made feasible by overdubbing—as double violin concertos performed by the same violinist (Borwick 1983: 1544).

Several social theorists have commented upon the cultural miracles that technologies such as the phonograph enable, and they have variously conceptualized them. It has been argued that the compression of time and space, and the virtual annihilation of time by space, has meant that the ordinates of daily life in the twentieth century became radically different from those of the past (Giddens 1990; Harvey 1990; Thompson, J. 1995). Further, one of the impetuses of phonograph-inspired change has involved the compression and extension of the technology, which has produced smaller, lighter, longer, more durable sources of music. This has led to the development of a compact musical culture: fifteen centuries of music from all over the world at a listener's fingertips (Hennion 2001: 18). Record players and records are also much smaller and more portable than they used to be, but not at the expense of their playing times, which have increased. A full symphony orchestra playing eighty minutes of music can be compressed onto a disc a mere five inches across. One offshoot of this development is the Discman, which has produced the musical *flaneur* (Middleton 1990: 99), that self-possessed being with music on his mind who strolls the streets of musical culture much as his Baudelairian ancestor strolled the streets of Paris.

The metaphysics of the absent-present is also a critical feature of epistemological practice, particularly in the sciences, where semiotic activities such as graphs and drawings dominate laboratory practice. Latour (1987; 1990) argues that these activities are at their most manifest in so-called "immutable mobiles," whose significance derives from their capacity to allow the absent to be present and the remote to be acted upon at a distance. Maps are a case in point, but so too are gramophone records, which also render the mutable immutable—in this case, the most mutable of physical forms, sound. Moreover, once they have done this, recordings have enough portability and durability to enable them to be transferred from the circumstances of their provenance. It is primarily this ability that has transformed the culture of sound, enabling its ephemeral nature, quite literally, to stand the test of time and be transferred to the present, thereby annihilating those constrictions that once fixed the experience of sound to particular places and times. This certainly gave a boost to the study of ethnomusicology, for it enabled specimens of music to be collected in the field and then analyzed after the event, far from the location of their performance. And just as the advent of the printing press led to the rise of literature in marginal European languages, the advent of the phonograph led to the preservation of "vernacular" music, particularly Afro-American jazz and blues, which eventually led, through the interest it generated, to the birth of rock music in the 1960s and 1970s.

Although Edison was an inventor rather than a social theorist, there nonetheless runs through his writings an appreciation of the spatial and temporal parameters that the phonograph could abrogate. For example, Edison noted that the phonograph had the capacity for the "gathering up and retaining of sounds hitherto fugitive and their reproduction at will" (1878: 527). With the aid of a phonograph, families would be able to retain the last words of their dying relatives, and the speeches of "our Washingtons, our Lincolns, our Gladstones" could be played endlessly, as long as the cylinder held out. In short, the phonograph had the capacity to "annihilate" (his word) the significance of "time and space" (Edison 1878: 536). To this end many of Edison's initial recording ventures involved prominent men and women. His representative in Europe, Colonel Gouraud, persuaded the likes of Florence Nightingale, Lord Tennyson, and William Gladstone to record their voices—for posterity's sake—and, in exchange, sought their endorsement of the phonograph (Johns 1958: 4).

According to an article dealing with the future of the phonograph, published in the *Illustrated London News,* it was envisaged that national voice galleries would soon be established that would contain "phonotype sheets," on which the utterances of "great speakers and great singers" would be "stored for thousands of years" ("Phonograph and Microphone" 1878: 114). Uppermost in Edison's mind was the idea that as an organ of sound preservation the phonograph's potential was limitless: animals, sermons, newspapers,

voices, and so on could all be consigned to the phonographic medium and retained forever. One 1899 catalog lists over forty uses of the phonograph, including serenading lovers, providing sermons, and chronicling the voice at
ages four, fourteen, and twenty-four (Briggs 1988: 392). Indeed, Edison envisaged that families would hold regular phonographic parties during which
they would listen to themselves and admire each other's vocal agility (Morton 2000: 136).

The capacity of the phonograph to subvert the effects of time was recognized to be particularly significant for music. Edison held that it would enable
future generations of musicians to hear Rubinstein's interpretation of Chopin, and that Dame Adelina Patti's singing would be "heard again on this side
of the ocean" (Edison 1888: 645–46). Thus the early discourses of the phonograph foregrounded the idea of auditory exhumation, the notion that the
phonograph could raise the voices of the dead and place the living in contact
with their ancestors—as if it was, quite literally, a mechanical medium.[7] In
fact, for a time there was a vogue for using phonographs at funerals so that the
"interred" might deliver their own eulogies (Brady 1999: 45). Thus, by the
early twentieth century, a discourse of the phonograph had emerged that reiterated this chapter's epigraph: that in the record "lies the *soul* of the whole of
Past Time," long after its material embodiment had "vanished like a dream."

The view that the phonograph had the power to exhume the past and provide a museum of music that would enable future generations to "hear" the
past was not an uncommon one among its early proponents. It was strongly
espoused by Edison's rival, Emile Berliner, who developed the gramophone
disc, which eventually superseded the cylinder. Its advent, he suggested,
would enable the utterances of the "long departed" to be preserved; hearing
them would be "like holding community with immortality" (Berliner 1888:
446). Indeed, Berliner envisioned that these audiences with the long departed would be encapsulated in what he called "tone picture[s] of a single
lifetime." Lasting about twenty minutes, they would provide a sound portrait of an individual, and evenings could be spent listening to them, much in
the way families had begun to derive pleasure from photographs of themselves. In fact, elsewhere in the same article Berliner envisaged phonographic
studios where individuals would have their "voices taken," and the resultant
"plate"—Berliner's original term for the disc—developed according to the
number requested (1888: 445).

Mediating the Phonograph through the Written Record

It is notable that these attempts to plot the future of the phonograph occurred in print, in the phonograph's textual adjuncts. In other words, early

speculations about the potential of recording were in large measure mediated through texts, which represented the technology to the world in lieu of its actual physical presence. In fact, these supplementary texts are an ongoing feature of the technology of recording, manifested in many genres and forms of documentation from advertising and record magazines to catalogs and discographies, just as in other forms of mass media such as film and television. Yet although there have been several histories of the phonograph (Day 2000; Gelatt 1977; Gronow and Saunio 1998; Kenney 1999; Millard 1995; Read and Welch 1976; Welch and Burt 1994), which owe much of their thoroughness to what has been written about the phonograph, to the many *records* of the record, they overlook the fact that the history of records and recording is as much a textual as a technological one. These "discographies" not only record the existence of recordings and provide constant guidance on their possible applications but also house the discourses relating to the significance of recordings in the culture as a whole. As has already been intimated, their existence predates by some considerable time and postdates by much less time the actual advent of the phonograph. Their aggregate impact has imprinted itself on the day-to-day practices of the record community and has framed the way records are received and regarded.

In fact, I will also present the notion in this book that the technology of recording constitutes a complex textual and narrative architecture that is, to a large extent, "intermodal," facilitated through the complex linkages of sound and word occurring through the aforementioned discographies. This architecture, as in the instances cited above, acts as a passageway through which the manifold concepts and practices associated with recording pass before their assimilation into the general sensibility. Thus it provides a sounding board for the polemic surrounding the phonograph, in which various debates about the nature of recording and its uses are promulgated. Indeed, as a particularly "cool medium" (McLuhan 2001), one that requires more active participation from its listeners, the recording demands these textual extensions for its comprehension.

It is ultimately useful to see these texts as just another link in the chain of transducers associated with the technology of recording that involves energy being converted from one form to another: cultural to mechanical to electrical, and back again. The chain begins with the sound waves generated by a singer or musical instrument, which are themselves expressions and interpretations of the cultural energies of a composer and performer working in conjunction with one another, and which are collected and then converted by a microphone into electrical impulses. In the case of analogue recordings—the processes are somewhat different in the case of CDs—these are in turn inscribed via a cutting head into the grooves of a record which, when played back on what was once, tellingly, termed a "transcription deck," generate in turn mechanical energy that is converted via the deck's "pick-up" into electrical energy. This energy is amplified and fed to loudspeakers, which convert the impulses back into mechanical energy that, depending upon the acoustic efficacy of the reproducing system, correlates more or less with the energy of the original sound. This leads to the expending of further cultural energy in the production of texts and documents about the recording, such as those found in record magazines, that further amplify and mediate its qualities. These texts are in their turn read by listeners and record collectors, who are then able to speak with more authority about records and recording and who might, as a result, engage in cognate cultural practices, everything from purchasing a better amplifier to acquiring a more representative collection of classical recordings, from joining a local gramophone society to writing a letter to a classical record magazine. In the process, energy is modulated from one form of reproduction to another: mechanical to electrical to textual to cultural and so on. This idea is encapsulated in the trademark of E.M.G., a manufacturer of state-of-the-art gramophones in the 1930s and 1940s, which shows a listener reading a miniature score, checking the authenticity of the musical "energy" emanating from the gramophone (see Figure 1.1).

The focus on the technological side of recording has detracted from the role of text as a transducer, and from the fact that much of the activity associated with the management and dissemination of recordings occurs through trade papers and magazines. Alongside these functional texts, which are integrated into the management practices of the recording industry at the everyday level, exists a body of more speculative literature dealing with the phenomenon of recording as recording, and on the particular qualities of its representation. Such texts form part of a large chain of signifying and inscribing activities that embed the technology of recording, enabling its practices to be represented and conserved, transmitted and regularized, amplified and elaborated, classified and ordered. They help to "contain" the epistemology of recording and the mundane knowledge associated with domestic listening; that is, the social practices and "literary" activities associated with the recording industry that are, in their turn, linked to other facets of music and sound culture.

The structure of the narrative architecture that is an integral part of the recording industry, then, is a complex and multifaceted one containing a distinctive narrative and set of textual practices. Thus the link between records and their related texts is essential, just as it is in other forms of technology, whose functions ought not to be downplayed. Yet to date no significant analysis of these texts has been conducted, something that this book, which focuses on the narrative architecture associated with recordings of "classical"

Figure 1.1 The advertisement from *The Gramophone* (June 1940) for E.M.G. Hand-Made
Gramophones Ltd. incorporates the company's telling trademark. The original woodcut,
designed by Michael Wickham, was based on an E.M.G. Model Xa. The proprietor of
E.M.G. at the time, Reggie Brayne, was captivated by the woodcut and used the "listening
man" as a feature of the company's stationery and advertising (James 1998: 66). It illustrates
the idea of the record as a textual transducer generating its own "reading" matter, in this case
a miniature score of the recorded music to which the man in the armchair, presumably the
best seat in the house, is listening. (Reprinted by permission of *Gramophone*.)

music and the way this architecture acts as a mediating force between recordings and the auditory practices of ordinary listeners, attempts to redress. Even though "classical" music continues to have a declining share of the record market—it was much higher in the days of the LP—and now only constitutes 5 percent of all unit sales (BFPI 2001),[8] it still represents the most "literary" part of the market, the one most imbued with textual mediation and exegeses.

Although earlier I pointed out parallels between the cultures of the book and of the phonograph, these parallels can be overdrawn. One characteristic unique to the phonograph—and it pertains to other forms of contemporary media such as film and video as well—is its twofold nature (Chanan 1995: 32), manifested in the division between the system of playing devices, such as a phonograph, and the devices that are played, such as LPs and CDs. Unlike a book, which exists more or less in its own right—and this is its main advantage over other types of information technology—the phonograph cannot do without the recording. A phonograph only has auditory significance when it enters into partnership with a record, when there is a merger between the player and the played. Moreover, this partnership requires some driving force, such as a clockwork spring or electricity, to be consecrated. Books by comparison do not require an outside source of energy for their literary power to be released. They are also relatively transparent technologies in terms of their construction and, beyond the need to be literate, do not require much technical knowledge. Few, if any, manuals exist on how to operate books.

Moreover, the actual processes of record reproduction are increasingly invisible, having undergone, since the invention of the phonograph—most of whose mechanisms were visible—progressive "internalization." With the surrender of the LP to the CD, the mechanisms of reproduction were secreted away. Thus reproducing technologies have required more textual support than the book. One obvious manifestation of this support is the technical manual, which accompanies the various components of sound reproduction: loudspeakers, compact disc players, and amplifiers. Then there are the various modes of "containment"—records, sleeves and jackets—that are the subjects of analysis in chapters 4 and 5—which act as a form of musical threshold where particular "readings" of a recording are pointedly emphasized and reinforced. Although Gerald Genette, on whose ideas these chapters draw, mentions in passing that his theory of paratextuality is applicable to a range of cultural texts, including phonographic ones (1997: 370), his focus is primarily "bookish." But records, be they cylinders or CDs, are also embedded in complex forms of paratext.

A True Record: The Etymology of the Phonograph

Though the analogy between book and record can be overdrawn, the idea that recordings are a form of writing is contained in the language of recording itself and the terms for its component elements, such as the "stylus."[9] New inventions always create a lexicographical vacuum, and the phonograph was no exception. The term coined for the new invention was developed by Charles Cros—though it was actually suggested by his friend Abbé Leblanc—and Thomas Edison, who first applied it to a sketch of his proposed talking machine (Read and Welch 1976: 6). In fact, Sir Isaac Pitman had first used "phonograph" for his system of shorthand in the 1840s, and it has been argued that the development of shorthand helped to catalyze an interest in developing a mechanical means for "representing" speech (Gitelman 1999: 25). And at one stage, three terms—only one of which has survived—emerged to refer to the various components involved in sound reproduction: the "phonograph" to denote the machine for recording, the "phonogram" to denote the record made by this instrument, and the "graphophone" to denote the instrument used to produce sounds from this record (Wile 1977a: 8). Emile Berliner subsequently coined the term "grammophone" (phonogram transposed) because Edison objected to his use of phonograph, a word over which he claimed proprietorship. In fact, when Berliner came to register his term, it was, much to the chagrin of classicists, minus one of its "m's"! But even this change was not enough to appease others with a stake in the embryonic gramophone industry; they slapped an injunction on its use—though it did not apply in the U.K.—and for some time Berliner was required to use the term "talking machine" in its stead. Berliner's business partner, Eldridge Johnson, hoped that the public might take to the name "Victrola," one of Victor's early phonographs, and they did for a time, but never in the way that "Kodak" became eponymous with the camera (Kenney 1999: 6).[10]

On other counts, too, the word "gramophone" riled. This was especially the case with its more odious inflections such as "gramophile" and "gramophobe." Indeed when Compton Mackenzie (1955: 72), a prominent figure in early record journalism, coined these "barbarisms" in the 1920s, he did so with tongue in cheek. He had not anticipated that they would eventually be vernacularized and appear in the London *Times* and the *Oxford Dictionary*. Mackenzie generally preferred the word "disc," for it produced more euphonious inflections and paralleled the bookish terms "bibliophile" and "bibliography." Like Edward Sackville-West and Desmond Shawe-Taylor (1951: 32), who also favored "disc," he thought that the use of "k" rather than "c," would repress the word's athletic associations. The adoption of the words "gramophone" and "phonograph" was not universal, however, and an Atlantic divide soon separated them. By and large, the English favored gramophone, which was channeled to Great Britain's colonies and dominions, whereas Americans, because the word "gramophone" was for some time the subject of litigation, favored phonograph (Wile 1977a: 9). And although terms such as talking machine and speaking machine were often used as alternatives, the etymology of gramophone and phonograph, which meant "sound writing," was consonant with the idea of a machine able to represent speech.

In fact, the inventors of the phonograph and the gramophone played on the parallels that existed between their machines and the technology of writing and printing. For example, Berliner likened the gramophone to a process of "etching" the human voice, and its original technology, which used zinc plates onto which acid was poured, was almost identical to etching itself (Berliner 1888: 445). And when Edison started to use wax to make recordings, he drew satisfaction from the fact that the processes were similar to those deployed by the Assyrians and Babylonians for their cuneiforms (Edison 1888: 641).

But the parallels did not end there, for the notion that the phonograph might serve as a language machine was foremost in Edison's advocacy of the phonograph. For although he was able to list at least ten other uses of the phonograph, including that of music, about which he was not "absolutely assured," he was adamant that first among them was the stenographic one (1878: 532–35). We must remember that Edison's phonograph could also record, a facility that Berliner's alternative machine lacked. Thus his machine was much more versatile than Berliner's; not only could its users create personal records of themselves but, when they had tired of them, they could use the "cylinder shaving attachment," with which all but the cheapest phonographs were equipped, to erase their recordings and make new ones.[11]

Aside from the fact that it was very difficult to make adequate recordings of music,[12] Edison simply assumed all along that the phonograph would be used primarily as a language machine, and he envisaged that "phonograms" would eventually become the main mode of human communication. Their advantages over conventional letters were said to be numerous and included the fact that they could be dictated, even at home, without a stenographer (Edison 1878: 532). Thus Edison thought that the advent of the phonograph would revolutionize office work, and he held that its widespread adoption would lead to dramatic reductions in secretarial costs. Early advertisements associated with the machine emphasized the phonograph's labor-saving potential and promoted it as a mechanical stenographer. One such advertisement that appeared in *The Phonogram* for May 1893 listed ten reasons as to why the phonograph was more efficient and reliable than a stenographer; these included the fact that it did not "grumble at any amount of overwork," always produced a high quality product, took dictation rapidly, and could outpace the stenographer. In fact, for many decades the letterhead of Edison's Phonograph Company carried the slogan "The Phonograph: The Ideal Amanuensis."

But initial trials of the "Ideal Amanuensis"—in this case, Bell and Tainter's graphophone—by the Supreme Court in Washington exposed the machine's chief stenographic inadequacy: it was not robust enough to cope with the volume of the court's work (Winston 1998: 264). Also, its introduction provoked industrial unrest among Washington's civil servants, who feared that the phonograph would lead to numerous redundancies (Gelatt 1977: 45). Indeed the first item for discussion at the inaugural convention of the National Phonographic Association in 1890 dealt with this issue and how to mitigate the fear of the phonograph generating "technological unemployment" (Read and Welch 1976: 44). Yet U.S. government departments, in the main, failed to adopt the phonograph as a secretarial substitute, which caused the companies associated with Edison some financial difficulties. Even so, Edison remained adamant that the future of the phonograph was primarily commercial.

Although phonographs were used widely in offices until the 1930s, this never took place on the scale that Edison had envisaged. Not that he was alone in misreading the future of the phonograph: like a number of other commentators, musicians, critics, and capitalists of the time, he simply selected the wrong "narrative" for it (Attali 1985: 94; Gitelman 1999: 132). The narrative chosen by the public concerned entertainment, and it emerged as companies involved in the embryonic recording industry sought to diversify their operations and interests. Records, for example, were used in "vocal commercials" to promote various products such as margarine (Moore 1999: 16; Jewell 1977: 22). Some of these uses, in fact, had Edison's blessing, such as using the phonograph as the "voice box" for clocks or dolls (Welch and Burt 1994: 47). The trouble was that these uses did not particularly enhance the cultural image of the phonograph, only confirming the widespread view among the musical elite that it was little better than a toy. But unbeknownst to Edison, who kept himself aloof from such developments, the phonograph was beginning to satisfy the public's appetite for popular music. This first became apparent in arcades, where coin-operated phonographs, prototypes of the modern jukebox, had been installed. These had been developed in 1889 by a San Francisco businessman, Louis Glass, and they enabled the public to listen to a range of recordings, mainly of vaudeville music, through prototypes of headphones called "ear-tubes" (Kenney 1999: 24–25; Schicke 1974: 25). They proved to be very popular in the United States and were soon exported to the saloons of Paris and London, where they also enjoyed considerable success.

It was as a sideshow attraction, then, that the phonograph captivated the public's attention, much to Edison's dismay; he deplored the idea that his invention would be used as a vehicle of entertainment. In a note written to his personal secretary, Alfred O. Tate, in 1894, Edison expressed his opposition to the phonograph being sold for amusement purposes: "it is not a toy. I want it sold for business purposes only" (cited in Read and Welch 1976: 55). Yet it is also true that his opposition softened as Edison recognized the ascendancy of phonographic amusement parlors and realized that it was toward frozen music, rather than speech, that the public's enthusiasm for the phonograph was leaning.

By the 1890s, another important concern had emerged in the discourses pertaining to the phonograph, one related to the phonograph's "cultural legitimacy," to the idea that it could promote musical enlightenment and serve broad educational functions. Arguably, the phonograph's struggle for cultural legitimacy paralleled that confronting the camera in its early decades (Bourdieu, et al. 1990). Some of the struggle was foreshadowed in the hostile reactions to photographs, which had begun to appear in prodigious numbers in magazines during the 1880s and 1890s. Many genteel readers feared that their appearance would eventually weaken the appreciation of the written word and its capacity to portray "truth" (Schneirov 1994: 67). An allied Platonist fear was that photographs did not idealize their subject matter: they left things as they were, in their unornamented state, though the proper function of art was to beautify, to uplift and add aesthetic improvements to the shortcomings of everyday life. Similar fears attached themselves to the phonograph: would it only conserve imperfect sounds and performances? In many respects, such fears anticipate the discourse conflict examined in chapters 2 and 3 that raged between realism and idealism, between the ideas that music on record should on the one hand aspire to and on the other transcend the conditions, imperfect though they may be, of the concert.

The Ascendancy of Music As a Divine Art

In the case of recording, however, this conflict between realism and idealism possessed particular features that had resulted from the repositioning of music in the arts during the eighteenth and nineteenth centuries. Music's former lowly status in relation to the other arts was challenged during this period, and it was eventually elevated. The interventions of the Romantic poets and philosophers, who held that music possessed almost supernatural powers, were responsible for this elevation. Hitherto, music had not enjoyed much esteem and was regarded, if not with contempt, as a mere accompaniment to other, more gratifying activities, such as eating and conversation. Music was not seen as worthy of contemplation in its own right, and, in many respects, it fulfilled the functions of contemporary muzak (Gay 1995: 14). Audiences, for example, generally talked among themselves throughout musical performances and rarely gave them their full attention. Music was not dignified with the high seriousness attendant to the modern concert, which is listened to in silence and where any unnatural interruptions (and natural ones, too) are regarded as impolite, very much in accord with the Romantic view of music as a sacred and divine art. Indeed, prior to the Romantic reevaluation of music, a quiet and attentive "audience" meant that a composer had made an impression. In fact it took many decades of "education" before audiences learned to affect the organized sobriety that now constitutes appropriate etiquette in the concert hall, to curb any instinct for exuberant expression, and to stop applauding at the end of movements.[13] Yet it is somewhat ironic that such etiquettes of repression are an integral part of concert protocol, for more than any of the other arts, music stimulates the rhythmic impulses of the body. Nevertheless, the bodies that listen to classical music are expected to maintain themselves in respectful docility throughout a performance, only giving license to their feelings at its end; even then, the applause is supposed to be subdued and respectful (Levine 1988: 178; Scholes 1947: 219). In the nineteenth century, then, a solemnity and asceticism descended on concerts that discouraged the arbitrary sounds and boorish behavior that would disrupt the experience of music in rapt silence, conditions that were commensurate with the belief in music's near divinity. Underlying this discourse was the notion that music, above all, should speak to the mind rather than the body.

The role of classical music as a marker of social difference and status was revisited at the same time as its aesthetic. Throughout the nineteenth century, in the United States and Europe, classical concerts became more socially exclusive, the prerogative of the elite and educated classes (DiMaggio 1987; DiMaggio and Useem 1982: 188; Weber 1975). Concerts were constituted as serious events in the calendar of metropolitan culture and played an important function in the consolidation of a socially divided society. They eventually became the centerpieces of bourgeois life; concertgoers were expected to dress in formal attire and exhibit the utmost decorum and respect for the newly promulgated musical etiquette (Scholes 1947: 191; Young 1965: 223).

But in so doing concerts also helped to establish the important hiatus between classical and popular forms of music: the so-called "great musical schism" (van der Merwe 1989). Before the emergence of this schism, popular and classical music had not been regarded as antithetical and often merged promiscuously together.[14] Classical composers drew on the popular and vice versa, and there was little discord between the types of music. But during the Romantic era this began to change; classical composers disparaged popular music, and classical music began to acquire its "overtones of culture and uplift" (Van der Merwe 1989: 19)—notions that eventually imprinted themselves onto the discourses of classical recording. Thus the schism became both musical and sociological.

Although listening to records is now taken for granted, it was not always so, and the modes of listening to them, like the modes for concert attendance, had to be invented, promulgated, and circulated. There was even an influential body of musical opinion—examined in the next chapter—opposed to listening to them at all, which held that mechanized music was anathema. When it was finally generally accepted that music, even classical music, and the phonograph were not mutually exclusive, the matter of their association was prescribed, as will be argued in chapters 7 and 8, in record guides and magazines, and it followed those protocols adopted for the live concert.

Elevating the Social Image of the Phonograph: Caruso and Advertising

Even though Edison downplayed the phonograph's musical potential, he was not entirely opposed to it and actually looked forward to the day when the phonograph would "transport" opera singers across generations. Yet it was Emile Berliner, in collaboration with Eldridge R. Johnson and Fred Gaisberg, who sought and eventually obtained cultural legitimacy for the talking machine. In so doing, these men undertook a program of social reconstruction for their gramophone that involved conceiving of it as an instrument of enlightenment as well as entertainment. Although it is hard to be precise about when a more receptive attitude toward classical recording emerged, it is plain that by the 1920s, with the advent of electrical recording, which dramatically improved the quality of its sound, a more favorable discursive context for recording had emerged (Brunner 1986: 494).

Prior to this development, the majority of, though not all, musicians had remained forthright in their opposition to the phonograph and its musical aspirations, only slowly coming to accept the inevitability of recording as a fact of modern musical life. The recording industry, particularly the Victor Company, began to counter these admonitions through a series of complex discourse maneuvers that they variously oversaw and undertook during the first decade of the twentieth century. Having launched a gramophone disc that offered unlimited reproducibility, Victor set about domesticating the gramophone, trying to ensure that it attained the status of an essential home appliance, as a source, as it were, of chamber music. Up until this time, the phonograph had been regarded as an unimpressive piece of furniture to be hidden away, and it was only admitted into polite company at partying times (Wilson 1926: 7). Improving the social credentials of the phonograph involved, among other matters, improving its design and acoustic capacities, a task that fell to Eldridge Johnson.

Upon first hearing the gramophone, Johnson likened its sound to a "partially educated parrot with a sore throat and cold" (1974: 40), which he cured through developing an improved sound box. He then turned to the visual presentation of the gramophone, which he thought most unappealing, particularly its horn attachment, which he considered "an affront to people of refined taste" (Johnson 1974: 73). He redressed this by producing the Victrola, which transformed the phonograph into an attractive item of furniture available in a range of styles, into which the unappealing horn was, even though it compromised the sound quality, enfolded. Other companies followed suit and advertised stylish phonographs in opulent settings as well (Frow and Sefl 1978: 39). These advertisements insinuated that the phonograph was an essential feature of the bourgeois home and as such deserved as much attention to its decorative features as the piano (see Figure 1.2). Indeed, some manufacturers produced phonographs that were designed to harmonize with their luxurious surroundings, even imitating the baroque ornamentation of keyboard instruments (Hayden 1923).

The phonograph was further elevated socially by way of its catalog of recorded music, to which Victor and the Gramophone Company added many more classical entries. This was achieved through a number of initiatives, including the appointment of Landon Ronald as an adviser to the Gramophone Company. Unlike many of his contemporaries, Ronald supported recording and made a number of classical recordings, including the first recording of a concerto, albeit one that was heavily cut (Duckenfield 1990). But it was the efforts of the company's peripatetic impresario, Fred Gaisberg, that went the furthest toward mollifying the musical establishment's animosity toward recording. A major breakthrough in this respect was that Gaisberg managed to persuade the Italian tenor Enrico Caruso to make a series of recordings.[15] This series perhaps more than any other initiative in the early history of recording improved the cultural status of the gramophone, for most of the other classical performers of the time had parried Gaisberg's overtures on the grounds that any professional association with the gramophone would irreparably harm their musical careers (Gaisberg 1943: 38). Caruso was an exception, and he thus set the stage for the phonograph, in spite of its acoustic limitations, to gain acceptance among classical musicians. Part of the

Figure 1.2 This advertisement (appearing in *McClure's*, February 1914) was part of a series designed to improve the social standing of the "graphophone" and convince the middle classes that it was a gadget essential to family life. To this end, the graphophone was restyled along the lines shown in the advertisement into a "handsome piece of furniture," one containing compartments to store records and, in the more expensive version, even boasting an "Individual Record Ejector." Note, too, the way the "listeners" are formally attired as if for a real concert. Interestingly, many of the advertisements from this period—this one is an exception—showed the performers in a "balloon" above the phonograph, as if their presence—such was the record's realism—was tangible.

reason for this acceptance, and for Caruso's enormous success as a recording artist—he was the first artist to sell a million records—in fact lay in these very limitations: in this era of acoustic recording, the methods of recording were particularly flattering to some operatic voices (Gaisberg 1943: 47).[16]

The other part of Victor's discourse strategy operated on the advertising front. Much of its advertising was directed at those social class "movers," who wanted to make classical music an integral part of their lives on the cheap. They recognized such music as one of the important signifiers of middle-class status, and records afforded them the opportunity to acquire this status without the inconvenience of leaving home or the expense of attending concerts. Victor's advertising played on this opportunity. Indeed, advertising was a key force in disseminating phonographic discourses and provided an important vehicle for encapsulating, in inventive and telling ways, the advantages of acquiring the phonograph (Millard 1995: 25; Siefert 1994: 209; Siefert 1995: 443; Thompson, E. 1995). One series of Victor's advertisements from the 1910s—featuring a range of operatic stars including Caruso and the soprano Geraldine Farrar—stated that records offered an experience equivalent to that of attending a "real" opera. The advertisements thus promoted the idea that the record and the soprano were all but indistinguishable from one another, and that listening to Farrar on disc "in your own home" was the equivalent to "listening to her in the Metropolitan Opera House." The ad also played with the idea of phonographic interchangeability; in its words, the record and opera star were identical ("Both are Farrar"). Furthermore, it presented the seductive idea that performances on record, unlike those occurring in real opera houses, could be mounted at any time of the day, according to the whim of the household, and be repeated *ad nauseam* (Boorstin 1974: 379). In this respect, records really did have a distinct advantage over opera performances. Finally, the option of mounting an opera in one's own home meant that opera was no longer the privilege of a social elite but could be enjoyed by anyone possessing a Victrola and a collection of opera records (Figure 1.3). Indeed, by the 1920s some industry moguls had come to believe their own advertising. HMV's Louis Sterling claimed that his company's gramophones had provided the lowest-paid with access to the music available in the finest opera houses, once the exclusive province of the wealthy (Sterling 1975: 390).

This emergent discourse of verisimilitude was also a significant feature of the trademarks and insignia associated with the early record companies. The inaugural trademark of Berliner's company was the "Recording Angel," which was designed by the manager of its Hanover branch, Theodore Birnbaum (Adamson 1977: 82). It was first engraved on Berliner discs in 1898 before being superseded by the more famous "His Master's Voice" trademark.

Figure 1.3 This advertisement (appearing in *McClure's*, April 1915), one of a series employing the same design, illustrates the discourse of verisimilitude: the idea that the record is an actual *record* of Geraldine Farrar's voice. It also implies that listening to the record at home is equivalent to listening to the soprano in the Metropolitan Opera House. The HMV insignia, in the bottom left-hand corner, also reinforces the idea of phonographic verisimilitude. Note also the globalization theme: Victor records can be demonstrated in any "city in the world."

Nonetheless, the image of the recording angel, still used by EMI in the United States—retains a measure of semiotic aptness, for it represents the initial, sound-writing phase of the phonograph that Edison favored, in the hope that the phonograph might one day displace writing and become the dominant mode of communication (Figure 1.4). But the angel also anticipates the theme of this book: that recordings would themselves become more "logocentric" and generate their own forms of writing, *off* the record but *on* the record. Thus the angel's quill would come to be utilized by phonographic critics, among others, who would record the deeds, both good and ill, of performers and producers and preserve them for posterity.

The HMV trademark (Figure 4.24), one of the most familiar in the history of advertising, was an adaptation of a Francis Barraud painting that had been inspired by a photograph showing Nipper—the name of Barraud's dog— cocking its ear to an Edison phonograph (Berliner 1977: 38). Thus its origins pay an oblique homage to the role of the Daguerreotype in the ascendancy of the phonograph. When the Gramophone and Typewriter Company expressed interest in using the painting—Edison's company had not—it required Barraud to replace the phonograph with one of its gramophones (Johnson 1974: 52; Petts 1983).[17] The HMV trademark was first used in the company's advertising in 1900 and on its records from 1909 onward, and it has been used ever since, partly because of its symbolic power, which like that of the recording angel transcends the signifying capacity of other, more recent, and more abstract logos. It provides a graphical illustration of the acoustic fidelity of the gramophone: such was the faithfulness of the sound emanating from the gramophone that the dog was unable to differentiate a record of its master's voice from that of his actual master! The HMV insignia, the angel, and EMG's listening man thus provide telling images— phonographic equivalents of the panopticon—that illustrate the power of the phonograph: HMV, the idea of verisimilitude; the angel, the idea of sound-writing; and EMG, the idea of the transducer.

Thus the notion that a record could raise voices from the dead and enable listeners to engage in séances with the past (Eisenberg 1988: 46), made familiar in the early writings about the phonograph, gradually began to be superseded by the ideas that a record could act in lieu of an opera, and that listeners to records should act and dress accordingly. Many advertisements for gramophones from the early twentieth century, for example, showed listeners in concert attire. Part of the allure of owning a phonograph was the promise that it offered an authentic musical experience that stood up to comparison with that of the concert hall or opera house. As Marsha Siefert has argued, the "terrier and the tenor" helped to give distinction to the gramophone and provided the type of musical credentials that enhanced its cultural legitimacy

Figure 1.4 Shown here is a millennial incarnation of the "Recording Angel," suitably made over for the times. She is featured in a brochure issued by EMI Classics in 2002 to promote its new budget label, "encore." All of the CDs in the "encore" series—at least those released in the United States—carry the insignia along with an issue-specific painting that complements the Chinese-box "framing" theme that is a central part of the cover's design as well as a pictorial encapsulation of the 'encore' idea. Their European counterparts carry the HMV insignia. (Reprinted by permission of EMI Classics.)

and helped to overcome the stigma that had been attached to mechanized music (1994: 197). In this regard Victor, whose example was soon followed by the Edison Company, had its eye on the phonograph eventually displacing the piano, which in the early parts of the twentieth century was still the prime source of entertainment in middle-class households in the United States and Europe (Chanan 1994: 27, 199). The only way to achieve this was to suggest that the phonograph possessed inherent advantages over the piano in terms of its versatility and capacity to offer performances that few amateur musicians could ever hope to attain. But, arguably, groundwork had already been laid for the acceptance of the phonograph in the home, along with other musical contrivances: the player piano was a step in the phonograph's direction, and even the piano repertoire itself, by the latter part of the nineteenth century, contained a substantial number of musical "representations," that were partially fungible with the real thing, including piano arrangements of important works in the classical orchestral repertoire, such as the Beethoven symphonies by Liszt, that provided alternative avenues of access to classical music (Van der Merwe 1989: 18).

It has often been asserted that the dominant character of contemporary culture is visual, and that the printed word no longer provides the main reference point for communal experience and values. Yet culture has always been visual—even the printed word is essentially a visual form—and, to a large extent, aural. The phonograph radically transformed the nature of aural culture, extending its purview through simulated and mediated forms of sound and music. It is not that contemporary culture is any more aural than it was in the past, but the diversity of its aural experience, and the modes of access to it, are the defining states of its contemporary nature. The phonograph in its various guises, both ancient and modern, has assisted in producing this diversity and accessibility. But it has not done so without the written and printed word, the products of diverse other recording angels. Though the phonograph was for some time called a talking machine, it could not talk about itself or provide speculative commentary on its cultural functions. That commentary came from off the record, from the myriad words written about the phonograph that made this most phonocentric of instruments progressively more logocentric. For the texts that eventually immersed the phonograph in their words of wisdom are as much an integral part of the culture of the phonograph as its technologies of reproduction and, as such, deserve a fuller account of their character than has thus far transpired. Their emergence as textual entities is, in a sense, a centrifugal one that follows the motion of the record, spreading ever onward and outward over its surface and into its various forms of containment, then through its manifold bibliographic representations until it eventually reaches the "best seat in the house." The remaining chapters in this book are devoted to providing an account of this motion and offer an analysis of the discourses and micropractices associated with the phonograph, including their emergence and evolution and the various texts that came to embed them: catalogues, discographies, covers, sleeve notes, essays, magazines, and advertisements.

CHAPTER TWO

Disconcerting Music
Performers and Composers on the Record

In John Sebastian Bach's day it was necessary for him to walk ten miles to a neighbouring town to hear Buxtehude play his works. Today anyone, living no matter where, has only to turn a knob or put on a record to hear what he likes. Indeed, it is in just this incredible facility, this lack of necessity for any effort, that the evil of this so-called progress lies.
—Igor Stravinsky, *Chronicle of My Life*, 248

Etymologies are often truthful, if only in an oblique way. Those of the "phonograph" and the "gramophone" are linked to the idea of a graphical representation of sound akin to writing. They assimilate the idea, illustrated in the "Recording Angel," that recording, by virtue of its chirographic features, is fundamentally textual in nature. Yet there is another way in which these etymologies are truthful, and that is in the degree to which the advent of the phonograph also produced a considerable body of "sound-writing." This writing encompassed everything from an inventory literature providing catalogs of discs to a dedicated polemics of sound production. As a body of work, it enabled phonographic knowledge to be managed and the discourses of recorded sound to be articulated and circulated. Therein lies another proposition, one concerning the degree to which inventions, the phonograph included, undergo a double invention through this writing, which gives them meaning and value, status and justification. At the heart of this writing are a range of intellectual tropes, figures of thought that stand the test of time and are regularly reproduced. The phonograph was no exception in this regard, and it is possible to trace the genealogy of these tropes in the "documentary reality" associated with recording.

In this chapter I will examine the sound-writing produced by professional musicians and music critics. Mechanized music, of which the phonograph was the ultimate expression, generated considerable animosity, which still persists, albeit in a more muted form, in certain quarters of the classical music profession. Indeed, among earlier generations of classical musicians there was a widespread tendency to demonize recording, to see the phonograph as a perfidious machine without musical peer, and although much of this animosity has now abated, there is still a tendency to regard recording as an inferior mode of musical representation.

This is evident in the fact that there is no coherent theory of recording, not even a universal term to describe the science of recording. Various neologisms proposed to typify this new science, such as "phonography" (Eisenberg 1988), "phonographology," and "gramophony," which appeared during the 1920s when an embryonic epistemology of recording emerged, have never caught on.[1] Any theories that exist, unlike those of film—recording's nearest analogue among the performing arts—are dispersed throughout the history of recording. There is no equivalent of *auteur* theory, for example, and what pockets of coherent thinking there are relate only to recording's effects, detrimental or beneficial, on the appreciation of music. Unlike film, which liberated itself from the proscenium arch of the theatre and utilized the camera to produce new forms of narrative representation, the recording of classical music has, by and large, remained deferent to the concert, which continues to be seen by the majority of musicians, for the reasons outlined in this chapter, as the apotheosis of musical expression. This is a view shared by record producers associated with classical music and the critics who evaluate their endeavors. Indeed, much of the polemic pertaining to classical recording surrounds the issue of whether it ought to defer to the acoustic conditions of a live concert, or whether it should be sufficient unto itself and apply more inventive forms of representation, a la the cinema, exploiting the many novel sonic opportunities afforded by phonographic technology.

The fact that the phonograph was not initially an object of universal adulation among musicians reflected the general disquiet appertaining to the mechanization of music as a whole. In part this was because the phonograph challenged the hegemony of prevailing musical practices and threatened their orthodoxies in powerful ways. These challenges were reflected in the discourse wars that followed in the wake of phonograph, which helped to generate ways of defending its aesthetic and musical pretensions. The discourses that survived from these wars provided mechanisms for seeing the phonograph in a new light, magnifying its musical significance and import and bringing to the fore dimensions of sound production and reproduction that had previously escaped attention. Typically these discourses emerged in the columns and editorials of the music press, in articles in record magazines, and in books on music and recording, the outlets in which the champions of recording typically pitted their arguments against those who saw recording in more perfidious terms, as a mortal enemy of music whose insipid attractions required rhetorical subjugation. That this rhetoric failed to quell the enthusiasm for Edison's invention demonstrated the machine's widespread appeal, for the opposition to the uptake of recording, particularly prevalent among some elite musicians, in the end was assimilated into the generally more sympathetic discourse on recorded music, where it nevertheless remains a powerful player.

The Phonograph in Fact and Fiction:
A Force for Good or Evil

As the group most likely to be affected by its advent, professional musicians were, from the first, ambivalent about recording, particularly in the face of its evident popularity and its capacity to act as a vehicle for types of music to which they were hostile. In spite of its myriad acoustic failings and its ability to provide only a reduced "picture" of music, the general public took to the phonograph with unabated enthusiasm. Much of the phonograph's success in the marketplace followed an adroit campaign of advertising (Harvith and Harvith 1987: 1) designed to establish it as the centerpiece of the modern home, as a vehicle of entertainment and edification. This had the effect of tempering its tawdry overtones and making it a more palatable investment for the middle classes, whose patronage helped enhance the economic success of the early record industry (LeMahieu 1988: 58). For though records and the equipment on which to play them were expensive, certainly by today's standards, this did not discourage their acquisition.[2] Even so, it still cost more to purchase a piano, even a mass-produced one.

Thus, by the early twentieth century, at least in the United States, the phonograph began to displace the role that the piano had played in the nineteenth-century household and had caused a dramatic decline in the sales of pianos and sheet music (Roell 1994). This caused considerable concern among musicians, for it was seen to threaten those values associated with "pianism," not all of which were musical: following from the "reconditioning" of music that had occurred during the Romantic era and saw classical music obtaining an almost "sacred" status (Frith 1996: 28–29), the piano was esteemed by its apologists as a source of moral strength that could provide therapy in the domestic sphere for individuals bruised by the excesses of modern life (Roell 1994: 90). Moreover, it had the capacity, allegedly, to steer individuals away from more "demoralizing" activities. But only if one worked at it: the moral dividends flowing from the piano were only acquired if it was played regularly. By and large, women were the pianists who helped to carry forth the moral benefits of the piano to the rest of the family (Foy 1994).[3] By contrast, the attractions of the phonograph were, in large part, derived from its capacity to provide an endless supply of music without much apparent effort. It was this that was held to threaten the piano's moral force, particularly because records, soon to be followed by radio, provided gateways to music held to be ribald, rebellious, and raucous (Fielden 1932).

The reaction of the musical establishment to the advent of mechanized music, if not wholly hostile, was certainly circumspect, and it was articulated in a number of telling ways in several realms of discursive endeavor. For example, prior to the advent of specialized retailers for selling records and gramophones, music shops, seemingly their natural home, for the most part refused to stock them (Batten 1956: 32).[4] Instead, they had to be acquired either through mail order catalogs issued by record companies or small shops whose primary trade was often bicycles, and whose proprietors were quickly irritated by constant inquiries about Chopin records (Sanjek 1988: 388; Wimbush 1973: 252).

Meanwhile, in domains of discursive endeavor such as encyclopedias and dictionaries, the entries on the gramophone and the phonograph, when present, often proved outdated and inaccurate. For example, the 1926 edition of *Chamber's Encyclopedia,* published almost fifty years after the phonograph's invention, only alluded to its amusement and amanuensis uses (Day 2000: 79). Even more revealing of the musicological insouciance toward the gramophone is the fact that until its most recent editions, *Grove's Dictionary of Music and Musicians* did not include a separate entry on the subject. And when it first mentioned the gramophone—in its 1942 edition—it was incorporated into the entry for "Mechanical Appliances." This indifferent treatment of recording also extended to the 1910 edition of the *Oxford English Dictionary.* The entry for "record," though two pages long, devotes a mere two lines to the disc sense of the word. Yet by 1910 this use had entered the vernacular and "outstripped all other forms of record" (Stone 1935: xi).[5] On the other hand, there were contrary signs during the 1920s that indicated a belated textual foothold for the phonograph in reference books. For example, Walter Cobbett invited Compton Mackenzie to write an entry on the gramophone for his projected encyclopedia on chamber music (Mackenzie 1929). And Percy Scholes (1924; 1925) had begun to compile a series of handbooks on music that endorsed the importance of the gramophone as a mechanical aid to musical appreciation.[6]

Yet many of the initial textual responses to the advent of the phonograph were literary rather than musical and occurred in a number of novels and short stories written soon after the initial public demonstrations of Edison's invention. In fact, there was a link between these more literary accounts and Edison's view of the phonograph as a language machine, for it was the potential of the phonograph to replace the written word that proved the main focus of fictional contemplation. In a Jules Verne novel set in remote China (1963) a phonograph was used to produce sound epistles, auditory love letters addressed to a prospective mistress. One of Edward Bellamy's "dream" stories (1889) pictured the phonograph as an all-round vocal automaton, a travel guide, speaking timetable, talking book and clock, child-minder, teacher, and so on. In other novels and short stories the phonograph featured as a narrative device, adding mechanical angles to their dénouements. These often focused on the phonograph's capacity to defy mortality and raise the voices of the dead—the discourse of resurrection that was popular during the first phase of the phonographic endeavor.[7] In James Joyce's *Ulysses,* Leopold Bloom speculates, complete with onomatopoeic effects evoking the gramophone's gravelly sound, that the living would use it to commune with the dead (Kern 1983: 39). And a husband in an Arthur Conan Doyle story turns this speculation into a reality and listens nightly to a disc of his dying wife imploring him to remain of sober habit. The narrator of the story, who knows the wife to be dead and overhears her temperance sermon, discovers its true origins; the "japanned" box of the story's title encloses a phonograph (Doyle 1929).

Such narratives demystified the phonograph and showed its potential, but they also highlighted its capacity to dissemble. They acted as moral tales for the unwary, cautioning them not to be taken in by the *trompe l'oreille* of the phonograph. But it is Bram Stoker's *Dracula,* a novel more renowned for its vampires than its meditations on the phonograph, that provides the most insightful account of the machine's limitations. In Stoker's novel, the psychiatrist Dr. Seaward uses an Edison phonograph to record the case histories of his patients (Stoker 1997: 288). When these were transcribed, his wife noted that they had removed the "beating heart" of their narrators. On the other hand, the transcriptions enabled the patient's psychiatric condition to be examined in a more penetrating way than was possible in their phonographic state. This served to underline the analytical superiority of writing over recording, and Stoker's narrative was a prescient one in recognizing that recordings would have to defer, in order to be managed, to writing's more encompassing explanatory power. The belief on Edison's part that the phonograph would eventually supersede the functions of writing thus undergoes a sort of deconstruction in *Dracula,* which intimates that the "phonic" part of the phonograph had a number of shortcomings that only the "graphical" representation of speech via writing could redeem.

But there was also another theme in the literary representations of the phonograph, as shown in George Orwell's *Coming Up for Air,* where the sound of an alfresco gramophone symbolized suburbia at its most crass and sordid (Orwell 1990).[8] In fact, members of the older, more "bookish" generation wanted to ban the newfangled instruments associated with mechanized music much as Pericles had wanted to ban musical instruments altogether. Their antipathy toward the gramophone joined a generalized antipathy among literary elites and intellectuals during the 1920s and 1930s toward the new media that sprang from a profound disdain for the effects of mass culture.[9] This was grounded in the fear that any move toward an egalitarian culture—also epitomized by universal education—contained the seeds of a barbarism that threatened genuine individualism and would eventually destroy the values associated with elite culture (Carey 1992: 71). Nor were these fears confined to politicized intellectuals: several contemporary composers—Arnold Schoenberg and Claude Debussy among them—shared these presentiments and were adamant that serious music was essentially an exclusive art whose popularization through radio and records risked its own undoing (Scott 1990: 388). Wanton commercialism directed at serious music, of the type exemplified by U.S.-based record companies and radio stations, during the 1930s, was seen as incompatible with the Enlightenment ideals underpinning classical music. According to Theodor Adorno, who criticized capitalist radio's appropriation of classical music, the egalitarian aspirations that were an integral part of, for example, Toscanini's NBC radio concerts were ideologically flawed (Adorno 1978). The concerts provided a measure of compensation for the widespread alienation that many individuals experienced in their modern lives, but at the same time they trivialized classical music and thwarted its potential to subvert the very forces of capitalism that had induced this alienation in the first place (Horowitz 1987: 224). Notwithstanding his fierce invective toward NBC and its radio concerts, which Adorno held bore all the hallmarks of the defective economic system that had produced them, he was, nonetheless, enamored with long-playing records and their capacity to interrogate opera in optimal conditions, particularly infrequently performed contemporary operas "shorn of the phony hoopla" encountered in the theatre (Adorno 1990: 64).

The Attitudes of Classical Musicians Toward the Phonograph: From the Acoustic to the CD Era

Much of the hostility toward the phonograph had its provenance in the fact that its musical pretensions were, at first, easy to dismiss. While many laypeople were mesmerized by recordings and chose to remain deaf to their sonic deficiencies, musicians generally found their capacities less than impressive. Although an editorial in *The Musical Times* of November 1887 had commented favorably on the musical future of Edison's "Perfected Phonograph" and looked forward to an era when Rubinstein would "make a tour of the world by phonogram," many musicians and composers remained defiantly anti-phonograph and, like Nikolai Rimsky-Korsakov (Craft 1957: 34), refused to participate in the production of records or feared, as Sir Arthur Sullivan did, that their advent would undermine music. Yet for all his animosity toward the new invention, Sullivan was not averse to participating in the phonographic parties that were fashionable in the 1890s (Jacobs 1984: 281).

There was a widespread tendency among musicians, then, to belittle the phonograph. Many of them saw it as a toy capable of bearing about as much resemblance to musical reality as nursery soldiers did to real soldiery (Swinnerton 1923: 52). Music struggled to be heard here against a backdrop of noise, and it was often viewed as "akin to looking down the wrong end of the telescope" (Johnson 1936a: 3). The resultant representation of music was unmistakably artificial; it was impossible, even, to distinguish any instrumental detail. Asked to comment, in 1921, on the impact of the gramophone on musical taste, several musicians and composers held that it had been mostly malign and suggested that a taste for the worst kind of music, defined as "ragtime" and "hedonistic jazz," had been thereby generated (Maitland, et al. 1921).

Electrical recording in the mid-1920s, which improved dramatically the sound of records and the manner in which they were made, served to mollify this widespread view, for during the acoustic era recordings were produced under the most exacting conditions and involved a range of compromises that served to tarnish their reputation. Instruments often did not sound like themselves and proved hard to identify. According to Sergei Rachmaninov, the recorded piano sounded more like a balalaika (1973: 99). Performances had to be repeated over and over again until the requisite number of recordings had been made. The Australian baritone Peter Dawson, who made many acoustic records, observed that most singers could not tolerate the demanding regimen involved: singing (though shouting was closer to the mark) a song over and over again into a bank of twelve machines for two three-hour stretches a day (1933: 315). Since it was impossible to correct any errors other than by rerecording the music, many musicians were fearful of making records at all. In letters written in 1919, the Italian composer Ferruccio Busoni complained bitterly about the hours it took to record and admitted that the constant fear of committing irrevocable musical errors inhibited his playing (Saul 1962: 257).[10]

Such fears were further exacerbated by the conditions of recording studios, the most debilitating of which was their uncomfortably high temperatures, required in order to keep the wax used for recordings "impressionable." Further, performers had to adjust their postures when emitting high notes to prevent what was called "blasting" (Moser, et al. 1978: 747). Cellists had to sit on specially designed chairs to project the sounds of their instruments and could not extend their bows to their fullest extents in the cramped conditions of most recording studios. Brass players with their surfeit of volume had to sit with their backs to the conductors and observe their instructions in specially mounted mirrors. Pianists, before the microphone was developed, could never play loudly enough (Moore 1962: 59). Whatever it was musicians were performing, it had to be fortissimo, or the recording horn would not harvest the sounds. There was no scope for musical subtlety. As Gustav Holst found when making a recording of *The Planets,* the experience was a trial to all, including the poor solo horn player in his orchestra, who broke down thirteen times for "lack of air" (Holst 1974: 60).

More to the point, though, was the fact that the conditions of acoustic recording involved making extensive musical compromises, even requiring the use of specially adapted instruments, such as Stroh violins that had diaphragms and metal trumpets to amplify their sound, that would allow a vague impression of an orchestra to be created within the exacting acoustic limits of pre-electric recording, which included a compressed frequency response and dynamic range, a poor signal to noise ratio, and so on. Not surprisingly, the results were disconcerting to many musicians, including the conductors Leopold Stokowski and Arturo Toscanini, who, once having encountered the indignities of the studio, which also included having their orchestras reduced to the size of chamber ensembles, vowed—they later relented—never to return (Marsh 1961: 46; Horowitz 1987: 416).

Of all of the compromises involved in early recording, the most pronounced was linked to the playing time of 78s—about four and half minutes per side. Since most classical works were much longer than this, the early catalogs only contained a limited representation of classical music and were dominated by abridged or specially arranged versions of the "classics" (Brunner 1986: 489). Sections were omitted or tempi adjusted to ensure a natural-sounding transition from one side to another. In a letter Herbert von Karajan wrote to Walter Legge concerning a proposed recording on 78s of Brahms' *Deutsche Requiem,* the conductor identified positions in the score where dramatic side-breaks could be obviated and made to sound less obtrusive and suggested that the tempo of the music be adjusted to facilitate this. Such "distortions" of the musical truth allowed works to be accommodated on discs in relatively felicitous ways (Sanders 1998: 170). Prior to the era of the long-playing record, such adjustment strategies were a customary practice in studios. Conductor Eugene Ormandy noted how stopwatches were employed to annotate scores and ensure that music did not overrun the borders of a 78 (1987: 143).

Such compromises did not endear themselves to musicians and held back the recording of uncut works until the late 1920s. But even the eventual appearance in the catalog of complete symphonies and operas—prompted by the embryonic record journalism of the time—did not allay those in the musical community who regarded the abolition of breaks between records as "the most needed reform in all gramophony" (Scholes 1933). Nothing sabotaged the sense of musical verisimilitude more than having to swap sides, or change from one record to another, which also involved needle replacement. Such actions left a vacuum of incredulity in the listening experience (Copland 1941: 245).[11]

As a response to the unendurable temporal failings of 78s and the accompanying "side-splitting" effects on the sense of musical continuity, the record industry embarked on the development of longer-playing records. As a stop-gap measure, automatic record changers were introduced that could stack upwards of ten records. These helped to reduce the intrusiveness of side changes and proved popular in the market place. However, their operation was not without its own form of incredulity: the "horrifying bumps" as one record replaced another (Robertson 1950: 4).

More satisfying solutions were in the wings. Though not the first companies to do so, RCA Victor and Bell Laboratories, in the 1930s, successfully demonstrated a long-playing record of Beethoven's Fifth Symphony. It lasted a full fifteen minutes per side. Unfortunately, the widespread interest created by this prototype LP was not accompanied by the development of an appropriate pick-up and record player that allowed the new recording format to be played at the right speed (Opperby 1982: 161). Moreover, the needles used to play these prototype LPs often wore out before they reached their ends (Haddy 1960: 14).

Instead, the public had to wait until 1948 for viable long-playing records to become available commercially, along with the requisite reproducing system to play them. Their appearance was greeted with approval by many musicians, including the conductor Anton Dorati (Badal 1996: 48), who accorded the many innovations associated with the LP, which included an extended frequency response and improved signal-to-noise ratio, as another pointer toward the holy grail of musical verisimilitude. Yet even allowing for the extra time available on LP, cuts were still frequently made or deemed necessary. For example, the first recording of Benjamin Britten's ballet, *Prince of the Pagodas,* was cut in order to allow the work to be issued on two LPs (Knussen 1990: 25). Such proposed cuts were compromises some composers were unwilling to countenance. When Decca approached English composer Gerald Finzi with a proposal to record his song cycle *Earth, Air and Rain* that involved dropping two songs to accommodate it on a single LP, he refused (Banfield 1998: 204).

From the late 1940s onward the use of tape recorders in recording studios altered radically the way records were produced. They enabled recordings to undergo complex editing techniques, permitting performance errors to be eliminated. But notwithstanding the dramatic improvements to recording that came with the advent of tape, some musicians continued to maintain a moratorium on recording. These included, most famously, the Romanian conductor Sergiu Celibidache, whose major objection to the phenomenon of recording rested on philosophical grounds; it represented to him a gross falsification of the musical experience, which required the presence of a live audience that was absent, by definition, from recording. He insisted that music was an experience that was essentially "organic" and intersubjective, which the past tense of recording negated. In the end, a record was like a photograph: a pale imitation of the real thing. Although he made a few recordings in the 1950s, Celibidache eventually ceased recording and even placed an embargo on the release of the audio tracks from films and videos (to which he initially had fewer objections) of his concerts (Badal 1996: 12; Moor 1976: 12).[12]

Even though the dramatic improvements in the technology of sound reproduction over the last one hundred and thirty years have bolstered the level of verisimilitude and removed many of the "fuzzier edges" (Day 2000: 33) surrounding early recordings, the resultant ameliorations have not drawn universal approval. Take digital sound, for example: conductor Kurt Masur insisted that its results were far from attractive, were too dissecting and penetrating; that they exposed more of the sound field than would ever be heard from the stalls of a concert hall (Badal 1996: 40). The recorded experience, for him, had become too akin to looking down the right end of the telescope: it offered *too* much musical detail. Others like pianist Alfred Brendel (1976: 137) have retained a nostalgia for the 78, which he insists offers more faithful reproduction than either LPs or CDs! Even the transition from acoustic to electrical recording was regarded as a retrograde step; the resultant "overamplification" destroyed the natural feel of the voice (Klein 1990c: 309).

Take One Versus Take Nine

Much of the present ambivalence, as opposed to that of the past, toward contemporary recording techniques is directed at overediting, at the fact that the "take one" of the concert still surpasses, imperfections and all, the "take nine" approach of the contemporary studio (Starker 1987: 185). On this matter the community of musicians is divided and forms two rival, irreconcilable camps: the "take ones," of whom Celibidache was the most famous, who believe in the inherent superiority of the concert, and the "take nines," who revel in the engineering opportunities afforded by the modern studio. In the view of pianist Glenn Gould, the most radical member of the "take nine" camp, the advent of the LP and tape recording rendered the concert obsolete.

The cadre of "take ones," though not large, felt that the techniques of recording led to manufactured and clinical performances devoid of the spontaneity attending a live performance. One reason for Brendel's fondness for 78s was that they were less subject to editing and therefore were more able to sustain the "horizontal" narrative of music. Most 78s were made with at most three takes, which meant that musical perfection had to be achieved almost immediately (Schuller 1987: 406). Modern editing techniques treat music *vertically*, as a series of discrete cross-sections that the performer aims to produce in note-perfect versions at the expense, frequently, of the music's *gestalt* (Brendel 1976: 137). Studio techniques do not recognize that classical music is more than just the sum of its "takes." That is why many performers often favor long takes in the studio, which provide the opportunity to achieve the seamless unity of a concert performance even at the expense of imperfect renditions. Conductor Edo de Waart even suggested that recordings actually benefit from the presence of minor imperfections, for they create the feel of a more lifelike performance (Blyth 1973a: 1303).

Still others favor the "take one" of the concert because it is more commensurate with the essential metaphysic of music. By its very nature, music varies from performance to performance. It is fundamentally ephemeral and transient; it lives and dies the moment it is born. Music was never meant to be "trapped in time" as occurs on record—at least that is the view of conductor Christopher Hogwood (Badal 1996: 93). This entrapment means that performances will inevitably go stale and become tiresome, lose their excitement and spontaneity, and exhaust their surprises, becoming predictable and monotonous. In contradistinction to those on records, every performance in a concert is unique and derives its "magnetic quality" from the fact that its musical surprises cannot be anticipated (Dorati 1979: 299). The concert performance is compelling precisely because it has not been heard in the same way before and will not be heard that way ever again. The "inspiration of the moment" means no two performances of a work are ever the same. The immortalizing power of the record thus is at loggerheads with the manifold contingencies of a live performance. This lay at the core of Celibidache's philosophical objection to recording: that music could not, prior to recording, transcend the present tense was what made its live performance special, surrounding it with an "aura" and sacred traits (Benjamin 1970a). Not all musicians thus have been impressed with the record's capacity to extinguish music's perishable nature and annihilate those spatial and temporal predicates that once limited its performance to the here and now.

Even the idea that, had recording existed in the past we might now be listening to Beethoven and Mozart's performances of their own works is not universally held as an attractive prospect. The absence of such recordings means that each generation of musicians must reinvent those compositions and impose their own interpretations on them (Turner 1933: 234). This is a privilege denied to current generations of musicians, for past recordings of a work—except in the increasingly rare instances where none exists—always shadow their own. Yet Edward Elgar, whose passion for the gramophone was unbridled, unlike that of many of his contemporaries, felt that future generations of musicians would derive benefit from these "shadows" (Moore 1974: 20). One conductor who did so was Georg Solti, who in the 1970s used Elgar's 1920s HMV recording of his Second Symphony as the inspiration for his own recording of it and was overjoyed to discover that it was refreshingly devoid of sentiment (Blyth 1972: 659).

In fact, many musicians now use records as exegetical reference points, to gauge the veracity of their interpretations in relation to those of authoritative ones from the past, much as Edison and Berliner imagined they would.[13] Recordings have enabled musicians to "tune into," and learn from, the performing traditions of the past. They have extended the anti-amnesic functions of notation into the area of performance and enabled the musical "voices" of the past to be resurrected. They have also enabled musicians to control their musical legacies. For example, György Ligeti, who is currently supervising a complete recording of his works for Teldec, sees recording as a means of ensuring the future survival of his music, and he has drawn a parallel to the way that, in the fourteenth century, Guillaume de Machaut supervised the preparation of the manuscripts of his own music (Ligeti 2001: 27).

Yet just as many painters feared the impact of the camera and took time to adjust to its aesthetic implications, many musicians feared the phonograph, especially its powers of immutability. Yet only a few have actually speculated as to the regard composers of the past might have had for recording.[14] An exception was the conductor/composer Igor Markevitch, who suggested that the generation of Romantic composers would have been especially enamored with recording, particularly its capacity to reveal the details of complex orchestral passages. By way of example, he cited Hector Berlioz's concerto tone poem *Harold en Italie,* whose extended viola part in a live performance is often overwhelmed by the orchestra; engineers can redress this effect and produce a balance that gives more "presence" to the viola (Kupferberg 1957: 44). Echoing this view and noting the "loquacious" inclinations of many composers, who "overwrite" for the orchestra and load their compositions with more notes than are ever audible, Schoenberg held that the clearer definition of sonorities on recordings would finally lead to more parsimonious scoring (Gould 1966: 58).

Performing music in a studio is of a different order than performing in front of an audience, whose presence some conductors believe—Pierre

Boulez is one—stimulates them to excel (Badal 1996: 130). Indeed many musicians, particularly ones unused to the studio, find the absence of an audience a disarming experience and have developed techniques to compensate for its absence. The Russian-born pianist and conductor Vladimir Ashkenazy, when he commenced his recording career in the West, coped with the disquieting affects of a "disembodied" studio by imagining a phantom audience (Parrott with Ashkenazy 1985: 139). Solti, despite believing that the concert was inherently superior to the record and would never be superseded by it, made countless discs by raising the level of tension in the studio and adding more musical expression, more dynamics, and more rhythm than would ordinarily be the case in a concert hall. This was by way of compensation for the contribution that audiences normally make to a performance (Blyth 1968: 528). Brendel also holds that audiences make a contribution, and that the "motionless listener is part of the performance." The complex social and psychological rapport that exists between the audience and performer is absent from a studio (Brendel 1976: 137), as is the element of risk present in a concert, which keeps the performer constantly in touch with, and alert to, the felicities of a score. For if a performance goes horribly wrong in a studio it can easily be rectified. The fear of failing to live up to the score thus makes its own tacit contribution to musical spontaneity, to the *liveliness* of the live performance.

Yet at least one performer, pianist Claudio Arrau, argued that the conditions of the concert are a social construction producing its own psychological and acoustical exigencies, unbecoming and irritating when repeated *ad nauseam*. Audiences have their own characteristics, depending on their size or even their ethnicity, that performers learn to respond and "play to" (Lehmann 1966: 17). And even though in the more clinical context of a studio, performers can now play wrong notes with impunity, knowing full well that they can be fixed, many musicians, including the pianist Alicia de Larrocha (Blyth 1973b: 654), still experience phonophobia and actually commit more errors than they ever would in a concert.

In all of these respects, then, "electric" performances are something of a misnomer, for they cannot, so to speak, be dialed up and switched on in the studio. There has been a longstanding animosity among classical performers toward the negative atmospherics of the modern recording studio. Otto Klemperer was one such performer and would have much preferred to issue recordings of his live concerts rather than go through the rigmarole of studio recording (Heyworth 1973: 124). In fact, in the last decade or so there has been a discursive shift in this regard, and many performers—Brendel (1984: 1157) is one—have begun to favor the issuing of recordings of their live concerts; notwithstanding the presence of such "take one" incidentals as the

sound effects of their audiences, these artists feel that these recordings provide a more authentic representation of musicianship than is possible in the
confines of the studio. This is a growing trend, exemplified by the number of
labels devoted to issuing live recordings. One is LSO Live, whose catalog is
drawn from recordings made at London's Barbican, the home of the London
Symphony Orchestra. Its recordings are said to "offer the energy and emo-
tion that you can only experience live in the concert hall."[15]

A problem—similar to the deflation one might experience upon seeing
the original of a painting after only ever seeing it in reproduction—is that in a
culture in which records have become the main vehicles for listening to
music, the auditory qualities of live performances often prove sonically dull
when compared with those of state-of-the-art recordings. Stravinsky feared
this eventuality and thought that the era of electrified music would spoil the
ear for natural sounds (1936: 244). The artificial sound of recordings, however, is but one facet of the phonographic phenomenon to perturb musicians. Benjamin Britten (1964: 20), for example, was ambivalent about the
consequences of the universal access to music provided by the phonograph,
and thought it had harmed, not benefited, the cause of music. Of particular
concern to him was the widespread practice of playing classical records as
background music at parties, which he regarded as an irreverent practice verging on profanity—a regression to the bad old days when audiences talked their
way through concerts. But as the technology of auditory reticulation has enabled music to be transmitted to virtually any environment, the option of insu-
lating music from such "abuses" has become increasingly difficult. In fact,
some would see them as yet one more symptom of the elision between elite
and popular culture that is a pervasive feature of the postmodern society,
where formerly sacrosanct categories such as the divine and the secular—at
least in Western cultures—have been abandoned (Huyssen 1986).[16]

Conductors and musicians have further suggested that much of the dramatic power formerly associated with music has been slowly undermined by
the pervasive amplification associated with recording. As a consequence, audiences have become blasé and desensitized to the amplitude of an orchestra,
and it has become more difficult to engender a response to orchestral extrem-
ism. When the "excessive sonorities" of the *Miraculous Mandarin* "can no
longer put people off their bridge," it was, suggested the composer Constant
Lambert, time to switch off the "universal loudspeaker," at least for the purposes of "propagating good music" (1934: 334). Furthermore, the fact that
the gramophone has produced a veritable cornucopia of music that is always
accessible has been held as not altogether a good thing, for it has produced a
new tyranny: that of being unable to escape the intrusion of music into
every facet of life—in effect, the very silencing of silence (Barzun 1969: 72).

The cumulative effect of such constant musical intrusiveness is that individuals are now so saturated with sounds that they have difficulty responding to the delicate and subtle nuances of music (Honegger 1966: 27).

Like several other habitués of the recording studio who took the view that the only true musical experience was a live one, Britten thought that recorded music had induced a measure of musical laziness, that the record made music *too* accessible. He argued that attendance at a real concert demanded effort and sacrifice: saving for the tickets, journeying to the concert, doing background "homework on the programme"—all of which provided a moral dividend (Britten 1964: 20). The gramophone was, by comparison, an instantaneous form of musical experience that required hardly any of the sacrifices associated with attending a concert. Records made music too easy! Allied to this was the fear that the phonograph would eventually render the processes of listening passive and inert (Stravinsky 1936: 244). It would thwart any desire to acquire the type of musical intelligence upon which the appreciation of serious music is predicated, and for which prolonged study is a necessary prerequisite. Pierre Boulez, who by all accounts never listens to recordings and does not own a gramophone, also espouses such a view. He argues that a score ought to be enough of a listening aid and that all forms of listening outside of the concert hall are of questionable worth (Day 2000: 222).[17] Here is the notion that the appreciation of "serious"—surely a telling epithet in this connection—music requires sustained attention and depends for its acquisition on a musical version of the work ethic to be anything other than superficial.

John Philip Sousa first propagated the idea that the phonograph might have a malign influence on the condition of music. He worried about what might happen to the vitality of live music if the phonograph were to take over. In a provocative essay published in 1906, he was critical of the invasion of the phonograph into the musical habitat, which he likened to the impact of the sparrow on the native bird population of the United States. He worried about, among other things, the intellectual property rights of musicians. "Canned music," he thought, would undo much of the grassroots musical activity that had effloresced in the United States in the latter parts of the nineteenth century. Because this activity required levels of application foreign to the phonographic milieu, Sousa feared that active music making would soon wither. That a machine might one day replace singing schools and country bands, put infants to sleep, even carol love songs was a development he decried (1906: 280). He saw the phonograph as a menace that threatened "American music and musical taste" and would never inspire the next young Beethoven or Mozart. It was a disease whose spread would suffocate such accomplishments as singing, which would eventually have dire consequences for the "national throat" and the "national chest" (Sousa 1906: 281).

But it is also true that by the 1920s and 1930s, many were increasingly sanguine about the prospects of the gramophone. Thomas Mann's *Doctor Faustus* is telling in this respect. At a gathering at an industrialist's home at which the composer hero, Adrian Leverkühn, was present, it was noted that good gramophone records had begun to be produced that had the capacity to move their listeners to tears. This prompts Leverkükn to indulge in the aesthetic observation that, *pace* Goethe, listeners should not be afraid of the sensual, even in music (Mann 1968: 396–97). Others at the time held that the gramophone had raised the levels of musical intelligence in the population and generated an almost universal enthusiasm for good music. There were a number of reasons for this. As English conductor Adrian Boult pointed out, prior to the gramophone and the radio, music—as if there were only *one* legitimate form of music—had remained the privilege of the wealthy, and the circumstances of the gramophone and radio provided far less intimidating environments in which to acquire musical insights than concerts did. Moreover, music on record and on the radio offered listeners access to better quality music—again, the assumptions are revealing—than that available in most concerts (Boult 1934: 432). According to Arthur Bliss, who toured the English provinces in the 1930s, records and radio, contrary to Sousa's presentiments, had generated a renaissance in music making (1991: 152). It was suggested that the transporting effects of recorded music had helped to produce this: recordings made classical music accessible to communities that formerly had had no such access (Daubeny 1920: 486).

A Tool of Composition:
The Phonograph as Musical Instrument

But it is the nature of the music preserved by the phonograph that has most perturbed some composers. Pierre Boulez, for one, has argued that the technology of recording, despite forever undergoing dramatic advancements, has generally retarded the "sound profile" of contemporary classical music. He has suggested that recording has produced a backward-looking musical culture propelled by a museum rather than a laboratory aesthetic, manifested in the fact that the "heritage" standpoint is hegemonic in the classical record industry, where musical preservation seems to be the primary goal. It is devoted to a permanent renaissance of older musical traditions, revivalism on a gargantuan scale.[18] Such "conservative historicism" has stagnated the type of acoustic progress that might have involved scientists and sound engineers in a complete reinvention of music and a radical extension of its acoustic possibilities (Boulez 1986: 492). Ironically, the hegemonic historicism that pervades the classical industry is less evident in popular recording, where the urge to "make it new" is part of the prevailing ideology and the idea of reviving popular music of the past is a much less dominant imperative.

Another prominent phonographic apostate, one who preferred listening to silence over records, was John Cage (1976: 106). Like Boulez, he thought that the almost pathological obsession with the faithful recreation of music on record, in the name of high fidelity, had squandered the potential inherent in the technology to extend the resources of sound. With the Zen-like simplicity that was his wont, he saw high fidelity as but one point on the circle of phonographic potential.

Thus although there came to be a begrudging acceptance of the reality of the phonograph in musical life, which sometimes likened its impact there to that of the industrial revolution on manufacturing, there was always a caveat: the concert or recital took precedence, and the record, no matter how good, would never surpass music in its live state (Dyson 1935: 115, 121). At best, then, mechanized music has been regarded as an inferior mode of music representation, sufficing only in the absence of anything better. The discourse of the concert hall thus slowly emerged as the keystone discourse to which classical recording should defer.

Yet not all musicians have been comfortable with the notion that the "take one" of the concert hall is necessarily superior to the recording. To the contrary, some musicians have argued that mechanized music should be encouraged rather than disparaged, for as Arnold Schoenberg noted in the 1920s, the blanket opposition to mechanized music obscured a truism: all music emanating from instruments is to some extent mechanical, and music's manifold mechanisms have always been subject to progressive refinement. These have usually ameliorated rather than impaired musical representation and articulation (Schoenberg 1975: 329). However, it is of course also true that the instruments remained, for the most part, in the control of the musicians. The advent of the phonograph added a new factor to the musical equation that shifted the locus of control from musicians to record producers and engineers and engendered a competition between the acoustic efficacy of the concert and of the phonograph.

Yet beginning with the composer Claude Debussy, the discursive conditions of early twentieth-century music were receptive to exploiting exotic sounds of all types, human and mechanical. Much of the excitement generated by Gamelan music—Debussy's passion—was prompted by a desire to reinvigorate Western music and liberate it from the shackles of exhausted compositional traditions. In this climate of experiment arose a fascination with new instruments and sounds, not all of them musical. The cacophony of contemporary life, for example, began to hold attractions for some composers as worthy of musical recreation—and not just among avant-garde composers.[19]

Factories, machines, and the "orchestra" of the modern city street were seen as authentic subjects for music, and a number of works, the tone poems of modernity, comprised sonic impressions of industrial and metropolitan life. Erik Satie's use of typewriters and pistol shots in his ballet *Parade* was typical of this urge to represent the acoustic timbre of the twentieth century, as was George Antheil's *Ballet mécanique* and Edgard Varèse's *Ionisation*, which used such mechanical sources as sirens and airplane propellers.[20]

More or less at the same time as these mechanical additions to the orchestra were being made, primitive electronic instruments were under development: the Dynaphone, for example, was a cross between a radio and modern synthesizer, and it was envisaged as a rival to the phonograph that would spread music via telephone lines "to towns, villages, and even farm-houses up to a hundred miles or more from the central station." Its inventor, Thaddeus Cahill, was motivated by egalitarian impulses and wanted to submit good music to the "democracy of enjoyment," to extend music's pleasures beyond the privileged sectors of society (Baker 1906: 293). Other early electronic instruments included the gargantuan Telharmonium—it weighed over two hundred tons—and the Theremin, both of which engendered interest among musicians. Stokowski collaborated with the inventor of the Theremin in a series of concerts held in New York during the 1920s (Dunn 1996: 90–91; Théberge 1997).

There was, then, during the initial decades of the twentieth century a growing view among composers that the future of music lay in the development of electrical and mechanical sources of sonority, and that the epoch of orthodox instrumentation might be reaching its end. Busoni had even suggested as much in casting around for a new aesthetic of music (Stuckenschmidt 1970: 137). For some musicians, then, mechanization was not an epithet of derision; to the contrary, it epitomized the very future of music.

The existence of this discourse environment, which ran counter to that delineated elsewhere in this chapter, provided an environment in which the phonograph was also adopted as a musical instrument in its own right. The fact that early phonographs were relatively portable and had a record function encouraged composers to collect "specimens" of exotic music from folk communities throughout Europe, which they then appropriated in their own compositions.[21] In 1905, Zoltán Kodály, followed a year later by Béla Bartók, began making regular expeditions into the countryside of Hungary and Romania, where he recorded samples of folk music; Bartók, for one, saw Thomas Edison as the father of ethnomusicology (Brady 1999: 80). Incidentally, because both were rather short of money, Bartók and Kodály initially used recycled cylinders that had been scraped clean of dance music that had "gone out of vogue" (Gergely 1955: 59). Percy Grainger was another composer who undertook phonographic expeditions, collecting specimens of English folk music that he later reworked. He was also impressed with the special qualities of the phonograph. His "folk singers and chantymen" (1997) appeared less inhibited by the phonograph than by the transcription of their songs onto paper. This was not unlike Bartók's singers, who also responded favorably to the phonograph, partly because they had the opportunity to hear themselves singing (Demény 1971: 119). Furthermore, by slowing down the phonograph it was possible to distinguish aspects of the music that were inaudible when the recording was running at normal speed. Even so, because musical notation was imprecise Grainger had to be satisfied with the "nearest writable [sic] form of what I actually heard" (Grainger 1997: 24). Indeed, Grainger hoped that a more sophisticated version of the "phonautograph" would one day be invented that would provide a "visible record on paper" of musical sounds.

Other composers used records as musical "reference books"—as sources of exotic forms of music that they eventually reworked into their compositions. Darius Milhaud used a number of Black Swan recordings of jazz he acquired in Harlem as the basis for his ballet La Création du monde (1952: 118). Ragtime records acquired in the United States by the conductor Ernest Ansermet prompted Stravinsky's enthusiasm for jazz, which eventually found creative expression in a number of works, including L'Histoire du soldat and Ragtime (Craft 1957: 35).

Sometimes recordings provided the sources that enabled composers to add auditory authenticity to their compositions. The more "exotic" passages of Madame Butterfly, it has been suggested, were derived from recordings of Japanese music—possibly made by Fred Gaisberg—presented to Puccini by the Gramophone Company (Klein 1990b: 281).[22] Likewise, William Walton was supposed to have filched the folk song "Bailero" for his score of Laurence Olivier's film of Henry V from the record Songs of the Auvergne, which Vivien Leigh purchased for him (Amis 1985: 56). When Ligeti was studying music in the postwar years in Hungary, recordings obtained from West Germany offered the only opportunity—radio broadcasts in eastern Europe were still jammed at the time—to hear the works of Schoenberg, Bartók, and Stravinsky (Griffiths 1997: 13).

The recognition that the phonograph could assist composers in various ways was also manifest in the fact that it was sometimes used as a "musical" instrument, either to augment the sounds of the orchestra or to propagate new types of sound. The capacity to change the pitch of sound through altering the rotational speed of a record, which provoked much hilarity at public demonstrations of early phonographs (it made tenors sound like sopranos), now became a means for synthesizing and altering musical sounds. Darius Milhaud and Paul Hindemith both wrote works that exploited this capacity

(Davidson 1994: 308).[23] Even more radical was the proposal of Bauhaus artist Lázló Moholy-Nagy during the 1920s that the phonograph be used to *produce,* not just reproduce, sounds, and that instead of using outside sources of sound to inscribe the "groove," that process might be carried out, direct to disc, by the stylus itself (Kaplan 1995: 33).

Occasionally composers employed the gramophone as an orchestral instrument. The first one to do so was Ottorino Respighi; his 1924 tone poem *Pines of Rome* uses a recording of a nightingale, and its published score identified the precise disc to be used, Concert Record Gramophone NR 61205. Interestingly, at the point in the score where the record plays, harp and muted strings are used to veil the record's surface noise (Chislett 1925: 277). The music critic for the *Sunday Times,* Ernest Newman, was not impressed with the effect and thought that the phonograph's crude realism clashed with Respighi's subtle orchestration (Lyons and Casey 1990: 8). Another composition that contains a part for gramophone discs to be played on variable speed turntables (anticipating the scratching techniques of modern hip-hop and techno) is the first work in John Cage's *Imaginary Landscapes.* In his 1927 opera *Der Zar lässt sich photographieren,* which helped to establish his reputation and led to his collaboration with Berthold Brecht, Kurt Weill uses the phonograph as a central "character." In fact, Weill uses two engines of verisimilitude, the camera (which doubles as a pistol) and the gramophone, in the opera's plot. A recording of "Tango Angèle," which was made under Weill's supervision and was part of the material issued to theatres by Universal for productions of the opera, acted as an instrument of distraction and saved the czar from assassination (Schebera 1995).

More or less at the same time as the gramophone was being included as an instrument in the orchestra, composers also began composing with the record in mind, recognizing its temporal limits as a Procrustean force. For example, some of the arias in Puccini's later operas were timed to coincide with the length of a 78 (Wilson 1997: 87). And though not at the time enamored of the phonograph, Stravinsky wrote a series of piano pieces collectively known as the *Sérénade en la* that could be accommodated on each side of two 78s. Occasionally, it has been suggested that the application of this same Procrustean force actually improved some compositions. When the first recording of Kodály's Cello Sonata was being undertaken, the work's performer, Janos Starker, suggested that the cuts necessary for the recording added much more cohesion to the sonata (Starker 1987: 188).

In their quest for cultural legitimacy, several American record companies began to court serious composers through various schemes in the 1920s and 1930s. These included a number of competitions for which lucrative cash prizes were offered. In 1929, RCA Victor offered a prize of $25,000 for the

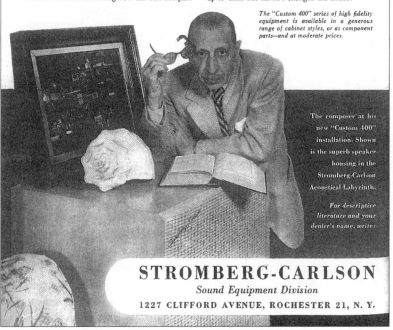

Figure 2.1 Beginning in the 1950s, composers and conductors endorsed audio components. This is a significant development and marks a departure from the 1920s, when most "serious" musicians disparaged the phonograph. The above advertisement (_Saturday Review,_ 27 February 1954) for Stromberg-Carlson's "Custom 400" loudspeaker exemplifies the new trend. Its copy suggests that a musician's ear is particularly attuned to "the most subtle nuances of music" and likens the loudspeaker to a "fine microscope" that has the capacity to bring out the "tiniest details of tone, harmony and musical timbre." There is also a reference to the decentered concert—"home listening as though the artist were in the same room"—an echo of the "Both are Farrar" theme.

composition of a symphonic work. Aaron Copland entered his *Dance Symphony*, a "scion" from his early ballet *Grohg* (Copland 1941: 228). Kurt Atterberg's Sixth Symphony, nicknamed the "Dollar Symphony" because of its "prized" origins, resulted from another of these competitions, one organized by Columbia as part of its celebrations commemorating the centenary of Schubert's death. In 1973, Deutsche Grammophon, commemorating its seventy-fifth anniversary as a company, commissioned a work from the avant-garde composer Maurizio Kagel. The result was *1898*, which used an ensemble of Stroh violins—inspired by a 1910 photograph of such an ensemble—that pays "recorded" homage to Deutsche Grammophon's prominent role in the early history of recording.

Some composers, as they came to value the gramophone's importance, entered into symbiotic relationships with the record industry. Edward Elgar's relationship with HMV was not atypical. In the 1920s Elgar embarked on a series of recordings of his own works, and in return HMV satisfied his requests for records and gramophones (Moore 1974).[24] Indeed, many composers by the late 1940s had begun to change their minds about recording. Stravinsky not only embarked on a complete recording of his works for CBS, but had begun to participate in product endorsement for the audio industry (as Elgar did in the 1920s for HMV). In one such endorsement, for Stromberg-Carlson, Stravinsky claimed that as a composer he had more than a passing interest in the "most subtle nuances of sound," and that the endorsed loudspeaker was like a microscope in terms of its capacity to reveal the hidden details of the music (Figure 2.1). Unlike the earlier examples of recording industry advertising that used indirect forms of endorsement, this ad cites the actual words of "the world-famed creator of *The Firebird.*"

Recording as an Indigenous Phenomenon: From Stokowski to Gould

From the mid-1920s onward, several prominent musicians commenced collaborations with the recording industry on a range of research and development projects. One was the conductor Leopold Stokowski, who went from being ill-disposed toward the phonograph to one of its most avid proponents. In the 1930s, he collaborated with the Bell Telephone Laboratories on a series of experiments investigating various aspects of recording, including the dynamic range of the orchestra, binaural sound, early stereo, and tracking problems, and played a decisive role in the development of the sapphire stylus. His Philadelphia Orchestra acted as a guinea pig for some of these experiments (McGinn 1983). One of Stokowski's concerns was that the technical exigencies of microphones demanded a set of acoustic parameters different from those normally deployed in the concert hall (Stokowski 1943: 173). In fact, Stokowski was never an ardent defender of the idea that the classical record should defer to the acoustic conditions of the live concert. He considered this principle a "meaningless criterion for music heard in the home" (Marsh 1961: 47). In order to better balance the orchestra on a recording and to adjust its various layers of sound, he experimented with the placement of instruments in the orchestra and altered them to optimize their sound on recordings. In the prewar period, he deliberately informed himself about the limitations of the recording and worked to make the best of them. According to Charles O'Connell, head of the Artists and Repertoire Department at RCA Victor during the 1940s, Stokowski believed that he could accomplish "more by manipulation of the orchestra than by revolving a rheostat" (O'Connell 1947: 291). And in the 1960s and 1970s, when the technology of recording began to offer many more auditory options, Stokowski became a strong advocate of quadraphony, which he also helped to pioneer, and Decca's Phase Four, which used a 20-channel console mixer (Opperby 1982: 175). This allowed for a sound "perspective"—outlined in an essay/interview with Glenn Gould (1987a: 266)—that could be adjusted to bring into sharp relief, when the musical argument demanded it, particular sections of the orchestra. Such techniques were in some respects the antithesis of concert hall representation, where the orchestra is treated as a smooth whole with no section subjected to unnatural accentuation.

Herbert von Karajan was another conductor who collaborated with the record industry, always keeping abreast of its developments and ensuring that his interpretations of the basic repertoire were available on the latest format of reproduction.[25] Toward the end of his career he collaborated with Akio Morita of the Sony Corporation on the development of the compact disc and encouraged Deutsche Grammophon—his record label—to establish a pressing plant for CDs in Hanover (Lebrecht 1991: 122). Like Stokowski, he also challenged the dominant discourse of the recording studio and urged the abandonment of the concert hall as the benchmark acoustic, arguing that it impaired one's ability to achieve more adequate forms of orchestral resolution. A case in point was his recording of Arnold Schoenberg's *Variations for Orchestra*. In Karajan's recording—part of a boxed set devoted to the music of the Second Viennese School—the orchestra is reorganized for each variation in a way that would be impossible in a live concert. This enabled the conductor to obtain the "right orchestral presence" for each variation and "to create the acoustic that one sees and imagines when one looks at the score."[26]

But while Stokowski and Karajan were notable advocates of phonographic technology and thought it was possible to extend the domain of musical representation on record beyond that possible in the concert, they never renounced concert performances. This was left to one of their admirers, the Canadian pianist Glenn Gould, who retired from the concert hall in favor of the recording studio, where he thought the musical future lay. His views are, in fact, not that far removed from the American composer Milton Babbitt, who also thought that the concert, at least for contemporary music, no longer communicated with audiences and so was an anachronism. Such music, he argued, would be better served by becoming the province of private performance (as it was prior to Haydn) and the electronic media. This would enable its composers to avoid the "unprofessional compromise and exhibitionism" forced on them by lay audiences lacking the expertise and fortitude to appreciate more esoteric musical practices (Babbitt 1958).

Gould's own reasons for deserting the concert hall stemmed from his long-held belief that recording was inherently superior to the concert. This superiority had been made possible by the tape recorder, which enabled a level of musical intervention into the recording process that had hitherto been impossible. In fact, its myriad interventions meant that making a recording was more akin to making a film than to playing a concert. And just as the process of editing had added new narrative options to the vocabulary of film, Gould argued that the performance and representation of music could be transformed by its own editing techniques. Indeed, he came to maintain that the processes of making music would increasingly weld the techniques of the engineer with those of the performer and represent intersections of science and art.

Gould's espousal of "take nine" discourse flew in the face of those musicians who believed that the art of music should be quarantined from too much technological and editorial intervention. Gould instead argued that the techniques of patching and splicing—to which many "take one" performers objected—actually enhanced rather than inhibited the coherence of a performance (1987b: 354). For Gould they enabled an error-free, note-perfect performance far in excess of that which was possible in a concert.

Such editorial interventions also posed a fundamental challenge to the metaphysical framework of music, that by virtue of its temporal extension music performances cannot normally be altered—at least in real time. However, with the assistance of the tape recorder these metaphysical constraints could be transcended so that even wrong or absent musical notes could be added or amended, even by sets of performers different from those originally present in the studio. Such techniques of phonographic "cheating" invalidated the idea of an "authentic" performance, of the record as a record of anything real at all. When Gould further discovered that listeners, even those with excellent ears, could not detect whether a recording had been edited or not—could not, in effect, differentiate the genuine from the fake—he beatified the Dutch forger of Vermeer paintings Hans van Meegeren as the patron saint of the electronic age (1987c: 341). Thus Gould came increasingly to advocate that recording be viewed as a different medium of music making, an "indigenous phenomenon" with its own particular hallmarks and characteristics that owed nothing to the conventions of the concert (1987d: 363). He then led by example and in 1964, after thinking about it for a decade, decided to cease giving public performances. His final recital was in Chicago's Orchestral Hall and included works to which he attributed special musical significance, such as Ernst Krenek's Third Sonata (Gould 1987e: 194). Until his untimely death in 1982, he dedicated the remainder of his musical career to a range of phonographic projects. This included a much-celebrated series of Bach recordings, the writing of liner notes for CBS, and the production of seminal articles analyzing the phenomenon of recording. It is of note, for it vindicates his sympathetic stance toward recording, that many of the latter articles appeared in the American magazine *High Fidelity*.

In fact, Gould predicted, in what continues to be one of the most exhaustive defenses of phonographic philosophy, *The Prospects of Recording,* originally broadcast on Canadian radio, that the concert would become moribund in the twenty-first century and that the main axes of music making would be electronic ones (1966). The original version of Gould's essay was edged with a series of annotations from "key figures in the worlds of music, recordings, and mass communications" including Aaron Copland, Leopold Stokowski, Milton Babbitt, and Marshall McLuhan, all of whom engage in a "marginal" dialogue with Gould's propositions in which they variously contest or affirm their cogency.[27] For example, Babbitt expressed incredulity that listeners still tolerated the physical inconveniencies of a concert when they could "sit at home" and hear it (Gould 1966: 44). Besides, as Gould pointed out in the main body of his essay, the concert could not compete with the acoustic "perspicacity" of the phonograph; microphones could penetrate the inner secrets of compositions and provide an auditory experience impossible in a concert hall, whose architectural inadequacies as a sound environment frequently blur and obscure the sonorities of complex compositions. Gould named Frank Martin's *Petite symphonie concertante* as an example of a composition that he suggested often failed when performed in concert but not on record. In fact, Gould could only see virtue in recording and characterized his antagonists as Luddites. But, interestingly, in the seventeen years since Gould had originally predicted its demise, it was the concert hall, not the recording studio, which was undergoing a renaissance. When confronted with this paradox, he suggested that it was a mere aberration and that come the twenty-first century the record would have superseded the concert (Gould 1987f: 457).

Of equal import to Gould's phonographic philosophy was his willingness to explore approaches to recording that unsettled the keystone discourse, of which stereophony was only the latest affirmation. In some instances, he also suggested that monophonic sound might serve the interests of some compositions more effectively than stereo's left/right channel separation (Cott 1984). Gould also questioned the slavish preservation of rear-end ambience in the interest of reproducing the acoustic of a concert, which transgressed the logic of music such as that of the Venetian composer Giovanni Gabrieli, which is spread around a space for its antiphonal effects. Gould had already experimented in a demo recording with four-channel sound—the results were never commercially released—in which the individual voices of a Bach fugue were each given their own channel.[28] Furthermore, Gould argued that in the case of a Scriabin sonata there were strong musical justifications for an unconventional recording process in which sections of the sonata would be recorded in different acoustics and with a measure of "pan-spotting," moving the sound sources around the room (Cott 1984: 91). Such techniques of "acoustic orchestration" are exemplified in Gould's own recording of Jean Sibelius's *Kylliki* (Stegermann n.d.: 11). Using multitrack tape and a battery of microphones located around the studio, the recording draws upon a range of sonic perspectives, shifting from long microphone "shots" to close-ups (Friedrich 1990: 254)—the acoustic equivalents of the analogous techniques used in film making.[29]

Further, Gould argued that listeners could add their own forms of "acoustic orchestration" to a recording. The dial twiddling—Stokowski's rheostats—that was possible on the panel of an amplifier facilitated this and enabled the processes of record reproduction to undergo further articulation in the home (1966: 59). Indeed, the proponents of this technological form of chamber music would be able to produce their own performances of a particular work from its existing recordings. By splicing together movements (or even different sections) from recordings made at different times and places, listeners could produce a unique combination of interpretations or even assemble the best possible recording of a work by splicing together the best sections available on record. Such possibilities provided listeners with a range of musical options denied to the members of a concert audience, where the interpretation of a composition is always from a single perspective: the performer's. Indeed, Gould argued that the individualization and privatization of the musical experience permitted by the phonograph meant that contemporary listeners could make musical decisions and judgments in the absence of any social and psychological pressure from the audience as a whole (1987g: 99).

* * *

Although the record has become an integral part of musical culture, this was not always the case, and there was for a time a tendency to demonize recording altogether. The discourse universe of recording has always been fluid and conflict ridden. The advent of the phonograph was not universally embraced, and many people doubted its musical capacities. A context of claim and counterclaim about its merits soon developed. A cultural war of sorts raged between those who wished to sustain the musical status quo, fearing the corrupting influence of the phonograph, and those who saw its impact as benign, arguing that the condition of music might even benefit from it. From this war emerged a series of benchmark discourses about the phonograph, epitomized by the views of two important musical figures. The conductor Celibidache felt that recordings negated the essence of music and that the concert is the apotheosis of musical articulation; the pianist Gould espoused the "disconcerting" view that records have rendered the concert obsolete, and that the forms of "acoustic orchestration" then possible in the recording studio offered more compelling forms of musical representation.

Notwithstanding the fact that the majority of music is transmitted through the medium of recording, many performers and composers still hold on to the belief that the "take one" of the concert—the keystone discourse—constitutes the supreme form of music making, and that reproduced music—even though it now can compete favorably with and may even surpass the concert experience—remains "flat and mediocre" at least when compared to live music. It is somewhat akin to experiencing a photograph of the Alps, beautiful in its own way but not in the same league as the actual Alps (Celibidache 2001: 71).[30] In many respects, then, the alliance between music and technology facilitated by the phonograph has been an uneasy one, with many musicians continuing to advocate the virtues of the live tradition in the face of longstanding challenges from recorded sound. In later chapters, I will argue that these discourses are more than just of passing interest but are central to the way records are produced and engineered, evaluated and judged.

CHAPTER THREE

The Best Seat in the House
The Domestication of the Concert Hall

At once, to my indescribable astonishment and horror, the devilish metal funnel spat
out, without more ado, its mixture of bronchial slime and chewed rubber; that noise
that possessors of the gramophone and radio sets are prevailed upon to call music.
And behind the slime and the croaking there was, sure enough, like an old master
beneath a layer of dirt, the noble outline of that divine music.
—Hermann Hesse, *Steppenwolf,* 246[1]

Although much has been written about the ways in which the phonograph
has transformed the conditions of listening to music, the nature of recorded
sound and its underlying discourses have not been subjected to the same degree of analysis. This neglect is particularly pronounced in the area of classical music, which has been insulated from those developments in cultural
studies that have shed light on the way recording has transformed the nature
of popular music (Frith 1978, 1996; Middleton 1990; Taylor 2001). Part of
the reason for this neglect stems from the cultural ethos that has embedded
the analysis of classical music, which has generally spurned contextual questions relating to music and the technology of its reproduction. The advent
of recorded sound was not one wholeheartedly embraced by classical musicians, who in some cases derided its impact and feared that it might undermine performed music. However, this antipathy toward recording was not
shared by the general public, who did embrace the phonograph, its relative
expense and technical limitations notwithstanding. This served to make the
early record industry among the most profitable in the world, a trend that
has continued despite the economic downturn during the 1930s, when the
Depression and competition from radio and the "talkies" threatened its viability (Jones 1985). The significance of recorded sound as a musical phenomenon, though, extends well beyond the part it has played in the growth
of the transnational media conglomerates.

Much of this significance is not economic at all but derives from the fact that, as a medium of musical preservation, the record has been as revolutionary in its impact as the printing press. What the latter achieved for writing in terms of facilitating its mass reproduction and circulation, the invention of the phonograph achieved for music. Recorded sound enabled those parameters of physics that had once restricted the circulation of music to the circumstances of its provenance to be transcended and reproduced *ad nauseam* and with ever-improving levels of fidelity. As such, the record shares features with other important technologies of preservation as well, such as maps and scientific figures. These technologies, or "immutable mobiles" (Latour 1987; 1990), enable the absent to be reclaimed in the present and cultural data to be translated across generations of time with a minimum of degradation. Such transporting effects are central to the social and material conditions of Western science and culture. They have enabled its epistemological deliberations to be conducted with increasing levels of exactitude and have provided a pragmatic foundation for mobilizing its resources and interests. Importantly, they have also provided a basis for consolidating its practices across the community. A core part of Bruno Latour's argument, which owes much to Foucault's notion of "panopticism," is the idea that the existence of "immutable mobiles" provided a basis for "optical consistency" across a community of inquiry or practice, normalizing its epistemological and ethical standards and drawing together its participants around common values.

Although Latour's insights were primarily directed at science, they can be applied to any field of practice in which modes of inscription are the dominant modes of cultural preservation and transmission.[2] The particular point of departure for this chapter, as for this book in general, is that the practices associated with the recording, be they in the home or the studio, are textually embedded. For while also being "an invention, an industry and a musical instrument" (Gelatt 1977: 11), the phonograph from the start has also encompassed a complex system of texts and inscriptions, everything from the logs kept by record producers to the contents of record criticism and journalism. This web of texts draws together the members of the record community around a common set of reference points and values. Also in among these quotidian texts is a more "reflexive" writing that articulates the keystone discourses associated with recorded sound. These encapsulate the underlying principles of phonographic culture and prescribe the way records are recorded and regarded.

As distinct from hearing, listening is *not* a natural process but one that is socially constructed, produced through the powerful discourses associated with sound, such as those concerning the presentation of music. Stravinsky developed the epithet "'phonogenic' sound," in the absence of a more apposite one, to describe the qualitative dimension of this discourse, and he suggested that it was epitomized in recordings that were naturally balanced (Craft 1957: 100) and that corresponded to the sound of music in a concert hall. Classical records, by and large, attempt to recreate the concert hall in a domestic environment and aim to make the best seat in the house the *best seat in the house*—a telling string of words in this connection, encapsulating the keystone discourse governing classical recording, that only a few have had the temerity to challenge.

Yet, as is clear from the day-to-day practices employed in recording studios, the idea of phonographic verisimilitude is an acoustical construct, "an ingenious form of *trompe-l'oreille*" (Canby, Burke, and Kolodin 1956: 17). For like the verisimilitude achieved in "representational" paintings and drawings (Gombrich 1960: 172), that of recorded sound also depends on techniques of deception, on the fact that engineers are able to provide enough suggestion of realism for listeners to complete the relevant sound picture for themselves. As such, engineers must anticipate listeners' auditory experience and shape the sense of musical similitude accordingly. In this sense, a recording is a joint creation between the engineer and the listener, who is tricked into thinking that its musical representation is real. It is with charting the genealogy of these practices of deception—whose combined impact supports recording's keystone discourse—that this chapter is concerned. For the adoption of these practices across the community of record engineers and producers has drawn it together around a common set of values regarding the desirability of concert hall sound.

Acoustic Recording: The Last Word in Absolute Sound?

Long before their actual invention, humankind had treasured the prospect of machines that had the capacity to preserve the transient beauties of music. However, for the most part these machines only existed on the page as literary invention, and it was not until the advent of such musical automata as the player piano that music could be heard in the absence of performers, and at any time or place. But, though they were impressive as organs of musical representation, such automata were essentially limited in terms of their sonic opportunities and were not able to transcend the auditory ambits of their mechanisms. A player piano could only "play" piano music. The gramophone, though it offered relatively unimpressive results in terms of its acoustic efficacy, at least in its earliest phases of development, was a more versatile medium of sound preservation and could, unlike other musical automata, preserve a much greater range of sounds.

In this respect, the cultural significance of the phonograph as a medium of preservation was understood from the moment it was demonstrated, and it quickly became the subject of manifold commentary. Indeed, as soon as Edison had lodged a patent for his invention, a percipient note appeared in the columns of *Scientific American* that extolled its virtues as a machine that enabled speech to be "immortalized" and music to be "crystallized" and "capable of indefinite repetition" (Johnson 1877: 304). Yet, as was noted in chapter 1, Edison was not overly enamored with the prospect that his invention would be deployed for musical preservation, holding that it had a more desirable future as a business machine. Certainly in its tinfoil version the phonograph proved incapable of preserving much at all. And even when the cylinder was developed, which proved a more robust medium for recording and reproduction, the phonograph's musical capacities were far from impressive. At best, it could only accommodate four minutes of music—not ideal, given that most music, certainly classical music, was considerably longer in duration. This, combined with the fact that the phonograph's frequency range was attenuated, meant that achieving musical realism was all but impossible. Even though by the end of its era the cylinder, in its Blue Amberol version, had achieved respectable auditory results for the time and certainly was better than those achieved by its rival, the gramophone disc, what finally did the cylinder in was that it proved difficult to replicate. This necessarily restricted its circulatory potential and made it prohibitively expensive. The great virtue of Berliner's gramophone disc was that it could be mass-produced, enabling music to be circulated wherever there was a demand for it, without end. Flat discs also made recordings more affordable (Gaisberg 1943: 20). With this potential portability added to its underlying immutability, Berliner's disc brought about Jacques Attali's "culture of repetition" (1985), which transformed the political economy of music and created a radically new relationship between its producers and consumers.

By the time of Berliner's innovation the idea of "good" music finding its home on the gramophone was no longer so inconceivable, and it was fervently promoted in advertising. Following the success of its Caruso records, Victor embarked on a campaign to domesticate the phonograph. This brought home the fact that it was an indispensable gadget of modern life. The advertising associated with this campaign also redressed the tawdry image of the phonograph and helped to sell the idea that it was capable of a range of cultural functions, including broadly educational ones such as the idea that the phonograph was able to satisfy the "universal" love of music and awaken its proper appreciation, or that recorded music could be therapeutic. At the same time, the important notion that the recording offered a degree of musical verisimilitude comparable to that of a live musical experience began to be promoted in advertisements and trademarks such as HMV's, which implied that listening to records was equivalent to listening to the real thing. They created the impression that the record was a *record* of actuality, and that the sound of a record was all but indistinguishable from its source.

These motifs, which emphasized the verisimilitude of recording, were also complemented through a series of public demonstrations, the so-called "Tone Tests" organized by the Edison Company. These demonstrations constituted early examples of the "annual sonic saturnalia" (Gelatt 1977: 259) that were a feature of high fidelity culture after World War II. The first of these tests was held in November 1919 in the Albany State Armory, and it involved a staged competition between the baritone Mario Laurenti, of New York's Metropolitan Opera, and a phonograph. The event and setting, complete with busts of composers, was designed to give the phonograph the bourgeois legitimacy that the industry sought (Thompson, E. 1995: 150). The audience consisted of six thousand teachers, principals, and superintendents, examples of the "fine, intelligent kind of men and women" to whom the nation had entrusted its children.[3] This audience (so it was claimed) was unable to distinguish the sound of the phonograph from that of the singer, for when Laurenti ceased singing and the phonograph played on, the audience was none the wiser. The demonstration thus extended HMV's trademark idea of verisimilitude and provided more proof that the phonograph, such was its convincingness, could "withstand direct comparison" with actuality. Yet for the most part these claims were hyperbolic ones. The sound that was actually achievable on record was subject to severe constraints and fell far short of being the absolute last word in reproduction. Acoustic recording, for example, could not cope with an orchestra consisting of more than forty players, nor could it capture the lower strings, whose parts had to be reassigned to trombones and tubas (Moore 1976: 130).

But there were many other compromises that also diminished the credibility of recorded music during the acoustic era. As has been noted, compositions were for the most part recorded in an abridged state, with whole movements from longer works such as symphonies omitted in order to cope with the fact that most records could, at most, only accommodate four minutes of music per side. Thus reviewers of classical 78s were expected to check their music against a miniature score and identify those passages that had been omitted or adjusted (Helots 1940). In fact, until the late 1920s, when abridged versions of the classics went out of favor, complete recordings of classical music were a rare event. Moreover, there were also mechanical handicaps inherent in the playback equipment that detracted from the realism of recorded sound, such as having to rewind the gramophone and change the needle between records. Indeed, there was a certain amount of art in selecting between the steel and the fiber needle; each left its own distinctive auditory imprint on the record, the former favoring a harsh but louder sound, the latter a mellower and softer sound (Wilson 1973a: 27).

There were thus a whole series of challenges that beset the quest for auditory realism, and meeting them necessitated radical changes to the technical, spatial, and temporal architecture of the record. These changes involved extending the record's playing time, frequency response, and dynamic range, as well as reducing the level of surface noise that bedeviled early records and further undermined their realism. Some of the changes were spatial and involved

Table 3.1 Various Phases of Recording Technology

Tinfoil, Cylinders and Discs		Electrical (Standard Play)	Long Player (LP + MP + EP + 45)	Stereo-phonic	Quadra-phony	Compact Disc (CD)
1877	1887	1926	1948	1958	1972	1983
Tinfoil, 60 rpm, Wax cylinder, 100 rpm	Disc	Shellac, 78 rpm; 7", 10", 12"	Vinyl, 33.33/45 rpm; 7", 10", 12"	—	—	Laser disc 200–500 rpm; 5"
Ear-tubes	Horn	Amplifier	LP player + special pick-up + amplifier	2 loudspeak-ers + amplifier + special cartridge	Amplifier + decoder + 4 loudspeakers	CD player + digital analogue converter (DAC)
4' p/time; s/n: 28 db	f/r: 1000–3000hz	4' p/time; f/r: 200–6000hz; s/n: 30db	20' p/time; f/r: 20–14000hz; s/n: 57db	30' p/time; f/r: 20–20000+hz	—	80' p/time; f/r: 20–20000hz; s/n: 110db
Acoustic		Electrical				
Analogue						Digital

Note:

p/time = playing time;   f/r = frequency response (herz per second);
s/n = signal to noise ratio (decibels)   rpm = revolutions per minute

This table shows the various phases of recording technology. Prior to its "electrification," recording was acoustic. From 1983 onward, analog gradually gave way to digital. Several formats in the development of recording—some omitted from this table—were only short lived, e.g. quadraphony. There is also overlap between rival recording formats; 78s continued to be produced until 1959 and LPs are still being produced for the "audiophile" market. The specifications stated above are approximate values only, particularly those referring to the acoustic era. Cylinders operated at a different speed than gramophone records, and it took some time for the speed of the latter to be standardized at 78 rpm. The discs used as a source of music for cinema intermissions in the 1930s, which played from the inside outward, like the modern CD, determined the speed of LPs.

"channeling" auditory signals in such a way that they were able to recreate the illusion of sound in space: the auditory equivalents of foreshortening and perspective in painting. In fact, the history of recording—outlined in a "figurative" way in table 3.1—is one of constant change centered on improving the record in such a way as to enhance its capacity to create an illusion of "reality."

Thus the contemporary CD, by no means the last word in recorded sound for it is already in the throes of being superseded,[4] can create the illusion of space, has a silent surface, and boasts enough playing time to accommodate, without interruption, most of the longest works (opera excepted) in the classical repertoire. In particular, the dramatic improvement in signal to noise ratio—infinitesimal on the contemporary CD—is indicative of the degree to which the intervening developments in the technology of reproduction have eliminated many of the problems that interfered with the realism of early recordings.

Meanwhile, while the various challenges to the basic fidelity of recorded sound remained unmet, many of the symphonic works in the Western canon—not to mention concertos, string quartets, and so on—still awaited their first recordings, complete or abridged. Indeed, those who wanted to acquire a working knowledge of the classical repertoire were better served by other mechanical contrivances, such as the aforementioned player piano, which had a larger range of "recordings" in its catalogs than were available on disc. For the most part, then, the era of acoustic recording, which lasted until the mid-1920s at least in the classical sphere, was preeminently a medium of the opera singer.

Realists and Idealists: The Search for the Absolute in Sound

It was, in part, to remedy this situation and encourage record companies to play a more active role in the realm of classical music that the well-known author Compton Mackenzie, with his brother-in-law, Christopher Stone, founded *The Gramophone* in 1923, the history of which is chronicled in chapter 6. From the moment of its launch, this magazine proved to be an influential feuilleton in the spread of phonographic culture and the development of the record review as a specialized genre of music criticism. Although the majority of its pages were devoted to such reviews, it did cover allied matters, including most importantly reviews of the equipment used to play discs. In fact, the editorial remit of the magazine was an electro-musical one, encompassing not just the qualities of musical performance on records but also their engineering. In order to encompass these two facets of recording, the magazine employed two sets of reviewers. The magazine was, quite literally, a sounding board for the advancement and elaboration of phonographic ideas and practices, providing an early forum for their articulation and formalization. Among other matters, debates about what constituted optimal recorded sound began to be mounted in its pages that led to the development of a range of criteria for judging one record and form of player to be superior to another. Thus emerged a series of secondary discourses that given *The Gramophone*'s authority as an influential magazine, served to regulate the way records were supposed to sound, mediating their audition by magnifying the importance of certain auditory qualities and disparaging others.

One noteworthy textual moment in the articulation of these secondary discourses preceded a well-known event in the history of recording. This was a competition in the mold of Edison's "Tone Tests" that was held at London's Steinway Hall in June 1924 to determine the most euphonious of the myriad available gramophones (Gilbert 1983: 96). In relation to this event, Mackenzie wrote a long editorial for his magazine that was subsequently reprinted in his "musical autobiography" (1955: 128–29). Entitled "Search for the Absolute," it divided gramophones into "romantic" and "realist" types that in turn reflected the prejudicial temperaments of their listeners. In characterizing the typical romantic gramophone, Mackenzie noted its tendency toward a "mellow tone" that, although quite seductive, particularly on first hearing, came about "illegitimately by a falsification of life," even making an oboe sound like a flute, a violin like a cello, and so on. By contrast, more acoustically faithful gramophones offered a closer approximation of the musical truth but in so doing were "apt to insist unduly on the unpleasant things in life," such as "Galli-Curci's nasal tone." In conclusion, Mackenzie drew attention to an alarming tendency toward widening the hiatus between the actual sound of music and that of the gramophone. He noted with alarm the "gramophonic Platonists," who wished to idealize sound and produce "a more perfect expression of music" than would ever be possible in the concert hall. Mackenzie insisted that the gramophone should not falsify the actualities of the concert hall but instead constantly defer to them and endeavor "to reproduce played music" (Mackenzie 1955: 128–29).

Mackenzie's binary between the phonographic idealists and the phonographic realists echoed the views of many musicians of the time. Importantly though, in later reviews and discussion of recordings and equipment it is increasingly suggested that departing from the sound of a concert—the keystone discourse—constituted unsound phonographic practice.

In the pages of *The Gramophone* during the 1920s and 1930s there was an ongoing debate utilizing Mackenzie's binary about whether records were superior to live performances. Percy Wilson, the magazine's technical editor and a prominent participant in this debate, concluded that live and recorded performances provided different kinds of acoustic reality. That this was so, however, did not mean that producers of records could be satisfied with "any standard of reproduction as long as it is not unpleasant." To the contrary, they had always to strive for "an illusion of reality" consistent with the acoustic qualities of a live performance (cited in Read and Welch 1976: 356). Thus, when electrical recordings were released during the mid-1920s there was intense interest in the degree to which these new techniques added to or detracted from the pursuit of phonographic realism.

Arguably, while the techniques of recording were only able to capture the sound of a symphony orchestra in an attenuated form, the matter of whether records were real or not was largely academic. Even though, from the earliest days of recording, it was regularly claimed that the last word in sound had been reached and that records were indistinguishable from their sources (Rabinowitz and Reise 1994: 286), in actual fact records fell far short of this. It was not until the 1940s and the coming of Decca's "full frequency range recording"—which was originally developed during World War II as a way to help pilots identify the sonic signatures of enemy submarines (Briggs, G. 1961: 158–59; Haddy 1968: 158)—that the record gained the capacity to capture the full amplitude of a symphony orchestra. When Decca first advertised its full frequency range recordings, it claimed that they could reproduce "every note with all its overtones and bring . . . *living music into the home*"(my emphasis).[5] The technique meant, in theory at least, that for the first time the complete sound of an orchestra, from an organ pedal to a triangle, could appear on a recording.

More or less contemporary with the development of full frequency range recording were two other significant technological innovations that radically reshaped recording culture: the long-playing record, created by U.S. Columbia during the 1940s under a team headed by Peter Goldmark (Scott 1998; Wallerstein and Botsford 1976), and magnetic tape recording. In fact, several other companies had developed longer-playing records prior to World War II. Edison, for example, had developed a record lasting forty minutes in 1926; however, it was deficient in terms of its capacity to reproduce either higher frequencies or a high volume of sound (Millard 1995: 195). From 1934 onward the Royal National Institute for the Blind in the U.K. had issued LPs for their talking books. These had more grooves than the normal 78 and played at 24 rpm (Wilson 1973b: 2138). Also, Bell Laboratories had patented an LP in the 1930s, but it lacked an adequate playback system.

Although musicians such as Leopold Stokowski (1943: 228) had for some time been exhorting record companies to develop records of longer duration, the technology to do so was not forthcoming until after the war, which provided other technological breakthroughs as well that the LP appropriated. For example, the shellac material from which 78s were made—which had become unavailable during World War II—was far too gritty for LPs, which required a finer material.[6] The finer material was eventually derived from poly-vinyl-chloride (PVC), which could accommodate the increased number of grooves per inch required for longer playing records (Read and Welch 1976: 333). It was also much quieter than shellac and served to reduce, though not eliminate, the "slime and the croaking" alluded to in this chapter's epigraph that had veiled the sound of 78s.

But it was the introduction of the tape recorder into U.S. recording studios after World War II that led to the most radical transformation of phonographic practice. Long contemplated as an alternative means of recording, the magnetic tape process underwent extensive development in Germany in the 1930s and 1940s (Angus 1973).[7] In fact, magnetic recording represented a different kind of sound preservation, the most popular form was the cassette, which paved the way for the development of Sony's Walkman, which was sufficiently small and portable to be pocketed, thereby allowing music to be "embodied." Prior to this, Grundig and Telefunken had designed reel-to-reel machines for the domestic market, spawning a whole audio-subculture of hobbyists. For a period in the 1950s, tape offered superior sound to LPs and also made stereo available as a domestic format prior to its appearance on vinyl. Several record labels including EMI developed extensive catalogs of tape recordings. Yet in spite of its superiority of sound, tape recording as an audio subspecies could not survive the processes of natural selection that followed in the wake of the CD (O'Connell 1992).

Recording methods during the acoustic era were cumbersome, and musical errors were difficult to eradicate. Although electrical recording and microphones improved the quality of recorded sound, studio practice remained dominated by the "take one" approach. The performance had to be right the first time, or not all. The advent of magnetic tape changed this and reduced many of the hazards that had hitherto hindered the accuracy of recordings. Although it had been possible to eliminate recording errors in the 1920s and 1930s,[8] tape recording offered a much greater scope for their rectification. Using a battery of editorial techniques such as multiple takes, patching, overdubbing, and splicing, producers and engineers could produce more or less faultless performances of musical works that were free of the mishaps that frequently bedevil concert performances. For good or for ill—good in the opinion of Gould, ill in that of Celibidache—such techniques provided the foundations for the "take nine" approach to recording and led to a further radical transformation of the metaphysics of musical representation; with the editorial opportunities afforded by tape recording, engineers and producers were able to defy still further the temporal and spatial parameters that had limited musical performance to the circumstances of its provenance. As a result, making a record came to be more like making a film and, indeed, adopted some of its vocabulary, such as the term "takes." In some instances as many as a hundred takes went into a recording (Frost 1987: 370; Revill 1987: 315). The need to keep track of these takes resulted in an important item of studio stationery—the producer's logbook, which had its own jargon and abbreviations that summarized each take's virtues (e.g. "NZ," which means "not together" from the German "nicht zusammen"; Grubb 1986: 11).

But it did not end there. The use of tape facilitated new types of musical correction, such as raising the pitch of a piano as needed through operating the tape at a fractionally faster speed (Grubb 1986: 137). Tape also permitted changes to be made to an error-afflicted or badly balanced recording, sometimes decades after the original session. Such interventions are commonplace in the modern studio and highlight the degree to which the pursuit of musical authenticity has always involved "creative cheating"—which Gould had cause to beatify—or what the conductor Otto Klemperer called "ein Schwindel" (Grubb 1986: 93). In fact, such incidents are more common than one might imagine and are often cited in histories of recorded sound. The most famous involved Kirsten Flagstad, who omitted a high C in a recording of *Tristan* that was "re-sung" by Elizabeth Schwarzkopf and dubbed onto Flagstad's recording (Chanan 1995: 133). Another such incident involved Sir John Barbirolli's recording of Mahler's Fifth Symphony. When it was first made in 1969, four bars of horn obbligato from the scherzo movement were omitted. When it was reissued on CD as one of EMI's "Great Recordings of the Century," those four bars were restored—remarkably, by the very horn player who had omitted them (Bettley 2001: 561).

Even "live" recordings have been subjected to such dubbing. Indeed, there are always unsuspected hazards involved in making live recordings. One of the first such recordings ever made—in which Gaisberg had a hand—has gone down in the annals of recorded history like Flagstad's high C. This was a recording of Elgar's *Dream of Gerontius* made at a Three Choirs Festival in the 1920s that had to be discarded because the microphones "eavesdropped" on a conversation in which the price of a "lovely camisole" was discussed (Gaisberg 1943: 176).[9] It had been forgotten that electrical recording could pick up off-stage whispers. Had tape recording existed at the time, it would have been possible to remedy the recording, as happened in 1970 at London's South Bank Festival. During a recorded performance of Beethoven's *Grosse Fuge* transcribed for piano four hands, the cuff links of the two pianists, Alfred Brendel and Daniel Barenboim, became entangled, which resulted in some very unmusical sound effects. The ill-sounding passages were retaken after the concert and then superimposed onto the live sections of the recording (Grubb 1986: 72–73).

Unless spliced with the utmost care, edits can be audible—contrary to Gould's observations (1987d)—especially on monitor speakers that are designed to expose crude edits and microphone replacements (Wilson 1957: 165). This problem became more pronounced with the advent of stereophonic recording, where the movement of singers has to be carefully planned and replicated from take to take so that jerks and discontinuities—similar to those observable on a badly edited film—are not audible (Grubb 1986: 26).

The capacity of the producer to vary quite dramatically the sound of a record led in the days of the LP to the production of so-called "white label pressings" that would be balanced in different ways. One pressing might have "too much top," another might be "too tubby in the bass" (Grubb 1986: 18). From these different pressings, each with its own distinctive version of the sound of the performance, the producer would eventually select a master disc that best matched the original music and from which the commercially available LP was eventually pressed. From these interventions it is clear that there are no absolute standards where the engineering of recordings is concerned, and the decisions about what constitutes an optimal recording involve myriad judgments.

The editorial interventions facilitated by the advent of tape recording have ensured that recordings of classical music, in terms of their accuracy and faithfulness to the original score, are always potentially finer than anything that is achievable in the concert hall, where performing errors, though not prodigious in number, are inevitable facts of musical life. Indeed, in the terms of Mackenzie's binary, the matter of whether overedited performances that are produced in the control rooms of studios constitute a form of musical realism linked to the way music is actually played or not is a moot point. They are plainly not on certain grounds, instead representing an ideal—the most perfect form of musical expression of which a group of musicians, at a given time, is capable. Indeed, in this connection the use of the word "record" is something of a misnomer, since a record does not ordinarily provide a *record* of a real performance at all (Eisenberg 1988: 89; Frost 1987: 368). Rather it represents a deliberate idealization of music, more or less constituting an exemplary interpretation of the music inherent in a score—an audio version of Plato's "immanent form." As was noted in the previous chapter, however, the pursuit of such forms of musical immanence led some eminent musicians to be dissatisfied with the recording process. They held that it had a malign impact on their musical performances. The most dramatic expression of this dissatisfaction was manifest in Celibidache's view that recording and music are contradictions in terms and that recording was a gross distortion of musical "truth." Any form of phonographic preservation transgresses the quintessence of music, that it lives and dies in time. Less dramatic forms of this dissatisfaction involve the complaints discussed in chapter 2, that the atmosphere of the studio is a sterile one or that playing to a control room hardly compares to playing to an audience and quashes the musical inventiveness that the audience's presence engenders. Moreover, the "take nine" approach of playing passage by passage until an entirely faultless performance has been achieved is said to destroy the spontaneity that an uninterrupted musical line induces. In order to neutralize the negative effects of "take nineism," some record labels have adopted a phonographic philosophy favoring single takes and minimal editorial intervention (Griffiths 1995: 35).

But for Glenn Gould, the most averred "gramophonic Platonist" in the history of the medium, the blanket condemnation of the "take nine" approach was unenlightened. He pointed out that the demonizing of the editing process was not present in arts such as literature and film, where these techniques were regarded as acceptable parts of the creative process. Indeed, Gould was a fanatical editor and believed that the musical improvements facilitated by "creative cheating" were among the main benefits of studio recordings. Interestingly, Gould's views had been anticipated in the 1930s by the critic Ernest Newman, who had looked forward to a musical "Eldorado," courtesy of the gramophone, in which individuals would be "freed from the maddening distractions of the concert room" to study exemplary musical performances within the intimacy of their own chambers (cited in Read and Welch 1976: 383). Gould saw the phonograph as extending the "catholicity of the repertoire," arguing that the inability to recognize the inherent superiority of recording was mere hubris, a failure to come to terms with the inescapable truth that the concert was no longer the main axis of contemporary music making. Overall, then, Gould's arguments established a new point on the trajectory of phonographic discourse, an offspring of Mackenzie's idealism that recognized recording as "an indigenous phenomenon" that offered alternative auditory conditions and opportunities outside of the "concert phenomenon" (Gould 1987b: 363).

The Best Seat Reupholstered: Stereophony and Quadraphony

For the most part, though, classical record producers and engineers—unlike their rock counterparts, who have treated recording studios as musical instruments in their own right (Cunningham 1998: 169; Middleton 1990: 93)—have been more circumspect in their approach to recording than Gould. They have generally adhered to the belief that the sound of recorded music should defer to that of the concert hall and should replicate, as far as possible, those conditions. Their practices in the studio and their judgments relating to good recording are broadly in line with the discourse of realism, which regards the concert as the apex of the musical experience. Walter Legge, who worked as a record producer for EMI in the 1950s, expressed it succinctly: he declared that all recordings of classical music should sound in the home as if they were being "heard in the best seat in an acoustically perfect hall" (Legge 1982: 73). However, the governing principle of this discourse was linked to the longstanding objective to domesticate the concert hall and make the gramophone, quite literally, a form of chamber music.

Legge's view in fact permeates most arms of the classical recording industry—the studios, the magazines and advertising, the design of audio components such as loudspeakers and amplifiers. An advertisement for a Pye high fidelity amplifier exemplifies the widespread prevalence of this view, which, as was noted in chapter 1, first appeared as an advertising theme in the 1920s, when the equivalence of the record to live music was first promoted. The Pye advertisement, however, actually suggests that listening to a record can be superior to a live concert. It points out that "the finest seat in the house" can be "reserved indefinitely," and the listening experience available from it, is free from distraction, and with the assistance of Pye's amplifier, can be adjusted for "individual mood," options not available to concert-goers (Figure 3.1).

Such claims were, in fact, quite common in the 1950s and 1960s and were used to promote the virtues of microgroove recordings. Following a review of one of its LPs by *New York Times* music critic Howard Taubman that lauded the "you are there" qualities and evocation of the "living presence" of the performers, Mercury adopted "living presence" as its slogan (Fine 1997: 2). The "you are there" sentiment was also "re-cited" in the technical manuals of the time, which emphasized the importance of "fidelity to the original sound" (Briggs 1956: 12), and not just any fidelity but "high fidelity," a phrase first coined in the 1930s that gained particular prominence during the postwar period. This remains a dominant discourse in the classical industry, especially among labels that continue to espouse the qualities of the original sound as their overriding objective (Seibert 1985: 98). For example, in a 1980s handbook dealing with the production and engineering of classical recordings, it is asserted that they should aim to "give the listener the effect of a perfect seat in a concert hall" (Revill 1987: 315). Or again, a 1999 advertisement for a high performance loudspeaker claimed that the listener's "sense of being there" was so strong he needed his eyes to convince himself that he was still in the living room.[10]

More or less while Legge was advocating his version of the keystone discourse, stereophonic sound arose, adding an important lateral dimension to the phonographic representation of music and enhancing its realism considerably. However, the extra speakers it required increased the physical presence of the phonograph in the household, placing a demand on domestic space at

Which is the best seat in the house? Orchestral tone in the concert hall is made up of a mixture of direct and reflected sound which changes from seat to seat. From one, the trumpet may be too dominant; from another, the double-bass may disappear. From perhaps just one seat the sound intensity and tonal relationship of the different instruments will match your own hearing characteristics. But how do you find it?—by prodding with a pin in a seating plan? The answer is very simple. The best seat in the house can be reserved indefinitely for you...in the comfort of your own home. With Pye High Fidelity Systems you can create the music of your choice, free from distortion or audience distraction, and exactly adjusted to your own individual needs.

The finest seat in the house

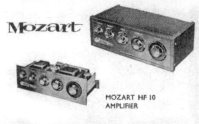

Mozart

MOZART HF 10
AMPLIFIER

For a thrilling new experience in good listening, good living
— see your Pye Hi Fi Dealer.

The Pye Mozart is one of the smallest and most compact amplifiers ever devised for home use. Ingenious design and brilliantly simplified circuitry have made possible no less than 10 watts undistorted output—sufficient for the largest home system—yet the Mozart can be comfortably contained on wall-shelf, bookcase or fireside table. It has facilities for high fidelity reproduction from records, tape and radio, and has separate volume and on/off switches. Features new 'dialamatic' pickup compensation. Installed in minutes. Printed Circuit production gives outstanding reliability.
The Mozart is available in chassis form, price 22 gns. (weight 8½ lb.) or in metal openwork case (9 lb.). Facia panel in copper finish. Dimensions: 10¼" wide, 3⅛" high, 5" deep. In conjunction with the Pye Bookcase Speaker and HFT111 FM/AM Radio Tuner, it offers today's most outstanding value in top-quality, low-price high fidelity.

HIGH

FIDELITY

SYSTEMS

PYE LIMITED ENGLAND

Figure 3.1 This advertisement for Pye High Fidelity Systems (*The Gramophone*, November 1957) illustrates the keystone discourse, that recordings offered an experience equivalent to "the finest seat in the house." Interestingly, Pye asserts that recordings and components are finer still, because they present music "free from distortion or audience distraction." There are three other matters of note in the advertisement: first, the Pye amplifier is named after Mozart, exemplifying the fusion between technology and high culture; second, the ad links "good listening" to "good living"; third, Pye lauds compression—through the use of printed circuitry (relatively new in 1957), Pye components were small enough to be "comfortably contained on wall-shelf, bookcase or fireside table." (Reproduced by permission of Philips and editor of *Gramophone*.)

a time—the 1960s—when houses were becoming smaller. This in turn stimulated the development of space-saving bookshelf speakers (Millard 1995: 216). Interestingly, one advertisement for such a speaker, again reflecting the ongoing prevalence of the keystone discourse, asserted that its "Concert Hall . . . is little bigger than an LP sleeve."[11]

Like other innovations associated with the development of the phonograph, precursors to stereophonic sound had been demonstrated early on in the history of recording. Something akin to stereophonic sound, for example, was demonstrated at the Paris Exposition of 1881 (Gray 1996: 69), and it had been the subject of speculation in manuals on sound reproduction in the 1920s. A particularly farsighted text of the period (it also anticipated tape recording) contained a chapter on stereophonic sound and discussed the need to recreate the spread of an orchestra on record (Gaydon 1928). Such textual speculations have always been important catalysts for technological change in the recording industry, furthering the desire for ways to improve the credibility of sound reproduction and lessen its artificiality. They led to experiments by Alan Blumlein, among others, in the 1930s that culminated in a stereo recording of Mozart's "Jupiter" Symphony with the London Philharmonic Orchestra under Thomas Beecham (Ford 1964: 183).[12]

However, it was not until the 1950s that the first commercial release of stereophonic recordings occurred, on tape in 1955 and then, when the cutting techniques had been perfected, on LP in 1958 (Ford 1964). At first, stereo was mainly used for demonstrating audio gimmicks and tricks: one channel playing Beethoven's Fifth, the other Ted Heath's dance band.[13] It was some time before the more creative sections of the industry began to appreciate the musical potential of stereo, which lay not only in its capacity to represent movement, which was particularly important in heightening the realism of operatic and stage works, but in its capacity to reveal "the complex threads of a score" and to "weave them into the composer's intended texture" (Culshaw 1981: 122). Stereo was a particular acoustic boon for those composers whose orchestral works were not clear textured but slightly muddy: Dvořák and Tchaikovsky, for example, posed particular problems for recording engineers (Grubb 1986: 59). In fact, part of the art of recording—and Grubb, an eminent record producer with EMI, insisted that it was an art, not a science—involves altering the balance of an orchestra so as to elicit its inner details, or at least those that are critical to the composer's musical objectives. And although one of the perennial preoccupations of recording engineers is to make the sound as euphonious as possible, eliminating all sources of distortion, sometimes the bad sound actually emanates from the music itself: much more harmonic distortion emanates from a live orchestra than from a good amplifier (Harlow 1964: 21).

This highlights the degree to which Legge's "best seat in the house" is not always a comfortable one for engineers. A microphone positioned in such a seat would not necessarily produce a superlative recording. In many instances, the inner parts of complex works would not be heard, even in that rarest of environments, the acoustically perfect concert hall, and if the recording engineer simply applied Legge's edict without adjustments the result would, in many instances, be a sonic catastrophe. Walton's First Symphony is a case in point: without appropriate interventions in the control room, some of its passages for strings and woodwind would be entirely overwhelmed by the timpani and brass (Grubb 1986: 72).

Producers and engineers have always had to tread cautiously with the classical performers who remain suspicious of their interventions and often countermand their injunctions. When the Russian pianist Emil Gilels undertook a recording of Grieg's *Lyric Pieces* for Deutsche Grammophon, he insisted that the *toningenieur* deploy a particular microphone that Gilels suggested had, in the past, produced a faithful representation of his virtuosity. The engineer disagreed and attempted to persuade him to change his mind, without success; he then did as the pianist insisted but left the offending microphone unconnected (Karwalky n.d.: 3).

At the beginning of the LP era, most tape recording was completed on simple machines, but as more tracks were added, the sound engineering possible in the studio became more sophisticated, and more sections of the orchestra were discretely "miked." This produced a fashion for "audiophile" recordings in the 1960s and 1970s that deliberately transgressed the keystone concert hall discourse by helpfully spotlighting particular sections of the orchestra or instruments at opportune moments. Their production utilized a special mixing desk that was able to blend up to twenty channels of sound. The recordings on Decca's Phase Four—many made by the conductor Leopold Stokowski—and EMI's Studio Two were typical. Though reviewers were impressed with their qualities of reproduction and sonic amplitude, others were perturbed by the degree to which they rejected the sway of the concert hall experience. One critic reviewing Stokowki's Phase Four disc of Rimsky Korsakov's *Scheherazade* described it as alternately a "musical crime," "like listening to a musical nightmare," and "a hideous mockery of orchestral sound," and then he reminded his readers that a recording should "aim to produce a result as close to concert-hall reality as techniques allow" (Heinitz 1965). Moreover, reviewers did not hesitate to praise those relatively fewer issues from Phase 4 that had avoided such a musical crime and adopted a naturally stereophonic perspective.[14]

In the early 1970s another innovation in the spatial distribution of sound was developed that also posed a threat to the keystone discourse: the relatively short-lived "quadraphony," sometimes called "four-channel sound" or simply "quad" (Borwick 1974). Like stereo, it changed the architecture of recording by providing two extra channels, further sources of musical and ambient information that had the potential to increase the stereo aspect of stereophonic sound and render it even more three dimensional. There was also a three-channel, allegedly more efficacious variant of quad called Ambisonics that a few labels adopted, including Nimbus. In fact, quad's multi-channel approach is currently undergoing a renaissance in the guise of the "surround sound" of digital video discs (DVD) and super audio compact discs (SACD), which can both encode several channels of sound. Part of the reason that four-channel sound was so short-lived, aside from its auditory shortcomings, was that it was issued in rival and incompatible formats, for example CD-4, Matrix, and SQ (Borwick 2000)—the death knell of any innovation in the recording industry. At most, only about three hundred fifty quad discs were ever released.

One prominent recording engineer actually hoped that quadraphonic sound would lead to "new techniques of recording" and the abandonment of the keystone discourse (Myers 1972: 23). He justified this on at least two grounds: one was that a lot of music was not written with concert halls in mind; another was that the adaptation of novels was quite acceptable in the cinema and theatre, so why not music through recording? In fact, several quad recordings did abandon the keystone discourse, most dramatically in those by CBS that used various techniques of "acoustic orchestration" to represent music. Bartók's Concerto for Orchestra, with Pierre Boulez conducting the New York Philharmonic, had different sections of the orchestra emanating from all four loudspeakers, challenging up front (or, so to speak, in a "roundabout way") concert hall realism (Marsh 1973). By and large, though, most record producers used the new system of recording with some trepidation. They used the two extra channels, which caused some sonic problems in quad's LP format, simply to accentuate the ambient information on a recording. This was to keep within the bounds of the British Trade Descriptions Act and thereby avoid possible litigation from disgruntled consumers, demanding their four channel's worth of music(Grubb 1986: 166).

Thus, despite the fact that it was technically plausible to depart from the keystone discourse with recordings that were sufficient unto themselves, the discourse remained dominant, reaching well beyond the studio to permeate the thinking of manufacturers of audio equipment as well. Although makers of recordings and of equipment have been separated from one another for some time,[15] they share the same phonographic values—at least, those serving the classical sectors of the industry do. This has been evident for decades; thus sound engineer Gilbert Briggs, for much of his career associated with the loudspeaker manufacturer Wharfedale, argued in the 1950s that the ultimate speaker would be one that let the music speak for itself without untoward intervention (Briggs 1950: 90). Other companies have shared this sentiment, most famously England-based Acoustical Manufacturing (now known as Quad Electroacoustics), which prides itself on the fact that its amplifiers and loudspeakers offer the "closest approach to the original sound," a slogan it first developed in the late 1950s and continues to use.

This same sentiment also pervades reviews of high fidelity equipment, which consistently emphasize the importance of acoustic neutrality and the absence of any coloration emphasizing particular sections of the audio spectrum. Even the initial response to digital recordings on the part of some manufacturers, for example turntable manufacturer Linn Sondek, was lukewarm—they were seen as endangering the auditory standards achieved in the analogue era (Borwick 1981). A reviewer of a high performance CD player in 1997 observed that though the player produced a seductive sound, a stringent set of quantitative tests revealed that it was attained at the expense of cutting treble and altering the natural ambience of recordings. The reviewer regarded this as a "dangerous road to embark on" since it compromised "the closest approach to the original sound" (Horn 1997: 131). Also telling, another reviewer from the same magazine commended a loudspeaker on the degree to which it was able to convey the listener to the "best seat in the house" (Fraser 2001: 113). However, this objective is not by any means a universal one. It is certainly more pertinent to classical than rock music, for which other design criteria apply. Indeed, some manufacturers specialize in producing equipment especially suited to rock music.

Moreover, the reviewers of classical LPs and CDs—certainly in magazines such as *Gramophone*—have been among the most fervent champions of Legge's "best seat" approach. This was itself a rearticulation of Mackenzie's 1920s advocacy of realism and was implacably opposed to any deliberate "falsification of life" done in the name of recording. Thus, reviewers invariably reserve most of their plaudits for those recordings that defer to the keystone and do not depart without good reason from the trajectory of natural sound. Those that do depart thus are subject to castigation. In fact, there is a particular affection for the standards of sound achieved in the late 1950s and 1960s, when at most three microphones and three tracks were used, and producers and engineers did not have access to multitracking facilities that might have tempted them into deviating from the "closest approach."

The keystone discourse is thus shared among the powerful sectors of the record world, and its hegemonic force is constantly reproduced and reaffirmed in the standards appertaining in the recording studio, in the types of amplifiers and loudspeakers that are manufactured, and in the magazine literature

dealing with recorded sound. It was also evident at those "spectacles" celebrating the achievements of high fidelity sound during the 1950s. These took
place in venues such as London's Royal Festival Hall and were designed to
demonstrate the increasing capacities of modern recording techniques and
reproducing equipment to recreate the original sound (Briggs, G. 1961).[16]
Using live and recorded sources of music, similar to Edison's "Tone Tests,"
such demonstrations again tried to show that the sound of LPs was all but indistinguishable from live sources. But these spectacles also had the effect of
further normalizing the keystone discourse across the recording industry and
large sections of the listening public, more or less without contestation. They
also led record critics to identify so-called "demonstration discs," recordings
that celebrated a sound-for-sound's-sake discourse by displaying the sonic
capacities of a domestic high fidelity system in the best possible light.[17]

In one sense, the existence of the keystone discourse reveals much about
the nature of musical power in the classical world. As the technology of recording developed and the efficacy of musical representation on disc improved, criteria had to be developed that would determine what constituted
truthful "sound," and differentiate it from less acceptable forms of musical
representation. This problem was less immediate during the early era of recording, when only monophonic forms of presentation were possible,
though even then, as I have pointed out, phonographic theorists were reluctant to condone forms of musical presentation that departed from a natural
sound. With the coming of stereo, which enabled individual strands of music
to be differentiated and sound to be dispersed and distributed in space, the
concern with truthful representation of music became more pronounced. In
the absence of a more defensible form of presentation, stereo phonographic
representation of classical music deferred to the concert—the discourse of
the best seat in the house. The idea espoused by Gould that the record should
liberate itself from this discourse and be an indigenous phenomenon was
knocked on its head. With the coming of quad, the temptation to depart
from the keystone discourse was even more alluring but nevertheless by and
large resisted. Although the incompatibility of rival systems was said to have
defeated the viability of four-channel sound, it is also true that most quad
classical recordings were never adventurous enough to fully justify the two
extra channels of musical information and were therefore redundant.

Such caution was not apparent in the film industry, which happily liberated
itself from the proscenium arch of the theater. Part of the classical recording
industry's failure to depart from the proscenium arch of the concert hall must
be attributed to the fact that it is performers and composers who wield most
of the power in the classical musical community, and who determined, early
on, that the phonograph should defer to their musical values—not the other

way around. Moreover, record companies, in the race to obtain their imprimaturs for recording, were quite happy to defer to them in this regard.

Compact Discs:
For an Even Closer Approach to Original Sound

Yet in reality the degree to which recording, at least during the LP era, was able to match the conditions of a concert hall was never absolute but, given the sonic constraints of LPs and their playback equipment, was, as Quad's slogan intimated, the "closest approach" possible. The most difficult of these constraints was the signal-to-noise ratio, which, though a marked improvement on the standards of the 78, was still large enough to interfere with the sound of LPs and attenuate their sonic range. Much of the extraneous noise heard on LPs was a product of their manufacture, deriving from tape hiss and surface noise that was further exacerbated by the dust-attracting properties of vinyl. Pianissimo passages in particular had to compete with a floor of unwelcome but unavoidable noise.

One incident involving Walter Legge exemplified the difficulties faced in engineering discs that could be played on domestic equipment. It involved a recording of Verdi's *Quattro pezzi sacri,* a work with a massive dynamic range that encompassed the full audio spectrum. Legge, ever the advocate of the best-seat-in-the-house approach, insisted against the wishes of his engineer upon recording the work just as it was, without any auditory compression or compensation. Only an edict limiting the dynamic range of recordings from EMI's top executives curbed Legge's desires and he agreed, albeit reluctantly, to the limitation. Had Legge obtained his way, the work's quieter passages would have been inaudible against the LP's background surface noise and tape hiss (Grubb 1986: 21).

What this telling incident reveals is the degree to which recording practices, in spite of the discourses emphasizing realism, are the products of compromises, and that a recording's realization of the "best seat" is always asymptotic, approaching but never quite reaching the ideal. Always, as in the Verdi work, the compromises are required by the technology itself, given the constraints of the existing studio parameters, which were still quite severe in the days of microgroove recording. The dynamic range from pianissimo to fortissimo of a standard symphony orchestra spans around ninety-five decibels, whereas most microgroove recordings in their heyday could only accommodate around seventy-five decibels and still remain playable on domestic equipment. Their sound was thus a product of making acceptable compromises involving a compression of auditory reality such that the relative "intensities" of the original sound were more or less preserved (Wilson

1957: 7). However, some record labels towards the end of the analogue era resisted this tendency to compress and issued LPs, mainly aimed at the audiophile, in an uncompressed state, complete with warnings about the damage that loudspeakers might incur at very high volume levels.[18]

The advent of digital sound eliminated many of the problems that had been associated with an inadequate signal-to-noise ratio. Indeed, in the years immediately prior to the advent of the CD, frustration about the noisiness of LPs—caused by the use of inferior stocks of vinyl arising from shortages caused by the 1970s oil crisis—had risen considerably. The letters pages of record magazines bristled with complaints about the bad vinyl as well as inferior LP pressing standards, articles appeared in magazines investigating these complaints (Borwick 1975; Lees 1974), and various electronic techniques were developed to eliminate the problems. These included direct-to-disc recording—a return to the days of acoustic techniques—in order to eliminate tape hiss; another fad of the time, the so-called "dbx," was also supposed to remedy hiss. However, most of these techniques were mere stopgap measures designed to prolong and sustain the life of the LP in the face of imminent competition from digital recording, first in its analog version on the LP itself, and then eventually on the compact disc.

In fact, digital recording, like the original tinfoil phonograph, was an offshoot of telecommunication experiments; it had resulted from successful trials conducted during the 1960s into ways of encoding speech sounds into digital information for transmission over telephone lines and radio channels.[19] When these techniques were eventually deployed in the recording studio, the advances were regarded as dramatic. Not only was the problem of worsening surface noise entirely eliminated, but digital technology offered a much greater dynamic range—upwards of 20 decibels—than had ever been possible on record, making it even more possible to "domesticate" the amplitude of a concert. However, the virtually silent background was the most valued feature of digital recording. When recording producers and musicians first heard digital sound, it seemed as though a veil had been lifted from the music; it no longer had to "fight its way through a mush of background noise" (Grubb 1986: 221). Even recordings made during the acoustic and electrical eras could, through the use of digital remastering techniques that suppressed their inherent noise, have their auditory signals updated and restored—like "an old master" having its "noble outline" revealed from "beneath a layer of dirt"—and could be made to sound very modern, as they had never sounded before on record, in fact.[20] And indeed the same auditory techniques of renovation—not restoration because the results of renovation in many instances sounded better than their LP originals—have been extended to LPs from the 1950s and 1960s. In fact, long after the major labels abandoned manufacturing LPs, a lucrative market in audiophile repressings appeared (and continues today) utilizing the heavy, high-grade vinyl of early era LPs such as RCA's "Living Stereo" and aimed at collectors who remain adamant that LPs offer superior sound.[21]

Notwithstanding these advances in technology that now present an orchestra on record much as it might be heard live, the production of recordings still involves myriad compromises, many related to the recording venue itself, be it a church or a concert hall. Few recording venues outside of the custom-built recording studio have perfect acoustics,[22] and the idea of a record representing the sound heard from the best seat in a concert hall is, for some music, a misrepresentation. For a start, much of the classical repertoire was never written with the concert hall in mind; such a hall was an eighteenth- and nineteenth-century architectural creation designed to house, with varying degrees of acoustic efficacy, the classical symphony orchestra. Properly speaking, as suggested by the musicologist and record reviewer Denis Stephens, music should be recorded in the acoustic environment for which it was written. It is simply wrong to record choral works in studios and symphony orchestras in churches: they provide the wrong acoustic frames (Stevens 1966: 25). Ironically, many famous concert halls are quite unflattering when it comes to recorded sound, pose manifold difficulties for recording engineers and producers, and are often avoided in favor of such nonmusical venues as churches, town halls, or even gymnasia. Some of the busiest recording venues, such as Watford Town Hall, which Mercury used for its "Living Presence" recordings of the London Symphony Orchestra, have become bywords for excellent sound. Even there, though, a variety of electronic and physical interventions have to be made to overcome acoustic idiosyncrasies and reduce the undue emphasis often placed upon particular parts of the audio spectrum. Whenever Decca recorded in the Concertgebouw, held to be a "natural hell" of a venue (Culshaw 1981: 110), the orchestra was placed in the auditorium, with most of the seats removed.

Even so, the results of such re-engineering often mean that the sound of an orchestra on record is often much better than that heard in most concert halls, particularly in terms of musical detail and overall balance. Indeed, some of the subtler sounds of an orchestra on record are impossible to hear in a concert hall. For in reality the best seat in the house is rarely that, and the concert hall sound that appears on record is an engineering construct (Moore 1987: 330). This is, again, due to the interventions of the recording engineer and producer, who often, contrary to Mackenzie's adjuration, falsify or at least refract the musical presentation in order to *enhance* its "truthfulness." This is one of the underlying paradoxes of recording.

Concerto recordings provide examples of such refraction in operation. Normally, a fortissimo orchestra can overwhelm the solo instruments involved, including even powerful ones such as a piano. The psychology of listening at a live concerto performance is complex, involving manifold visual cues that enable momentary imbalances of sound to be corrected through eye contact with the relevant instruments (Pfeiffer 1987). These cues have the effect of directing the ear toward sounds emanating from the solo instrument, thereby "equalizing" the overall presentation. Through careful balancing in the recording studio's control room, engineers and producers mimic this visual equalization, especially through the use of stereo effects so that the contribution of the solo instrument is brought into the foreground of the concerto "action." The same is true of passages in complex orchestral works, in which music emanating from the depths of the orchestra can be brought to the fore, thereby achieving more acoustic "perspicacity" than is possible at an actual concert. Indeed, part of the interpretive function of the producer and the conductor is to determine whether the composer would have desired such acoustic readjustment to occur.[23] In the absence of the relevant visual cues that are available to the listener in the concert hall, then, producers and engineers tend to create an acoustic illusion that compensates for the disembodied nature of recorded sound. Interestingly, Mercury's recording team, in deference to the psychology of listening, would locate their control room out of the sight of the orchestra they were monitoring, thus preventing the incursion of visual cues that might upset the natural balancing process of the recording (Rooney 2001: 14).

In short, deception and falsification play a significant role in the processes of achieving musical fidelity on record; simulation on record is achieved in no small measure through acts of dissimulation. Thus, the discourse of realism is a qualified one. If anything, the ruling principle of recording is a discourse of "super-realism," where through careful studio engineering, recording producers and engineers are able to "reupholster" the sound heard from the best seat in the house.

Recording as the Theater of the Mind

One record producer who was conscious of the powers of super-realism possible on stereo recordings was John Culshaw, at least during the latter parts of his career with Decca. He was particularly taken with the potential of stereophonic sound, which he felt could add new dimensions, especially to opera, offering a more dramatic and faithful recreation of the composer's intentions. He championed Gould's idea of a record as an "indigenous phenomenon" that ought to go beyond the transcription of a performance, arguing that careful studio "retexturing" could provide new modes of musical presentation. In this respect he felt that recordings afforded opportunities to access musical experiences that were impossible from the best seat in the house. To this end, he experimented with recording techniques that went beyond adhering to the keystone.

Culshaw's recording of *Rheingold* was his first sustained phonographic exploration of these possibilities and was intended to demonstrate how techniques of sound engineering could augment the Wagnerian aesthetic.[24] He further developed these techniques in the remaining parts of his complete recording of the *Ring* cycle. Such stereophonic interventions were supposed to substitute for the absence of visual information in a recording, engulfing the listener in ways that "drew them closer to the characters of the opera" than was possible in the theatre (Culshaw 1967: 17).[25] This "theatre of the mind," as Culshaw described it, went further than just being a "transcription of a performance"; it was also the "recreation of opera in aural terms," one that could more faithfully convey immersion in the operatic drama (1967: 17). Indeed, through techniques that were only available in the studio, recordings could provide an alternative way of staging opera. However, while many were impressed with Culshaw's results, some, including the record critic Conrad Osborne (1976: 308), suggested that these techniques took unacceptable liberties with opera's quintessential theatricality.

Yet to fully take advantage of these various forms of phonographic representation, be they of the keystone or the Culshaw variety, the cooperation of the listener is required. The domestication of the best seat in the house cannot be attained without the adoption of commensurate listening habits, which have changed as one recording format has superseded another. For example, when stereo superseded mono, listeners had to be encouraged to adopt new listening modes, such as removing speakers from a room's corners, which was satisfactory for mono but not for stereo. The two speakers also had to be situated at the proper distance from one another—too close, and the effect of stereo was neutralized, too far and a hole appeared in the middle of the sound stage. Stereo speakers also had to be slightly angled—60 degrees, to be precise—into the listener. It was also important to ensure that the speakers were connected properly and in phase, otherwise they sounded indistinct and amorphous. The geometry of stereophonic realization was regularly reproduced in the high fidelity handbooks and magazines of the time (Gardner 1959; McIntyre 1969), when stereo etiquette could not be taken for granted. Magazines and advertisers in this respect shared a community of interest. For example, one of Mercury's advertisements from the beginning of the stereo era identified, lest they be new to listeners, the location of the instruments of an orchestra: "violins sitting on the *left* are heard from the *left*," and so on.[26] Listeners who had no experience of the spatial configurations of an orchestra or chamber group had to be informed about them so as not to understand the sounds emerging from left and right as merely the arbitrary decisions of the record producer and engineer. In effect, listeners were being briefed on the conventions of the keystone discourse, and unless they configured their systems in ways that were commensurate with these conventions, they would have not the opportunity to sit in the best seat in the house.

Test records were also issued that had special tracks to demonstrate. among other things, phase and balance problems, and that were designed to assist listeners in setting up their equipment to optimize its acoustic potential. These test records invariably used samples of music from the classical repertoire. *The Enjoyment of Stereo* is a good example; originally issued in 1970, its sleeve notes, which contain instructions on how to avoid the pitfalls of setting up a stereo system, make direct reference to the concert hall discourse: with the system set up correctly, the listener should have "the feeling of being present at a 'live' concert."[27] The keystone discourse thus does not operate in isolation: it generates secondary discourses and micropractices that in turn buttress it.

Importantly, such handbooks and test records have helped to extend the dominant discourses of the recording studio into the home while also disseminating high fidelity jargon such as "woofers and tweeters" or the technical specifications associated with amplifiers and speakers. They have imprinted these discourses on the sensibility of listeners, who have been encouraged to "re-tune" their high fidelity systems as if they were real musical instruments and "tweak" their various components to make them even more "phonogenic." They have "set the record straight," in short, correcting misaligned speakers and ensuring that the acoustic of the listening room complemented the demands of the high fidelity system. This even went so far as to involve replacing furniture and drapes with items that could absorb reflections and reduce a room's acoustic liveliness (Stock 1978). Those listeners who chose not to observe these homilies of auditory life were implicitly chastised for not making the most of their opportunities to experience "one of the greatest of civilized delights" (Gardner 1959: 111). Thus the keystone discourse gradually infiltrated the acoustic habits of listeners.

But occasionally listening habits could depart from the keystone discourse; listeners could be encouraged to follow Gould's prescriptions and re-produce a recording in keeping with their own personal tastes and home acoustics (Culshaw 1966: 27). This had been an option available to listeners since the 1920s, when the advent of amplifiers introduced a measure of control over the envelope of sound that personalized its auditory character. This control has only increased. With the aid of a CD player's keypad, music can be "ordered around," movements transposed, repeated, interleaved with other music, even randomized. The sound can be subjected to a range of acoustic and organizational interventions that are impossible in the concert hall.

Yet in reality home listening practices rarely parallel those of the concert hall in terms of the layout of the sound and its associated listening etiquettes. The circumstances in which individuals listen to recorded music are not always optimal; records are often used simply as background music, or they are played through inferior equipment that lacks the capacity to reproduce complex scores. Indeed, part of the problem with high fidelity listening practices is that they can be antisocial, are frequently only optimal from one position in a room, and require levels of loudness that are incompatible with social intercourse in most households. This can generate a certain amount of in-house altercation, especially since high fidelity behaviors are primarily the province of men (Keightley 1996: 165). In addition, high fidelity manuals, which sometimes acknowledge the antisocial nature of sound perfectibility (Borwick 1982: 63), often recommend that the lights be dimmed or even switched off to focus the senses on the sound spectacle, a further disincentive to normal patterns of social intercourse. Inevitably, then, except in the rare instances of the audiophile who is able to dedicate a listening space away from the disrupting effects of normal domestic life,[28] home listening practices tend to be travesties of those that are required to compete with the acoustic conditions of a real concert hall and opera house. Free of such disruptions, though, the recorded acoustic experience can offer listeners unparalleled access to musical detail (Robertson 1946: 90).

The account of recording offered in this chapter has stressed the degree to which the practices of sound production and engineering have been systematically articulated around two contradictory discourses, one emphasizing realism, the other idealism. The first asserts that recordings should defer to the sound of a live performance in a concert hall; it emerged in the 1920s and constitutes a keystone discourse in the classical recording industry. It has pervaded many areas of recording practice, from the engineering of audio components to the advertising copy used to promote recordings and equipment. The fact that it does so helps to maintain its predominance. It developed at a time when recording still faced enmity from professional musicians, and it was reflected in public demonstrations intended to prove that recorded music was impossible to differentiate from the "real thing." It even drove the technological development of the phonograph and led to such audio developments as the LP and stereo, which further added to its force.

The second discourse—mostly associated with Glenn Gould—implies that recorded music should be a medium unto itself and provide an alternative aural landscape to that of the concert. It treats the record as an "indigenous phenomenon," challenging the idea that records should necessarily act as surrogates of the concert. It even suggests that the record can achieve a form of auditory "elucidation" that is impossible in an opera house or concert hall. However, for the most part this discourse has remained frustrated in the classical recording industry—it is far more prevalent in popular music recording—and has not been able to supplant the keystone discourse. Indeed, because its development is negatively correlated with the keystone, it has been given short shrift by many in the classical recording industry. In truth, though, the idea that a record should provide an account of music as it is heard in a concert is not reflected in the way records are actually produced. In reality, the much-vaunted best seat in the house is, on or off the record, a fake one.

CHAPTER FOUR

Creating the Right Impression
An Iconography of Record Covers

◆

> I myself dislike the glossy surfaces used by some companies. These are said to be
> popular as they do not show dirty fingermarks. It is interesting to know that the
> great unwashed go in for the purchase of records, but most of us manage, with the
> aid of soap and water, to avoid soiling our books, or music, or record sleeves. There
> is, certainly, an obvious difficulty in providing artistic designs for records of non-
> programme music, and I, personally, prefer a plain cover with well-executed
> lettering and perhaps the signature of the composer, or a portion of the
> score, etc., to exotic flights of the imagination.
> —Alec Robertson, editorial in *The Gramophone* (1956), 342

In spite of the many claims that are made about the capacity of recordings to recreate music more or less as it is heard in the concert hall, they are manifestly deficient in one important respect: the musicians responsible for the music are invisible. Listening to records remains in the era of the CD, as it was in the earliest days of the phonograph, a disembodied experience, heard but not seen, whose contributing musicians must be imagined, a fact that many in the past felt degraded the musical experience offered by the gramophone (LeMahieu 1988: 229).[1] Moreover, except in a very limited sense there is no way of "reading" from their surface markings the sounds encrypted into a record (O'Reilly 1999: 51; Ranada 1983: 59). Nor does a record carry anything equivalent to a "running header" to enable readers to know precisely what it is they are reading and where they are positioned in a book relative to the beginning and end.[2] The indecipherable semiotic of the record, at least in its unplayed state, has made an exigency of textual supplementation and prompted a "documentary reality" to *cover* the record.

Yet much of the literature on recording, perhaps because it has concentrated on analyzing auditory features, has eschewed the manner in which recordings also provide *records* of themselves and are underwritten and overwritten with a range of typographical and pictorial forms of supplementation.

This text is found on the label of the record and on the various forms of packaging that have evolved to enclose it—a sleeve or jacket for the LP, and the so-called "jewel box" for the CD. In the past this packaging was relatively unimpressive and unrevealing, but with each change of reproducing format it has become more elaborate and expository. Even so, the function of this supplementation remains the same: to provide information and explanatory comments about the record it accompanies. It thereby forms another important link in the chain of transducers associated with recording, by way of its narrative architecture, which contains myriad features. These range from a graphic design on the front cover—the subject of this chapter—to a detailed description of the record's contents and its performers, the so-called "liner notes." The nature of these notes and the role they play in the listening process will be the subject of the next chapter. In the meantime, it is sufficient to suggest that both "surfaces" of the record's cover inform the listening process and play an important role in mediating the way the music is heard and understood. In this respect the cover acts like the miniature score shown in the E.M.G. advertisement, reinforcing the same underlying idea of the textual transducer; the cover converts the listening process into sets of meaningful mediations with the music. In particular, the cover engenders sets of significations correlating more or less with the musical programs for which the cover acts as a material form of containment. In its optimal form, it ultimately serves to reinforce the discourse of seriousness that frames classical music. This has deterred classical record imagery that abrogates this seriousness or provokes indignation, of which this chapter's epigraph is a classic example.

The Containment of the Record: From Paper Bags to Jewel Boxes

Records might occupy a domain of modality different from that of books, but the aesthetic of their containment is analogous and performs similar functions. Parts of their narrative architecture, such as the label, are a constituent element of of the record itself. But most of this architecture, at least in the instance of more recent disc formats, is not bound to the record in any direct sense but forms part of its containment, of the packaging and coverage that can be detached from a disc. Nevertheless, it is still linked to and conditioned by the surface geometry of the recording, which with the exceptions of cassette and reel-to-reel tape—which remain outside the province of this book—has taken the form of a flat disc of varying diameters and weight. The exception was Edison's relatively short-lived cylinder, which was housed in a box with a detachable lid, on which was inscribed the name and number of the recording and its time and speed: "4 minutes and 100 revolutions per minute—not faster or slower." During the period of analog recording, most 78s and LPs were issued on double-sided 7", 10" and 12" discs.[3] The 78s, which were made of brittle and fragile shellac, were much heavier than the LPs. Their relatively short duration meant that whole symphonies and operas occupied several 78s of them, which were often issued separately. Thus music broadcaster John Amis's appreciation of César Franck's *Symphonic Variations for Piano* was for a time limited to its third and fourth movements, the only ones that, as a teenager, he could afford (1985: 30).

When LPs were launched, one of the ways they were advertised was through the deployment of a "six versus thirty-four" comparison that emphasized the increased musical carrying capacity of LPs that occupied much less space than 78s and were easier to handle and transport (Figure 4.1). Not only that, they played for a longer time.[4] This compression and extension of the disc's carrying capacity has continued into the era of the CD. Whereas a complete recording on 78s of *Die Meistersinger*—the subject of Decca's ad—occupied sixty-eight sides and six and a half inches of shelf space (Davidson 1994: 367), or ten sides of five LPs, it now occupies a mere four CDs.

As their name suggests, CDs are much more compact and also more robust and lighter than their analog predecessors. More importantly, though, their compactness did not come about at the expense of their playing times. Indeed, as the size of the disc has reduced, its recording time has increased. Thus Decca's complete recording of Haydn's string quartets, consisting of some forty works that occupy over twenty-four and a half hours of playing time, can be accommodated in a five-inch-square box a mere two inches wide, provoking one reviewer to recall Blake's "holding the world in a grain of sand."[5] To their greater duration can be added durability, because unlike their predecessors, CDs are not subject to degeneration. When Philips launched them, they were promoted as promising "perfect sound forever" (Rohan 2002: 105).[6]

But the dramatic reduction in the disc's surface area—a CD is about one-fifth the size of an LP—has not been unanimously applauded. There is now much less surface area for iconographical invention than during the era of the LP, the halcyon days of "phonographics" that have since seen the efflorescence of a subculture of "vinylphiles" who have a passion for microgroove recordings and collect little else (Gilroy 1993: 241; Plasketes 1992: 118).[7] Indeed, there has been a growing disenchantment with the "plasticity" of the jewel box developed to house the CD, which collectors consider unappealing. Many labels, spurred on by the example of independents such as Winter and Winter (Anderson 2000), have developed new ways of containing the CD as part of an overall commitment to bettering its presentation qualities. These formats are "classier" and more aesthetically pleasing than their plastic

six *versus* **thirty-four!**

At last you can possess a complete performance of Wagner's *Die Meistersinger von Nürnberg** on six Decca long playing records — a set which employs all the resources of the Vienna State Opera to produce one of the most splendid achievements in operatic recording of our time. Heading the list of distinguished artists is Paul Schoeffler, whose Hans Sachs is probably the finest in the world today. Hilde Gueden is the delightful Eva, and the part of Pogner, her father, is sung by Otto Edelmann, one of the most distinguished of the younger generation of singers. Günther Treptow's Walther shows that there are still Helden-tenors who can combine robust tone and lyrical beauty in their singing, while Karl Dönch makes a suitably cantankerous Beckmesser. The minor rôles are also excellently cast, and the orchestral playing by the Vienna Philharmonic Orchestra under the sensitive and experienced bâton of Hans Knappertsbusch reveals all the beauties of Wagner's score — beauties which are so abundant that the opera must be heard again and again if they are to be fully absorbed. That is why *Die Meistersinger* is an ideal work for the gramophone, especially when it occupies only six Decca long playing records as against thirty-four ordinary seventy-eights.

*We suggest you order this magnificent recording now so that you are sure of obtaining your copy immediately it becomes available. Decca ffrr Long Playing Records Nos. LXT 2659-64. Price £11 17s. od. For those who have already purchased Act II—issued a year ago—Acts I and III are also available on five more Decca long playing records, Nos. LXT 2646-7 and LXT 2648-50. Price 39/6d. each record.

The above prices include cost of art container with notes, and Purchase Tax.

DECCA ffrr

REGD. TRADE MARK

LONG PLAYING 33⅓ r.p.m. RECORDS

THE DECCA RECORD COMPANY LTD., 1-3 BRIXTON ROAD, LONDON, S.W.9

Figure 4.1 This advertisement from the Decca Record Company appeared originally in *The Gramophone* (January 1952), just after the launch of the LP. It is one of a series of advertisements showing the comparative advantage of LPs over 78s, especially in the case of operas: six discs instead of thirty-four for the same opera! It is also suggested, humorously, that LPs had a weight advantage over 78s. Such comparisons were a regular promotional stratagem at this time. The dogs allude to the HMV canine able to appreciate his master's sound sense. The same self-satisfied dog is found in other advertisements in the series. Note also the "ffrr" ear—another famous phonographic emblem. (Reproduced by permission of the editor of *Gramophone*.)

rivals and owe much to the gatefold packaging that was sometimes used as an alternative to the sleeve in the days of the LP, particularly by American labels; they also utilize cardboard facing instead of plastic as well as better quality graphics and papers.[8] In this form of packaging, the booklet whose cover doubles as the outer face of a conventional CD occupies a special pocket, generally inside the gate of the album's folder. Some labels also use cardboard slipcases to contain their plastic jewel boxes, often for special editions of their CDs (see figure 4.8), which has the effect of generating new surfaces of meaning for further pictorial and textual embellishment. It is, perhaps, a matter of plastic engendering the wrong material connotations for classical music, of its being the wrong "substance of expression" for its containment (Gottdiener 1995: 28). Indeed, some labels have adopted retro forms of containment, harking back, even if only in a symbolic sense, to pre-CD materials. While the albums of 78s recalled leatherbound books, those of CDs recall LPs. Indeed, the perimeters of Archiv's CDs simulate the linen covers used on its boxed LP sets. Linen appears to be a material metonym for so-called pre-classical music—Supraphon also used it to cover its Musica Antique Bohemica series (Melville-Mason 1996: 40).

Another imperative influencing packaging—less necessary in the case of the relatively robust CD—has been the need to protect the disc's surface. This was particularly important for LPs, which attracted dust, which in turn caused extraneous noise. And although several preparations and cleaning cloths were developed to mitigate this problem (Wilson 1972), the main line of defense was the LP sleeve, a literal dust cover, plus the inner sleeve, which added a further layer of protection. That this inner sleeve contained a range of homiletic texts stressing the need to keep records scrupulously clean only served to emphasize the degree to which the outer and inner jackets of the LP served, first and foremost, protective rather than decorative functions. Indeed, one cover designer suggested that sleeves were invented to stop LPs from rolling off their shelves (Lake 1996: 262).

Dust on 78s was never as troublesome as it was on LPs, for its "sound effects" were silenced by their inherent surface noise. As a result, their packaging was more perfunctory. Only long orchestral works and operas were given more "luxurious" forms of containment, the so-called "album," which owed its design to the photograph album (Smart and Newsom 1977: 21). This contained several pockets, into which individual discs were inserted. Discs could also be bound in folders with bookish features such as leatherette spines and gilt-edged titles (Garlick 1977: 780; Weidemann 1969: viii).[9] Single 78s, by contrast, were slipped into brown-paper, often called "Kraft-paper," sleeves, which were neither eye catching nor especially pertinent to the music they wrapped.[10] Instead, the sleeves provided a billboard on which record labels and retailers could regale consumers with a range of inducements and advice (Raynaud 1978: 132):

SPEED IS IMPORTANT . . . use the HMV Instantaneous Speed Tester
Sir Edward Elgar, OM says: "Without doubt the most important invention in the history of the Gramophone"
Drysdales Music Store: The House of Happiness
Never use a steel needle twice

However, when Kraft paper was employed to cover LPs it left unsightly marks, particularly when the LPs were piled on top of one other (McKnight-Trontz and Steinweiss 2000: 53), which was another reason why a specially designed cardboard sleeve was developed to house them. But even prior to the LP, Columbia had employed cover designs in the 1930s on its 78s as a way to stimulate demand for records (Heller 1994/1995). The strategy worked. Eye-catching covers aroused consumer interest and improved Columbia's record sales. Thus a mercantile imperative underwrote the shift to more decorative styles of record containment.

Interestingly, once such covers, which were relatively expensive to produce, became the norm, at least one label, Harmonia Mundi, adopted a design strategy counter to them. For its budget label Musique d'Abord, plain covers, devoid of excessive decoration, were employed. These were promoted as a means of reducing production costs and of materially demonstrating that for Harmonia Mundi, at least, music was more of a priority than packaging. Of course, in a context of over-decorated covers their unassuming "design" often attracted attention (Figure 4.2).

These initial observations suggest the ways in which record packaging serves a number of functions and has changed as one format of recording has superceded another. They also highlight the decades that contemporary forms of packaging took to develop, as they continue to do. The parallel with an analogous cultural technology, the book, is worth revisiting, for the book also took several generations before its current architecture emerged from the shadow of the illuminated manuscript, which had provided its template during the period of the "incunabula." The modern cover had yet to be developed and positioned, as did the conventions associated with the page and pagination. The protocols associated with the pre-text regions of the book also had to develop. But once the basic conventions and material fabric of the book were invented, they were systematically deployed throughout the publishing industry and have been retained ever since (Steinberg 1974: 28). Much the same has happened to the record: it too went through its own incunabula phase, when the presentation of the disc underwent a series of innovations, before being systematized into its current format. This was also the period in which the various divisions of labor associated with the record

Figure 4.2 This advertisement for Harmonia Mundi's budget label, Musique d'Abord, first appeared in *Records and Recording* (September 1978). It attempted to take market advantage of its low-cost covers—an example of which is included—because the covers on other, less budget-conscious labels could cost as much as the LP itself. It is implied that these excessive costs would have been better directed toward putting the "music first," which is exactly what Musique d'Abord means. (Reproduced by permission of Harmonia Mundi.)

industry emerged, including specialists such as record producers and engineers, record critics and journalists, and designers of record covers and writers of liner notes—textual "engineers." But a more compelling parallel is the fact that the narrative architectures of the book and the record display many features in common; in short, the architecture of the book has imprinted itself onto the disc.

The Narrative Architecture of the Record: Labeling Conventions

According to Gerald Genette (1997), the narrative architecture of the book consists of two discrete textual zones: the text itself, with which most literary criticism is concerned, and a series of surrounding, supplementary texts, the so-called "paratexts," that are part of the text and yet not part of it. This idea is similar to Jacques Derrida's "parergon," which literally means something that is outside of or beyond the main work but is also a constituent element of it, as in the title of a painting (Duro 1996). In addition to its main text, the structure of a book also consists of "pre-textual" and "post-textual" zones that occupy its outermost regions, its beginning and end, and are much less subject to critical scrutiny—as if they possessed only peripheral significance. Into the former category fall such textual phenomena as the cover, title, and contents pages, and into the latter fall endnotes, indices, and appendices. In addition, there are a range of sub-textual features that occur at regular intervals within a book and help to frame a page or a set of pages. These various narrative subunits include chapter and section headings, which calibrate and enumerate a text as the bookish equivalents of a map's longitude and latitude. Lastly, there are a series of "rhetorical" interventions such as acknowledgments, prefaces, and epigraphs that variously help to orchestrate predispositions toward the text they embed and frieze (Genette 1997).

The term that Genette uses to describe these "thresholding devices," which again stand outside of a text yet are also integral parts of it, is "peritextuality." This is distinct from the second category of paratextuality that Genette identifies, called "epitextuality," which is located outside the actual architecture of the book but is linked to it through various representational forms such as press releases, advertising, brochures, interviews, and articles about its author. In order to enhance its profile in the marketplace and to act as a promotional vehicle, epitexts are often generated when a book is about to be, or has just been, published. They are also a prolific feature of literary and review magazines (Genette 1997: 344–48).[11]

Genette has argued that the notion of paratextuality can be extended to records, where the disc itself is the text, and its containment devices the peritext and epitext. Although these texts occupy a modal universe different from the book, they exhibit analogous features of paratextuality and perform many of the same functions as those associated with books. If anything, they are more indispensable than their bookish equivalents, because the contents of a recording cannot be ascertained from its surface. A record, in this respect, is a black box whose "blackness" is even more pronounced on the silver disc, where no audible traces are discernible, not even tracks, even though CDs are more "tracked" than ever.[12]

From the first, records needed to carry titling devices identifying their contents and provenance. This was inscribed rather crudely at the hub of the disc, where the playing surface ceased until Berliner hit upon the idea of pasting a printed label onto the hub. This could be read because a hole was cut out of its paper cover. This label, the most important peritext relating to the early disc, lay at the heart of the disc's identification system and provided a space, albeit small in area, where information not inscribed elsewhere was "encircled." This included details relating to the particular record, such as its title and catalog number, and to records in general, such as the rules pertaining to copyright (the latter were usually placed around the rim of the label so as not to interfere with the more specific information relating to a disc). How much information was cited was a matter of company policy. In 1915, for example, Edison decreed that labels on his records should not divulge the names of performers, and any description of their contents should be presented on their "B sides" (Welch and Burt 1994: 145).[13]

In bookish terms, then, the label fulfills many of the same functions as a title page. An important focus of the label is the trademark, a semiotic device consisting of visual and typographical elements. Those employed by record companies reveal much about the cultural impression they wished to create and were often embossed with classical, musical, or religious emblems that were designed to symbolically enhance the status of recording. It has already been noted that the Gramophone and Typewriter Company initially adopted the "Recording Angel" as its trademark, an icon redolent with religious connotations. The name of the German branch of the Gramophone Company, Odeon—the first company to manufacture double-sided discs—reflects another distinctive "trace" in phonographic nomenclature: it was named after a "concert hall," depicted on its label, from ancient Greece. In fact, many labels have turned to "classical" culture for their names—Argo, Mercury, Naxos, Orfeo, Erato, and Hyperion, for example—to underwrite their own classical endeavor. For the names of recording companies, unlike those of many publishers, were not often those of their founders—the Edison Company was an exception. This was because the small companies associated with the early recording industry quickly merged into larger companies, and the names of their founders were lost. In such a depersonalized climate the industry adopted other names.

But such names also illustrate the way the culture of the high street—an English phrase denoting a shopping district—has become increasingly fused with high culture (Whiteley 1994). Decca's discs in the 1930s, for example, carried a portrait of Beethoven, even those that contained popular music! And because it was relevant, record labels such as Columbia's Society Issues carried a picture of the composer whose work was featured on the particular album. Such strategies employing the cachet of the past have assisted in conferring distinction on classical recording and offsetting any lingering doubts about its cultural credentials. But they have also served to create a sense of history for the record, a modern commodity that is devoid of one. This is an aspect of the record's "invented tradition," a history that is spurious but appears to be genuine (Hobsbawn 1984), which tries to include those consumers impressed by commodities that are embossed with the symbols of history, assuming them to be the hallmarks of prestige and status.[14]

Another semiotic feature of the early labels was that they were color coded for particular types of music. HMV, for example, reserved its "Plum Label" for its prestige performers. Indeed, the prestige that the Australian soprano Dame Nellie Melba commanded was such that she was granted a label to herself. Melba's 78s came in an opulent package with her name in gold lettering and a glassine window that, when withdrawn, displayed a picture of the diva (Marty 1979: 181). Victor's flagship was its "Red Seal" label, whose trademark simulated a traditional wax seal—another icon of the invented tradition. At the other end of the musical spectrum, vaudeville songs and comedy were assigned to the company's "Black Label" (Kenney 1999: 31). And attesting to its importance at the hub of the record is the fact that the word "label" has become a synonym for a record company, the industry's equivalent of the publishing house.

With the coming of the long-playing record, many of the identifying functions of the early labels were transferred onto the sleeve. Still, the label retained many of its 78 identifiers, ensuring that, should the sleeve be mislaid, the information relating to a disc's contents would be retained. However, some new features were added to the label, such as those pertaining directly to microgroove recordings, such as their particular playing speeds. Labels also began to sport the "signs" of high fidelity, which had its ascendancy during the LP era. In the immediate postwar years, Decca's discs carried an iconic ear, designed by F. E. Attwood, a member of the company's Art Department (Lewis 1956: 89), that was graced with the letters "ffrr," short for full-frequency range recording (see figure 4.1). With the advent of stereo, this became "ffss," full-frequency stereo sound. On some of Decca's sleeves from the 1950s, the ear was encircled with the words "True High Fidelity" (see figure 4.3), as if that emanating from other labels was less "true." In fact, the Decca label was a veritable site of LP propaganda, alluding not just to the LP's higher fidelity but also its longer duration and its flexibility and hence durability. Although these symbolic micropractices might seem inconsequential in themselves, their presence on every Decca disc, in conjunction with the label's advertising, which dwelt on similar themes, helped to inculcate belief in the inherent superiority of the LP and erode any resistance to its adoption. Even the use of the quasi-technological word "microgroove" conferred a measure of scientific distinction on the LP.

Not that Decca was alone in resorting to such symbolic strategies. Capitol, Philips, and RCA all at one stage or another included a range of symbols on their labels denoting high fidelity and stereo. For example, forms of typographical "figuration" were often employed to visualize the acoustic advances of high fidelity. For example, the letters of the word "stereophonic" could be spatially configured to convey the enlarged sound stage of stereo. The word "stereo" on CBS LPs was situated between two outward pointing arrows, to achieve the same effect.[15] These "turns of imagery" also reflected the ascendancy of a sound-for-sound's-sake discourse: record consumers had become impressed by such badges of sonic advance.

Another important development occurring during the LP era was the increasingly differentiated price structure for recordings, which eventually led to the so-called "budget label"—the LP equivalent of the paperback. This was created—and all of the majors eventually had one—because of competition from another postwar phenomenon, the record club, which offered substantially cheaper discs. Typical was Decca's Ace of Clubs, a label name selected to suggest that it was in the process of trumping its opposition in this area of the market (Patmore 2000: 47); it drew its list, like other budget labels, from the company's large back catalog of recordings.

But there were also many smaller labels—Vox and Connoisseur were two—that lay outside the network of majors and specialized in more recherché repertoire (Day 2000: 93). Also in the LP era, joint ventures began to emerge between composers' organizations and record companies to promote the interests of new music. One such venture was the Composers' Recordings Inc. (CRI). Formed in 1954, its declared mission was "the discovery, circulation, and preservation of the best music of our time" and the promotion of works by American composers. It was the first label to record Henry Cowell and Roger Sessions (Brunner 1986: 507). It was an initiative anticipated in the U.K. by the Special Committee for the Promotion of New Music, which was launched in 1943 and sponsored recordings of the works of younger British composers, such as William Alwyn and Malcolm Arnold (Adamson

1995: 358). The emergence of these ventures reflected a significant shift away from the phonographic agnosticism prevalent among earlier generations of composers.

With the coming of the CD, which unlike preceding formats has only a single playing surface, the mode of labeling underwent further dramatic changes. Though not much larger than an LP label, the non-playing side of the CD has, in effect, become the label, which is now printed directly onto its surface. One mandatory requirement is that all CDs display the CD logo, usually embossed on the jewel box. This was a precedent set by the inventors of the Dolby Noise Reduction System and is a symbolic allusion to the fact that the price structure of every CD includes a small fee paid to its inventors, Sony and Philips, who continue to hold proprietorship over its patents. Indeed, the record label has always provided a site for a range of statutory declarations. Thus the information relating to copyright and unauthorized public performances generally occupies the rim of the CD's label, a positional practice inherited from the 78 and the LP. This is not because such information is in any sense marginal: after all, it is a legal requirement that it be there! It is simply that, positioned thus, it makes room for the information that does not appear on every CD, that is instead specific to a particular recording.

Label designs sometimes recuperate the history of recording. Those for the CDs of Deutsche Grammophon's "The Originals" series, digitally remastered recordings from the company's back catalog, recuperate the original LPs themselves, which are reproduced, even down to the play of the light on the grooves. This visual simulation is, in turn, matched—and it is a practice employed in other retro series emanating from the majors—with a reproduction of the cover on the original sleeve, with its titling suitably reworded to reflect the actual program of the reissue, which can be different from that of the source LPs (see figure 4.9).

Cover Versions: Visualizing Music for the Consumer

The record's sleeve—sometimes called "jacket," "cover," or at one stage, though the terms never caught on, "envelope" or "container"—is the other significant threshold device associated with the disc. Like its bookish equivalent, the dust cover—a late addition to the architecture of the book—it also exhibits both pictorial and textual features on its two major surfaces. For although Columbia had begun to issue some of its 78s with covers in the United States during the 1930s, it was not until the coming of the LP— the first batches were released by Columbia (who patented the term) in the United States in 1948 and by Decca in the U.K. in 1950 (Wallerstein and Botsford 1976)—that covers became a standard element of the disc's narrative architecture. This also extended to the other microgroove formats, the extended play (EP) and medium play (MP). Their covers' emergence reflected two imperatives: the need to insulate microgroove recordings from the "noisome" effects of dust, and the recognition that attractively covered 78s helped to attract consumer interest (Herdeg 1974: 25). However, such coverage was not extended to single-play 45s, the main format of popular music, which many in the industry saw as essentially the province of ephemeral music that had no need of long term protection and therefore received only paper sleeves.

One of the important developments in retailing following World War II was self-service, which was expressed in its most extended form in the supermarket, whose various protocols consumers had to learn for themselves (Humphery 1998: 135). Record shops also adopted self-service modes of retailing and introduced browsing boxes and racks containing LP, MP, and EP covers for the purpose. Because 78s only came in "dingy brown, blue, grey or green paper covers," record shops prior to the LP's advent were rather unattractive environments (Chislett 1960: 7), and records were hard to distinguish from one another. The advent of covers changed this, and they were soon shown in the windows and on the walls of record shops, much like paintings in art galleries. Indeed, cover designers often viewed record shops as their art galleries (Garlick 1977: 784).[16] Eye-catching covers had a distinct market advantage in the self-service environment, where looks counted, as they could excite or quash consumer curiosity (Witteloostuyn 1997: 105). The fact that they could do this had an influence on cover layout, particularly in terms of locating important information relating to the disc that consumers would be looking for. Thus the composer's name and the works on a recording were located toward the top of the cover, where they would stand out in a browsing box (McKnight-Tontz and Steinweiss 2000: 139). This practice was apparent on HMV covers from the 1960s, which had a white band across the top few centimeters of the cover where a summary of the record's title was located alongside the label and recording format (see figure 4.4).

Thus, the momentum for cover design was driven by the need to dominate the symbolic economy of the retail environment by utilizing various forms of pictorial rhetoric. In addition to promoting the longer playing times and quieter surfaces of LPs, their advertising also drew attention to their "colorful pictorial containers" and "authoritative notes about the music."[17] Yet it is possible to overdo the economic motives underpinning the new mode of phonographic presentation and overlook the expository advances engendered by covers, which the reviewers of early LPs were among the first to appreciate. To have the notes accessible on the obverse of a "beautifully designed cover" was generally regarded as a mark of progress in the evolution of gramophone containment, worthy, *pace* Musique d'Abord, of the extra costs involved.

These "beautifully designed" covers had their provenances in the art departments of the record companies, and, as with much design in the immediate postwar period, were not usually subject to attribution. The failure to name designers should not downplay their significance as a new form of narrative architecture, in which there is an innovative textual interplay between the musical, the visual, and the typographical that provides novel synergies across a range of cultural domains, particularly music and painting. It is generally held that Alex Steinweiss, who worked for Columbia before joining Decca, helped to pioneer many of the graphic conventions associated with record covers (Heller 1994/1995: 71). His graphic style (exemplified in the over five hundred covers he designed) emphasized bold shapes and forms and a distinctive typography, the so-called "Steinweiss scrawl." He argued that this "scrawl" was an integral part of the visualizing process and that an attractive calligraphy could also arouse interest in an LP's contents (Heller 2000: 38).

Early LP covers in the Steinweiss tradition for the most part used simple designs to pick out, in visual terms, the music they "covered." They were not overly colorful, at most using only three or four colors mainly as highlighting devices to establish semiotic hierarchies between dominant and subsidiary lines of information. For example, on a Decca LP of *The Planets*, the title is the core element of a veritable solar system of information. This comprises profiles of the planetary "gods" along with a central sun/corolla where *The Planets* is spelled out in a bold font. More peripheral information is located toward the "outer reaches" of the cover's solar system (see figure 4.3). The resultant illustrative correlations of the early designs, though using basic shapes and forms, were often effective, operating in subtle ways across a number of planes of meaning. They enciphered the qualities of the music they covered using a form of pictorial shorthand combining simple imagery and telling forms of typography. Thus an LP cover from the early 1950s of Chopin's *Les Sylphides* and Jacques Ibert's *Divertissement* (see figure 4.5) consists of a diptych, each of whose panels utilizes relevant signifiers evoking Chopin and Ibert. From the tree, which separates the panels, blossoms fall that are figuratively transformed into ballet dancers (Chopin) on one side and a Parisian street café (Ibert) on the other. The title fonts also provide a semiotic correlation of sorts with the music: copper plate for *Les Sylphides* and modernist for *Divertissement*. The overall iconography, though simple by today's standards, continues to exert charm and allure, and is very telling.

Yet the record cover was not an entirely original design genre, for it represented an application of principles originally developed for the covers of sheet music and the concert program, which are also mediating texts. Its

Figure 4.3 Planetary System: A sleeve typical of early LP cover design. Although the reproduction is primitive by today's standards, it remains effective through its use of bold colors and shapes. Also note the technical information and logos at the bottom of the sleeve, another common feature in the early days of the LP. (Reproduced by permission of Universal.)

Figure 4.4 Top Information: A typical LP sleeve from the 1960s. Basic information is situated in a band across the top of the sleeve, where it is easy to see. The cover draws on one of Marie Laurencin's designs for the first production of *Les Biches*. The institutional stickers at the top of the cover are indicative of the disc's "career." (Reproduced by permission of EMI.)

Figure 4.5 Double Coverage: Early London LP showing the designer's attempt to "visualize" both items of music on the program as blossoms falling from a tree. Different typographies are used to represent the distinctive qualities of the music. (Reproduced by permission of Universal.)

Figure 4.6 Logocentric: A cover typical of DG's "serious" phase, when words and words alone were considered to be all that was needed in the way of a cover design for classical music. Observe the stains and wrinkles on the sleeve, symptoms of the aging process. Covers never stay pristine. (Reproduced by permission of Universal.)

graphic imperative parallels that of Mussorgsky's *Pictures at an Exhibition*—the quintessential work of musical illustration—but in reverse: the images represent the music, adding a visual track to its sound, albeit one embedded in a range of entitling and corporate emblems. Such emblems have become especially preponderant in the last two decades. From the 1980s onward, as many music ensembles have been forced to seek additional streams of funding to support their endeavors, sponsorship signs such as logos have become a design feature of many covers.[18]

Arguably, too, the whole discursive environment of the recording industry, well in advance of the LP cover, had pioneered visualizing techniques for promoting records through evocative advertising and merchandising (Schwartzman 1993). In the 1920s, for example, RCA placed a series of advertisements for its classical albums in the magazine *The Etude,* which had a wide circulation amongst musicians (Figure 4.7). These ads graphically illustrated the music they were promoting and represented the precursors of postwar cover iconography, as did the covers of catalogs issued by record companies between the wars (Witteloostuyn 1997: 121–122).

In fact, for much of the era of the LP cover designers had, more or less, *carte blanche* in their design briefs, unlike some of their present-day successors, who, like many in the record industry, now defer to marketing departments. Marketing's influence has not necessarily been a beneficial one, particularly in terms of the design values and standards of covers. This is evident in the number of howlers perpetrated on covers, including mistitling and misattributed photographs. One LP cover from the 1970s has André Previn conducting the Chicago Symphony Orchestra, when he was actually conducting the Pittsburgh Orchestra (Grubb 1986: 165). Furthermore, as marketing departments began to gain a foothold in the recording industry, most famously at Decca in the 1960s, the budgets of art departments were slashed, which led to unsightly results such as the "coverage" of Karajan's landmark recording of *Aida.* This came in a red plastic folder instead of the customary black box associated with opera sets, that "looked and felt cheap," with "a transparent window through which you see an ill-defined still from (I think) The Ten Commandments." (Culshaw 1981: 220). Culshaw recounts another problem he had with Decca's art department at this time, in relation to obtaining a germane design for Britten's *War Requiem* cover; the department failed to produce one that was "serious" enough for Britten's work. In the end, Culshaw elected to follow the example of Boosey and Hawkes, Britten's publishers, who had adopted a jet-black design with white lettering (Culshaw 1981: 314–15). The adoption of visualizations used elsewhere to illustrate a musical work is, in fact, not all that common. One of the few other examples is an EMI CD of Frank Bridge's works, which includes the orchestral

Figure 4.7 This is one of a series of advertisements appearing in *The Etude* from 1927 onward that promote Victor's Red Seal discs and their "new method of Orthophonic reproduction." They foreshadow the graphic designs employed on LP covers, and their style owes much to a modernist aesthetic. Note also the way the advertisement extends the idea of verisimilitude. In this case, it is suggested that "no matter where you live," Red Seal records can bring "into your home the best of the concert and the operatic stage" whenever you like. Lastly, the advertisement also promotes one of Victor's publications, *A Musical Galaxy*, which provides a commentary "upon six of the greatest moments in music"—presumably in the manner extolled in the advertisement, by personalizing music via the lives of its composers. (Reproduced by permission of Theodore Presser.)

tone poem *The Sea.* Its cover is an adaptation of the title page from the full score of Bridge's work, whose frieze is used to frame a painting of the sea (see figure 4.10).

In contradistinction to Decca's parsimonious tendencies, CBS's president in the 1960s and 1970s, Goddard Lieberson, encouraged his cover designers to adopt an avant-garde aesthetic. To this end, he enjoined them to keep abreast of developments in experimental theater and film and design covers that reflected the directions of contemporary art (Codrington 1996: 53). But prior to Lieberson's recognition that cover art should move with the times, some companies had already commissioned contemporary artists to design covers, as opposed to merely reproducing their work (a much more common practice), particularly if there was an existing association between a painter and the composer. Recognizing such a link between the English painter John Piper and Benjamin Britten—Piper had worked on the stage designs of several of Britten's operas—Argo invited Piper to design the LP cover for the composer's second set of *Canticles.* For the cover of Alessandro Scarlatti's opera *La Dama spagnola e il Cavaliere romano,* Decca turned to Salvador Dali, who had designed the sets of the opera's Venice production. Famously, the LP included a sachet of the Guerlain perfume that was used to mask the odor emanating from the carcass that was a feature of the production. Other artists involved in cover designs during the LP era included Ben Shahn and Marie Laurencin, who painted a watercolor for L'Oiseau-lyre's recording of John Blow's opera *Venus and Adonis* (Davidson 1994: 376).[19] Although the majors now no longer seem to commission artists on a regular basis—they mostly use graphic designers instead—this is not the case with the more "aesthetic" independents, such as ECM, Winter & Winter, Col Legno, and Arts.[20]

Just occasionally a performer with some capacity for painting or drawing has been invited to design a cover, particularly for a recording in which they have had a hand, or, in this instance, a voice. The tenor Gérard Souzay designed the cover for his Philips LP of Poulenc songs. And on at least one occasion record companies have used the paintings of the composer they were recording, as Chandos did for its William Alwyn cycle, an apt choice since the composer saw his paintings as an integral part of his creative endeavor (see figure 4.11).[21]

Significantly, however, the art of record design has not been accorded the same status and kudos as that of the book—a reflection of the disc's continuing struggle for status in the hierarchy of the arts. Many modern artists including Picasso and Matisse have been involved in the design of books, either from cover to cover or through cover illustrations alone (Bloch 1987). Many of these same artists, at various times during their careers, also enjoyed creative relationships with classical music, particularly ballet and opera. Several

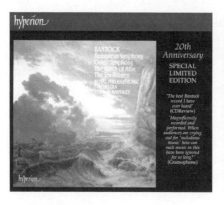

Figure 4.8 Limited Edition: Much used in book publishing and the visual arts, the limited edition is a rarity in the record industry. For its Twentieth Anniversary Hyperion reissued its twenty bestselling CDs as a "limited edition." They were featured in cardboard slipcases based on the original covers, on which excerpts from laudatory reviews of the original CD were placed. (Designer: Terry Shannon.)

Figure 4.9 "The Originals": A typical retro cover exhibiting a series of features: "ethnic" imagery evoking Dvořák's dances; a reproduction of the LP sleeve, set at an oblique angle to differentiate it from the cover of the *actual* CD; and a "seal" encircling the words "legendary performances." In the left hand corner appears some technobabble ("Original-Image Bit-Processing") designed to counter the perception that "original" signifies *original sound*. (Designer: Hartmut Pfeiffer. Reproduced by permission of Universal.)

Figure 4.10 Cover to Cover: From EMI's "British Composers" series, this Frank Bridge CD uses part of the cover of the score of "The Sea," which is in turn used to frame a painting of the sea originally appearing in the *Girls' Own Paper.* The template used in this series incorporates a "silvered" map of the British Isles as its signature motif. The "EMI Classics" logo is a semiotic offshoot of the 1970s, when the company "corporatized" its image and dropped its traditional insignia. (Reproduced by permission of EMI.)

Figure 4.11 Autograph: For its cycle of Alwyn CDs, Chandos drew on the composer's paintings, which he regarded as an integral part of his artistic project. The presence of the composer's autograph thus works in a double sense, emphasizing the authenticity of the CD ("recorded with the assistance of his wife") and the cover painting, "Dartmoor," which was reproduced the wrong way round on the CD. This has been corrected. (Designer: Jacquetta Sargeant. Reproduced by permission of The William Alwyn Foundation.)

major twentieth-century painters were commissioned by Diaghilev to create stage designs for the Ballets Russes, most famously Picasso for Erik Satie's *Parade*. No one, however, did a record cover.

By comparison, most contemporary artists, with the notable exception of those who have used recording as part of their work,[22] have found a closer affinity with rock musicians, particularly those who came to prominence in the 1960s and 1970s and had art school backgrounds, such as John Lennon or Brian Eno.[23] This has been reflected in much of the iconography associated with rock music of the time, not just record covers but also posters and couture, whose styles were indebted to the Pop Art aesthetic (Walker 1987). Two of the covers for Beatles' albums, said to be "groundbreaking in their visual and aesthetic properties" (Inglis 2001: 83), were produced by two prominent artists of the time, Richard Hamilton *(The Beatles)* and Peter Blake *(Sergeant Pepper)*. Certainly, by and large, rock art has been far more adventurous than its classical counterparts.[24]

It is also important to note, since it bears on what cover designers have been able to marshal in the way of iconographical resources, that from the LP to the CD, printing and graphic design underwent radical change. Record covers, in fact, provide a graphic illustration of this change, the most dramatic being those associated with computer-assisted design and image digitalization. Cover designers now have at their disposal data banks of iconographical resources, including everything from portraits of composers to facsimiles of scores, to which they increasingly resort (Johnson 1994: 42). As a result, the graphics of CDs are visually more complex than their LP predecessors, incorporating a wider range of imagery and more chromatic gradation, as well as complex forms of "separation" in which color is used to position and punctuate information. This is manifested in "stratified" layouts, in which figure, through subtle changes of color, becomes ground and vice versa. Images often meld with one another, and the result is a subtle gradation of images and words, emblems and colors—almost akin to an iconographical fugue. Designs cross from one surface to another and exploit the transparency of the CD case, which has now dropped the black ribbed bar that was a feature of the early jewel box. Images can shadow images across the whole box—from the CD booklet through to the jewel box and back again—in a constant and ongoing pattern of iteration alternating between foreground and background (see figure 4.12). Increasingly, these images, or some fraction of them, continue onto the "livery" of the CD itself, which frequently displays distinctive and unique features. Forms of record coverage thus carry the technological "fingerprints" of their times.

But even before these changes, graphic design had been subject to the revolution of offset printing, which enabled photographic images to be imported into graphic designs with relative ease (Witteloostuyn 1997:118–19). Other changes included the use of cardboard laminates for sleeves beginning in the late 1950s. These enabled a spine to be added to the flat jacket, providing a third surface on which to inscribe information, albeit in a small font, relating contents of a record. This was a significant addition, particularly since LPs were supposed to be stored upright on shelves in the manner of books, with their spines outward. When Decca introduced its controversial plastic container, one reviewer thought that the lack of a "title down the spine" was a major inconvenience (Shawe-Taylor 1960: 341).

Exotic Flights of the Imagination: Getting Off the Musical Track

One of the important functions of a record cover is rhetorical. It acts as an arousal mechanism, designed to make the music it houses more alluring, for in many instances, a record is seen before it is heard. In this respect, covers act as mediating discourses, helping to frame and generate initial impressions that whet the appetite and induce the desire to listen. While a book can be opened at random and its contents more or less determined, records afford no analogous opportunities. Moreover, they do not have titles, at least the bookish type that are also designed to excite interest and provide clues about contents, approach, or style. A record's "title" addresses its putative listeners in far more oblique ways than a book's title. Genette's exemplary title, that of James Joyce's novel, *Ulysses,* reveals considerably more information about the "character" of its novel than the names of most musical works, which, with the exception of the titles of program music, are far less forthcoming (Genette 1997). For example, even the nicknames of symphonies and concertos are comparatively unrevealing and in some instances positively misleading, as in Haydn's "Miracle" Symphony. The nickname "miracle," allegedly, refers to an extra-musical happening at the symphony's first performance. Just after the audience had left the auditorium, a chandelier fell to the floor and its members were spared certain injury.

In spite of the modal dissimilarities between writing and music, records have acquired the architecture of the book through adopting, sometimes literally, its iconography. For example, Penguin's "Music Classics," a series that attempted to popularize classical music in the way that Penguin Classics have popularized literary classics, shares its design template with the book series (see figure 4.13). Penguin's involvement in CDs is itself unusual; only a few book publishers, including those specializing in scores and music works, have extended their operations into the realm of recording. The

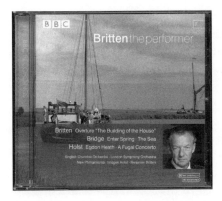

Figure 4.12 Transparency: The BBC series "Britten the Performer" consisted of recordings made at the Aldeburgh Festival. Their covers show "Britten country" across all of their surfaces. Their designs, like most CD designs of recent provenance, exploit the transparency of the case. In dropping the black bar found on the left of older cases, another area for inscription was created. (Designer: Tobasgo Design London. Reproduced by permission of IMG Records.)

Figure 4.13 Record Book: The design follows a classic book cover, thereby affirming the idea of the culture of the book imprinting itself, in this case quite literally, onto the record. Note also the two simulated "palimpsests": the band "Featuring an original essay by Douglas Coupland" and the seal of approval "Recommended in the Penguin Guide to CDs."

Figure 4.14 Nashville Classic: A Paul Nash painting "Wood on the Downs" forms the basis for Conifer's CD of early-twentieth-century English piano concertos. Nash is the Constable of modernist English landscapes and thus an appropriate visual "echo," so to speak, of the program. The cover information also includes the fact that the performance of Walton's *Sinfonia* is the "first recording" of its "original version." (Designer: R. W. Graphics. Reproduced by permission of BMG.)

Figure 4.15 Retro: One of EMI's "Great Recordings of the Century" "recovers" EMI's history in iconographical terms from its "dog days," represented by HMV's "Nipper," located bottom left, to the days of the LP, a section of which is reproduced alongside the LP cover of the "great recording," Richard Strauss's *Don Quixote*, and then to those of the CD. (Designer: Enterprise IIG. Reproduced by permission of EMI.)

Paris-based Editions L'Oiseau-lyre, which was established in the 1930s by Louise Hanson-Dyer, originally specialized in scores of renaissance and baroque music.[25] Hanson-Dyer launched the record label in the late 1940s because she considered records to be a natural extension of music publishing (Davidson 1994: 309).

An apposite visualization has traditionally provided, then, one of the main vehicles through which recorded music is mediated. In the early days of cover iconography, designs were more abstract, but at least they were original designs. Secondhand images such as paintings were not often utilized, nor were photographs, partly because the technology remained insufficiently developed. When offset printing arrived in the 1960s, this changed, and graphic designers turned to other sources of imagery for inspiration. Paintings, along with photographs, began to be widely used on covers, and the Steinweiss pattern of design began to recede.

Yet some in the industry questioned the need for such visualization. They argued that it was incompatible with classical music, that the use of cover imagery, no matter how tasteful, debased the music's qualities. Hans Donialoff, who headed the art department at Deutsche Grammophon during the 1950s, was adamant that pictures were inappropriate "fronts" for classical music and that words alone would be sufficient (see figure 4.6). Popular music, meaning recordings that sold more than 2,000 units, were exempt from this embargo (Marcowicz 1995: 26). Symptomatic of the prevailing ethos of seriousness and abstraction associated with classical music, this view was to some extent shared by Alec Robertson, along with a number of correspondents to record magazines who have at various times declared their abhorrence of inept imagery. In the same editorial from which this chapter's epigraph is extracted, Robertson complains about covers becoming glossier and resorting to lurid, "cheesecake" motifs utilizing "exotic flights of the imagination" that were unrelated to the recording. Like many in the classical industry, he felt that the covers of classical LPs should endeavor to present a tasteful front to their contents and lend distinction to the music. They should avoid the wanton commercialism employed by other sections of the popular media—an illustrative manifestation of the great musical schism. But this is also a manifestation of classical restraint: music should speak to the mind, not the body, and covers, accordingly, should not be "loose" in their modes of presentation. By contrast, the covers of rock albums have often tested the boundaries of pictorial permissiveness, whereas classical covers, even those fronting music that deals with prurient subject matter, such as Ligeti's *Le Grande Macabre,* have generally displayed decorum and restraint.[26] Robertson felt, like Donialoff, that "well-executed lettering" or a "portion of the score" was illustration enough (1956: 342). And indeed the latter has sometimes been used as a cover design, if for no other reason than that the scores of some contemporary composers like Ligeti have considerable aesthetic interest.

Covers thus are expected to create the right atmospherics, setting an appropriate musical tone that is revealing but not revealing and commensurate with the ascetic aesthetic of classical music. In fact, these "flights of imagination" have always been constrained to a degree; the layout of an LP or CD cover contains necessary if sobering fixed properties relating to the placement of such obligatory design features as the company's trademark and livery, in which "release-specific" imagery was expected to be embedded (Witteloostuyn 1997: 95, 105). In the case of Deutsche Grammophon, the fixed element comprised the label's cartouche, which occupied the top two-thirds of the cover and provided the disc's titular setting (see figure 4.9). In fact, the need to include this cartouche troubled many of the label's designers, who felt it interfered with their inventiveness (Marcowicz 1995: 26).[27]

In fact, following Robertson's advice, a goodly number of LPs and CDs have used lettering and typography as their main imagery. For example, a Pianissimo CD of Chabrier's piano works uses the autographs of several impressionist painters set around a piano keyboard, both to evoke the "impressionistic" style of the Chabrier's music and to acknowledge the fact that Chabrier—as Felix Aprahamian's liner notes point out—was an avid collector of impressionist paintings. Yet it has been "exotic flights of the imagination" rather than "well-executed lettering" that has dominated, notwithstanding the practice at Deutsche Grammophon, which was finally abandoned in 1955.[28] And while there have been literally thousands of LP and CD covers produced, their "flights" (never mind their exoticism) nevertheless fall into several main categories.

First, there are those that utilize types of portraiture, drawn from paintings—in the case of older composers—and photographs, which, though relatively neutral in expository terms, attempt to place a recognizable face on the music and "profile" it in terms of a countenance, be it of a performer or a composer (see figure 4.16). Second, there is landscape imagery, which draws its aptness from its topographical relevance to the music; Scottish symphonies invariably attract Scottish landscapes or subjects (see figure 4.17); New World symphonies, American ones; English concertos, English ones (see figure 4.14), and so on. Third, there is imagery that takes its cue from the type of music on the disc: for example, religious music generally attracts religious paintings or architecture, such as cathedrals, which are particularly preponderant on discs of organ music. Fourth, there is imagery that reflects the era during which the music was composed: contemporary music, for example, utilizes contemporary paintings (see figures 4.14 and 4.22), and so on. Recordings of opera and ballet often adapt stage designs (see figure 4.4) or actual scenes from a "live" performance. Finally, there are covers that utilize multiple categories of imagery in a form of montage. Those CDs from the BBC series "Britten the Performer" are typical and utilize the same design template and color register, which makes them recognizable as a series. In their bottom righthand corner is a photograph of the composer, to the left of which is a listing of the works on the CD. These are placed on a greenish background that overlays a photograph of the Suffolk countryside (see figure 4.12). Exploiting the transparency of the case, this design creates a series of narrative and iconographical planes that can be "seen through," as it were, engendering a dialogue between figure and ground, titles and photograph, and constructing a visual commentary on the music and its composer. Thus word and image here form a laminated text of musical and topographical references suggestive of "Britten country" and its contribution to his music.

EMI's "Great Recordings of the Century" also employ laminated texts using a series of emblems drawn from EMI's century of recording: the cover of the "great" recording that forms the program of the CD, embedded in a "quadrant" of an HMV LP (see figure 4.15). The same image is also reproduced on the back cover. When the CD is detached from its jewel box mount, HMV's trademark appears (see figure 4.24). This is a symbolic affirmation of EMI's longevity as a company: one hundred years in the business. More to the point, though, the cover also encapsulates a discursive emblem of the phonographic endeavor, linking music to engineering so that recording comes to constitute a technical art. This is epitomized in the outer regions of the cover: in the LP disc itself and the "duplicitous" logo "ART," an acronym for "Abbey Road Technology" that also points up the complex art of the CD, as epitomized in the sleeve, the product of a graphic designer, and the performers and composers who created the CD in the first place (see figure 4.15).

With the exception of LP covers produced for Nonesuch and Vox-Turnabout in the 1960s and 1970s, humor is not often deployed on classical covers, supporting the dominant idea that classical music is essentially a serious endeavor that only rarely lets its hair down.[29] One cover that does deploy, however—and even it has a serious side—is United's *Hypothetically Murdered,* whose rebus elements complement Dmitry Shostakovich's burlesque music. In the background of the cover is a shadowy profile of the composer and in the foreground a definition of the word "hypothesis," torn from a dictionary, which has a dagger through it, adding to the murderous tone of the image (see figure 4.25). Cartoons and visual jokes are not much in evidence on covers either. Maurizio Kagel's '1898' is a *trompe l'oeil* design that places the actual LP on a parquet floor, broken into five pieces, which also alludes to the fragility of the 78, whose sonic qualities are reproduced on the recording (see figure 4.18).

Thus the images on record covers operate much like the titles of paintings, sometimes deferring to and sometimes dominating them (Foucault 1983: 32). But there can also be a productive reciprocity between the title and the titled, wherein meanings are shunted back and forth between them in the process of deciphering their significance. Arguably record covers operate in analogous ways: the music evokes the cover, and the cover the music. But rarely does a cover function as an autonomous explanatory unit, comprehensible without reference to other parts of the disc's narrative environment. The cover of a Virgin Classics recording of Camille Saint-Saëns's chamber music, which includes *Le Carnaval des animaux,* is a case in point. Predictably, the main design theme draws on animal imagery, which overlays a picture of Saint-Saëns and an almost indistinguishable architectural drawing from the cover's brown background. The initial reading is that this must be a drawing for a zoo, but in fact it is adapted from one by the Regency architect John Nash. Thus it acts as a visual pun paying heed to the performers on the disc, the Nash Ensemble, operating on a number of planes of meaning that are not obvious until one reads the liner notes.

But unlike the title of a painting, which remains outside of its frame, thereby constituting a parergon, the title information associated with a recording is a design element of the cover. Indeed, with the exception of those covers in which the "painting" is framed and provided with a space to itself (see figure 4.14), the title invariably violates the cover's aesthetic integrity. It is often placed over the image as a panel, as in the case of Deutsche Grammophon's cartouche (see figure 4.9), or it forces the image to seep through its interstices (see figure 4.17). Thus the painting no longer stands alone as an object to be contemplated in its own right but becomes an object to be contemplated *alongside* the music. Thereby the painting, normally an ergon, is transformed into a parergon—a musical parergon at that. Indeed, the reproduced painting functions somewhat similarly to a quotation in a text: it illustrates the music while taking a new set of meanings for itself that spring from the music. The titles on the cover, so to speak, also retitle the painting. Sometimes this is a result of "detailing"—not an uncommon practice—wherein only a small portion of the painting is utilized that evokes the most musical resonance (see figure 4.19).

In fact, there is a certain aesthetic rationality in appropriating paintings for covers, as record companies commenced doing in the late 1950s, and they have even utilized them as a marketing ploy. In 1955, RCA released a series of albums that were promoted as "deluxe art packaging" and included "a beautiful color reproduction of a world famous painting . . . READY TO FRAME"—

Figure 4.16 Composed Portrait: This cover was an Axel Poignant photograph of the composer, Michael Tippett, at work in his studio. The image is an inviting one that seems to take the viewer into its confidence and cajoles them into wanting to listen to the LP that it "fronts." (Reproduced by permission of Universal.)

Figure 4.17 Topographical Cliché: Covers frequently use images that correspond to the "geography" of the music, in this case Mendelssohn's "Scottish" works are suggested through an engraving of Edinburgh originally drawn by J. M. W. Turner. (Reproduced by permission of EMI.)

Figure 4.18 *Trompe l'oeil:* This cover is actually atypical of Deutsche Grammophon and is one of the few LPs to use the record as its central image, though many CD retro designs do (see figure 4.15). The "broken" record is a visual signifier of Kagel's '1898', a work commissioned to commemorate the label's seventy-fifth anniversary. The image recalls an era of phonographic history when records were easy to break. Incidentally, the recording itself attempts to simulate the sound of records from the acoustic era. (Reproduced by permission of Universal.)

Figure 4.19 Fragment: This example of an appropriation, from Pieter Brueghel's *Wedding Feast,* provides an apt (if geographically remote) impression of one of the works on the LP, *Les Noces.* Note that this title is not given in full, presumably because it would disrupt the symmetry of the design. (Designer: Jacques Vatoux. Reproduced by permission of Erato.)

yet another case of the high street utilizing high culture in the ongoing elision between the two.[30] But outside of these economic motives, the subjects of many premodern paintings correlated with those of "classical" music and therefore obviated the need to execute an original design when one already existed—for example, Poussin's *Judgment of Solomon* for Handel's oratorio *Solomon* (Barker 1958a: 13).

This logic was applied in the case of an LP program of French contemporary ballet including Francis Poulenc's *Les Biches,* for which Marie Laurencin created the original stage designs, one of which forms the basis of the cover (see figure 4.4). This logic is also apparent, albeit in a more oblique way, on a CD cover of Richard Strauss's *Symphonia Domestica* and its musical offspring, *Parergon,* which is based on a photograph of Strauss's family and thus acts quite literally as a visual parergon to the music. Tone poems of the type composed by Strauss, which often have direct literary connections, have always proved easier to illustrate, partly because these literary connections have also been the subjects of many Western painters and sculptors (see figure 4.15).

The same logic applies to those compositions like *Pictures at an Exhibition* that provide a musical evocation of paintings. These include Hindemith's *Mathis der Maler Symphonie*—a musical recreation of Grünewald's Isenheim altarpiece, a veiled version of which appears on Abbado's recording of the work.[31] In such instances the cover provides an accessible image for the listener attempting to establish links between the music and the paintings from which it is derived. Curiously, though, very few recordings of *Pictures at an Exhibition* have used the paintings of Victor Hartmann that inspired Mussorgsky's work; one of the few to have done so was the Capitol recording of the work by Leonard Pennario (Wittleloostuyn 1997: 475). Generally, its covers—a notable exception is Arthur Wills' transcription for organ, which adopted a white cover with gilt lettering—are imagined versions of these paintings or are paintings of other *pictures at an exhibition*.

But paintings also link with music on recordings in a more indirect way, through their style rather than their subject. Even though Hector Berlioz admired the Flemish painter Antoine Weitz, the more "painterly" covers of his music on LP and CD have generally drawn on paintings of the French Romantic school, including those of Eugène Delacroix and Théodore Géricault. The recordings of work by members of Les Six—who were active in Paris during the 1920s and 1930s—often adopt the paintings of Raoul Dufy, André Derain, Henri Matisse, and Pablo Picasso, suggesting a visual affinity between the music of Les Six and the painters belonging to the Paris School. In due recognition of this affinity, the cover of a CD of Poulenc's piano works deploys a pastiche of Dufy's work (see figure 4.26). Such pastiche is not uncommon in cover design; each CD cover in Neeme Järvi's Prokofiev cycle of symphonies for Chandos is a pastiche of Kasimir Malevich's paintings as well.

The same aesthetic stereotyping has applied to other music from the twentieth century, such as that of the Second Viennese School, particularly the early works of Schoenberg and Berg, which are often associated on covers with German expressionist painters, especially Oscar Kokoschka and Max Beckmann. This has also applied to the music of the so-called impressionists Claude Debussy and Maurice Ravel. In other contexts, however, the aptness of the imagery is not always immediately apparent. A Hyperion LP of the works of the British composer Alan Bush uses L. S. Lowry's "Industrial Scene" (see figure 4.20), whose appositeness derives only from the composer's membership of the Communist Party.

With the coming of the LP, which led to mixed programs of music from the same composer, the imagery often focuses on one work, usually that which is likely to excite the most interest. Thus, the covers of discs that include Honegger's *Pacific 231* as parts of their programs invariably sport express trains. Some LP or CD covers select the work with the most visual potential. In the case of an HMV recording of Ravel and Prokofiev piano concertos, the cover features a Utrillo painting of Montmarte. This is relevant to the Ravel but not the Prokofiev, for even though Prokofiev spent several years composing in Paris, he wrote his first piano concerto—the one featured on the LP—while still a student in Saint Petersburg (see figure 4.21).

Much cover imagery applies the *zeitgeist* principle that all of the arts reflect the spirit of their times. This was deployed in Philips "Modern Music," a series notable for including the early works of avant-garde composers Boulez and Stockhausen. Its covers sported hand-mounted prints of avant-garde paintings from the 1960s, mostly abstract expressionism, or at least its European variants, Tachism and Cobra (see figure 4.22). The link between painting and music underpinning the presentation of the series was evident in the fact that brief biographies of the painters were included on the LP (see figure 4.23). But the paintings also proclaim by illustrative example something about the "tone" of the music in the series, its surface disorder and chaos.

Similar principles apply in the case of ECM—short for "Editions Contemporary Music"—a label that has specialized in contemporary and medieval music but also jazz and is committed to the importance of the phonographic ideal, of which its covers are an integral part. ECM has a well-developed design philosophy that clears the decks: the label feels that there is too much information in contemporary culture, and covers should not add to this burden. Hence its covers reflect a minimalist style owing much to the aesthetics of the 1980s, as manifested in Op Art, Art Povera, and

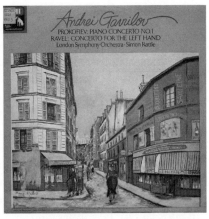

Figure 4.20 Political Ideology: The L. S. Lowry painting on this LP, an industrial landscape with anonymous figures, alludes to Alan Bush's Marxism. The music on this LP, however, is not in any direct sense a representation of proletariat life, although the title of one of its works, *Dialectic,* hints of Marxism.

Figure 4.21 Separate Coverage: The Utrillo painting exemplifies the way covers sometimes give visual priority to one work, in this case the Ravel. Observe, also, the way in which the pianist has top billing, evidence of the influence of performers, and the way technical information relating to the LP is omitted from this cover. This is relevant here because the recording used EMI's much criticized SQ system. (Reproduced by permission of EMI.)

Figure 4.22 Hand-Mounted Print: An example of a cover from Philips "Modern Music" series, which set new standards of design in the early 1960s, particularly when compared with the "appalling" standards (said one reviewer) of Columbia and Decca. The series used contemporary paintings for its covers, in this case one by Frank Avery Wilson, to provide a visual correlation with the music. (Reproduced by permission of Universal.)

Figure 4.23 Pictures at an LP Exhibition: The reverse side of a Philips Modern Music LP features reproductions of the front covers of other LPs in the series. A brief biography of the current painter is included on the right-hand side of the sleeve. Note also the way the perimeter of the actual LP is imprinting itself on the cover as a black arc—a palpable sign of the LP's age. (Reproduced by permission of Universal.)

color field painting (Kemper 1996: 8). But they also provide visual echoes of the minimalist music associated with the label.

In fact, paintings, as well as images from other visual arts such as photography, have been systematically plundered, at least since the 1960s when the techniques of color reproduction were perfected, as a source for record covers in the worlds of both popular and classical music (Shaughnessy 1996: 45). Among other things, the use of paintings or photographs brought about the eclipse of the more "autographic" sleeve. In fact, some labels, most notably the independent Hyperion—a label that also pays close attention to the textual environs of its discs—use them almost exclusively. One reason, presumably, is that a tasteful and apposite painting is more in keeping with the tone of classical music. But another is that the independents often use, for reasons of affordability, performers and ensembles with less of a "profile" in the classical industry, who are not usually interested in the extra visual coverage on CDs that the big names associated with the majors often demand (Shaughnessy 1996: 46). In fact, the phonographic practices of the majors are now heavily oriented toward performer representation, as their marketing departments begin to deploy those strategies that have been widely used to promote rock music (Pollard 1994), which center on "individualizing" and highlighting artists. Hence the covers of the majors have tended to spotlight performers in various ways. This can take the form of giving added typographical and pictorial emphasis to their names rather than the music titles on the sleeve, which seems to defy the natural order of precedence where music is concerned (see figure 4.21).[32] Or the conductor's autograph might appear on the CD, a device employed on some EMI Classics. It has also involved the deployment of some of those un-classical "cheesecake" poses that were much criticized in the past. Thus covers featuring some female performers have been subjected to an erotic emphasis and continue to be seen, even in an era of pictorial permissiveness, as unjustifiably tasteless and incompatible with the aesthetic sobriety of classical music (Symes 1997).[33]

Nonetheless such portraiture can operate without titillating imperatives and be used for artistic reasons or for much the same reason that a picture of an author might appear on a dust jacket, to satisfy one's curiosity to see the face behind the music. The photograph of Michael Tippett on an LP of his Second Symphony shows the composer in his studio, looking out of the sleeve with a score in his hand. Its composition has the effect of inviting its viewer into Tippett's studio, the domain of his creativity, an invitation that also extends to the LP itself (see figure 4.16). But in another example of such composer portraiture, on a CD featuring the work of the Erich Korngold, the visual presentation makes spurious connections. The film sprockets that dominate the sides of the CD (see figure 4.27), as well as its label allude to

Korngold's years as a Hollywood composer. The trouble is that the two works represented on this particular CD, the Suite and Piano Trio, antedate his Hollywood period. Supraphon's designers, presumably with an eye more to the market than to music history, are hoping that the greater popularity of film relative to chamber music will boost the sales of the CD, but in doing so they have committed a historical error.

Indeed, cover designers often exploit opportunities afforded them by other media contexts, such as when an excerpt—and usually it is only that—of classical music is used as a signature tune in a film or television commercial and has gained, as a result, a degree of popularity it might not otherwise have enjoyed. For more than three decades Mozart's C-major Piano Concerto has been known by its associations with the Swedish film *Elvira Madigan* and was tagged that way on many LP covers, including even a recent reissue of the concerto, long after the film had disappeared from cinemas.

Such strategies reflect the need to secure positional advantage in the marketplace, particularly one surfeited with many recordings of the same work, and any means, fair or foul, that lead one recording to be special and distinctive merit this semiotic spotlighting. For example, in the 1950s the titling on covers was often used to disguise metonymically the "true" contents of LPs. Recordings of Aram Khachaturian's ballet *Gayenah* were often labeled the "Saber Dance," overlooking the fact that this dance, made well-known in other contexts, occupied but three minutes of a ballet lasting over an hour (Windreich 1956: 29). This spotlighting also applies, for example, to recordings in which a composer has been in attendance as an adviser and which therefore have special significance and authority ("Recorded in the presence of the composer"; "Performed on Greig's piano at the composer's villa") or which are world premieres of a newly discovered version of a score ("Original Version, First Recording"; see figure 4.14).

Of course, there is no single way of visually interpreting a musical work, and sometimes covers, even from the same label, adopt the same paintings to illustrate different compositions. A recording of Samuel Barber's piano works issued in 1980 on Helios, Hyperion's budget label, utilized the painter Edward Hopper's *Nighthawks*, which appeared again several years later on a recording of American piano concertos from the same label. Likewise, the painting titled *Number 5* by Charles Demuth has been featured on several covers of contemporary music, including Dorati's Mercury recording of music from the Second Viennese School. The LP includes Schoenberg's seminal *Five Pieces for Orchestra* and Webern's work with the same title, which, presumably, provides the iconic justification for the "figurative" cover. But the same iconic logic has applied to other "major fifths" in the modern repertoire, such as Prokofiev's Fifth Symphony, Ashkenazy's

Figure 4.24 His Master's Voice: The backdrop of the CD in figure 4.15 shows the classic trademark of recording, which was based on a painting of Francis Barraud. It alludes to the discourse of verisimilitude associated with recording; the dog, Nipper, is unable to tell the difference between a gramophone record and the voice of his master. (Designer: Enterprise IIG. Reproduced by permission of EMI.)

Figure 4.25 Rebus: Classical covers are not conspicuous for their levity, but this one is, utilizing a visual way of defining a hypothetical murder. Such imagery accords with the music's burlesque character. The profile of the composer underlying the text adds a ghostly presence and a suggestion that Shostakovich might himself have been "hypothetically murdered," at least in an ideological sense. (Designer: Roy White & Hands on Design.)

Figure 4.26 Pastiche: Recently, cover imagery has shifted away from using original paintings. In this instance, though, the design, a cross between a Matisse and a Dufy painting, pays heed to Poulenc's breezy and colorful piano music. Note the band across the top corner of the CD, which was released at a time when digital recording was still new and there was a market advantage in "badging" CDs this way. (Designer: Hilary McManus. Reproduced by permission of Universal.)

Figure 4.27 Film Clip: An interesting cover that, so to speak, distorts the musical record. Korngold was a well-known Hollywood film composer, but only later in his career, after the programmed works were composed. Thus, the cover's film imagery is a "misrepresentation." (Designer: Jan Webber. Reproduced by permission of Supraphon.)

recording of which uses the Demuth, with added Cyrillic lettering to insinuate its Russian characteristics.

Indeed, one of the problems flowing from the fact that the same works are recorded over and over again is that the same type of imagery is often adopted. Recordings of Slavonic or Hungarian dances, such as those of Brahms and Dvořák, often utilize folkloric imagery (see figure 4.9). In the same way, recordings of quintessentially English music, such as that of Elgar or Vaughan Williams, invariably attract images of the English countryside of the type epitomized by the paintings of Constable and Turner. Such covers—even though they are, musically speaking, anachronisms—engineer a certain image of these composers' music: that it is as English as Constable, first of all, and that the sound of the Constable landscape can be heard in the *Enigma Variations*. But such visualization has also been seen as part of a process of heritage building, affirming England's cultural history particularly during periods when it has been strategic to reinforce emblems of national culture (Blake 1996: 230). The trouble is that the frequent use of such imagery can be counterproductive and lead to the peddling of "design clichés" (Shaughnessy 1996: 44). Thus many covers of Vivaldi's music are based on postcard pictures of gondolas and San Marco or the paintings of Canaletto or Guardi, suggesting that Vivaldi is Venice and Venice, Vivaldi. Interestingly, for the cover of a recent CD of the *Four Seasons* the Italian label Opus III abandoned such clichés and used only the figure 4, a sign that in the Vivaldi bin a "4" can mean only one work.

Covers thus are a phonographic form of impression management and exploit many of the same techniques of desire and arousal that are integral to advertising (Williamson 1978). Music is an abstract art from which it is difficult to elicit any direct or palpable meanings, and covers provide the meanings that listeners are often seeking, enabling them to see the music in a certain way and evoking a host of secondary associations with which they might identify. Equating Vivaldi with Venice builds on the more generic experiences that the musical novice might possess. One might know that Venice is an attractive city and assume that those attractions might have flowed into the music of Vivaldi.

Yet covers do not always provoke immediate recognition, and Ginette Niveu's recording of Sibelius's Violin Concerto is a case in point. It features one of Matisse's paintings of Nice interiors. While the work incorporates a violin and reflects Niveau's nationality, it is in other respects at odds with the image of Jean Sibelius as a Finnish composer who is associated with his own visual clichés—pine forests and fjords, lakes and snow scenes. Similarly, a recent cycle of Mozart piano concertos on original instruments for L'Oiseau-lyre, whose design incorporates antique ornamentation in keeping with the label's authentic performance philosophy, features the paintings of Paul Klee. These are seemingly anachronistic choices that work against Mozartian clichés, but in the context of the many other recordings of Mozart's piano concertos, they certainly attract the eye. Indeed, covers quite often make spurious connections with the music: Mercury's LP of Respighi's *The Birds* and *Brazilian Impressions* "covers" both works but only in a partial sense: neither of the birds featured on the cover is the subject of Respighi's work, but they are rainforest birds. Covers then inevitably take liberty with truth, and often only evoke a vague resemblance to the musical actuality.

Covers are also used as palimpsests, sites of "overwriting" of texts. This overwriting is added to a cover to further spotlight a recording's qualities among rivals and competitors; it might include the prizes and accolades that are now a feature of the classical recording industry and are manifested in a textual way in the honorific stickers (*Deutscher Schall Platten Preis, Grand Prix du disque*) that now figure on many CDs. Since they are often awarded after the cover is printed, they are placed on the cellophane used to wrap the modern CD — which then provides another layer of symbolic ornamentation.

The record cover is also used to illustrate the record itself, as a quotation device representing it in a variety of textual contexts, including advertisements, brochures issued by record labels, or reviews in magazines. This practice started in the 1950s in magazines such as *Records and Recordings,* which often featured covers, explaining their significance and then using them in the manner of a rubric to head the disc's review. This marked a turnaround from the days when the review copies of LPs came in "plain brown covers" (Robertson 1956: 341), which were not often the subjects of commentary. But even though it is part of the reviewers' responsibilities to evaluate covers (Robertson 1973), they tend only to do so in instances of particular excellence ("Fine colour picture of an old lute provides an apt sleeve design for Mercury's fine recording . . . of Ancient Airs and Dances for Lute") or execrableness ("Why Opus III has illustrated the cover with an irrelevant catwalk model is not easy to understand: Polverelli has no need of such marketing").[34] Instead, it is the correspondents to record magazines who are more likely to comment on the effectiveness of cover designs ("Such sleeves as that by HMV for their *Peer Gynt* are visually repulsive"), even calling for the standardization of all covers.

Covers are a strategic element in the narrative architecture of recordings and constitute important textual extensions of the record, whose various dimensions have conditioned the methods of containment that have been deployed on and around the record. Originally developed as marketing devices at the end of the 78 era, covers did not come into their own until the LP era, and they are now an inseparable part of the narrative architecture of the disc.

Through apt and cogent visualizations they have helped to render an abstract art form more approachable for its record collectors. At their best, covers provide a complementary aesthetic that is in keeping with the moral penumbra that has shadowed classical music: one that is serious and sober and avoids gratuitous showiness and exaggerated forms of self-expression.

Covers began as relatively simple designs mostly produced in the art departments of record labels, gradually incorporating paintings and photographs as the technology developed to make this possible. Notwithstanding the greater range of options for graphic designers that developments in offset printing have created, cover designs on classical recordings have generally reinforced the discourse of seriousness that is an integral part of classical music. When it has been abandoned, the offending label has drawn fire from record critics and collectors. Yet aside from providing a tasteful face to the record, the cover functions chiefly as a parergon that interposes itself between the record and its listener. It might entice a shopper in a record shop or prepare the listener in relevant ways—above all else, it provides a lens through which recorded music is filtered and mediated, creating the right impression all around. Yet in the end it is important to recognize that the cover is only a cover, a threshold to the other elements in the textual ensemble that is the record: its liner notes, the music itself, and so on. For whatever else the graphic elements on the cover contribute to the listening process, they remain only a "front" for the music itself.

CHAPTER FIVE

Off the Record
Some Notes on the Sleeve

> The notes that accompany musical recordings or even simply the
> information provided on record jackets or CD cases, are a mine of
> paratextual information. Other researchers, I hope, will work that vein.
> —Gerald Genette, *Paratexts: Thresholds of Interpretation,* 370

Sleeve notes or "liner notes" have appeared in formats ranging from a slip of
paper to a richly illustrated booklet. Like other framing devices such as a
book's dust cover they remain separate from yet integral to the disc's narrative environment. They are, structurally and materially speaking, *off* the
record, yet their contents, for the most part, are *on* the record. But they also
occupy a modal universe different from that of the record, and much of their
efficacy as a textual form depends on their capacity to accord with its contents
and minimize any distortion that might flow from transferring between
modes of "meaning." The topographical status of this second order of texts
is thus ambiguous, hence the term "parerga." Yet this apparent ambiguity
also underlines their significance as rhetorical markers in the social world,
where they assist to parenthesize cultural phenomena, marking their boundaries in contexts that are otherwise undifferentiated (Duro 1996). The
frame around a painting isolates an aesthetic domain and sets it apart from its
immediate milieu; it defines a visually significant space. It has been argued
that such markers have particular importance for contemporary works of art
(Danto 1981), whose actual matter and subject matter are often aesthetically
ambiguous or hard to isolate from their immediate environs. Framing devices help to punctuate the cultural world, placing inverted commas around
objects considered worthy of extended contemplation. A record sleeve performs a similar function: it denotes a domain of musical significance and at
the same time differentiates it from other sleeves and from other types of

textual architecture such as books and paintings. For while covers might resemble paintings, it is clear from their frames that, first and foremost, they hope to "charm the ear" rather than the eye.

But these same frames also mark the onset of a make-believe world, one requiring the temporary suspension of credibility along with mundane conducts and habits. In a theatre, for example, the dimming of lights in conjunction with the raising of the curtain enjoins the audience to cease its conversation and to become engaged with the events on stage (Goffman 1986: 128–31). It is similar with records; for all of their claimed ability to recreate the concert hall, recordings are still illusions. They involve a measure of make-believe and willingness to enter into an imaginary universe of sound without the conventional social scaffolding associated with the concert hall, such as "embodied" musicians and audiences, and the various forms of playacting that occur at concerts (such as acquiring a program, applauding when the music ceases, and so on). Recordings also engender germane phonographic etiquettes that are observed whenever a record is played, such as sitting in an appropriate spot between two speakers and listening to the music as one would in a normal concert, more or less in silence, though, in due recognition of the "dehumanized" nature of recordings, without the applause. Only rarely are these etiquettes rendered explicit, for they are mostly transmitted through the manifold encounters with recording that individuals have in their lives. In some instances, though, they are, and sleeve notes are a case in point. In effect, these notes are hearing aids that display a distinctive narrative architecture designed to enlist the attention of the listener along the lines, quite literally, specified on the sleeve. But the notes, in the end, only defer to what is contained in the record.

Sound Explanations:
From Concert Programs to Record Programs

As has already been argued, the record occupies a modal universe different from that of the book and cannot, except in a very limited sense, be "read" from its physical surface. Instead, it requires a stylus or a laser beam acting in conjunction with an amplifier and loudspeaker to make sense of its surface indentations. In the absence of the technology able to realize the musical potential mapped onto the record's surface, a complex framework of "telling" texts, called liner notes, acts in its stead, giving identity, meaning, and reference to the contents. These texts are members of an important class of "electrical" discourses whose main *raison d'être* derives from their links to technological gadgets, as they provide their users with guidance on to how to derive the most from these gadgets. In particular, they provide performing scripts that enable their users to enact their myriad functions. In fact, these texts are central to the discourse universe associated with the recording industry, which lends meaning to records and their listening habits. For though recorded music might be the "central fact of lay culture" and represent a mark of the generalized "retreat from the word" said to be a feature of contemporary culture (Steiner 1967: 43), its experience is, in large measure, mediated through the printed word, as manifested by the voluminous pages devoted to recorded music. The retreat into recorded music is enriched through these pages, which span everything from sleeve notes to musical reference books, record magazines, HMV catalogues, and the notebooks of musical information that are sometimes compiled by collectors (Steane 2002).

Chapter 4 examined one manifestation of these enrichment texts: the record cover and the way it visualizes music through various forms of iconographical articulation. But this articulation represents only one layer of meaning in the expository universe enclosing a record, for it was also noted that the record is fundamentally a laminated text whose meanings are deployed across different planes of sound, vision, and word. The visual plane is but one aspect of the cover environment, the one that the LP and CD expose to the world. Another, more "telling" side occupies the back of the sleeve, the domain of liner notes that impart the "inside story" of the music. In the textual environment of the CD, these notes occupy a small booklet that combines the functions performed by the front and back covers of the LP sleeve and has the further advantage of being detachable from the jewel box itself. Yet these notes, which are now an integral part of the record's narrative environs — another facet of the recording angel's "chirography" — have for the most part been overlooked or, at best, only subjected to the most perfunctory of analyses. One comprehensive survey of classical LP covers makes no mention of the "other side" of the LP and its important expository functions (Wittleloostuyn 1997). The same goes for a well-known encyclopedia on records and recording, which is otherwise comprehensive in its coverage of phonographic phenomena (Marco with Andrews 1993).

The notes that accompany CDs and LPs interface with the recordings themselves in a range of ways, of which the calibration and descriptions of their contents is one of the most important. This distinguishes their function from that of the front cover, which while trying to create the right musical impression was designed to arrest the attention of consumers in retail environments. Arguably, the functions of the liner notes are more inward-looking than the cover design, more concerned with giving a different, essentially expository form of coverage to the record. In these respects there is less scope for freedom of expression there than on the front cover, since the liner notes must accurately reflect the contents of the record and provide some appropriate account of its nature. Yet the way this function is fulfilled still exhibits a range of expository approaches.

The tradition of listening to classical music through texts began with the advent of the concert program, a development that coincided with the rise of the modern concert. This occurred in the eighteenth century, at a time when music was being shifted from its court settings into more public arenas; this shift also saw the rise of music journalism and criticism. This was manifested in the more extensive coverage given to musical events in newspapers and weeklies, where reviews of concerts were a regular feature (Young 1965; Stauffer 1986). Even though they are intended for a different context of listening, liner notes share many of the textual features embedded in concert programs. In this respect, they could be said to derive from a common genre devoted to the analysis of music in performance. Both formats, for example, contain a list of featured musical works, highlighted in various ways to draw attention to their relative importance in the program environment. This includes spatial highlighting, such as having a page or section devoted to themselves, as well as various forms of typographical underscoring, such as capitalization and the use of attention-seeking fonts. Alongside the named work in both formats, and usually in a plainer font, is a brief profile of the composer and the music. There is also usually (certainly in the case of a concert program) a brief description of the performers, a practice that was uncommon in the early days of the LP but has become almost universal on CDs.

However, prior to the advent of the LP, most 78s were devoid of explanatory notes, even though their major competitor at the time, the piano roll, included "explanatory matter alongside the perforations" (Scholes 1935: 19). Indeed, at one stage it was common practice on early recordings for singers to introduce the work they were performing, much as if they were giving a conventional recital, a practice that has been occasionally revived on LP and CD.[1] The development of an off-the-record note was relatively slow in coming. Prior to Odeon's introduction of its double-sided discs in 1904, which had been postponed for fear that few consumers would be interested in having two works on the same disc, the unrecorded side of the disc had either "carried an etched trademark" or "a square of paper with the words of the recorded song" (Moogk 1975: 33). Such squares of paper were a feature of Berliner's early discs as well, and it has been suggested that without them the songs on recordings would have been unrecognizable (Gitelman 1999: 155). These texts were, in effect, prototypes of the modern liner notes, as were the "descriptive notes" (as they were called) included in albums of classical recordings from 1925 onward. Descriptive notes invented by Herbert C. Ridout (1942: 145), who wanted to explain "the music in a simple fashion to the uninitiated," which entailed being as nontechnical as possible. The trouble was that these notes were invariably lost (Lieberson 1947: v). Sleeve notes were also part of the generalized repackaging of the 78 that occurred in the years immediately preceding the advent of the LP. They were featured on Decca's recordings of *Desert Song* and *Oklahoma,* and much of those recordings' success on the market was attributed to this verbal wrapping (Garlick 1977: 780). With the arrival of microgroove recording, the practice was transferred to LPs, and later it appeared on reel-to-reel tapes and cassettes as well. And although in the early 1960s an Australian company contemplated manufacturing discs that were textually self-sufficient, in that the cover and the notes would be printed directly onto the disc, thus eliminating the need for sleeves, the idea never reached the manufacturing stage.[2]

As just one among several innovations associated with the LP, the cover was nevertheless the one to which the reviewers in the early 1950s responded with unqualified enthusiasm. The added convenience of a program note on the reverse of an aesthetically presented cover was regarded as "a great step forward" and another reason for the LP to be lauded as a "new page in recorded history"—a somewhat telling metaphor, given the thesis of this book.[3] The LP also permitted many classical works to be accommodated on a single side and heard without interruption, which led to different forms of musical program than hitherto possible on 78s, ones where, time permitting, there were often two or three compositions on the same disc. Moreover, these programs, at least where orchestral works were concerned, were of an order different from those ordinarily performed in the concert hall, where one would not expect, as was often the case on LPs, programs devoted entirely to overtures, often from the same composer. In fact, the normal mode of programming the LP—which has continued through to the CD—is to program like with like: overtures with overtures, concertos with concertos, and so on, often by the same composer. Another feature of LP programming was the so-called "fill-up": a short work of between ten and fifteen minutes, not often programmed in concerts but ideal for filling the unrecorded time available on an LP containing, say, a thirty minute symphony.

The LP also led to the programming of compositions that shared aesthetic affinities with one another, such as the Grieg and Schumann piano concertos or Mendelssohn and Bruch violin concertos, something that rarely if ever happens in a concert. Heterogeneous programs crossing musical genres did not often appear on LP, nor did works from radically different traditions or epochs of music, unless, that is, there was a musical justification for doing so. Aside from the naturalness of combining like with like, much of the imperative for homogeneous programs was, and continues to be, driven by performance factors: recordings are made by soloists and instrumentalists, particular ensembles and groups who tend to record the types of works with which they are associated. Hardly ever does a string quartet record on the same disc with a string trio, although it is not uncommon for a string quartet to enlist the services of a cellist to record string quintets. And even though there have been occasional attempts to break with these patterns of homogeneity by issuing recordings of different conductors and orchestras on the same disc, these have not proved a commercial success (Dearling and Dearling 1984: 202). Notwithstanding market considerations, however, there have been, even during the LP era, relatively adventurous compilations—so-called "concept albums" whose existence is often prompted by factors outside of the recording industry. EMI produced one such compilation in 1970, entitled the *Stamp of Conductors,* which was issued to coincide with the release of a set of stamps commemorating British conductors.[4] Tellingly, few LPs have ever been issued that cross the "great musical schism," though many have been released that treat rock music "seriously" or that "beat up" the classics.[5]

Another programming trend emerging in the LP era was the omnibus set of recordings—sometimes called the *intégrale édition*—devoted to a complete cycle of works, for example Sibelius's symphonies or the complete works of Beethoven or Mozart.[6] This trend began in the late 1960s with so-called "limited editions," as Deutsche Grammophon called them, boxed sets of recordings offered at a discount price, generally at Christmas time. Sometimes these sets were issued with lavishly illustrated books, as was the case with a special edition of Elgar recordings (Martland 1997), released in 1972 by EMI. Indeed, around this time there was a certain vogue for book/record hybrids that combined word and sound in inventive and instructive ways, as in "The Great Musicians" series, which provided "the complete life and times" of a composer in a "beautifully illustrated book" with "fine recordings of their music."[7]

Yet the greater programming capacity of LPs was not universally acclaimed. It was suggested that it coerced collectors into acquiring works they already owned. One music critic reviewing the LP's first decade suggested that its coming had produced too much needless repetition in the record catalog, leading to the unavoidable necessity of having to buy a recording of *Don Quixote* with *Don Juan,* when one already possessed the latter (Mann 1960: 3). Behind Mann's concern—and it was one voiced with increasing frequency—was the fact that large parts of the repertoire still remained unrecorded, and yet another *Don Juan* in the catalog squandered disc space that could have been better deployed on works still waiting their first appearance on LP. This concern, which had already been voiced in the days of the 78, served as an injunction to record companies to redress the musical omissions in their catalogs. But it was also a concern that had various other aspects. One emanated from Glenn Gould, who justified owning more than one version of the same work on the grounds that it enabled record collectors to "edit" their own version of a composition, abstracting a movement from conductor X, another from conductor Y, and so on (1966: 59). Another aspect was that listeners eventually grew tired of listening to the same performance of a work over and over again and yearned to hear a different version of it. American composer Roger Sessions recalled hurling just such an offending disc of Debussy's *Images* right across the room. (Sessions 1970: 52).

Yet contrary to Mann's fears that the LP would lead to an explosion of "more of the same," it actually led to the exploration of new territories of musical repertoire, such as early or Baroque music. In fact, during the LP era the industry became like "a vast suction machine, which took up anything of an age that would adhere to tape long enough to make an LP" (Barzun 1969: 76). There was, for example, a vast expansion of the spoken word catalog, in which the labels Caedmon and Argo were preeminent.

With the arrival of the CD these tendencies toward more adventurous programs have gained more momentum, if anything. Its increased playing time—almost eighty minutes—has enabled longer programs to be assembled and works to be "tripled" rather than merely "coupled" with one another. For in the classical market, at least, partially filled discs are disparaged. Although several labels issued discs of shorter playing time at a reduced cost, in the mold of the extended-play (EP) and medium-play (MP) records, they were not popular, especially when budget CDs came along. Thus CDs of the aforementioned concertos now often include a third work. A recent Decca recording, for example, of the Mendelssohn and Bruch concertos includes the latter's *Scottish Fantasia* as well. Indeed, the extra recording time available on the CD has prompted more original couplings than were possible on LP, such as Mendelssohn's Violin Concerto with Elgar's, or Bruch's with Goldmark's. But the novel program trajectories of the CD extend beyond new groupings—one of the distinctive features of the CD catalog, which started in the 1980s, is "retrospection," the reissue of a back catalog, generally in a budget format. Indeed the bulk of new releases from the majors, these days, are re-releases. This latter trend began with the reissuing of highlights from Mercury's catalog. These reprocessed the original tapes into the digital format and issued them on CD using facsimile versions of the original covers and notes, scaled down to suit the new format. RCA ("Living Stereo"), Decca ("Legends") and Deutsche Grammophon ("Originals") followed with their own retro-labels, as did, in recent years, Philips ("50 Great Recordings") and EMI ("Great Recordings of the Century"). Following from the omnibus editions of the 1970s that were devoted to complete recordings of a composer's symphonies or string quartets—many of which have been transferred to CDs—the new focus of completeness is on ensembles and performers. Such omnibus series are targeted at a specific type of collector, the so-called "completist"—a new word in the phonographic lexicon[8]—who wishes to own every composition, regardless of its quality, that a performer or ensemble committed to record.

Not that the exploration of more esoteric repertoire has been entirely suspended. A number of independents, particularly those dedicated to unearthing this repertoire, have their versions of "completeness" as well. Over the last decade Hyperion, a label specializing on the "outskirts of musical life" (Soames 1990: 504), has been undertaking an omnibus recording of Schubert songs that parallels its complete recording of Liszt piano works. In addition, it has a series devoted to the "Romantic Piano Concerto"—concertos that have either never been or only rarely been recorded at all.

Sound Commas and Full Stops: Punctuating Discs

Notwithstanding these changes to the modes of programming music on discs, their acoustic topography, the way the music is "punctuated" on disc, has displayed considerable uniformity over the history of recording. Except for the brief period when performers announced the contents of a disc, a practice many listeners considered a waste of precious recording time (Gitelman 1999: 155), silence has been the primary mode of phonographic punctuation. Thus a few seconds of silence is used to mark the onset of a work, the recorded equivalent of indenting a paragraph, and the same at the end: silence to mark the "offset" of the music, its conclusion, the equivalent of a full stop. Classical recordings, except when live, rarely use the electronic fades deployed on recordings of popular music. They favor a natural decrescendo— and it is consistent with the keystone discourse—as the music is dispersed into the acoustic of the concert hall or studio. Silence is also used between movements, but it is of shorter duration than that at the beginning or end of a record of a whole work—a comma, as it were, instead of a full stop. This even occurs on some live recordings, where the effect seems at odds with the "sound effects" of the audience evident elsewhere on such recordings. These electronic punctuation marks, also relate to the way the record is calibrated via tracks that represent, to use another analogy, the equivalents of book chapters and which are visible on the surface of the LP, and whole sides. But they also serve to cue the listening etiquettes mentioned earlier, providing an acoustic border between the sound of the room and that of the record. They mark the onset and offset of a musical make-believe, the acoustic equivalents of the conductor raising and lowering her baton.[9]

As has already been argued, much of the imperative for technological change in the recording industry has focused on extending the length and longevity of records, increasing their duration while compressing their dimensions. This in turn has influenced the "dividing practices" associated with recordings. Because 78s offered approximately four minutes per side of playing time, most classical works, songs excepted, were many "sided," occupying three or four or more records. LPs, about the same size as 78s but able to store more musical information, made it possible to accommodate on a single side most classical compositions, except for operas and longer works, with their individual movements separated by tracks or divided between sides.[10] CDs, by comparison, are featureless, with no observable tracks or divisions. But they are nevertheless, albeit invisibly, tracked and calibrated, often to a much greater degree than LPs ever were. But unlike LPs, whose tracks were accessible by the manual means of moving the playing arm to the required location, the CD's tracks are only accessible electronically, via a digital keypad either on the panel of the compact disc player or its remote control. In addition, many CDs have index points, tracks within tracks that enable particular subsections of a musical work to be accessed. CDs, then, contain many more forms of calibration than their analog predecessors. In addition, the keypads of CD players have many additional functions that enable tracks to be played in any order, fast-forwarded and reversed, memorized, paused, skipped, repeated, and on some players, randomized. Hence the enumeration of tracks and index points has more significance on a CD than an LP, as does their precise timing, another mode of calibration new to the phonographic environment. In fact, by using the fast-forward facility and the time display it is possible to access particular points on a CD very precisely by noting the time at which a musical passage commences. Interestingly, though reviewers often avail themselves of the facility ("After the big, momentous climax of the finale (8'21"—bar 212)"), the authors of CD notes rarely, if ever, do. Indeed, in most instances, they only infrequently use even the track numbers as expository reference points.

These various ways of tracking recorded music are, nevertheless, significant parts of the narrative architecture of a record. The cover notes defer in various ways to the titling information and provide a detailed listing of the works on a record, information which is best situated on its label. Such informative domains are the equivalents of the pre-text sections of a book. One important element of a record's pre-text is the calibration of the disc, which identifies sides and tracks (sometimes called "bands") by letter or number and enables listeners to navigate the musical program. These track numbers are usually listed, along with the relevant titles and movements as well as the names of their composer and performers, at the head of the sleeve. They are framed and emboldened to stand out, both to emphasize their importance and to separate them from other regions of the sleeve's geography. This is less of an imperative in a CD booklet, where the different parts of that geography have come to occupy different pages: most often the back cover and one of the inner pages.

In 1981, the International Association of Sound Archives prescribed that LPs—and similar prescriptions now apply to CDs—should display, at the very least, the following information: date and location of recording, the musical edition used in the performance, any cuts or changes to the score, the performers involved, the duration of items on the disc, and the names of the recording producer, balance engineer, and editor (Dearling and Dearling 1984: 199–200). In addition, CDs are also required to display so-called "SPARS information," a series of abbreviations that denote whether a recording has a digital (DDD) or analog source (ADD; AAD). In the first decade of the CD, these abbreviations were always spelled out along with other facts and figures relating to the digital technology, but most labels have discontinued this practice.

But unlike the book, whose pre-text regions sometimes occupy many pages, those of the LP, because of its limited surface area, were more confined. Even so, there was still enough space, at least in the early days of the LP, for labels to promote their other products (Frankenstein 1954: 59). Early Decca LPs not infrequently listed company publications such as *Decca Book of the Opera*. Thus, although the liner notes defer mainly to the contents of the record, they often also refer to off-the-record products. The fact that the notes were accessible on the reverse of the sleeve helped to increase the allure of the LP, since potential buyers could learn more about the recording and its music from simply turning the cover over. One of the disadvantages of CDs is that their liner notes are often locked away in a sealed container and are thus impossible to consult. In order to circumvent this difficulty, Naxos follows the practice of book dust jackets that on their back covers a summary account of their contents.

Even the CD booklet cannot accommodate endless amounts of text. It rarely if ever exceeds twenty-five pages, many of which are devoted to the various translations of the notes that are now standard features of the record's narrative architecture. Hence, there are generally no equivalents on records of such frontispiece elements as acknowledgments, forewords, prefaces, and dedications, though the latter are frequently found on discs of popular music.[11] Genette argues that such prefatory devices are important elements of the book's threshold rhetoric, providing a context for its text and helping to frame particular predispositions toward it (1997). This is a reminder of the degree to which a record as a cultural technology is not a book but one with bookish components.

Nevertheless, the pre-text regions of the record are, like those of the book, subdivided into distinct zones and geographies. Indeed, the sleeve notes constitute a whole latticework of texts that has acquired new and distinctive elements as the technology of reproduction has progressed. CDs emanating from the early twenty-first century carry the signs of their digital times, bar codes and websites, just as the LPs of the 1950s carried theirs, high fidelity, full frequency range recording, and so on.

There are also certain timeless features of the cover's textual architecture. One is that the textual design of the discs from particular labels exhibits distinctive properties as part and parcel of a coordinated semiotic associated with the label, which ensures that the CDs of Decca are readily distinguishable from those of Philips (even though they are from the same media conglomerate, Universal). Thus the notes of LPs, even those from the 1950s, and CDs are framed within a distinctive template displaying particular emblems and insignia that appear on each and every cover from the label—the phonographic equivalent of the colophon. It is within this template that the text for a particular record is situated. Thus the back cover—like the front cover—is an amalgam of the generic and the specific.

In fact, much of the generic text (which might also be repeated on the front cover and on the record's label) relates to the record itself and is vital for the accreditation of a disc and for inventory texts such as record catalogs. This text includes the number of the record, a long chain of letters and numbers that once encrypted whether the record was mono or stereo, LP, MP, or EP, and so on. To this has been added the bar code, which is different for every disc. This is a digital recognition signal that can be read by point-of-sale terminals and used to monitor disc sales and reorder stock. Many of the catalogues issued by the recording companies these days reproduce bar codes alongside an illustration of the CD's cover, and stock is often reordered using a laser gun that connects directly to the point-of-sale terminal—the communication heartland of the contemporary retailer—via this bar code. The use of bar codes has helped to automate many aspects of retailing and enables dealers to determine the last time a CD was stocked, how many it sold, and its price. It has also enabled the monitoring of the buying habits of record consumers (Du Gay and Negus 1994). But unlike books, CDs have yet to be assigned ISBNs, another indication that their status as cultural objects, even though they have sometimes been assigned Library of Congress numbers, continues to remain ambivalent. This ambivalence also extends to the fact that in the U.K. and Australia, at least, there is no compulsory legal deposit, as there is with books, requiring record companies to make a copy of every new CD available to the relevant national collection (Day 1981: 127).

Though information about the provenance of a recording might appear trivial, it has proved to be quite telling in the past. For example, with regard to the country of manufacture, when the 1970s oil crisis caused the price of vinyl to skyrocket, some labels were induced to cut manufacturing costs by pressing their discs on inferior vinyl. As a result, the quality of pressings could vary dramatically from country to country. A record manufactured in Germany (where the standards of pressing were higher) was regarded as a plus, for German pressings were much less afflicted with the flaws that plagued LPs from other sources, such as Australia, where pressing standards were lower. In fact, the words "imported pressing" and "pressed in Germany"—"hurrah phrases" of the time—were often capitalized on LPs.

Capitalization and textual emphasis—a mode of typographical rhetoric using the expressive capacities of letters—is often found on cover architecture, where space is at a premium and "alphabetical" accentuation is an economic way of highlighting important information. A typical sleeve from the early days of the LP—which was not much different at the end of its days—had three separate areas of text devoted to information about the label, whose various axes in and around the sleeve and at the margins provided a template into which the more "programmatic" parts of the LP were located. These programmatic parts, in their turn, formed two main areas of text: one containing titular information relating to works on the recording, one dealing with the works themselves. In the absence of the pagination that would ordinarily separate these areas of text in a book, the textual separation of a sleeve occurs on the horizontal plane, across its whole surface area. Thus its texts form a lattice structure whose various elements are isolated from one another using position, lines, columns, and other spatial devices, and even differentiated fonts, to emphasize that they belong to a distinct textual area. Sometimes there is continuity between the two sides of the cover, such as through identical fonts, particularly in the titling sections.

This structural punctuation also expresses the political economy of music and the recording industry, and the degree of status accorded to its key players, such as composers and performers, who in the early days of the LP were the only ones who warranted "billing." Since then, in line with the increased sensitivity to intellectual property rights, and with some pressure from record critics (Blyth 1974: 1350), the roll call of those contributing to a record's production has been increased, particularly since the advent of the CD. Thus discs now credit, though not in large fonts or in prominent areas of the sleeve, the recording producer and balance engineer. The textual engineers responsible for the various parts of the cover architecture, such as the liner notes and cover design, are also identified, as are, increasingly, the various audio components used to produce a recording ("Monitored using B & W loudspeakers"). In the case of many piano recordings, the piano tuner present at recording sessions, who has always played an important role in maintaining the "temperament" of the piano (Brendel 1976: 137), is also sometimes named.

This marks a turnaround from the past, when major companies such as EMI routinely refused to identify the record producers and engineers responsible for their discs, in spite of the fact that it was their endeavors and interventions that frequently turned indifferent recordings into superior ones (Grubb 1986: 120). It also reflects the emergence of discursive conditions in which naming the most important protagonists and technologies involved in a recording have become telling factors in the evaluation of recordings, which can make some CDs more desirable than others. Thus some recordings are purchased on the strength of their producers and engineers alone, something of which Pianissimo was conscious when it named well-known producer and engineer Bob Auger on the front cover of one of its CDs—moreover, in the same sized font as the pianist![12]

In fact, some labels such as Telarc—particularly during times of phonographic change—have made a point of including essays on their recording techniques. One of the first LPs that Telarc issued—Frederick Fennell conducting the Cleveland Symphonic Winds in a program of Holst and Handel—included an article extolling the virtues of digital sound. Telarc was actually the first label to use the term "digital" (Brown 1993: 38). The article draws attention to the deficiencies of magnetic recording, which digital recording, so it was claimed, overcame. Thus sleeve notes can be the sites of phonographic propaganda as well, normalizing the uptake of new reproducing technologies.

Just occasionally sleeves contain "writerly" elements. Those of Australia's World Record Club came with a panel of dial settings, one for volume, one for treble, and another for bass, which the listener could "inscribe" for future reference—indices of the degree of rheostat control that listeners potentially had over their recordings.

Cautionary Notes: The Homilies of Recorded Sound

But it is the list of works and their composers, as befits their role in the musical endeavor, that is largest relative to these other players (when they begin to appear) and the other text on the back cover. Even so, this list is often not as large and bold as the name of the company, which on one Decca cover from the early 1950s reigns supreme, along with the word "flexible," over the lower regions of the cover! The presence of the latter is itself telling of the degree to which cover notes are also period texts that can provide traces of the technological changes in the record industry that consumers have been reminded about. One of the virtues of the LP over the 78 was certainly greater robustness, which provided an imperative of sorts—along with the promise of "full frequency range reproduction," also emblazoned on the sleeve—for its acquisition. But once these advantages of LPs became better known, the need for their inclusion on the cover ended. The same has happened with the word "digital," which hardly ever appears on the exposed areas of CDs these days.

Consumers were also informed about practices associated with the treatment of LPs, which did not have a terribly wide circulation during the early 1950s. Thus the word "Decca," for example, is surrounded by a series of injunctions, highlighted in italics to emphasize their importance, relating to such things as the fact that LPs must be played with a "pick-up designed for long playing records" and "at 33 1/3 revolutions per minute," and they should be cleaned with a "barely damp cloth." These notes tended to figure on most record sleeves of the period, when microgroove records were still new and the conduct associated with their maintenance unfamiliar. Some labels, for example, included instructions on how to store LPs when they were not in use, upright and with the opening of the sleeve "facing the back of shelf or cabinet." Still others carried warnings with suitable typographical emphasis, about the need to use a stylus tip of a certain size ("not exceeding .7 mil") and advised that it be checked "for replacement at least every SIX MONTHS." The language was hortatory in tone and served to script appropriate vinyl behaviors—though there was often wide variation among labels about the precise nature of this behavior (Brown 1963: 63)—and to spread the word about long-playing practices. They helped, in other words, to inculcate the micropractices associated with microgroove recordings.

But they also helped to prescribe and normalize a new playing regime that was different from that of 78s. They drew attention to the ways that LPs need to be treated if long-term and irrevocable damage to their surfaces of a kind that would eventually degrade their sound was to be avoided. Interestingly, much of the prescription involved, which occupied space that could have been used for further explanatory notes, was eventually transferred to the inner sleeves of LPs, where it had closer proximity to the disc and where it provided a "topical" reminder—that is, just as they were about to be played—about the need for disc care. Not that 78s—which came to be known after the advent of LPs as "standard play"—could be treated in an entirely carefree way. The authors of one early "discography," for example, cautioned listeners not to smoke when playing the gramophone and to place the needle on the record "as if you were making a cast with a fly," this last piece of advice providing clear evidence, if any were needed, of the gender and social class of its authors and of putative gramophone users (Mackenzie and Marshall 1923: 14).

Although such advice might seem a mundane part of the disc's textual environment, it helped to harness through its omnipresence on every sleeve, new phonographic behaviors involving not just the investment in flexible, full-frequency range LPs but also the new types of equipment required for their reproduction. Thus the text of the sleeve was a disciplining one designed to proscribe the transfer of those habits associated with standard play to the LP. But, as with the references to LPs being "non-breakable" and possessing "silent surfaces," once this gramophonic conduct had become the habit in the record community it was deleted, thus creating room for other information.

But it never disappeared altogether. In fact, as the technology of the LP underwent further developments during the 1960s and 1970s, including the arrivals of stereo, quad, digital analog, and so on, the advice ("PLAY THIS RECORD WITH STEREOPHONIC PICK-UP ONLY"; "IMPORTANT: This record is intended for use only on special stereophonic producers") took new forms of expression. Consumers were told that if they wanted to take full advantage of the new format of recording they would either need to upgrade their systems ("The disc, when played back through an SQ QUADRAPHONIC decoder, will display the original four channels through the four speakers in the listening area") or, in the instance of the hybrid digital/analog recordings issued at the end of the LP era, not upgrade them, for those recordings were fully compatible with existing equipment ("THIS DIGITAL RECORDING IS FOR USE WITH CONVENTIONAL RECORD REPRODUCING EQUIPMENT"). Even so, they were informed that the improved quality of the digital reproduction was more likely to be apparent on "HIGH QUALITY PLAYING EQUIPMENT." Here again the tone is hortatory in its call for better reproducing equipment.

With the advent of CDs much of the tone of these texts was mollified and limited to relatively benign remarks about the general care of CDs, such as what to do if they became "soiled by fingerprints, dust, or dirt." This more abstracted tone reflects the fact that the CD was a more resilient recording medium whose playing surface was hard to damage, certainly when compared with its predecessors. And the technology involved, at least for the user, was relatively straightforward and did not require speakers and amplifiers to be replaced or upgraded. All that was needed was a CD player, which did not even require that its "stylus" be checked. The operational logistics of digital reproduction were comparatively straightforward, though consumers were cautioned against using solvents, which were often used to clean LPs, because they can damage CDs. They were also sometimes cautioned about the dynamic range of some CDs. Some labels included warnings—in red capitals, no less—exhorting their owners to be prudent when playing them. Telarc, which promoted itself as a label that did not subject the dynamic range of its discs to compression, cautioned listeners against playing its CDs at "excessively high levels," especially those like the *Nutcracker Suite* containing artillery shots, lest they damage their "speakers or other components." The very presence of such warnings, though, might have instead engendered a great deal of "masochistic" interest in recordings that, potentially, could imperil speakers.

Modes of Entitlement:
Naming Conventions and Other Notable Developments

With the exception of song recitals (*The Maiden's Prayer*) and mixed programs of shorter works from several composers (*Czech Avant-Garde; Censored by Hitler*), most classical recordings adopt "rhematic" or generic titles, much the same way that classical poetry did (Genette 1997: 86). Indeed, Mackenzie had argued in the 1920s that the popularity of classical music might be increased if more compositions were nicknamed along the lines of the "Moonlight" Sonata (1939: 22). In fact, many novelty albums of classical music that have been issued in the last few years employ such titles (*Rule Britannia!; Concert a la carte*), as have those CDs that employ programmatic rationalities different from those that determine conventional classical CDs. Teldec's *From My Home* consists of a diverse program of music from Baltic composers such as Arvo Pärt and Peteris Vasks, devised by Gideon Kremer— one of a series of such discs from the violinist—to be a musical evocation of his homeland. Such programs are another manifestation of the increasing focus on the performer in the classical recording industry. Although this trend is not new and can be traced back to such endeavors as RCA's complete recording of Jascha Heifetz (Pfeiffer 1976), two recent series of recordings, Philips's "Great Pianists of the 20th Century" and IMG's "Great Conductors of the 20th Century," also exemplify this shift.

Such discs manifestly reflect the cult of the performer in their expository environment, which is often differently ordered from that of more orthodox discs. For example, the first pages of the CD booklet's notes are more than likely devoted to a description of the interpreter rather than the works they interpret. In the case of Sony's "Masterworks Heritage" series—a retro label drawing on CBS's back catalog of recordings—the notes include detailed accounts of the recording sessions. Those accompanying conductor George Szell's recording of Bartók's Concerto for Orchestra recount how the conductor—who had a reputation for being a martinet—made the percussionists feel so intimidated that they were unable to execute, at least to Szell's satisfaction, the extensive part for snare drum in the concerto (Charry 1999: 8–9). The notes for such recordings thus tend to have an "implied reader" different from those of the conventional CD: by and large, those who acquire retro recordings are already familiar with the music on the disc and keen to acquire more insight into the manner and mode of the interpreter than the nature of the interpreted.

The hierarchies of "onymity" (Genette 1997)—who is named and to what extent they are emphasized—are important aspects of the cover's titular environment, where, before the advent of the thematic title, composers and their compositions were always sovereign. Indeed, until the latter parts of the LP era, the performers who were billed in this environment were generally not subjects of account. They did not have, as is the case today, a section assigned to themselves: a short history of an orchestra, for example, complete with musical biographies of its conductor and any soloists who might be involved, including their career highlights and a list of any other recordings made with a particular label. This is another reflection of the degree to which the documentation associated with classical recordings has become more exhaustive and comprehensive in the era of the CD.

In spite of the fact that more and more facets of recording are now subjected to record keeping, the majority of the text associated with the sleeve is still devoted to musical explication. For this purpose, EMI employed a panel of fifty or so music critics in the 1950s who had the freedom to write more or less what they liked, providing it came within the requisite word limit: 1200 words for LPs, 750 to 800 for MPs (Barker 1958b: 11). In fact, one of the notable differences between the expository environments of popular and classical music is that the former are generally bereft of explanatory notes; their texts are, in the main, restricted to lyrics from the vocal tracks.[13] Indeed, what is most telling about pop texts is the degree to which images dominate them, mediating the music through less literary means. In the past, it should be said, popular recordings were issued with liner notes, though their quality was, for the most part, execrable (Packer 2003). By contrast, the notes accompanying classical recordings have always adopted a more literary and scholarly style, in keeping with their functions as phonographic libretti. There is an implicit assumption that listeners to classical recordings, by and large, wish to be informed about the music and will sit down and listen to a recording as they would in a concert, in relative quietness, with their ears attuned to the musical structures identified and discussed in the notes. As such, the notes are designed to produce a more attentive and reflective mode of listening, one that might be at loggerheads with other, more diverting modes of listening, such as when music is employed to induce emotional solace or revelry. Indeed, there are many "classical" albums now in the catalogue—several have become hits—that are specifically designed with such diverting modes of listening in mind, and are clearly titled to identify their function, for example Decca's *Music for Relaxation*.The notes for such CDs—musical versions of Prozac—pay but scant attention to the musical claims of their contents, which in accordance with their mood-altering effects are rarely subject to review.

Although listeners often oscillate between one mode of listening and another, the notes accompanying most classical CDs are written with "expert" listening in mind (Chanan 1994: 102). Their prevailing mood reflects the serious attention to music required by the keystone discourse, which they support. But the notes also help to sustain the cultural legitimacy of recording as a vehicle of classical music, which in the past was never assured, facing opposition from many phonographic apostates. Thus many musicologists and critics at first saw writing analytic notes for albums as a vulgar activity and accordingly resisted any overtures to do so; it was therefore considered a coup on the part of Walter Legge to persuade Ernest Newman—in the 1930s, the world's leading expert on Hugo Wolf—to compile the notes for an album devoted to Wolf songs.

In fact, the surface area of the sleeve note—which is a limited one—has never been restricted to one plane. Even during the era of the LP, when the cardboard sleeve was the dominant form of record enclosure, some labels, mainly American ones, issued LPs in gatefold sleeves (with one or more pages behind the front cover) or presentation boxes, particularly when, as in the case of an opera recording, the recording occupied more than one LP. In the early days of the LP, the libretto of an opera was often issued separately, some months after the recording's initial release and then only by customer order and at a price. In some instances, though, consideration was given to not issuing a libretto at all on the grounds that sales of the opera were likely to prove small and would not warrant the extra expenditure required to print a libretto. This was the case with Decca's *Rheingold*, which caused its producer some angst until the decision was rescinded (Culshaw 1981: 220). Generally, though, boxed sets of recordings included presentation booklets that were often illustrated and, in the case of operas, contained a complete libretto along with explanatory notes and essays. Some labels such as Mercury even used specially imported Italian paper for these booklets (Morgan 2001: 26), providing material planes of meaning that underwrote the quality and character of the music. For example, the rag paper used for the booklet accompanying Krzysztof Penderecki's *St. Luke Passion* could be seen on one level as a material expression of the music's apocalyptic nature.

Some LPs issuing from labels such as RCA's Soria, which specialized in deluxe forms of LP presentation, were "packaged for the perfectionist" in cloth-covered boards that were weightier than the normal sleeve, with a leatherette spine, gilt-edged lettering, and a lining. The recording of Darius Milhaud's *La Création du Monde* and *Suite Provençale* contained a booklet from the Swiss art publisher Skira.[14] Its contents included an excerpt from the composer's autobiography dealing with the significance of jazz, and an essay on Milhaud by the musicologist Edward Lockspeiser. The booklet was lavishly illustrated with hand-mounted prints of Cezanne paintings, apt visual backdrops for the *Suite Provençale*.[15] It also included illustrations of Fernand Léger's costumes and set designs used in the first stage production of *La Création*—one of which figured on the album's cover. Furthermore, the sleeve notes were comprehensively referenced, which is unusual for liner notes but enhances their utility as artifacts of scholarship and historical documentation. In this sense, the whole packaging was more akin to a book with a record as an insert, providing a sound exemplification of the text.

The inclusion of insert slips and pages was another strategy for increasing the surface area of the sleeve and extending its expository realm. These inserts were a special feature of the LPs emanating from Deutsche Grammophon's historical division, Archiv Produktion; they combined the gatefold sleeve with insert cards specifying the exact score used for the music, which was tabulated with scholarly meticulousness.[16] Such inserts were often included in the LP jackets of contemporary music, which often required far more exposition than more conventional music and often demanded, by way of illustration, excerpts from the score. The reverse of the sleeve, freed of text, was then used for photographs, generally of the performers or the composer. Other labels also specializing in contemporary music, such as Nonesuch with its computer music series, located some of the explanatory text on the *front* of the sleeve, thereby incorporating liner notes as a cover feature.

CD formats for notes also vary. The CD booklet is not universally used. Some labels have adopted various folder formats, which open out into a single field of text. But these are the exception rather than the rule, at least for classical releases, whose notes usually occupy between twenty and thirty pages of text—though not in the same language. Much to the annoyance of many CD collectors, who often complain about the matter in letters to record magazines, the size of the font is excruciatingly small—"pretty eye-straining," one correspondent bemoaned[17]—certainly when compared to that used on the LP, whose presentation, in this respect as in others, is often recalled with nostalgia. Even extracting the booklet from its jewel-box housing, which is sometimes difficult, has irked some collectors.

The fact that most classical CDs are intended for a global market rather than a national one, as tended to be the case in the days of LPs, means that most notes are multilingual—usually French, English, and German, the order depending on the CD's country of origin—which is one reason why they now occupy twenty or thirty pages. Yet multilingual notes had their origins in eastern Europe prior to the raising of the Iron Curtain, when many classical LPs issuing from companies such as Supraphon and Melodiya, which were targeted at Western markets, had English as well as Russian and Czech texts. In the late 1960s the practice spread to Western Europe, when EMI, perhaps as a way of textually reinforcing its claim to be "The Greatest Recording Organisation in the World," introduced trilingual notes, which forced a considerable reduction in the font size, one comparable, in fact, with that used on many contemporary CDs.

Liner Notes: The Case of Alan Bush and Sergey Prokofiev

With respect to the notes themselves, the completeness of their exposition ranges among labels from almost no relevant musical documentation at all on some budget labels[18] to a comprehensive accounting and detailed analysis of the disc's music. This is because some labels regard the accompanying notes as an integral part of the disc's presentation, demanding the same scrupulous attention as the recording itself. The Swiss-based independent Claves—and the independents, as a rule, are generally more conscientious with matters of documentation than the majors—believes that the "literary backing" of their CDs (including a concern with its readability) is an essential part of the development of a "flawless product." To this end, Claves only commissions "specialists in the field" to compile this "backing," which is also illustrated with appropriate "iconographical materials," such as facsimile examples from scores and photographs of performers and composers (Johnson 1994). Just as the front cover of the record sleeve was always, and remains, a wordy environment, CD liner notes represent an increasingly pictorial and colorful one.[19]

In fact, record companies have always turned as best they could to appropriate scholars for their liner notes.[20] In the absence, though, of "freelance" scholars willing to undertake the task, labels employed their own writers. Following the example of the Gramophone Company in the 1920s, who produced a series of booklets written by well-known record critic Alec Robertson, then an employee in its education department, Decca issued extended versions of its sleeve notes under the guise of its so-called "Music Guides."[21] These dealt with the symphonies of Beethoven and Mozart. At least two other prominent figures in the record industry, Walter Legge and John Culshaw, also began their careers preparing notes for record albums. And once such notewriting became more respectable, music scholars were less hesitant to undertake it; during the LP era, music critics of the ilk of Neville Cardus and William Mann regularly did so.

This itself was another marker of the way in which the discourse conditions of recording had achieved a measure of respectability, and recording was becoming regarded as an acceptable contribution to music that could constitute an important reference point in chronicling the history of music. Complete recordings of a composer's work were beginning to be seen as the auditory equivalents of the variorum edition. One such was Decca's recording of the Haydn symphonies with Antal Dorati conducting the Philharmonia Hungarica, for which the scholar H. C. Robbins Landon, who had prepared the contemporary edition of the composer's symphonies used in the recording, was commissioned to write the accompanying notes. It has now become a common practice for contemporary composers to be invited to compile notes for discs of their works—most famously, Alfred Schnittke for BIS. Unfortunately, his notes were sometimes unflattering about the performances of his own works, which brought the composer into conflict with BIS's director, Robert von Bahr, who regarded such comments as unwarranted (Ivashkin 1996: 196).

Notwithstanding the fact that they are often written by scholars, it has been argued that notes should be written with musical neophytes in mind and should be readable rather than recondite. This is because the practice of reading notes while listening to recordings is sometimes deplored as impairing musical concentration (Cudworth 1962: 113). Not that classical notes always provide much in the way of musical explanation. A set written by Karlheinz Stockhausen for an LP of his *Klavierstücke I–IX* includes extensive details about the recording sessions and remarks about the gastronomic excesses of the performer, Aloys Kontarsky, but it features a complete lack of musical analysis. Most liner notes, though, adopt a more constructive approach and provide notes, of varying degrees of relevance, according to the particular contents of the recording. Those accompanying a BIS disc of both versions of Sibelius's Violin Concerto are painstaking in their detailed analysis, complete with musical examples. And a recording of Bruno Walter rehearsing Mozart's "Linz" Symphony includes a full score of the symphony, which enables the listener, Cudworth's admonitions notwithstanding, to keep track of the results of the conductor's injunctions.

Notes tend to employ different rhetorical strategies when the music is new to the catalogue or its composer is an undeservedly neglected figure in the history of music. In the case of one such figure, the English composer Alan Bush, the notes with a Hyperion LP of his works employ a "revivalist" rhetoric, championing the long-overlooked Bush ("It has been the fate of major composers to be largely ignored in their lifetime through reasons that have little to with their intrinsic worth as creative artists"). In this case, the neglect is attributed to Bush's membership of the Communist Party. The notes then characterize Bush's works in various ways and attempt to make them palatable, brushing past mild dissonances of the kind found in Britten's music that will pose no apparent difficulties for the listener. In fact, this exhibits another rhetorical strategy commonly employed to introduce an unfamiliar composer: likening their works to another, better-known composer, thereby mitigating any fear engendered by the former's relative obscurity. The notes to the first recording of the Violin Concerto of Miklós Rózsa employ this strategy, suggesting that it is a neglected masterpiece ranking with no less than the violin concertos of Prokofiev and Bartók. Sleeve notes are also often used to raise the reputation of a composer and draw attention to works that have been unjustifiably overlooked and unrecorded. Peter Lamb, the author of the notes on Alan Bush, identifies one such work, the composer's "Nottingham" Symphony, that he holds to be a "superior composition" to the much-admired Symphony No. 7 ("Leningrad") of Shostakovich.

Sleeve notes also change with the times, and a work receiving its first recording is likely to be written about differently than after it has "matured" and been absorbed into the mainstream repertoire. Historical perspective and hindsight add new accretions of scholarship to the appreciation of a work, and liner notes often take advantage of this. For example, Prokofiev's Fifth Symphony, has been the subject of many recordings since its first public performance, in January 1945, under the direction of the composer in war-torn Moscow (Gutman 1999). The notes accompanying early recordings of Prokofiev's Fifth are more bound to their times than those of more recent origin, which turn their attentions to the significance of the symphony in terms of the composer's complete musical output, which could not be assessed at the time, when the composer still had eight more years to live.

After the "Classical" Symphony, with which it is often coupled on CD, the Fifth is Prokofiev's most recorded symphony. It is a work notable on a number of grounds that justify its many recordings and its status as a major Soviet symphony of the mid-twentieth century, including the unpropitious circumstances in which it was composed. These circumstances relate to the demands placed on artists and composers in the Soviet Union from the 1930s onward, when they were expected to celebrate and glorify the Soviet state and apply to their music the hackneyed aesthetic associated with Communist ideology, at the risk of being persecuted, imprisoned, or sentenced to death. The ideological forces that had marginalized Alan Bush in the United Kingdom for being an overly devout Communist could lead to a Soviet composer being marginalized for not being devout enough. Also vital to its popularity are the particular musical qualities of the Fifth and the ways that these contributed to the development of the contemporary symphony.

As one might expect, the notes accompanying the recordings of the symphony pay heed to the political hazards Prokofiev faced and staved off. They also emphasize the composer's precocity and his disenchantment with the Bolshevik revolution, which led him into exile. He spent many years in France, where he soon gained the patronage of Diaghilev, which was relevant because many of Prokofiev's symphonies derived elements from his ballet scores. Most of the notes mention the homesickness that eventually drove him back to the Soviet Union in 1934, at the height of the Stalinist purges (from which he was spared), and most mention his encounters with Stalin's cultural aide-de-camp, Andrey Zhdanov. The punitive cultural regime of the Soviet Union impressed itself on Prokofiev's musical radicalism, which his sojourn in Western Europe had nurtured and his return to the Soviet Union tempered. In this respect, the Fifth Symphony is a significant work in Prokofiev's compositional trajectory and represents a toning down of his radicalism and the adoption of a more ideologically deferent musical style.

As one might expect, the notes on the Fifth from the Soviet Union's official record label Melodiya play down any suggestions of political straitjacketing and play up the symphony as a glorious essay celebrating the triumph of Soviet will in the face of wartime adversity, one that combines "lofty thoughts about the Motherland" with an ardent "belief in the invincibility of man's spirit." In fact, this was more or less commensurate with Prokofiev's own account of the symphony—often cited in notes and itself a manifestation of his ideological deference—as an essay in human affirmation, exploring the "grandeur of man's spirit." Most of the notes also refer to the fact that the symphony was composed at the height of the "Great Patriotic War," when Prokofiev, along with a number of other artists, was evacuated to a place of refuge in the northern Caucasus. They also describe the circumstances of the symphony's first public performance, citing pianist Sviatoslav Richter's account of the portentous artillery salvos that burst over Moscow as Prokofiev marched onto the podium. In fact, just three weeks after conducting this performance, Prokofiev suffered a mild heart attack while descending a staircase, from which he never fully recovered; it led to his premature death in 1953—ironically, on the same day that Stalin died. Some of the notes also report the death threat to a conductor of the work in Salt Lake City during the McCarthy years, when the celebration of Soviet art was seen as unacceptable, to which Prokofiev reacted with utter disbelief, regarding such persecution as an ironic editorial on the "free world," that for all its proclamation of free expression, some still felt threatened by a "hymn to the free and happy man."

But during the Cold War years, music was no more exempt from ideological mongering than other cultural endeavors. Another example from the world of recording is the cover of Ormandy's recording of Shostakovich's Symphony No. 13 ("Babi-Yar"), a setting of poems by Yevtushenko, which is embellished with Cold War rhetoric ("The courageous 'Symphony of Protest' by two of the Soviet Union's most important angry young men"), as is the cover of the same composer's Tenth Symphony. As well as detailing the many occasions on which Shostakovich violated the dictates of Stalin's cultural *apparatchiks,* the cover makes clear that "no part of the proceeds from this recording enures [*sic*] to the benefits of the Union of Soviet Socialistic Republics, or to any of its agents or representatives."

Some of the liner notes accompanying Prokofiev's Fifth only deal with biographical and historical background (e.g. Dutoit's on Decca), allowing the music to speak for itself without the scaffolding of musical analysis. However, this is unusual; most notes provide detailed comments on the symphony's structure and development, identifying its main themes as they are introduced and passed from instrument to instrument, from one section of the orchestra to another, then one movement to another, through to the conclusion of the symphony. Sometimes, as on the Telarc recording, musical excerpts from the score are included, but this is not common. Often, relevant links to the composer's other works—in this instance, the ballet *Romeo and Juliet,* from which a discarded melody was retrieved—are made. Some notes deal more extensively with a conductor's relationship with his symphony, as is the case in Karajan's much-admired recording. In addition to recounting the way in which the work was assimilated into the repertoire of Karajan's Berlin Philharmonic, the notes allude to the conductor's political stance during World War II. The notes, in effect, defend Karajan's wartime reputation. They point out that while he was rehearsing the symphony in Berlin, during the last days of the war, he worried that a proposed trip to Italy would whisk him away from the human price about to be exacted on the city by the Soviets. Moreover, it is noted that Karajan's particular genius as a conductor was displayed to its greatest extent in works that "reflected his experiences of war."[22]

Of particular interest, though, are the extremely informative notes accompanying Ormandy's 1977 recording, which were written by Christopher Palmer. They include an anecdote from the composer Dmitry Kabalevsky about the piano run-through of the symphony in the Caucuses, which notes the symphony's profound impression on the other musicians present. Then there are some remarks about the distinctiveness of the Russian symphony in general and Prokofiev's Fifth in particular: it is more episodic than holistic, cast without the overarching spans of musical logic that characterize the Germanic symphony. This preamble leads into a detailed account of the symphony's structure that departs from others in that Palmer anthropomorphizes the music's thematic strands and their various transformations. The first movement, for example, is said to display a "pert little tail piece of re-peated semiquavers" and conclude with a "coda of iron might and majesty." The second movement is a blend of "roguish naïveté and laser-keen irony" that does not evolve "symphonically," the grist for Palmer's opening mill, but instead undergoes a "kaleidoscopic transmutation." The finale is a "merry throng" of May Day conviviality (presumably not its Soviet incarnations) be-fore a coda of "glittering dynamism" whose "chief *agent provocateur*"—and how it could be put otherwise for a work so colored with political intrigue and innuendo?—is the "laughter of the violins, peal after peal."

In this instance, then, Palmer's commentary acts as a textual amplifier, bringing to the fore certain passages of the Fifth for closer auditory examina-tion. In this manner the pathways of listening are channeled and molded, mediated and disciplined, and given auditory directions and instructions as the music progresses. The piece is heard as Palmer wants it to be heard, though how much so depends on the listener's preparedness to adopt the notes as a frame of reference. What is more, there is implicit in the explana-tory code a correlative injunction: the need to develop a pattern of listening consistent with that of the concert hall—the keystone discourse—in which the music is heard in a context of quietness, without the distraction of con-versation or any diversion that would subvert the possibility of "perspica-cious" auditioning—anything less, and the Fifth's symphonic narrative as outlined by Palmer would be meaningless.

But there is by no means unanimity about the explanatory efficacy of liner notes, and some in the industry hold that their musicological pretensions add yet another level of intimidation and obfuscation to the reception of classical music. Partly to redress this and partly to capitalize on what it perceives as being a "flight to quality" in the contemporary consumer environment, Pen-guin Music Classics employed different explanatory approaches and commis-sioned authors better known for their novels, for example Douglas Adams and Edmund White, to write the notes for their "classics." These writers tend to adopt a mode of musical exposition different from that of the conventional musicologist, one that proffers a more direct response to the music that is free of musical jargon and analysis. The notes written by *Generation X* author Douglas Coupland for a CD of the *Goldberg Variations* liken its first hearing to the noise of a conveyor belt in a factory—of course, alongside Coupland's lay "analysis" is a musicological examination of the work as well.

The founder of Winter and Winter, Stefan Winter is also disenchanted with the expository conventions and style of liner notes. He argues that music should be emancipated from too much written explanation and that words are not the only mode of communicating apposite musical insights (Anderson 2000). To this end, the notes with a CD of Maurizio Kagel's

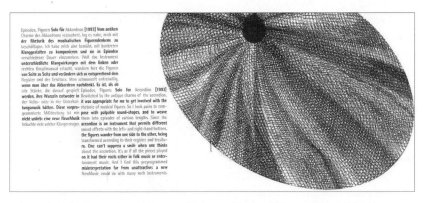

Figure 5.1 The above, from Winter and Winter, a label well known for its painstaking attention to CD presentation, exemplifies liner notes as line drawings. The label's founder has questioned the "logocentrism" of liner notes, arguing that a drawing can be equally telling, as in the above example, taken from a CD of Maurizio Kagel's accordion and piano pieces. (Reproduced by permission of Winter and Winter.)

piano and accordion compositions (black and white instruments) are illustrated with black and white drawings, the creations of Ursula Burghardt, the long-time associate of Kagel responsible for the stage designs of his anti-opera *Staatstheater*. And in another Winter and Winter recording, Uri Caine's version of the *Goldberg Variations,* the text is entirely "typographic," each variation being identified with different fonts, differently colored and positioned in a nonlinear way.

Thus far the analysis appertaining to the cover has treated the record as a pristine object, free of any of the adulteration resulting from its circulation or use. Yet there is a need to recognize the telling effects of this circulation and to acknowledge that the "life" of an individual record only commences once it is acquired. This acquisition impresses its own signature properties on a disc, which provide a material *record* of its use. For records are dynamic artifacts that have, after leaving the factory, "careers" of their own as well as distinctive profiles of ownership and possession. Contrary to the view expressed in the epigraph to chapter 4, records, even ones that are only infrequently played, rarely retain their pristine state—and, if they do, that too can be telling. Their various forms of coverage and their surfaces always provide a trace of the types of misadventures of poor handling or overplaying that have befallen a record; they come to comprise a résumé of sorts of the way the record has been used. The signs can be quite dramatic in the case of an LP—less so with the jewel box, though even it eventually loses its shine—the record has cut through the sleeve, or the glues dry out and become brittle, so that it has had to be rebound with sticky tape. Even LPs that are handled only infrequently eventually, by dint of pressure from their "neighbors," leave impressions of their circumference on their covers (see figures 4.6 and 4.23).

More dramatic, though, are the ways institutional settings such as libraries use a sleeve as a "palimpsest," as a surface on which to apply other texts usually concerned—as in the case of a library—with the administration and circulation of the record, such as date stickers and call numbers. Some of these other "texts" are used as tracking devices to regulate the circulation of discs, such as the magnetic strips—electronic versions of the panopticon—that set off security alarms if a disc is illegally removed from the library. To this end, discs are also registered and classified, which means that their covers are stamped with the signs and stickers of officialdom and proprietorship. Sometimes there are stickers for when an LP was last washed (see figure 4.23), a practice that has largely died out with the advent of the CD. Then there are a variety of institutional and personal "autographs," where a user of a record (and it only generally applies to LPs) has penciled in the playing time of its tracks or some remarks about the quality of a track, that it is damaged at a particular point, for example. Further, in the context of an academic library with a large cohort of music students among its borrowers, a record's cover will be further affected by whether its composer figures on a syllabus or not. At the University of Sydney's Conservatorium of Music, for example, the LP covers of Granville Bantock's music are, by and large, pristine, a sign that they are borrowed but infrequently, whereas those of Bartók—a composer who has a much higher profile on the contemporary music curriculum—are mostly tattered and undergoing "deconstruction."

Although they are often a neglected element in the recording phenomenon, cover notes are an integral part of the sleeve's narrative architecture and are far from peripheral to the record's "documentary reality." Certainly, many labels have taken the compilation of notes seriously and regard them as significant adjuncts of the way records are presented and packaged; to this end, they have commissioned eminent musicologists to compile them. But their realm embraces more than these explanatory texts, for they have also included prudent advice relating to discs and their maintenance. In all of these respects, cover notes help to frame and focus the conduct of the listener, both while handling and playing records and when listening to them. They thus constitute another transducer extending the envelope of the record experience beyond merely passive and inarticulate modes of listening. They are also significant sites of peritextual and parergonal devices, and they represent the equivalents of the pretext regions of books, containing the information relating to a recording and its provenance, thereby providing invaluable information for dating and placing a recording. Thus the functions of protection and consumer arousal that were the main *raison d'être* for the cover have been partnered with other functions, principally explanatory and informational. Sleeve notes, like cover designs, act as mediating texts that provide a particular reading of the music that interposes itself between the loudspeaker and the listener. However, there are many other texts that are still more distant than those of the sleeve—that are, as it were, even further *off* the record. To those we now turn.

CHAPTER SIX

Just for the Record

The Narrative Architecture of Gramophone Magazines

Papers like the Exchange and Mart for instance, or Cage Birds or the Oracle
or the Prediction or the Matrimonial Times only exist because there is a definite
market for them, and they reflect the minds of their readers as a great national
daily with circulation of millions cannot possibly do.
—George Orwell, "Boys' Weeklies," 176

Record magazines might have short shelf lives, but their impact on readers is
enduring. By virtue of their ephemeral nature, it is easy to eschew their significance and overlook the fact that their very regularity has assisted in enlist-
ing enthusiasm for recordings and spreading the word about their merits.
Nor is it possible to overlook the sheer number of such magazines, which is
testimony to the important functions that they have played in the recording
industry. At rough calculation, upward of five hundred fifty titles have been
published in the last one hundred thirty years (Velez 1993: 646), and their
manifold contents provide, in more senses than one, a graphic illustration of
the changes that have beset the industry during this time, and the way these
changes have been "sold" to record consumers. Magazines have provided a
means by which consumers have been able to keep themselves informed
about developments in recording—not just the continuous streams of discs
released every month and the dramatic changes to the industry associated
with the developments of new formats of reproduction. Magazines have
played a central role in mapping these changes for consumers. They have also
been the main mechanisms through which the phonographic "laity" has acquired the "epistemology" of recording, its vocabularies and values, jargon
and ideas. Their constant citation in record magazines has helped to repro-

duce and domesticate, regularize and normalize the myriad habits associated with acquiring and listening to records.

The envelope of the magazine's influence on records is somewhat analogous to that of record covers, except at one step removed, after the judgment of relevant experts in the field have been cast upon the record's qualities. The magazine's texts are both informative and normative; moreover, the zone of their influence is more extensive, because they examine a broader conspectus of phonographic issues. As will be argued in this chapter, record magazines are not just mechanisms for procuring interest in records and recording; they also constitute another link in the chain of reproduction, another transducer through which recordings are mediated. In this case, though, the transducer/magazine constitutes a form of *re*-production that adds new planes of meaning to the record above and beyond that appertaining to its acoustic reproduction. The advent of a magazine culture thus exemplifies the way in which the authority of recording has shifted from the phonograph to the printed word, yet another example of the recording angel at work, another form of the *written* record.

Words to Buy:
Magazines and the Production of Consumer Capitalism

Record magazines are not unique in keeping their readers abreast of developments in their field of interest; their functions and rhetorical maneuvers in this respect were pioneered in the mass-circulation magazines that appeared throughout the nineteenth century in the United Kingdom and the United States, which evolved through several generations before achieving their current narrative form. Their very existence was one of the offshoots of the mechanization of the printing industries that occurred at the end of the eighteenth century and led to the mass production of "literature" on an unprecedented scale (Williams 1962: 23). This productive capacity was deployed in manifold ways but most notably in the establishment of mass-circulation magazines that were within the financial reach of working people. In the first phase of their development, these magazines favored content espousing creeds of self-improvement and moral amelioration. This was intended to act as an ideological foil to the politically subversive literature then circulating in chapbooks and broadsheets (Anderson 1991). Only slowly did the mass-circulation magazines develop a consumer orientation, such that by the middle of the nineteenth century they were including significant advertising content along with relevant subject matter championing the virtues of commodity acquisition. Thus by the latter parts of the nineteenth century the self-improving functions of magazines, though not entirely superseded, were increasingly conflated with consumerist functions. Such magazines were one of the mechanisms used to cajole the population, particularly in the United States, to accept the logic of consumption and the domestic utopia it promised.

It was no accident that these more consumer-oriented magazines appeared during an era when the nature of work was undergoing a radical reorganization and the onus of the economy was shifting from production to consumption. Prior to this period, many of the necessities of life, including entertainment, had been produced within the sphere of the home (Ohmann 1996: 9, 58). The new order of work, which was increasingly undertaken outside the home and under temporal regimes that undid domestic self-sufficiency, increasingly required households to purchase what they needed, which in turn stimulated the demand for new types of consumer goods. But there was also much more to know about managing the home, and this information lay outside the realm of the traditional domestic lore passed on from mother to daughter or father to son. Magazines filled this epistemological void by providing advice on the new modes of domesticity, both inside and around the home; hence, the popularity of home and gardening magazines. At the same time, a new order of leisure emerged that complemented the easier home life accelerated by the development and deployment of labor-saving devices. There was more free time available and more ways of "spending" it; the new leisure came at the price of a not insignificant investment in gadgets of various kinds, which were also increasingly a pivotal element of recreational practice and thereby helped to fuel the expansion of consumerism.

But operating at a "prophylactic" level around the fear that the expansion of leisure might not be unequivocally beneficial, a strong moral impulse also underpinned the leisure literature that was strongly manifested in magazines. It has even been argued that leisure was constructed in such a way that, rather than constituting a suspension from work, it constituted an extension of work, for many of its most favored forms required the types of diligence and application also required by workplaces (Moorhouse 1987: 244). This idea—to be revisited again in chapter 8—is associated with so-called "serious leisure" (Stebbins 1992) and holds that the deployment of active work principles in leisure activity produces character development. Moreover, because much serious leisure has also required the investment in technological gadgetry—and on a regular basis, since this gadgetry has been subject to constant obsolescence—the leisure economy has emerged as an important sector of productive activity in the modern capitalist economy. The pursuits of free time are rarely free, after all, and recording is no exception in this regard; records and the equipment on which to play them require a not inconsequential outlay. Thus the adoption of the leisure ethic—one increasingly expressed in the consumption of gadgets—has come to augment the work ethic (Bauman 1998; Martin 1999).

Magazines have been important in spearheading the enthusiasm for the "toys" of technology, particularly when they are new to the marketplace and knowledge about their nature has yet to saturate the community. Thus the impact of leisure via its various magazine expressions is twofold: it helps bolster the economy by stimulating new domains of consumer desire, and it services the moral economy through the cultivation of more productive and morally palatable leisure habits. The latter is significant because such habits foil interest in those forms of immorality characteristic of "dark leisure" (Rojek 1995) that have at various times lured working men and women into squandering their free time on otiose pursuits (Cross 1993). In the case of cultural hobbies, of which collecting records is but one example, there is another dimension to this moralizing, and that is the degree to which these hobbies are underpinned with an aggressive aesthetic politics targeted at undermining forms of cultural expression this politics opposes. Magazines, such as those associated with the recording industry, have always been important conduits for such politics.

Yet in spite of the moral penumbra shadowing other types of serious leisure, such as reading or nature study, that appertaining to records was not unequivocally embraced. As was argued in chapter 2, it was feared that the phonograph would threaten the active musical culture that had emerged in the United States in the nineteenth century, which many held had improved the moral and musical milieu of America. Yet this fear was to a large extent misplaced, for although it was often said that the phonograph had led to a diminution in active music participation, it also generated compensatory forms of musical activity (Barzun 1955: 33).[1] These forms were not always strictly musical in Sousa's sense but merged technology and music, and then were modeled in and transmitted through record magazines, which also helped to convince their readers that it was natural to own a record player and records and that, contrary to the critics, an active musical life could be obtained from the phonograph (Katz 1998; Marvin 1988).

Though not alone in orchestrating radical changes in the organization of the leisure economy, the mass-circulation magazines of the nineteenth and early twentieth century were, nonetheless, instrumental in championing mass-produced goods and the science and technology that underpinned them. The editorial remit of these magazines generally "sought fulfillment in the future" and projected a new social order founded on prosperity and abundance (Schneirov 1994: 2). The magazines were thus forthright in their promotion of new inventions and machines, including the phonograph.

Much of this promotion was achieved through advertising, for which the new magazines, as apostles of progress, provided propitious sites. Indeed, their unalloyed espousal of the new technologies was mutually reinforcing, serving the organ of advertising and advertiser alike and attracted a range of manufacturers and industries. From 1904 onward, for example, Victor advertised its phonographic products in all of the quality magazines of the time (Schneirov 1994: 175; Siefert 1994: 187). Given the demographics of their readerships, this was important in enhancing the social status of the phonograph—as it was for other commodities. Victor's advertisements, which at first were relatively crude, merely asking readers to "Look for the Dog," gradually gained in subtlety. Victor's advertising eventually came to employ complex forms of persuasion utilizing a combination of images and solicitous copy that brought home the importance of the phonograph for the whole family. Interestingly, advertising for the phonograph occurred in a narrative context in which short stories and feature articles on the record also appeared, which underlines the ways in which the advertisements cannot be disaggregated from a magazine's other contents.[2]

In fact, the nexus between advertising and magazines is critical, particularly at the economic level, because the income derived from advertising helps to subsidize the cost of their production; without it, they are not viable (Ohmann 1996: 25). For example, a high percentage of the contents of a magazine, sometimes as much as 50 percent, is devoted to advertising space, and typically advertisements are woven through, into, and around the rest of the magazine. Mass-circulation magazines thus have provided an important "crucible for modern consumer capitalism" (Wilson 1983: 42), as well as a hospitable climate for the circulation of consumer habits, through complicated narrative structures that have endorsed the ownership of a range of commodities (Ohmann 1996; Schneirov 1994). Importantly, magazines have enabled their readers to fantasize about these commodities and fostered desires to own them by allowing them to shop at a distance without the need to engage in their acquisition right away.

Yet it is possible to overdo the shop talk at the expense of recognizing the "critical" functions of magazines; after all, magazines also represent the interests of their readers. They are significant sites of *caveat emptor* discourse that, through their careful appraisal of commodities, have countervailed the hyperbolizing blandishments of advertising. This is particularly true of those specialized magazines that have become important adjuncts of popular culture (Peterson 1964; Williams 1962) and whose diversity and profusion are evident at newsstands. Indeed, the organization of these shops—the textual emporiums of contemporary leisure and recreation—sheds light on the dominant categories of leisure activity: sports, electronics, cooking, and so on. They remain divided along gender lines, with women's magazines being predominantly about the projection of the self through beauty and fashion, these magazines invoke work on the self (McCracken 1993; Scanlon 1995) or on behalf of others. The majority of men's magazines, on the other hand, invoke the projection of the self through commodities such as cameras, cars, and electronics.[3]

But irrespective of their gender dimension, specialized magazines generate a readership around emergent or traditional hobbies and thus help define a constituency of interest whose membership includes those requiring regular guidance and information on how to extend and consolidate their hobbies. Because the members of various microcommunities associated with hobbies are widely dispersed and not often in contact with one another, at least in any formal sense, the magazine also acts as a forum for, and bond of invisible communication between, the members of what is a relatively specialized and dispersed "social world" (Unruh 1980). Such magazines have been a feature of the social world of music since at least the eighteenth century and have been variously devoted to the diversified interests of musicians and music educators as well as hobbyists. Those magazines that emerged around recording and music technology have served to further extend the print-based nature of much musical activity (Théberge 1997: 100).

The emergence of hobby magazines as a distinct group of periodicals is also reflected in the increasing diversification of related markets and commodities (Ohmann 1996: 357). The magazines' existence provides a documentary manifestation of the shift away from the mass production that dominated the first half of the twentieth century to the more specialized forms of production associated with post-Fordism that emerged in the last quarter of the twentieth century. These forms in turn reflected the individualization and diversification of consumer habits around niche commodities and services, that require specialized knowledge and information for participation (Featherstone 1991: 18–19; Piore and Sabel 1984). Magazines have provided one of the vehicles by which consumers inform themselves about what they should own and how they can they obtain the most from what they already own or propose owning. Record magazines fulfill this function, of course, and their individual titles reflect the dominant factions of interest populating the phonographic community.

Whereas in the past record magazines encompassed most domains of musical repertoire and were aimed at a mass market, they now come in a range of specialist titles that reflect the increasingly diverse and specialized nature of contemporary music culture. This nature is also manifested in different types of record journalism and scholarship appertaining to the field of music and its reproduction. Record scholarship, for example, is largely the province of academic journals dealing with the culture of recorded sound and its upkeep and preservation; in the absence of any specialist academic journals devoted to the subject,[4] it tends to be embedded in journals devoted to media and music. By and large the most scholarly musical journals have, not unexpectedly, been circumspect in their coverage and analysis of phonographic culture. Even in the 1950s, music scholars were still reluctant to grant cultural legitimacy to recording and its study. An editorial in one eminent music journal evaluating the cultural achievements of the phonograph declared that while much progress had been made in broadening the repertoire of recorded music, there was still an ongoing need to ensure that the disc remained the servant of music and to reiterate the view that recorded music is inferior to performed music (Lang 1952: 428).[5]

Then there is a body of periodical literature variously produced by record societies and clubs, such as the *Hillandale News,* the official journal of the City of London Phonograph and Gramophone Society, aimed at the "phonoquarian," which deals with matters of historical interest to collectors of vintage recordings and gramophones. In addition, the major record companies have, in the past, published magazines, for example the *Victor Record Review* (RCA) and *The Voice* (HMV). These magazines were primarily intended to keep the public informed about new products, but they also played a role in promoting musical appreciation and disseminating knowledge about classical music (Horowitz 1987: 210). In this chapter, though, it is the mass-circulation classical record magazines with a global readership that are the principal subjects of examination.

In fact, there has always been a certain amount of periodical coverage associated with the record industry, though much of this representation occurred originally through trade magazines such as Edison's *Phonogram,* whose interests tended, by definition, to be partisan and in large measure promotional. Outside those produced by the industry, the first independent magazines dealing with the phonograph appeared in the 1890s in Tsarist Russia, where the recording industry soon acquired an enthusiastic if short-lived following (Lotz 1983).[6] The content of these incunabula magazines was in the main devoted to lists of recordings, interviews with recording artists, and sundry technical matters (Velez 1993: 646). Only rarely did the magazines engage critically with the record industry or seek to challenge its directions. One exception to this was the Berlin-based *Phonographische Zeitschrift,* which in 1909 drew attention to the omissions in the record catalog and noted that the more demanding music lover was ill-served by the phonograph (Gelatt 1977: 174–75). This was a well-justified criticism, for at the time there was little classical music available on disc, and what there was of it was often abridged. Criticism like this established an important principle that is manifested in the editorial remits of subsequent magazines: an interest in encouraging the industry to pursue more adventurous and serious recording policies. It also reflects the mediating function of record magazines which provide an authoritative voice for championing and representing the interests of record consumers. For prior to their appearance in the 1920s, there were no magazines in the marketplace that were directed at the average collector (Gronow and Saunio 1998: 33). The record journalism that existed was embedded in other print media, mainly newspapers and music magazines, and only appeared irregularly.[7] Newspapers, even quality ones, still did not have columns devoted to record reviews.

The Textual Invention of the Gramophone: Early Record Journalism and Criticism

However, this was beginning to change. In September 1922, Robin Legge, the music critic for the London *Daily Telegraph,* invited a recent convert to the gramophone, the novelist Compton Mackenzie, to write a brief article on the subject. In this article Mackenzie described his recent discovery, urged readers to forget "the ancient outrages" visited upon music by the gramophone, and asked them to listen to a perfectly rendered recording of Fritz Kreisler playing Brahms's *Hungarian Dances,* for they will be agreeably surprised at the vast improvements that have been made in the interim. The article aroused considerable interest and generated many letters of support, including one from another prominent "gramophile," the critic Percy Scholes, whose magazine *The Music Student* had carried articles promoting the educational and musical potential of the gramophone since 1919. The story of how Mackenzie acquired "gramophilia"—oft told in his prodigious oeuvre—demands retelling, as it reveals, once again, the struggle for classical credentials that the gramophone continued to face even into the 1920s.

Hoping that it would allay his chronic melancholia, Mackenzie decided to invest in an Aeolian Organ, which duly arrived at his remote home in the Channel Islands with an unexpectedly reduced catalog of rolls: "the symphonies of Beethoven and Tchaikovsky I remembered were no longer listed" (1955: 64; 1973:1).[8] In desperation he wrote to the Aeolian Company, expressing his disappointment and asking if he could withdraw from the transaction. They refused but offered an alternative deal involving the purchase of the company's Vocalion Gramophone, together with a representative selection of records; Mackenzie accepted with some hesitation, since hitherto he had, like many of his contemporaries, dismissed the gramophone's musical pretensions as exaggerated. He thought of it as "nothing but a detestable interruption of conversation and country peace" (1922: 5). Indeed, the world of records was so alien to him that he had to ask an engineer friend what the letters "HMV" stood for (Mackenzie 1955: 65). His wife, Faith, was of little help; she could not even spell "gramophone" and considered it a "below stairs" activity, a "strident toy" for the "nursery or servant's hall" (Mackenzie, F. 1940: 111).

Included in the selection of Vocalion records Mackenzie purchased was a two-disc set of Schumann's Piano Quintet. He was thunderstruck: "I had expected to hear nothing more that the scratchy buzz of a violin record in 1910 and piano sounding like somebody tapping a tune on his front teeth. Instead, I heard music" (Mackenzie 1966: 218). It was the Schumann album, more than any other, that awakened Mackenzie's passion for the gramophone. It led him to invest a small fortune on a large collection of records, many of which, disappointingly, proved to be "duds" to which he felt the general public needed alerting (Stone 1933: 57). This feeling, plus the excitement generated by his *Telegraph* article, convinced Mackenzie that the moment had arrived to take the gramophone "seriously" (Mackenzie 1940: 111) and that a proper vehicle was needed to champion its interests. Thus emerged the idea of a magazine devoted to an unpartisan discussion of records, which would review them in the same way that a "literary magazine reviews books" (Mackenzie 1966: 243).

Although many around Mackenzie expressed some skepticism about the wisdom of his scheme[9]—they thought the radio would render records obsolete, among other things—he persisted. Representatives from HMV and Columbia, however, were more encouraging and pledged their support. They helped to defray some of the magazine's initial expenses by taking out a number of advertisements at the cost of "seven guineas for a page." They also agreed to supply the magazine with review copies of new records (Mackenzie 1966: 249–50).

The first issue of *The Gramophone* appeared on 20 April 1923, three weeks later than had been planned (Mackenzie 1966: 250). It was a mere twenty-three pages long, six of which were devoted to advertising. It had a print run of six thousand, small by today's standards but sufficient to create a flow of congratulatory letters and subscriptions that proved hard to staunch (Mackenzie, F. 1940: 124). The response convinced its editor that there were, after all, "enough gramophone enthusiasts" wanting the "organ of candid opinion" he had promised in the magazine's first editorial (Mackenzie 1923a: 1). In June, a second issue appeared. Since then, its readership has steadily increased, along with its stature as a magazine at the forefront of record criticism. Right from the start, it was recognized that it occupied a more elevated critical plane than its more sycophantic competitors *The Sound Wave* and *The Talking Machine News*. For unlike them it set recordings in their musical contexts and applied the same standards of criticism granted to other manifestations of music (LeMahieu 1982: 379). The standing of *The Gramophone* as a record magazine stems not just from the fact that it was the first in its field but also that it pioneered the narrative architecture associated with the record magazine. Its sheer longevity in a field of publication where magazines come and go often is also worthy of note; its contents encompass most of the most important phases of recording, at least for classical music, and thereby provide a unique conspectus of the history of the recording industry.

Over the eighty or so years of its publication, the magazine's narrative architecture has undergone regular renovation: it is now a more voluminous and less monochromatic magazine than when it was launched. Many of these changes echo those evident in the graphic design of record covers and reflect the dramatic changes to printing technology that have occurred since the 1920s. The first issue of *The Gramophone* was a short black and white production dominated by the printed word. Current issues, by contrast, feature large numbers of illustrations. About the only sections of the magazine that remain monochromatic are the review sections, and even they use colored panels for textual emphasis. This reflects the increased tendency in magazine design to use color as a form of punctuation, paragraphing, or highlighting. Except for a short period during World War II, when it shrunk because of severe paper shortages to a mere nineteen pages—its font went from ten point to six as well, to compensate for the fewer pages (Pollard 1998a: 42)—the size of the magazine has steadily grown and it is now between 140 and 150 pages. Its circulation, at the time of writing, is around 55,000.[10]

Other magazines—with the exception of the *American Record Guide,* still going strong after sixty-five years of continuous publication—have proved much less resilient, despite taking their inspiration from *The Gramophone.* In fact, many more record magazines, as is true of magazines in general, have failed in the long term than have succeeded. Much of this has to do with the timeliness of their publication. It is of note, for example, that the majority of record magazines come into existence at the time of "paradigm switches" in the industry, a fact reflected by their titles. Those magazines such as *Gramophone* that have been able to transcend this timeliness are handcuffed to titles reflecting the period of their provenance. For example, the developing interest in home theater systems in the 1990s led to the publication of appositely titled new magazines such as *Home Theatre.* These magazines claimed territory that the older, more established audio magazines had not colonized in any specialized sense and endeavored to cultivate a readership that was otherwise poorly served by them. It is a common strategy not confined to the record industry.[11] During the 1950s, for example, when the interest in high fidelity burgeoned, a separate group of periodicals emerged that catered to it.

For although the established magazines had always analyzed the techniques of sound reproduction (and still do), they remained subsidiary to their main preoccupations with classical music and its performance on record. Thus whereas their editorial remit was "sound for music's sake," the high fidelity magazines favored "sound for sound's sake." This was reflected in their titles (*Hi-Fi News & Record Review; High Fidelity*) and the hierarchical ordering of their contents. In high fidelity magazines, audio matters occupied the front of the magazine, whereas in record magazines they occupied the back.[12]

Redefinitions in magazine readership are engendered by the ongoing format changes that are a perennial feature of the recording industry. For although there is a certain amount of editorial "infection" between record magazines, each new magazine that enters the market reinvents the genre. Its genetic structure undergoes editorial mutation, so to speak, in the hope that this will produce a significant amount of title switching in the marketplace. For example, soon after the launch of CDs a number of new magazines sought to take market advantage of the specific interest in the new format (*CD Review; Classic CD; What CD?*), but they only lasted, in an intensely competitive market, for a short time. Magazines that do not survive are often absorbed into their more resilient competitors, or another characteristic of record magazines, particularly during the 1950s and 1960s, is that they often merge. *Records and Recording,* a U.K.-based magazine that was launched more or less at the same time as stereo LPs, absorbed the *Record Times* before being itself absorbed into *Music and Musicians,* from which it had originally sprung. In 1960 the U.S.-based *High Fidelity* absorbed the more hobby-oriented *Audiocraft* and *HiFi Music at Home,* and some time later *Music in America,* before being itself absorbed into *Stereophile.* Record magazines also frequently undergo changes of editorial identity. *American Record Guide,* which first appeared under its current title in 1932, began as an advertising newsletter for the New York Band Instrument Company, only including record reviews in an appendix (Cooper 1978). *High Fidelity* had begun as a "nuts and bolts" magazine catering to audiophiles. But as more and more of its pages became devoted to reviews of classical records and articles on their performers, it became more "musical," eventually promoting itself as "America's *Gramophone*"(Long 1971).[13]

Other record magazines, however, have sought to distance themselves from the narrative architecture of the *Gramophone* through the development of different editorial emphases. The bimonthly *Fanfare,* which resembles a scholarly quarterly in appearance and whose subtitle, "The Magazine for Serious Record Collectors," positions its readers in a more elect group than its rivals, is notable for its long and penetrating essays on performers and record companies. By contrast, the *International Record Review,* as its title intimates, places the emphasis on reviews—over two hundred per month, its cover proclaims. In line with this emphasis, it is free of the features found in most other record magazines, including the cover-mounted CD, which became a "sound" addendum of many record magazines in the 1990s. This was of course a notable development in their narrative architecture, providing, at least in the case of *Gramophone,* excerpts from esteemed new releases that served as auditory "footnotes" for their reviews.[14]

But the redefinitions of readership occurring around new magazines are not just driven by technological change. Some of the changes relate to matters of musical repertoire and the types of music reviewed in the magazine, as is evident in the large number of magazines devoted to specific strands of popular and rock music (e.g. *Juice, Radiohead*). This is another aspect of the "flexible specialization" associated with post-Fordist production, which has produced commodity niches within niches. In the instance of recording, the proliferation of musical repertoire that the advent of the record helped to generate, which has engendered ever more specialized forms of musical taste, is reflected in magazines catering to those tastes, which in turn increase the demand for more recordings to satisfy these tastes, and so on. For example, there are now record magazines, most appearing since the arrival of the CD, that deal particularly with historic, piano, opera, early music, and world music recordings.[15]

Aesthetic Politics: The Gramophone and Jazz

Such repertoire diversification marks a dramatic turnaround from the early 1920s, when *The Gramophone* was determined to redress the lack of catalog of classical music on records. Indeed, Mackenzie's attitudes toward the gramophone were underpinned by a proselytizing mission directed at several fronts: record companies, the skeptical musical establishment, and the musical tastes of the general public. The nature of this mission was outlined in *Gramophone Nights,* which Mackenzie co-authored with Arthur Marshall, who was then writing occasional articles on the gramophone for the *Morning Post.* In Mackenzie's contribution record companies are derided for not dedicating themselves more resolutely to building catalogs of impeccable music, that is, "entire symphonies and concertos of Beethoven." He suggested that they too readily pandered to popular taste, identified as "rubbishy so-called ballads, schoolgirls' violin pieces and hackneyed orchestral compositions." The lesson to be drawn from the book industry was that "publishing rubbish" made poor commercial sense, particularly with radio in the ascendancy, which he feared would purvey continuous rubbish (Mackenzie and Marshall 1923: 9). If they were not to be usurped by radio in the musical garbage realm, record companies had to rethink their catalog philosophy and concentrate on recording music of the highest quality.[16] In treating the gramophone record as a musical equivalent of the book—a rhetorical strategy he often deployed[17]—Mackenzie was also trying to offset concerns in the musical establishment about the cultural status of the record. For he was implying that what had been true of books *could* also be true of records: that they did not have to select their contents from an inferior menu of music. However, part of the blame, Mackenzie recognized, lay on the demand side: he observed that too many owners of gramophones were lazy in their buying habits and needed to devote the same diligence to records as to books. If they would do so, there would be far fewer skeletons in record closets, for "the greatest economy in music . . . is to buy the best" (Mackenzie and Marshall 1923: 12).

In fact, Mackenzie began to see the gramophone (in its upper- and lower-case versions) as a bulwark against the spread of inferior musical taste, and he found John Reith, the first managing director of the British Broadcasting Company (BBC), to be a comrade-in-arms. Mackenzie in many respects was the Lord Reith of the gramophone record, and he shared Reith's cultural ambitions, which included raging a war on popular music. Reith had determined that radio would *not* be the organ of majority taste, and he resisted succumbing to Fleet Street's taunts about the "miseries of chamber music and Bach cantatas" having a dominant place on the network of the public broadcaster (Mackenzie 1966: 251–52). He aligned his philosophy of radio to the same civilizing principles espoused in an educational context by Matthew Arnold: wherever possible, radio should contest the proclivities of mass culture. He proclaimed that the radio should feature the "best there is," be it in the domain of amusement or instruction, for he feared that entertainment without edification on the air waves would suffocate the ameliorative potential of radio (Briggs 1965: 75; Doctor 1999: 26–27).

Yet although both Reith and Mackenzie saw radio and records operating in an alliance against the common enemy of bad taste, records, because of their sonic limitations, were initially banned from the BBC. As a matter of principle, live musicians were hired in their stead, and if musicians were unavailable, then a player piano—and most studios were equipped with one—was used (Briggs, A. 1961: 260). This embargo was not lifted until the advent of electrical recording, whereupon the BBC appointed, in 1927, its first "disc jockey"—Christopher Stone, co-editor of *The Gramophone* and brother-in-law of Compton Mackenzie (Mackenzie 1967: 116). The possibility of furthering the alliance between radio and records led Mackenzie to pilot a publication parallel to *The Gramophone* that would be devoted to radio, but the short-lived *Vox* was soon absorbed into the master magazine.

But it was in Mackenzie's monthly editorials—or "causeries," as he called them—from the mid-1920s to the outbreak of World War II, that he delineated the precise nature of his aesthetic politics and projected his agenda for elevating the musical taste of the general public. In these "fireside chats," he pictured the gramophone as leading the war against the main musical foe of the time: jazz. His hatred of jazz was in fact shared by cultural commentators and intellectuals across the complete political spectrum, from Theodor Adorno on the left to Wyndham Lewis on the right. Like them, Mackenzie railed against the rising tide of musical vulgarity epitomized by the growing enthusiasm for jazz, and he made bold claims about the elevating powers of classical music. Beethoven, for example, had increased the mercifulness of modern society (Mackenzie 1939: 87), while Bach had engendered a revolt against the noise of "trains, trams and omnibuses." But he directed most of his commentary at the deplorable standards of mass entertainment, as exemplified in most (not *all*) light music and dance music, which he regarded as the "work of pickpockets, not artists" (1939: 32). Jazz and swing music were prime examples. Their only saving graces were their capacities to act as a "carminative" and offer an outlet to the gymnastic instinct. They could not claim to be music at all, for genuine music would evoke emotional and intellectual feelings, and they did not. Jazz was mere noise posing as music, a debased and infantile form of expression generated by the "sickness" of an era that encouraged the mind to surrender to the excesses of sensuality (Mackenzie 1939: 290–97). That some music could act as an aphrodisiac was further deplored and in need of countermanding via music whose appeal was more cerebral. Throughout his diatribes against jazz there was more than a hint of racism as well; in fact, with its allusions to Zulus and "funny nigger noises," it was at times, even for the times, very overt.[18]

For Mackenzie, chamber music constituted the zenith of good music and was one of the "major delights of mortal life," but its presence on radio required a vigorous defense in the face of Fleet Street's invective. In describing the virtues of César Franck's D-minor String Quartet, he derided a correspondent to the *Radio Times* who complained about the "beastliness" of chamber music. He called her a "jackass" and asserted that she and her ilk should not be given the opportunity to proclaim "their deficiencies" in print (Mackenzie 1939: 146–47). Elsewhere Mackenzie turned upon the "turnipheads" at the BBC who, notwithstanding Reith's entreaties, were undermining its cultural contract to the people, which included an obligation to "persecute the people with beauty." Those who failed to meet this obligation and hindered, either through word or deed, the habit of chamber music deserved to be annoyed, harassed, persecuted, even tortured.

Mackenzie freely acknowledged that the zeal for good music, which he was eager to impose on the rest of the community, was not an easy one to acquire.[19] Egged on by the gramophone, the musical habits of the era had, in fact, encouraged the opposite: lazy listening. The gramophone had produced a labor-saving approach to music that offered instant musical gratification, realizing the fears Sousa had voiced decades earlier. The appreciation of "good" music, on the other hand, placed exacting and constant demands on the listener and required the application of an aesthetic version of the work ethic that involved regular exercise and attention. Listeners had to immerse themselves in the sounds, soaking up melodies as "they might saturate themselves in a bath" (Mackenzie 1939: 35). Repeated listening was the key, which is why Mackenzie was such an ardent apologist for the gramophone, for it allowed music to saturate the sensibility through constant iteration.

Given that Mackenzie held jazz in such contempt and hoped that its gradual withdrawal from circulation would convert the public to the cause of "good" music, it is ironic that his magazine was not averse to reviewing jazz. But this was always against his better instincts. When the magazine's readership had begun to flag, it was decided to incorporate strands of popular music into its review sections as a strategy to acquire new readers. Mackenzie tried to veto, but was overridden by his editorial board, the appointment of Edgar Jackson, the founding editor of *The Melody Maker,* to the magazine's panel of reviewers; he then held the position for twenty-eight years, during which time he edited his own column, "Jazz and Swing" (Pollard 1998a: 38–39). In another attempt to make the magazine "swing" with the times, Jackson persuaded Christopher Stone to modernize the magazine's layout (LeMahieu 1982: 390). In fact, Jackson often used his column to promote the musical merits of jazz and, at one stage, accused Ernest Newman, one of jazz's fiercest critics, of musical myopia (1933).

In fact, by the late 1930s Mackenzie's curmudgeonly attitudes toward popular music, jazz in particular, had mellowed, and his musical "idealism" become tempered with "common sense." He came to accept their pervasiveness as a necessary evil. He recognized that his causeries had not reformed musical taste and that the economic facts of recorded life were such that, without the profits accrued from the discs of popular music and jazz, fewer classical records could be produced (Mackenzie 1931a: 112).[20] He comforted himself by introducing initiatives on other fronts to increase the representation of classical music in the catalogue that placed some of the financial onus on its listeners, such as the subscription schemes variously established under the aegis of the National Gramophone Society.

Thus it was only from the 1970s onward that *Gramophone* began to focus exclusively on classical recordings, its periodic nods in the direction of jazz and film gradually fading from coverage in the intervening years. Its renewed focus on serious music is evident in the slogans that have appeared on the magazine's masthead, which are always signifiers of the magazine's prevailing musical concerns. The first of these slogans, posted in 1990, was "Reviews of New Classical Recordings." This changed in 1995 to "The Best Classical Musical Magazine in World," and in 2002 to "The Classical Musical Magazine." The latter suggests that the magazine is in the process of extending its remit beyond classical recordings to encompass classical music in general.

Opera and Soap Opera: Record Magazines as Time Machines

Magazines occupy a territory of narrative located somewhere between the newspaper and the book. They appear with less frequency than newspapers and usually in glossier and more alluring formats. Their articles are more bookish than newspapers in their analytical scope and depth but their sequencing is more discontinuous than a book and exhibits less discursive unity. Their more specialized subject matter is more predictable and less concerned with the day-to-day, exhibiting more temporal distance than a newspaper. Readers come to know what to expect from a magazine and "script" their lives around its features. In this respect, magazines are more "writerly" than "readerly"; that is, they provide their readers with opportunities to engage with the magazines' texts in more active ways, by writing themselves into or out of their texts—writing a letter to the editor, for example, or taking the magazine's advice and purchasing a highly recommended LP or CD.

Magazines share with newspapers, as distinct from books, a respect for punctuality; they come out on time, at regular (monthly, bimonthly, or quarterly) intervals. Much of their content is also event related, chronicling the here and now as well as the heretofore and hereafter. Many of their features and feature articles are worked out over time and continued into subsequent issues, or they refer back in time to "issues," in both senses of the word, of the past. This is especially true of *Gramophone,* whose contents appear more "regular" than those of its competitors, which, outside of their review sections, tend toward more stand-alone articles. Moreover, the purview of these competitors' subject matter is often more extensive and draws on a less select band of authors. Take *High Fidelity,* for example: the volume for 1963 included feature articles on such subjects as the psychology of sound, learning French from discs, record clubs, room acoustics, and the American composer Harry Partch. And while it employed, like *Gramophone,* a panel of in-house reviewers, composers and musicians of the stature of Aaron Copland, Robert Craft, Glenn Gould, and Milton Babbitt also occasionally wrote for the magazine. Their articles helped to underwrite the musical credentials of not only the magazine *High Fidelity* but also high fidelity in general.

In the mid-1950s, by which time there were a number of magazines "devoted to the growing cult of the gramophone record," it was important that any new related magazine "do a job that is not done elsewhere." At least that was the view of *Record and Recording*'s first editor, who thought it was the duty of his magazine to bring the readers' attention to "news and opinions, information and illustration"; this was endorsed by a selection of letters from his intended readers (Senior 1957: 5). And while the majority of its narrative environment, like other magazines of its type, was devoted to record reviews, it also covered more facets of the recording phenomenon than did, say, in *Gramophone*. Thus its inaugural volume included articles on sleeve designs, record reviewing on air, and record care. LP sleeves—which were also often the subjects of separate commentary—were used to illustrate reviews, and the magazine pioneered modes of "charting" classical records such as the "Record of the Month" and "Records You Bought" lists that other magazines eventually adopted.

By comparison, *Gramophone* was, and still is, more inclined to draw its content from the immediate or distant past. It constantly chronicles and re-chronicles itself, constructing a history of the record from its own *record* of that history. But nothing ever really remains the same, or if it does, it is re-framed and renamed, undergoing reinvention for the new times and new generations of readers. It is notable, for example, that the language of the magazine is much plainer than it was. For example, the rather Proustian feature title "Things Remembered," which first appeared in June 1940, became "Looking Back" and lately "Hindsight." "Trade Winds and Idle Zephyrs," a column of news on the record industry, became "Here and Now" and lately just "News." Some features have disappeared altogether, such as the poetic "Swish of the Scythe" listing discs about to be deleted and "Nights at the Round Table" reviewing recordings of lighter music.

Some of the timeliness of *Gramophone* has always been seasonal. Issues for the month of December inevitably have a Christmas flavor; the typography of the magazine's masthead was, at one stage, even capped with snow. The December issue is also more "present" centered than other months, containing features that review the year in records. For the annual "Critics Choice," reviewers selected their six favorite records of the year. And because so much of classical music celebrates the events of the Christian calendar, the magazine is notably more religious at Easter and Christmas as well, reflecting the releases of the record companies.

Magazines are thus "time machines," texts that are date conscious but that, like those of newspapers, quickly date. Some sense of this datedness, as was noted earlier, is preserved in their titles. That of *The Gramophone*—the definite article was dropped in October 1973—employs a dinosaur of a term, a textual legacy of the 1920s long since superseded by hi-fi equipment and stereo, terms that were chic in the 1950s and 1960s and contributed to magazine titles from that era (*High Fidelity; Stereo Review*). Sometime these titles could backfire and create the wrong impression about their contents. When Roland Gelatt, at the time primarily a music critic, was invited by *High Fidelity* to be one of its feature writers, he initially hesitated on the grounds that he saw his interests as exclusively musical. He had to be assured that those of the magazine were compatible with his and not *just* high fidelity (Gelatt 1961: 39).

The timely orientation of magazines is also manifested in a tendency to be chronically retrospective and take their own *records* seriously. They are forever looking back on their pasts or drawing on back issues in columns of the "hindsight" type. They also celebrate phonographic anniversaries and their own publishing milestones. Thus, the centenary of Edison's phonograph was given generous reportage in many record and audio magazines in 1977, as was EMI's centenary in 1997, which was marked by publication of a special supplement in *Gramophone*. At the "ideological" level such textual celebration normalizes change in the recording industry and consolidates the profile of certain companies who instigate that change. Magazines also do the same with anniversary issues of their own publication, thereby celebrating their durability in a domain of publishing not noted for such. Those that prove the exception generally mark their prolonged presence in the marketplace with anniversary volumes. *Gramophone*, for example, marked its fiftieth and seventy-fifth years of continuous publication with anthologies whose contents drew on representative articles from the magazine's past (Pollard 1998b; Wimbush 1973). Its American equivalent, *High Fidelity*, produced a similar anthology to mark its twenty-fifth anniversary (Clarke 1976).

By making the dimension of time such a prominent feature of their narrative structures, record magazines have, over the years, built a community of readers that have become *chronically* dependent on their contents and cannot cease subscribing to the magazine lest they lose the "thread" of those narratives carried on through time. The piquancy of magazines owes much to the sense of anticipation that they orchestrate through their focus on an implied future. The fact that each issue of the magazine is engineered through references to the past, the present, and the future means that the reader's sense of affiliation is engaged through a temporal commitment, through various forms of episodic "hangover," akin to those used in soap operas. This leads readers of *Gramophone* to try to anticipate how other reviewers will evaluate much-lauded recordings and guess about whether they will be elected into that most rarefied of categories, the critic's record of the year.

Thus the magazine works episodically on its readers and insinuates itself into their expectations and into their lives, providing temporal coordinates for their own phonographic existences. It operates on the "tense" of their musical experiences, aligning those of the past to those of the present and future. The letters pages of *Gramophone* bristle with examples, of readers who have read the magazine for forty and fifty years ("I have been a reader of GRAMOPHONE from the first issue of the halcyon days of Sir Compton Mackenzie and Christopher Stone . . ."). During this time these readers' musical experiences have come to intersect with their records, and the contents of the magazine act to engage these experiences and stimulate mnemonic loops between the past and the present. One correspondent recalls attending a concert of the Sydney Symphony Orchestra in November 1946 in which Charles Mackerras played the first oboe, another purchasing a 78 of Tito Gobbi in Trieste just after World War II, and on and on.

The Narrative Architecture of Record Magazines

But magazines first and foremost are "living" documents — at least during their immediate shelf life, before they are "bound" into history. A proportion of their contents consist of "epitexts" (Genette 1997) that are variously aligned to records in the news, onto which they turn their critical spotlight. This might be an extended profile of or interview with a performer, designed to arouse interest in and sell one of their recent discs. Take the profile of the pianist Maria João Pires, which appeared in the pages of *Gramophone* coincident with the release of her Beethoven CD. The profile not only "recorded" details of her career and musical philosophy but also described — in the editorial spirit of the more life-style oriented magazine *Classic FM* — her farm/studio as a venue for "cultural tourism" (Finch 2002: 10). The effect of these mediations is to suggest that though musicians of Pires's ilk might be capable of feats of musical virtuosity beyond the dreams of the average *Gramophone* reader, their everyday tastes are not so very different from that of the reader. Such articles constitute not much more than "advertorials" and are part of the machinery that record labels use to promote their star performers and keep them in the public eye. In the past, the "human side" of the performer was dealt with in less effusive ways. It was always there in such features as obituaries, but as the cult of the performer has grown, more and more aspects of their lives are celebrated, even mundane ones. For example, a recent *Gramophone* feature is "My Month," in which musicians chronicle their professional activities for four weeks.

The narrative architecture of record magazines displays a department structure consisting of a series of discontinuous narratives of varying lengths and genres that are arranged into sections. This segmented structure is framed with a range of "peritextual" devices that identify and partition a magazine's various departments—where they begin and end. These dividing practices are a dominant feature, as are the range of navigational aids such as contents pages that enable readers to find their way around the reviews and features. Given that magazines tend not to be read in a linear way from cover to cover, these navigational aids "streamline and manage the reading process" (Wilson 1983: 43). Readers thus become comfortable with a particular narrative design and layout for a magazine and when some radical restructuring occurs, as when a magazine begins a new volume or undergoes a change of editorship, it causes reader discontent. For example, when *Gramophone* introduced its cover-mounted disc in 1993, readers expressed ambivalence about its value: some saw it as an opportunity to hear what they had only read about, while others saw it as yet another "deeply unwanted CD" (Pollard 1998a: 179–81).[21] The fact that the list of records reviewed in each issue of the magazine is positioned at the rear is something many readers find not just inconvenient but counterintuitive.

Running through the many thousands of issues of record magazines that have been published since the 1920s, though, there is an underlying structure for which the early issues of *Gramophone* provided the ground plan. The main feature of this plan are those centrally located pages devoted to the record review, whose narrative architecture will be the subject of chapter 7. To either side of the reviews are the editorials, feature articles, and news items, together with the magazine's main navigational aids, its content pages and, in the case of *Gramophone*, indexes to reviews and advertisers. The way this text is ordered constitutes a textual hierarchy of sorts, with important narrative such as the editorials located in the magazine's front regions and more marginal narrative such as the classifieds in the back. Here it is important to differentiate between text generated within the confines of the magazine, such as the reviews and feature articles, and text generated outside them, such as advertisements, which are themselves prominent and telling parts of the magazine's architecture and reveal much about their readers' musical tastes. For example, those ads appearing in *Classic FM*, a magazine that promotes the idea that music is a pivotal part of an "epicurean" lifestyle, are by and large related to travel, food, and wine. To this end, the magazine's interviews with musicians often focus on epicurean matters; that with Norwegian pianist Lief Ove Adnes elicited the fact that he was a fan of noodles and Japanese cuisine and even included a recipe for his favorite dish (Fox 2002).[22] By contrast, the ads appearing in *Gramophone*, whose readers see music as the *sine qua non* of the good life and for whom there is no need to travel much beyond the "best seat in the house," are almost without exception devoted to records and high fidelity equipment. Indeed, when the magazine was enjoining its readers to subscribe to the National Gramophone Society in the 1920s, it suggested that sacrificing an aspect of this good life, namely "two gaspers a day," would be more than enough to pay for ten of Hugo Wolf's songs (Pollard 1998a: 40).

The percentage of pages devoted to advertising varies between magazines and, according to the vagaries of the market, over time. The percentage in *Gramophone* is higher than in equivalent magazines but not as high as it was in the 1970s.[23] This suggests that the markets for records and their reproduction, which did not yet have to compete with other forms of electronic *divertissement,* had reached a peak during that period. On the other hand, a dramatic reduction in this percentage usually signifies that a magazine is in financial trouble. Just prior to its re-merger with *Music and Musicians, Records and Recording* was almost totally devoid of advertising for its last seven issues. Its last issue only carried two advertisements—one for cigarettes, the other for a book club—hardly a vote of support from the record industry.

The other form of "external" text is drawn from the readers of record magazines. It is manifested in at least two quarters: the classifieds and letters pages. The former were modeled on the exchange and mart format and first appeared in *The Gramophone* in October 1931. They have traditionally serviced a range of wants and needs ("15s OFFERED for perfect copy of Paderewski, DB 3183 Haydn Variations"), including personal ones ("Young man would like to meet others interested in classical music").

Readers' letters generate a feeling of connectedness across the record community, among readers, record journalists and reviewers, and record industry staffers.[24] They also provide a conduit for readers/record consumers to air their phonographic grievances, as well as a forum for exchanging ideas about the state of recording. They comprise a consumer editorial on the industry that often exercises its right of reply. They also provide a dialogue with the contents of the magazine—an opportunity for readers to reprimand and correct reviewers when they are guilty of factual error or ill-judged assessments. In other words, through the letters pages of record magazines the record collector can strike back with his own chirography: the reader, at the outer regions of the record, so to speak, can set off a chain reaction that might eventually lead to a label issuing a work that a letter writer has suggested is long overdue for recording. Not infrequently, series of letters dealing with themes of topical concern extend over several issues of the magazine, in which readers "dialogue" with one another. One feature of the narrative architecture of record magazines is thus the degree to which their readers are able to write themselves into their texts and become themselves the subjects of the magazine's contents. Nor is this limited to the letters pages. A recent addition to *Gramophone* is the feature "One to One," in which readers have the opportunity to interview a well-known recording artist. Another is the "Audio Clinic," which enables readers to have their high fidelity systems undergo a "health" check by the magazine's "audio doctor."

In *Gramophone*, at least, in line with its long-standing commitment to extending the record catalogue into "undiscovered" regions of music, a significant quotient of letters have dealt with neglected repertoire. They have urged the recording of unjustly overlooked works and bemoaned the release of yet more versions of the "warhorses" ("So with Gungl, Linke, Eysler and Zeller I suggest EMI have ample material for more of their entertaining records"). But as the catalog has expanded, particularly during the CD era, this theme has moved to the backburner. Like much else in their contents, then, the letters page of record magazines is a powerful index of the times, registering the major issues of concern among record consumers. The deteriorating quality of LPs was a frequent issue of complaint during the 1970s, until they were superseded by CDs. The many letters on the subject eventually inspired articles that examined their claims and found that LPs were not what they once were and at least 25 percent of them were faulty (Borwick 1978). This concern also evinced responses from some record labels, including countervailing advertisements. For example, the independent Saga attempted to take market advantage of the climate of execrable LPs and championed the idea in one of its advertisements that its LPs were quieter than those of its competitors; it included a letter from EMG asseverating this claim.[25]

In fact, there is a complex dialogue between the various departments of the record magazine. Letters, articles, advertisements, and editorials are all subject to regular claim and counterclaim. Advertisements especially provide instances of this intratextual dialogue. They play out, visualize, and crystallize the rifts existing between various phonographic discourses, giving them pithy and succinct expression. Two advertisements from the 1970s demonstrate the nature of such complex textual interplay, in this case the ongoing conflict between music in its preserved and live states.

The first, from Decca, exemplifies the nature of the conflict using a pecuniary "illustration" that contrasts the price of two tickets for superb seats at Covent Garden, a minimum cost of £30, with Decca's new recording of *I Puritani*. "Hear the same artists"—Sutherland and Pavarotti—"from the *best seats in your own house* [my emphasis] and permanently yours for only £9.75." The second, from Quad, interrogates this claim and raises the matter of whether the concert hall can ever be fully "domesticated." It asks its readers why music still sounds better in a concert hall than it does at home. It thus provides a counterdiscourse to the Decca advertisement, suggesting that the best seat in the house can never fully replicate the *best seat in the house*—that

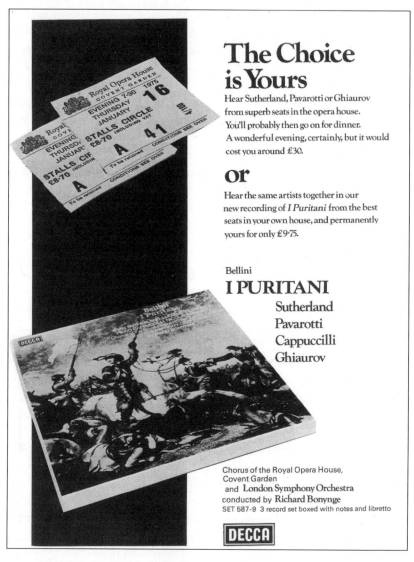

Figure 6.1 This advertisement, originally appearing in *Gramophone* (July 1975), explores the pecuniary advantages of owning an LP set of *I Puritani:* it is much cheaper than a "wonderful evening" at the opera followed by dinner at around £30 total, and it provides a listening experience equivalent to that available from the best seat in an opera house (as represented by Tickets A40 and A41, where most members of an opera audience would not be able to sit). Moreover, the experience—unlike that of the opera house—is "permanently yours." (Reproduced by permission of the editor of *Gramophone*.)

If QUAD amplifiers are so perfect, why does it still sound better in the concert hall?

In real life, the sounds from all the instruments and sometimes parts thereof are independently radiated and so are not 'phase locked' together nor are they subjected to common eigentones.

These mutually incoherent wavefronts are subjected to tiny but important reflections at the pinna and finally end up as just two channels representing the pressure at the two ear drums. It is not possible to achieve this transfer accurately by means of loud-speakers or headphones however good these components may be.

Nevertheless with good amplifiers and loudspeakers (and on those occasions when the people at the recording and transmitting end get it right) a musical experience can be achieved which is extremely satisfying and one of the greatest pleasures of our time.

For further details on the full range of QUAD products write to: The Acoustical Manufacturing Co. Ltd., Huntingdon, Cambs. PE18 7DB.
Tel: (0480) 52561

QUAD
for the closest approach to the original sound
QUAD *is a Registered Trade Mark*

Figure 6.2 This defining moment in audio advertising from Acoustical Manufacturing Company (Quad) appeared in *Gramophone* (December 1979). It expresses some reservations about the viability of the keystone discourse. Note the bolded slogan "for the closest approach to the original sound," whose appositeness the preceding copy helps to explain, and also the two concert tickets, metonyms of the keystone discourse, which are "overshadowed" by the Quad amplifier. (Reproduced by permission of Quad and the editor of the *Gramophone*.)

the keystone discourse is, in fact, a flawed one. It provides a scientific explanation for this: musical instruments radiate their sounds discretely, as "mutually incoherent wavefronts" that can never be represented accurately "by means of loud-speakers or headphones[,] however good these components may be"—and those of Quad, it is purported, are "good." However, these limitations notwithstanding, recordings can provide "a musical experience . . . which is extremely satisfying and one of the great pleasures of our time." But they will never be enough to completely displace—*contra* Glenn Gould—the concert, metonymically represented in the advertisement by two tickets. Thus recordings might be "permanently yours," but the impermanency of the concert remains superior. In revealing the truth about the keystone discourse, Quad hopes that it can still sell its speakers and amplifiers to those consumers interested in an auditory event that approaches the reality of the concert hall (Figures 6.1 and 6.2).

Thus, magazines constitute an active discourse in which phonographic "truths" are always contested and recontested, shaped and reshaped. They are not inert texts but strongly interactive, encouraging their readers to write in, and to write themselves into their texts. In doing so, magazines are able to monitor the demographics of their readerships, rendering them more transparent in terms of social profile and location. Thus it was known by 1925 that *The Gramophone* readership already had a global reach that extended from "China to Peru, from Spitzbergen to Invercargill" (Mackenzie 1967: 70), and that it included a few aristocrats, including the young Viscount Lascelles (later Lord Harewood)—a regular correspondent to the magazine while at Eton—and the Maharajah of Mysore. It was also known that, by and large, the readership of *The Gramophone,* as with other magazines of its ilk, was an overwhelmingly male one, a recognition that the gramophone constituted as "much a male hobby as bowls" (Mackenzie 1955: 137).[26] This continues to be the case today. A check of the forty-one letters published during the first six months of 2001 indicated that only two were from women.

Two other devices have been used to elicit information about a magazine's readership: the competition and the survey. The *Gramophone* has deployed both in its history. Two examples of the former will suffice: in December 1927, a competition invited readers to identify the "best electrical recording"; in August 1939, another asked readers to nominate which among their favorite musical works they would most like to see recorded. A regular feature of *The Gramophone* in the prewar years, competitions nevertheless disappeared from its pages in the 1950s and have only recently returned with the advent of the cover-mounted CD, which includes a competition with it ("Identify the seven Second Symphonies"; "Identify the five works depicting musical storms").

Regular surveys of *The Gramophone*'s readership began in September 1931 and have continued to the present. In the 1931 survey, 460 "opinions" were received in response to a questionnaire regarding how readers felt about the various contents of the magazine, which revealed that most readers regarded the "Analytical Reviews of New Recordings of Big Works" as supremely valuable (Mackenzie 1931b: 111).

The general absence of competitions from classical record magazines reinforces the ethos of seriousness that is a mark of classical music. Yet in its early years, *The Gramophone*—and *High Fidelity* even more so—displayed a degree of levity, with cartoons and humorous stories as regular features, especially at Christmas time, when even serious music lovers allow levity to enter their lives. Generally though, record magazines are not notable for their irreverence or self-deprecation. And in spite of Mackenzie's own literary preoccupations, only a few poems and short stories have ever appeared in the pages of *Gramophone*.[27] Indeed, the tone of the magazine is preeminently technical and musical, with few textual opportunities to exercise fantasy. Whatever fantasies readers enter into relate to the commodity realm, to the products advertised in its pages. The only respite from the serious business of record analysis occurs in the occasional advertisements that draw attention themselves through visual and verbal puns (Redfern 1984: 131). Those accompanying the launch of Decca's LPs were typical; via a series of comic motifs, they pressed home the LP's inevitable ascendancy to the phonographic throne and implied that those who hold out against it will eventually be laughed out of court (see Figure 4.1).

Games such as quizzes and crosswords, often found in other magazines, are also generally absent in classical record magazines as part of their prevailing seriousness. When they are present, it tends to be a one-off rather than a regular event.[28] Nor are self-discovery texts—those personality inventories enabling individuals to profile themselves in popular women's magazines—present in record magazines. This might reflect the fact that those who write for record magazines are mostly male, as are their readers.[29] A recent survey of *Gramophone*'s readership showed that it was not only male but also aged between 45 and 65 and earning substantially more than average as members of the "professional classes." A quarter of them owned more than 500 CDs and one-tenth owned reproducing equipment worth more than 4000 pounds (Jolly 1994: 1). Not much has changed. The 1931 survey revealed that a quarter of *The Gramophone*'s readership belonged to the "scholastic classes": "clerks in holy orders, music teachers, and journalists" (Mackenzie 1931b: 111). However, its overwhelmingly male readership is not manifest in masculine iconography. There are no scantily clad girls, a feature of other male magazines (e.g. *Sports Illustrated*), and if there were, it would be seen in the same vein as a décolleté woman on an LP cover (Windreich 1956), as a severe lapse of taste.

The Technologizing Process: Magazines as Etiquette Manuals

In some respects record magazines play a similar role to the etiquette manuals of the past. These assisted to produce the conduct of a civil society, which had developed from court society and which codified ways of deporting the body. Among other matters, these manuals led to the suppression and internalization of what were seen as unseemly conducts, helping to further the "civilizing process" (Elias 1994). This process now continues in the columns of magazines, for they help their readers to acquire appropriate modes of behavior in unfamiliar domains, including those of technology. For while magazines have provided guidance in a world of bewildering choice regarding commodities and activities (Schneirov 1994: 100), they also tell individuals how to act in relation to these commodities and activities, many of which are new and alien. They perform educational functions and are part and parcel of the "technologizing process," advising individuals on how to relate to their gadgets and optimize their performance.

One can see the technologizing process taking place in the contents of record magazines. Advice columns abound, such as the aforementioned "Audio Clinic," where readers seek solutions to problems besetting their equipment. The phonographic novice, for whom the various protocols and vocabularies of the record culture are new, is one of the readers that all magazines attempt to address when framing their editorial remits (Schneirov 1994: 96). It was for this reader that *The Gramophone* in January 1930 launched its "Novice Corner," which appeared on and off until the 1950s and was aimed at the "complete beginner." It gave advice on a range of technical and musical matters and covered the basics of gramophones and music, such as describing the virtues of "fibre needles" and explaining the correct way to pronounce "Yehudi Menuhin." Its purposes were didactic and designed to protect the novice from committing a phonographic *faux pas*. But "Novice Corner" was also admitting that person into the society of "gramophiles," moving them by degree from its periphery to its center, from knowing how to pronounce its basic terms to the meanings and values associated with its "magisterial discourses" (Bourdieu and Passeron 1977: 108–109). Such novice corners, though not often as transparently basic as the *The Gramophone*'s, are a frequent feature of record magazines and have taken a variety of forms, from advice on what to include in a basic record collection to how to care for LPs. They have also included information on how to "domesticate" stereo equipment.

In the 1960s and 1970s *High Fidelity* published many articles on home acoustics and "stereo décor," including floor plans that showed where and where not to locate speakers. Many of these articles were intended to appease the "wives" who, as was often alleged, were unhappy about the amount of space records and speakers "colonized" (Mackenzie 1955: 136; Horn 1978).[30] They were also illustrated with actual homes that had been able to tastefully accommodate a stereo system—moreover, in a way that did not compromise its sound. One such article suggested that the best solution was to incorporate a hi-fi system into the actual fabric of the room and align its components "with other aspects of the good life." It was suggested that it be incorporated into the bar, alongside the television, as part of the home's "pleasure center." The intent of such articles was to "naturalize" stereo and give the impression that its various components were normal parts of the 1960s home; though they were admittedly not *objets d'art,* they could nonetheless complement other furnishings in a modern room (Anderson 1964).

One of the other implied readers, at least of *The Gramophone* in the first few years of publication, before Christopher Stone leavened its content, was the aesthete steeped in the traditions of a liberal education, who was comfortable with the magazine's affectation of "magisterial discourse." For example, Mackenzie's "Prologue" (1923a: 1) came with Latin tags, and the magazine's letter column originally carried the epigraph *de gustibus non est disputandum* (there is no arguing about matters of taste). Mackenzie's editorials were imbued with erudite allusions and excess pedantry. The monolingual reader could expect to struggle with their polyglot register, for the most part a product of a classical education. How much the exhibition of erudition was rhetorical, intended to proselytize the phonographically apostate and to convince them that there was a cadre of "learned men" who were in no doubts about the musical merits of the gramophone, is a moot point. One suspects instead that the register was regarded as natural for the times. For forty years later, in the context of the United States at least, the linguistic registers of record criticism were more vernacular and more conscious of the alienating effects of a magisterial register. In the interests of maintaining their readerships, such magazines valued accessible and readable prose, and they were apologetic when this was absent. When *High Fidelity* published Glenn Gould's *The Prospects of Recording,* it was accompanied with an editorial *mea culpa* acknowledging that many readers might find Gould's language objectionable but urging them, in the interests of being exposed to its rich insights, to persevere (Gould 1966). Incidentally, one who found

Gould's sesquipedalian prose objectionable was record producer John Culshaw (1966).

Record magazines are defined by their times. This is reflected not just in their articles and reviews—whose growth in numbers is a powerful index of the sheer numbers of records now being produced across the world—but also by their advertisements, which provide telling epitaphs, simply by their absence, of labels and companies, retailers and manufacturers long since departed, along with much of the equipment and the technologies with which they were associated. At the same time, they also provide evidence of phonographic longevity via advertisements for those companies that have survived almost the entire history of the phonograph, albeit in merged states, such as HMV and Deutsche Grammophon. The retail industry is another prominent "player" in the pages of record magazines, certainly from the 1930s onward when specialist dealers of the ilk of EMG and Henry Stave regularly advertised in such magazines.

Record magazines also provide sites where the genealogy of the recording industry and all its various material progeny are paginated and given textual inscription: cases for carrying LPs, furniture and cabinets for storing records and hi-fi equipment, software for managing record collections, and so on, many of which are quaint curiosities now obsolete. The pages of record magazines thus record the life and death cycle of many of the commercial ventures associated with the recording industry. In the "thick description" of their pages the record industry is textually re-incarnated and is given a form of permanency long after its material manifestations have passed.

Thus the broad intent of record magazines, and magazines in general, is to incorporate their readers, to act on their behaviors and conducts, and to insist that if they are to obtain the most from records and music they must change their attitudes, rearrange their rooms, and pronounce "Menuhin" correctly. Record magazines have been instrumental in the formation of requisite phonographic habits and have helped facilitate the shifts to new paradigms of recording. With the coming of LPs, for example, the wisdom associated with needles was replaced by that of the LP, wisdom that was, and continues to be—at least its modern-day equivalent—transmitted via the record magazine. Through their manifold texts the many processes associated with recording are produced, reproduced, and re-produced in conjunction with the advent of new formats. Magazines are one of the important organs of osmosis through which the discourses and grammars of recording are generated and regenerated and then given textual form and shape—they infect their readers with an enthusiasm for records and recording and convey the "working knowledge" associated with recording into the life of the ordinary record collector. And each time their readers turn their pages and make records and their various accessories an integral part of their phonographic lives, they are also helping to produce and instantiate the discourses that lie at the heart of the record industry and its operations. To end where the chapter began: it is not so much that record magazines "reflects the minds of their readers" as it is that they help to create those minds in the first place; this is where most of their significance derives.

CHAPTER SEVEN

Compact Discourse
The Review of the Gramophone

◆

> In succession I tried half a dozen editions of Tennyson by as many different
> elocutionists, and by the time I had heard "Where Claribel low lieth" rendered by a
> soprano, a contralto, a bass, and baritone, each with the full effect of its quality and
> the personal equation besides, I was quite ready to admit that selecting phonographed
> books for one's library was much more difficult as it was incomparably more
> fascinating than suiting one's self with printed editions.
> —Edward Bellamy, "With the Eyes Shut," 743

Although the recording industry has transformed musical culture in dramatic
ways, appraisals of its impact have, for the most part, concentrated on the paradigm shifts undergone by the industry, which have rendered whole formats
of recording obsolete in the pursuit of the holy grail of absolute sound. This
has obscured the fact that the industry has also been associated with myriad
cultural practices as significant in their own ways as these continuing shifts.
These complementary practices have been much less subject to description
and analysis. While on the surface they might appear peripheral to the recording industry and its own practices, they have been, and remain, central to
elaborating the culture of the phonograph beyond its various technological
manifestations. The emergence of a specialized retail industry to market
records and stimulate consumer interest in their acquisition was one of the
more important of these phenomena. It was to service its various needs and
act as a go-between for the consumer and record producer that a corpus of
"literature" emerged in the latter parts of the nineteenth century, when the
sheer numbers of recordings had reached unmanageable proportions. At first
much of this literature consisted of inventory texts, catalogs of the recorded
repertoire that now provided "traces" of the range of music available on disc.

But once the musical potential of recording was realized and much of the
hostility toward recording on the part of the musical establishment had mellowed, a more analytic literature emerged that contained the critical tools to

scrutinize rather than merely *record* recordings. This more critical discourse, which was equipped with an indigenous language and epistemology for evaluating recordings, had its ascendancy during the 1920s, when specialized magazines devoted to recordings and their audition began to appear. Those magazines have gone on to become even more specialized, either in terms of the parts of the recorded repertoire that they examine or the musical propensities of their readers, which divide into two distinct camps: those more interested in the sound aspects of recording, and those more interested in the musical aspects. As was noted in the previous chapter, a core part of the narrative architecture of the record magazine is the record review, which has become a specialist genre of music criticism with its own community of textual engineers—connoisseurs in the art of judging records.

Histories and analyses of record culture (Gelatt 1977; Gronow and Saunio 1998; Millard 1995; Read and Welch 1976) have, for the most part, overlooked the role that record reviews have played in the development of the record industry. The failure to examine this aspect of phonographic culture has been particularly pronounced in the domain of classical music, whose paradigms of scholarship have tended to eschew analytic approaches that highlight the importance of contextual factors in the culture of music (Green 1988; Negus 1999). When applied to that of rock music, for example, contextual approaches have illuminated the ways "fanzines" and other musical texts have contributed to the codification and dissemination of rock music, for the circulation of rock music is a mediated process involving many types of textual intervention that are critical for advancing some recordings while retarding others. The matter of musical preference is a complex phenomenon, difficult to predict and determine, let alone control and manage, as many in the industry have found to their cost (Frith 1996; Hirsch 1990).

The choices of the record consuming public have their origins in a variety of sources, of which record magazines are but one. Such magazines assist in determining the record preferences of their readers and provide much-needed information about the appreciation and audition of records. In the case of classical music there are, currently, a number of such record magazines that have considerable authority among collectors and dealers and consist, in the main, of reviews of compact discs and audio equipment. I will argue in this chapter that these reviews provide insights into the discourses of musical reproduction and the ways in which various qualities of discs have been evaluated and enunciated. Indeed, record reviews constitute ideal textual sites for identifying and tracing the discontinuities and continuities apparent in the discourses of record reproduction. This chapter examines the morphologies of record reviews and argues that as a normative genre they utilize a variety of rhetorical tactics not all that different from those exercised in other realms of "tasteful" judgment. In the end, compilers of record reviews

are skilled and professional exponents of musical judgment, that least understood of critical processes (Frith 1996: 11), and the way it is exemplified in reviews reveals much about how recorded music is regarded.

A Review of the Record Review

The record review's narrative architecture is similar to that of the book review, a "literary" genre that only emerged in the periodical of the eighteenth
century before spreading to newspapers and political weeklies in the nineteenth century (Walford 1986). Although record reviews are mostly concentrated in specialized record magazines, they can also be found in general interest magazines, newspapers, periodicals, and scholarly journals. Most of
the "quality" broadsheets and lifestyle magazines in the United States,
United Kingdom, and Australia have at one time or another carried record
reviews as part of their remits to provide a broad coverage of the culture industries. Some U.S. magazines that originally boasted a "literary" focus, such
as *Atlantic Monthly* and the *Saturday Review,* also eventually published
record reviews.[1] When Irving Kolodin assumed the editorship of the *Saturday Review*'s record supplement in December 1949, he created a record magazine within a magazine. But the presence of record reviews in what were
fundamentally literary magazines also reflected the alliance between books
and records that early record journalists had fostered.

Record reviews are also to be found in specialist instrument magazines
such as *The Strad,* where the focus of attention, as one might expect, is
mostly on recordings of string music. In more scholarly journals devoted to
music, the practice of reviewing records is more sporadic and has, in the past,
been actively resisted, another reflection of the scholarly ambivalence toward
mechanized music. As was noted in the previous chapter, the *Musical Quarterly* only commenced reviewing records in 1952, and then only within strict
guidelines that emphasized the evaluation of their musical merits (Day 2000:
228). For example, one of its first record reviewers observed that "senseless
cuts"—which had become rare by the 1950s—would not be countenanced
and recordings "thus disfigured" would never be commended. And following the precedent set by E.M.G.'s *Monthly Letter,* some record dealers have
published review magazines and newsletters as well. London's Henry Stave
was one; its magazine *Consensus* claimed to offer "original and unbiased cri-
tiques of current records."[2]

Record reviews have also been featured on radio programs.[3] They have
drawn on their magazine equivalents as models, with one notable difference:
they were able to provide sound excerpts to illustrate their reviews. John
Lade's *Record Review,* first broadcast on the BBC in 1957, was such a pro-

gram. Reviews were only one part of its remit, which also included regular news items on the record industry and features such as building a record library, similar to those found in record magazines. Due to time considerations, of course, Lade had to be more economical than a magazine in selecting recordings to illustrate his reviews. He could never, in what was a short program, hope to review—let alone provide sound examples of—the hundred or so recordings issued each month, a high proportion of which were reviewed in the record magazines of the time (Lade 1958: 2).

However, for the most part record reviews have been concentrated in record magazines, which have an international circulation despite mostly emanating from Europe and North America, the global centers of record production and consumption. The narrative morphology of these magazines, like that of magazines in general, is segmented and differentiated. This derives from the nature of the magazine itself, which is fundamentally a serial publication that strives to be informative and current through a montage of narrative forms, including news items and feature articles, illustrations and advertising. This montage is not continuous or linear but sectionalized, with strong demarcations around a series of microtexts dealing with the major subject matter of the magazine and providing a literal "context" to its cornerstone text, in this case the record review. The magazine's narrative montage also has a strong temporal focus, marked not just in terms of the frequency with which it appears but also by the fact that many of its narratives are episodic within the magazine's periodic structure. Thus feature articles continue over into subsequent issues and sometimes into volume after volume, and readers come to anticipate their presence as part of the ongoing "historical" saga that is recording. For part of the temporal compass of record magazines is also worked out through their contents—through articles that deal with the present, past, and future of the recording industry. The record review, because it deals with new releases, by and large reinforces the magazine's obligation to the present tense.

Record reviews belong to a special category of texts called "dependency texts." Like book and film reviews, the record review is not entirely autonomous but predicated upon the pre-existence of another "text" upon which it casts judgment. Without records, there would be no reviews—or, for that matter, reviewers, not even imaginary ones such as poor demented Claude Hummel, who was finally unhinged by "too many records and, especially, too many album notes." "The last entries in his diary recall the effects of reviewing as many as eleven records a day, which leaves Hummel in a state of utter gloom and despondency" that eventually drives him to take his own life. (Mayer 1961: 153).[4]

The record review exhibits a distinctive narrative morphology that easily differentiates it from other departments found in record magazines. This morphology has a number of structural and temporal parameters relating to the length of the review and the time in which it must be completed in order to maximize its relevance in relation to when a disc is released and when it is likely to be under the critical spotlight. A review cannot be overlong or over-due. Structurally speaking, the text of the review is situated between a head-ing protocol that is magazine specific and a cognomen identifying or disguis-ing (e.g. "Discus") its author. Following the practice of other review magazines and papers, *The Gramophone* did not at first identify its reviewers, only doing so on a regular basis from the late 1940s onward and then only by initials that were spelled out elsewhere in the magazine. In fact, it was only in the 1990s that reviewers began to be named in full at the end of their reviews. Although occasionally some of its reviewers used pseudonyms ("Newman Passage"), particularly in the magazine's early days, this was never a common practice (Walker 1998a: 195).

The relationship of a review to a record is fundamentally interfacial; the review provides an interpretive lens through which to "see" a record. It vari-ously proclaims the record's presence in the world. However, unlike an entry in an inventory text such as a catalogue, which serves a similar function, a re-view performs something extra: an evaluative function, drawing attention to a record's various strengths and weaknesses. In doing so—and not all record magazines follow the practice—reviewers also undertake a comparative analysis of a recording relative to others of the same work in the catalogue, both current and past. The review thereby performs normative and informa-tive functions, combining the acts of promulgation and evaluation. But the latter is the preeminent function of the review and derives from the fact that recordings are rarely perfect but exhibit a range of material, technical, and in-terpretive failings of varying magnitudes of severity with which listeners might or might not be able to live.

The raison d'être of the review derives from the fact that in a world of commodity oversupply, consumers need to be able to make informed choices about their purchases, and in order to do so they need access to professional determinations of the commodity's merits. In many magazines—*BBC Music Magazine,* for example (though interestingly, not *Gramophone*)—these processes of qualitative judgment are subject to semiotic calibration, which enables readers to determine at a glance the recording's merits. This is facili-tated through the use of a three- or five-point calibration scale that has been used since Karl Baedeker's travel guides pioneered it to grade and rank serv-ices and commodities: three for an outstanding product, one for an inferior one. Most record magazines, in fact, utilize two scales: one to calibrate a record's performance, the other, its engineering—a phonographic version of the great musical schism. To these the *BBC Record Magazine* has added a third, a "value for money" scale, along with other "symbolic" judgments consumers might find useful and pertinent. For example, the CD considered the "best available version" of a work—the so-called "benchmark recording"—is identified with a trophy alongside its title and catalog number.

When *The Gramophone* appeared, it was the first magazine of its type to be exclusively devoted to record reviews. Among the contents of its inaugural issue was a "Prologue" in which its editor summarized the magazine's philosophy and obligations. These included the statement that the magazine was primarily an "organ of candid opinion" whose first loyalty was to the "numerous possessors of gramophones" who needed protection from the exaggerated claims of record advertising. For example, an advertisement that Columbia placed in the first issue of the magazine described one of its discs as featuring "Britain's Greatest Basso" and "perhaps the most awesome song on record—a triumph of vivid reproduction." The magazine set out to assay such claims, and if they could be sustained, endorse them (Mackenzie 1923a: 1).

Interestingly, this desire to protect consumers from the unscrupulous tactics of advertising copywriters was still being used to justify the existence of new record magazines fifty years later. An editorial in the short-lived *Gramophone Record Review* claimed that the "hidden persuaders"—a reference to Vance Packard's pioneering work on advertising—were dominating the record industry and subjecting consumers to the tactics of "psycho-seduction," against which the new magazine supposedly afforded protection. It was also suggested that LP covers were part of these tactics and that they exerted undue influence over consumers; more honesty would prevail if records were issued in plain brown paper bags (Hibbs 1960: 381).

In the case of *The Gramophone*, which provided the evaluative framework for subsequent record magazines, the function of being an "organ of candid opinion" was fulfilled in a number of ways and in a number of domains. But these took some time before they were regularized and have been subject to regular alteration and redesignation ever since. For example, at first Mackenzie felt an obligation to review piano rolls, since they also represented mechanized music, but following reader complaints decrying the practice, he dropped them (Mackenzie 1955: 115). The choice of records that were sent out for review encompassed recordings of popular music. In fact, right up until the 1990s *Gramophone* had always reviewed popular records, in spite of Mackenzie's hostile attitudes toward such music; these records included, at one stage, rock, as well as forms of music occupying the borderlands of "serious" music, such as jazz and world music. Indeed, the ambit of recordings that the magazine has reviewed during its long history has even included nonmusical areas such as wildlife and spoken word recordings. However, by the end of the twentieth century its review ambit had become more avowedly classical in focus. Thus many recordings on the classical "borderlands" that would have been reviewed in the past, albeit within separate departments of the magazine, are either not reviewed at all or incorporated into its main review sections. In the past, film music, for example, would have had a department to itself.[5] However, this exclusion has not applied to audio equipment, which began to be reviewed in the third issue of the magazine.

Thus as an "organ of candid opinion" *The Gramophone* had from its outset a broad range of editorial obligations whose satisfaction, it was hoped, would result in its readers exercising more discretion when acquiring discs and equipment (Pollard 1998a: 27). In an approving letter written to Mackenzie soon after the magazine's launch, Gordon Bottomley, poet and self-proclaimed "gramophil [*sic*]," noted that prior to the publication of *The Gramophone*, purchasers of records for the most part had remained in the dark about the wisdom of their choices (Mackenzie 1967: 140). Thus reviews, in theory at least, have always stopped collectors from purchasing records with which they would eventually be disappointed and have thereby helped them to avoid wasting their money. Indeed, record magazines in the past have been formally promoted as having the pecuniary welfare of record consumers in mind. An advertisement for *High Fidelity* headed "Just for the Record," appearing in various magazines in 1970, claimed that a subscription to the magazine made sound economic sense, since it could potentially save its readers "a fortune in records and tapes" and a somewhat bigger (and the word was capitalized) amount in stereo equipment.[6]

Thus record magazines have been championed in terms of their caveat emptor function, which is at its most pervasive in their review departments, which are subject to various forms of categorization. The most general level of categorization divides the reviews of audio equipment from those of the various recording formats, including in the past tapes and cassettes and these days DVD. Typically, more sound-oriented magazines have favored audio equipment reviews by positioning them forward in the magazine, always a telling index of editorial priorities. The reviews of CDs, generally much fewer in number than in record magazines yet covering more segments of the musical spectrum, including rock and jazz—audio superiority is not only the preserve of classical music—are positioned toward the back.[7]

On the surface, this positional "rhetoric" might appear trivial, but it actually carries deep significance in the overall fabric of the record magazine's narrative environment and is revealing of the hidden "orders" governing musical values and culture. The highlighting of certain texts relative to others, their placement in favored positions, and the percentage of pages devoted to them are all potent symbols of the hierarchies pervading music. Noting their comings and goings can help decode the powerful reworking of these hierarchies.

The Gramophone Record Review from 1923 to 2003

In the first issue of *Gramophone*'s eightieth volume, in which its narrative architecture, as sometimes happens at a publication milestone, underwent layout "surgery," twelve out of 138 pages were devoted to the review of audio equipment and thirty-seven to CDs and DVDs. This translates into 125 reviews—moreover, "by the world's greatest critics," a fact emphasized on the magazine's cover as it seeks to dominate a market in which other magazines have claimed numerical superiority in the review department ("150 CDs Reviewed and Rated"; "Over 200 CDs Reviewed"). It is also of note that as the number of reviews has increased, their arrangement has been reset to facilitate more alacritous modes of accessing them, a change that recognizes demands on the reader's time. This recognition is also evident in *Gramophone*'s current highlighting of reviews of significant releases, usually those selected as "Records of the Month," and its placement of review extracts in its "pretext" regions near the contents pages. Oddly, in spite of the fact that record reviews are a core part of their narrative architectures, the various anniversary anthologies drawn from such magazines have not to date included representative examples of them.[8]

The narrative guidelines governing the content of record reviews were established at an early point in the magazine's history. These included the need to provide historical commentary on the music, an estimation of the proficiency of its performance, and, finally, an assessment of the technical merits of the recording. An early correspondent to the magazine originally suggested these guidelines (Robertson 1973: 21)—another example of the way magazines obtain guidance from their readers. To these was added, at the beginning of the LP era, commentary on the accuracy of the cover notes and the aptness, if any, of the cover design, to whose errors of presentation reviewers often drew attention.[9] Thus the reviewing guidelines have always kept "in tune" with the changes to phonographic presentation. In spite of these changes, though, the function of a record review has remained what it always was, to "characterise a performance with such vividness that the reader takes over from the critic as the final arbiter" (Jolly 1998: 202).

Gramophone reviews can be categorized into two main types. The first comprises the individual reviews devoted, in the main, to new releases and re-releases—though these days, except in the case of exceptional recordings, the latter rarely have reviews to themselves. The number of these individual reviews per month has increased steadily from the 1920s, when it was around twenty. This is a textual vindication of the dramatic growth in the number of records released each month in the past eight decades, for in spite of the perennial crises said to afflict the classical recording industry, the number of individual releases each month, many of them from the independents, has increased dramatically. The growth in the size of the magazine, summarized in the previous chapter but worth reiterating, also provides a dramatic index of this expansion. The inaugural volume (1923/4) was a mere 261 pages; volume seventy-nine (2001/2) was close to 1800. Furthermore, as is clear from the lists of new releases included in *Gramophone,* many more discs are released per month than are ever reviewed.[10] Some record labels, such as Nimbus, refused for a period to submit records for review on the grounds that the magazine's reviewers rarely displayed much sympathy for the "chamber acoustic" that was a hallmark of its recordings (Griffiths 1995: 187).[11] By contrast, Telarc, with its reputation as a sound-for-sound's-sake label, faced a different problem: *Gramophone* (like the *New York Times*) would not review—it now does—its discs (Brown 1993: 42).

The second major category of review is the "essay" review. Much longer and more probing than that devoted to a single CD, it takes as its purview a series of recordings exhibiting a common theme or musical genre. Starting in the postwar period and continuing through to the present, such essays have become a regular feature of the *Gramophone*—part of its episodic architecture. They appear every quarter. Reviewers long associated with the magazine compile them using their expertise in a particular realm of musical repertoire ("Early Music Retrospect"; "Carols"; "French Baroque Music"). Then there are the various *reviews* of the reviews, which provide a second evaluation of new releases focusing on specific aspects of their production. The now defunct feature "Sounds in Retrospect" was typical. First appearing in December 1971, it responded to the growing interest in the "technical aspects of gramophone records," and its contents dealt in a more exhaustive way with the sound of LPs and CDs than was possible in the "regular reviews" (Panel Review 1971: 1007). There are also the essay reviews focusing specifically on musical matters and undertaking comparative reviews of particular compositions. Their function has become more exigent as the catalogue has expanded ("The Gramophone Collection"; "Master Class"). Finally, other types of essay review deal with particular categories of recordings, such as budget reissues ("Replay"; "Heliodor Reissues"; "Classical Reissues"), which typically offer short, pithy assessments.

The section in *Gramophone* originally devoted to single reviews was entitled "Analytical Notes and First Reviews"; the title, like many aspects of *Gramophone,* was preserved for many decades, until 1970, when it was retitled "Classical Record Reviews." In 1975, when the magazine's layout was revamped, this title was embedded in a panel of faces made up of composers from Monteverdi to Shostakovich, a telling reflection of the canon of music to which the magazine was committed.

One of the magazine's other longstanding conventions is the system of categories under which the reviews are grouped. It was adopted in the magazine's first issue and has remained more or less unchanged to the present. Sometimes categories were added, such as "Electronic Music" or "Gregorian Chant," but these were temporary departments existing outside the main review departments, which have remained the same: orchestral, chamber music, instrumental, choral and song (now "vocal"), and opera. What is more, other classical magazines have adopted much the same categorical architecture, though not always in the *Gramophone* order. Those categories of music outside the bounds of classical have typically been reviewed in separate departments; eventually, as mentioned previously, they were dropped. These other departments were usually located in the back regions of the magazine and had many fewer pages devoted to them, a revealing symbol of their place in the magazine's musical hierarchy.[12]

In association with these basic classifications, there have been other notable changes to the "settings" of the reviews, many of them reflecting the changes, chronicled elsewhere in this book, to which the industry has been regularly beset. Records were once classified in *Gramophone* by label—Parlophone, HMV, Brunswick—a practice that continued until November 1949, when classical recordings were alphabetically ordered by composer's name.[13] Interestingly, up until that point, the information protocols accompanying reviews placed the name of the composer last (see table 7.1). The name of the orchestra (always bolded), the conductor, and the compositions on the record preceded the composer. Another early listing protocol, also later relinquished, was that recordings of instrumental compositions were listed under their instruments: guitar, piano, cello, and so on. In this instance, the composer's position was relegated to a position even "lower" than that of the performer, for it was immersed in the body of the review and did not figure in its headings at all.

During the 1920s reviewing involved drawing attention to the myriad imperfections associated with 78s. Their short duration meant that they could not accommodate longer musical works, which inevitably meant that they were often cut, even severely so. This was a practice that the editor of *The Gramophone* abhorred, and much of the initial crusading undertaken by his magazine focused on changing it (Mackenzie 1940: 111). To this end, reviewers were unforgiving of lax performing standards and, from the first, enjoined companies to be rigorous in their faithfulness to the score and to avoid, without good reason, needless omission and recomposition (Goodchild 1924). However, until the technological conditions governing recording underwent the relevant development and the practices of abridgment were abolished—which, arguably, Mackenzie's magazine stimulated—reviewers were expected to identify precisely where recordings departed from the score and what parts of the music had been omitted or adjusted (Helots 1940). This also involved indicating how many record sides a movement occupied and at what point in the score each side ended. For this purpose Mackenzie acquired, at the time of the magazine's founding, a small library of miniature scores (Mackenzie 1940: 111).

Indeed, one of *The Gramophone*'s early contributors, W. A. Chislett, encouraged the consulting of scores when one listened to records—as illustrated in the E.M.G. trademark—and wrote a series of articles for the magazine on how to do so (1961: 71). To this end, many record dealers specializing in classical music—E.M.G. was one—also sold miniature scores (Amis 1985: 56). A handful of discs have been issued with scores, and even the odd baton for the listener to exercise their conducting skills.[14] And in an advertisement from the 1970s, the music publisher Boosey and Hawkes suggested that such scores, which were "often a good deal cheaper than records" and represented the "ideal yardstick by which to judge records," should, as a matter of course, also be collected.[15]

In the shellac era, when notes were not commonly supplied with albums, reviewers were also expected to describe the music they were reviewing, especially when it was unfamiliar. Much of the review of *Pétrouchka* in *The Gramophone* of April 1924 is devoted to recounting Stravinsky's ballet and its musical interpretation—the type of description that the advent of liner notes rendered, to some extent, obsolete. Some early readers of the magazine found this practice irksome, feeling that properly speaking a magazine ostensibly devoted to reviewing gramophone records should concentrate on discussing their technical merits.[16] The review also encourages listeners who might find Stravinsky's "peculiar methods of expression" not to their liking to persevere, for with "repeated hearings" the music grew on one. Indeed, the opportunity afforded by the gramophone to rehear complex works was dear to the heart of Mackenzie and something that his magazine used every opportunity to promote.

Thus even in the early days, reviews operated on a number of rhetorical fronts, broaching a range of matters not all of which were strictly musical. In a long August 1927 review of an HMV album of the "New World" Symphony and Weber's Overture to *Der Freischütz,* the reviewer casts a number of aspersions on Dvořák's "American" compositions, particularly their use of "negro tunes," which the reviewer deplored. The reviewer's various remarks, which have an Anglophile fervor verging on the jingoistic, are interleaved with racist comments typical of the eugenics movement, to which many intellectuals subscribed in the 1920s, and entirely consistent with Mackenzie's denigration of jazz. Mention is also made of the inferior brain capacities of the Slav races relative to those of the British, which are musically epitomized in the more sophisticated compositions of Elgar; this provides the explanation for Dvořák's musical failings, as exemplified by the "New World." Reviewers in the past were not taciturn in their espousal of backward ethnic ideologies.

Notwithstanding the reviewer's racist leanings, the one paragraph in the review actually dealing with the merits of the recording displays several salient features typical of the genre. He mentions, for example, that the same orchestra and conductor, the Royal Albert Hall Orchestra under Landon Ronald, had recorded the symphony on a previous occasion but that the one submitted for review is "infinitely more interesting." Much later in the development of review discourse, this process of comparing different recordings of the same work was subject to more formalization. Further, in discussing the performance of the symphony, the reviewer resorts to a range of colorful metaphors to illustrate his impressions of the Dvořák symphony: the recording has the "right sheen upon it" but does not capture the "finest shades of tone." Further, he remarks that the woodwind displays "grace and lissomness," though not of the consummate "delicacy" that, presumably, some other orchestra might have attained.

One of the ongoing features of recording, I argued at the commencement of chapter 4, is that it "disembodies" music, meaning that it lacks the physical and material cues present in a live concert. Reviewers try to compensate for this absence. Through using visualizing vocabularies, the recordings, so to speak, are re-embodied, given a corporeal form that allows the music to be imagined in more palpable ways. Such linguistic strategies also reflect the fact that the language of hearing is less discriminating and differentiated than that of seeing. For example, there are no ways of describing sounds equivalent to the terms of their color and shape, at least not without resorting to the abstract, and less commonly understood, nomenclatures of music and physics.

Then the reviewer remarks about the engineering of the recording, which is able to capture the "scale of the music" and "do ample justice to the lovable work" but on the debit side "droops" when it comes to the "right portrayal of the finest shades of tone." In the case of the Weber overture, the reviewer suggests that the "string tone" is not entirely lifelike, yet the balance between the brass and the strings is good. Reviewers regularly espoused this benchmark of "lifelikeness," often expressed in the phrase "a natural recording." For example, when the first electrical recordings were released, reviewers were interested in their capacity to recreate the acoustic of the concert hall. Records that did not do so were criticized on the grounds that they bore as much "resemblance to an actual orchestra as a cinema does to life."[17] Thus the keystone discourse was evident even in the earliest reviews, and reviewers

Table 7.1 Various *Gramophone* Review Heading Templates

Acoustical/Electrical	Long Player: Mono	Long Player: Stereo/Quad	Compact Disc
His Master's Voice D683–D684 Brandenburg Concerto in G, and Air on the G String	FOERSTER. Cyrano de Bergerac, Op. 55. Brno Radio Symphony Orchestra conducted by Bretislav Bakala. Supraphon Mono LPV382 (12in., 30s. plus 9s. 9d P.T.)	★ GLAZUNOV. Birthday Offering—Ballet Music (excerpts arr. Robert Irving). ★ LECOCQ. Mam'zelle Angot—Ballet Music (arr. Gordon Jacob) Royal Philharmonic conducted by Robert Irving. H.M.V. Stereophonic CSD1252 (12in., 25s 9d plus 8s 4d. P.T.) Mono: (9/58) CLP1140 Mam'selle Angot: Royal Opera House Orch., Covent Gadn. Fistoulari (7/59) SB2039	ADAMS. Shaker Loops (1982–3) REICH. Variations for winds, strings (1980) San Francisco Symphony Orchestra/Edo de Waart Philips Ⓔ ① 412 214–2PH From 412 214–PP14 (12/84)
His Master's Voice D1250, 1251, 1252, 1253, 1254 (12in., five records in album, 32s. 6d.). Royal Albert Hall Orchestra, conducted by Landon Ronald: "New World" Symphony (Dvořák)	—	BEETHOVEN. Piano Concerto No. 4 in G major, Op. 58. Wilhelm Backhaus (piano) Vienna Philharmonic Orchestra conducted by Hans Schmidt-Isserstedt, Decca Stereophonic SXL2010 (12in. 28s. 9d plus 11s 2d P.T.)	Ⓡ Mozart. Concertos for Piano and Orchestra—No. 23 in A, K488; No. 24 in C Minor, K491. Sir Clifford Curzon (pf), London Symphony Orchestra/István Kertész. Decca The Classic Sound Ⓜ ① 42 88–2DCS (57 minutes: ADD). From SXL6354 (11/68)
—	BEETHOVEN. Concerto No.3 in C minor, Op. 37. Edwin Fischer (piano), Philharmonia Orchestra. H.M.V. BLP 1063 (10 in., 27s. 3d.). Backhaus, Vienna P.O., Bohm (2/51) LXT2553 Kraus, Vienna S.O., Moralt (7/53) PL270 Arrau, Philadelphia Orch., Ormandy (12/53) 33CX1080 Gilels, Conservatoire, Cluytens (11/54) 33CX188	ISHII. So Gu II for gagahu and symphony orchestra* TAKEMITSU. Cassiopeia†. Gagaku Ensemble*, Stomu Yamash'ta (percussion)†, Japanese Philharmonic Symphony Orchestra conducted by Seiji Ozawa. EMI Quadraphonic Q4E MD 5508 (£1.29)	Lambert Ⓝ Concerto for Piano and Chamber Orchestra[a]. Merchant Seamen Suite. Pomona. Prize Fight. [a] David Owen Norris pf BBC Concert Orchestra/Barry Wordsworth ASV White Line Ⓜ ① CDWHL2122 (66 minutes: DDD)

Table 7.1 *(continued)*

Acoustical/Electrical	Long Player: Mono	Long Player: Stereo/Quad	Compact Disc
B.B.C. Symphony Orchestra (Boult): **"The Planets" Suite**, Op. 32 (Holst). H.M.V. DB6227–33 (12 ins., 64s 5d). Auto DB8904, DB8995–9000. Recorded under the auspices of the British Council.	—	**BRUCKNER.** Symphony No. 4 in E flat major, "Romantic." **Vienna Symphony Orchestra** conducted by **Otto Klemperer.** Turnabout TV 370731 (£1.29) From Vox mono PL6930 (11/53). Electronic Stereo.	Ⓝ TUBIN Symphonies – No 4, "Sinfonia lirico"; No 7 Estonian National Symphony Orchestra/ Arvo Volmer Alba Ⓕ ABCD 155 (63 minutes: DDD) **Symphony No 4**—comparative version Bergen SO, Jarvi (10/86) (BIS) CD227 **Symphony No 7**—comparative version Gothenburg SO, Jarvi (1/89) (BIS) CD401

Note: Illustrated here are the various heading templates covering *Gramophone* reviews from electrical recording to the CD. There are a number of matters to note. One is the way in which each of the headings incorporate format details in either abbreviated or symbolic forms, e.g. Ⓛ = CD, Ⓝ = new recording, Ⓡ = reissue. A ★ is used to denote a new format and is eventually dropped once the format becomes the norm. Also note the pricing details, which reflect the emergence of a more diversified market. Records no longer have a fixed price as they did in the past and now fall within brackets, e.g. super bargain Ⓢ, bargain Ⓑ, mid-price Ⓜ, and full price Ⓕ. The latest addition to the "legendary" devices is the Ⓝ symbol, indicating that the recording is new to the catalogue, which reflects the fact that a large number of current releases are so-called "reissues."

reprimanded recordings that eschewed it, in effect helping to consolidate its benchmark status in the evaluation of classical recordings.

The *Gramophone* reviews of the 1920s and 1930s were often effusive, perhaps because there was much to be effusive about in the way of phonographic breakthroughs. When the first complete recording of Brahms's Third Symphony was released, its reviewer remarked that he was in a state of absolute joy and that his prayers had been answered.[18]

By the mid-1940s their tone and content was more sober, more informed and erudite, and less prone to be judgmental. Take Alec (A.R.) Robertson's August 1945 review of *The Planets* with Adrian Boult conducting the BBC Symphony Orchestra, an early example of Decca's full-frequency range recording. The review begins with an account of the work's composition and notes Gustav Holst's own ambivalent assessment of his work. The reviewer then proceeds to examine, in some detail, its first public performance. He notes that the charladies of the Queen's Hall danced in the corridors as the sounds of "Jupiter" wafted through. Regarding "Neptune," the reviewer brings up Richard Strauss and Claude Debussy, who had also attempted to depict "mysticism" and whose efforts the reviewer thinks are less convincing than Holst's. At the time, Robertson rated Decca's recording, one of the first to be sponsored by the newly instituted British Council, as "state of the art" and extolled it as a superlative essay in sound presentation, "more actual than anything we have had before"; its "excitement" could induce apoplexy "even in the hardened gramophile."

The review, which refers to a miniature score, contains many technical details regarding the work's instrumentation, which it describes as huge, diverse, a "box of magical delights." Reference to scores was still common in the reviews of the 1940s and 1950s, though there were no excerpts in *The Gramophone* as there were in more "musical" periodicals such as the *Musical Times*. To this end, reviewers would include details of the publishers of the relevant scores presumably to help those readers who, in the E.M.G. tradition, wanted to determine the accuracy of the reviewers' pronouncements. Surface noise, even on Decca's full-frequency range discs, could still obscure significant musical detail, which then might be the fault of the recording or the conductor. The climactic "quadruple forte discord" in Mars "must be heard to be believed," but A.R. cannot hear the "genuine double piano at the start of Part 2," which he attributes to the recording rather than Boult.

To accommodate the various paradigm shifts besetting the record industry, the morphology of the record review has undergone various forms of modification and development. Reflecting this, the information protocol heading each review, which incorporates the specific facts and figures relating to a disc, has become more detailed and informative (table 7.1). The medium of recording has not been restricted to a single format since the days of the 78, for example, but has at various times and often concurrently encompassed LPs, cassettes, CDs, mini-discs, videos, and so on, all of which have required additional specification. One way of facilitating this specification was to create separate departments for each recording format. For example, quadraphonic LPs were, for some time, reviewed separately from stereo LPs, a practice that is currently followed with the review of DVDs. More mainstream formats such as LPs and CDs have always been kept together, and their particular subvariants identified using different symbols generally specific to a particular magazine. Thus, whether a recording is fully digital, new to the catalogue or a re-release, available only at full price, and so on can all be ascertained from the information protocols. When examined over several decades, these protocols also provide a chronology of sorts of the innovations occurring in the record industry and the amount of time they took to be mainstreamed. The appearance of certain information within these protocols can also reflect *caveat emptor* concerns. In the early days of CDs, reviewers complained about the ungenerous "timing" of CDs and suggested that many were half-filled and did not make the most of their potential duration.[19] In direct response to this criticism, the playing time of a CD was added to the protocols. In addition, the protocols have encoded information about the cost of discs and are therefore telling about the changing economics and price structures of records, at least in the United Kingdom. Some of the encoding was applied only for a short time, as in the case of "starring" stereo LPs, and was dropped once they became the norm.

That such information appears in the review's "pre-text" serves an important economic function, obviating the need for reviewers to squander words—and words are a precious commodity for them—on format information and instead place most of the focus of their review on matters musical and technical. Other magazines have adopted similar templates but have sometimes presented additional information. For example, *High Fidelity* included, beginning in 1977, the name of the record producer, yet another reflection of the changing discursive conditions of record production.

But these information protocols were not always used. In the prewar years this information was supplied in a more perfunctory way and further parenthesized in the main body of the review. The development of a relevant information template "outside" the review took several volumes to develop in *The Gramophone* and only took on its contemporary "design" in 1949. Since then, other features have been added; the most notable, introduced in December 1999, is the color reproduction of a CD's cover that is "indented" into the first paragraph of the review. The effect—and it is a reflection of the increasingly visual nature of *Gramophone*—is akin to a rebus. In fact, it is another device that assists in increasing the expeditiousness with which the magazine can be read, at least for those who recognize the livery of certain labels and are attracted to their particular CDs. The BBC "Legends" series is a case in point; their presentation renders them instantly recognizable, even in the relatively compact magazine reproduction. This, combined with the added practice, recent for *Gramophone*,[20] of "headlining" reviews, means that the review section occupies a number of planes of accessibility, from the most succinct to the most extended, and the reader can track them with alacrity according to their immediate musical inclinations and interests.

Another telling part of the review's information protocols is the listing, for purposes of comparison, of alternative recordings, along with the dates of their reviews. This textual practice, introduced in December 1954, reflected, as the accompanying editorial explained, the complicated question of duplication that the advent of the LP had exacerbated. It immediately obligated reviewers to refer to the merits of alternative recordings ("We do not see, hear and smell of the sea, as in Toscanini's and Karajan's performances. My own preference is very slightly for the Karajan").[21] But at a more generalized level such recorded comparisons were a textual response to the increasing tendency of labels—even more pronounced in the LP era—to record the major works of the classical canon over and over again, so that the market became saturated with certain titles—the so-called "warhorses." This practice is not reserved for the transition to a new recording format such as the CD, when it is assumed that collectors will automatically want to reinvigorate their collections *holus bolus* by replacing perfectly serviceable LPs with the new medium. It is instead an ongoing issue. Comparative reviews thus can counter the zeal to "renovate" a collection and discourage the oft-held view of these technophile times that the newest recording necessarily supersedes its predecessors. Such reviews often earmark recordings from the past as still worthy of possession, as having stood the test of time. The fact that an older version might also be available at a cheaper price might be an additional virtue in its favor ("I do feel material of this kind is more acceptable in the form of a medium-price LP than a top-price Compact Disc").[22]

Record Reviewers: Those that Can, Do; Those that Can't, Review

The record review belongs to the same strain of music criticism as the concert review (Frank 2000: 50). One of its salient features, aside from being "done against the clock" (Wimbush 1964: 321), is its concision—a reviewer never has an unlimited number of words. Most reviews, with the exception of those dedicated to multivolume sets, are approximately four hundred words in length. This means that reviewers must compress their evaluations and avoid repetition and circumlocution, which results in an aphoristic style devoid of the usual pointers characteristic of more discursive writing, such as introductions and conclusions.

Most record reviewers tend to have backgrounds in classical music rather than journalism, and reviewing is one among a range of musical "engagements" for them. Many, for example, also write sleeve notes. The reviewers associated with the *Gramophone* are, by and large, drawn from the main bastions of the U.K. musical establishment. One has edited *The New Grove Dictionary of Music and Musicians;* others hold or have held academic appointments in music faculties at British universities.[23] Several commenced their careers in the BBC, either in its Music Department or Gramophone Library, and many have had a prolonged association with the magazine (one current reviewer began at *Gramophone* in the 1940s). This helps sustain the "chronological" tone that is a feature of the magazine's style and extends into the genealogical style of its reviews, which constantly compare new releases with their immediate and long-standing, often forgotten predecessors. Although in the past an individual reviewer would cover most segments of the musical spectrum, now he or she will stick to a specific area. Reviewers thus become known for their erudition as well as their idiosyncrasies, which readers eventually come to identify and value. The late Lionel Salter's reviews, for example, exhibited erudition and pedantry alongside an acumen for musical error and inept interpretation ("Beecham's idiosyncrasy of making unmarked *ritardandi* . . . will upset some Mozart-lovers"). Reviewers mostly adopt the first person, reinforcing the fact that their judgments are their own. Yet although a considerable measure of subjectivity enters the matter of judging recordings, there is consensus, among reviewers, about the merits of some recordings, certainly those that are held to be the greatest ever made, such as Carlos Kleiber's recording of Beethoven's Fifth Symphony or Pablo Casals's recording of Bach's Cello Suites. As to what qualities such recordings exhibit, it has been argued that they "withstand constant repetition and yet still reveal new facets of a composer's mastery" (Layton 1967: 5).

In the end, though, reviewing is generally held to be a grueling and exhausting task involving checking scores and evaluating the interpretive felicities of a particular recording (Robertson 1961: 115), the results of which are likely to be despised by other members of the music industry. Indeed reviewers are often regarded as hacks, second-class musical citizens who had their ambitions to be proper musicians thwarted and thence air their frustrated ambitions through reviewing (Strevens 1961: 16).[24] Yet in spite of the general animosity toward reviewers and their pronouncements, the record industry has never been hesitant in harnessing their pronouncements to promote its

Figure 7.1 Part of a series from Enigma Records that uses the same "strap-line," this advertisement originally appeared in *Gramophone* (December 1977). It recognizes the cynicism pertaining to the claims of advertisements ("Don't take our word for it") and asks its readers instead to accept the words of reviewers, some examples of which are shown. At a more generalized level, though, this advertisement encapsulates the idea that record sales, in the end, defer to the authority of the written word—that the pen is mightier than the stylus. (Reproduced by permission the editor of the *Gramophone*.)

discs (Figure 7.1). However, the practice common on book dust jackets of citing adulatory reviews has not been adopted by many labels—or, if they have, it is only in the inner pages of the liner notes. The exception are the retro series of CDs, which, to justify their re-releases, increasingly cite original review notices—often on their front covers (see Figure 4.8). However, there are signs that even this is changing; Martha Argerich's much-acclaimed recent CD of the Rachmaninoff and Tchaikovsky Piano Concertos has the words "THE BEST RECORDING OF RACH 3" emblazoned across it in red, together with the magazines that have named it the best, which makes it stand out in the browsing box environment.

The classical musical background typical of reviewers has had a number of consequences. Reviews are invariably in a magisterial discourse that distances its readers, by requiring an advanced understanding of musical epistemology: its common genres, nomenclature, and taxonomy. True, this density stems from the need for brevity: reviewers do not have the space to be informative, other than when it makes rhetorical sense to do so. Still, the gratuitous displays of erudition found in reviews alienate readers, including those with a musical background (Strevens 1961). The highbrow tone of reviews has also meant that they tend to reinforce rather than transgress musical orthodoxies. Records falling into unconventional music categories, such as "crossover" genres, "Glassical" music, or music in the style of Philip Glass, are either not reviewed at all, or churlishly so.[25] This is particularly the case when such music appears on a label usually associated with upholding classical traditions ("This is not so much a crossover disc as a pop one in classic(al) designer clothing").

But reviewers do not just focus on musical matters. Some of their attention is also focused on the engineering aspects of a recording, particularly at times of format change, when consumers are often exhorted to embrace the new format without interrogating its claims. Reviewers feel dutybound to comment on the strengths of the format and weigh them against the hype of the record industry. This is designed to protect the consumer against investing in equipment and recordings that might in fact prove inferior to existing formats or that might not endure in the long term. After all, the history of audio equipment is a checkered one, with several formats, notwithstanding their auditory virtues, proving to be technological cul-de-sacs that failed to attract public support and were eventually phased out. Four-channel sound and digital audio tape (DAT) were just two of these short-lived wonders.

Whatever the case, though, the shift to a new audio format invariably produces reviewer ambivalence and, sometimes, outright opprobrium. Reviewers often raise questions about the efficacy of the new format, wondering whether it is really required and whether consumers are not better served by existing formats. When stereo LPs were launched many reviewers complained about their auditory defects ("The sound . . . is somewhat hard and even with the top heavily cut, it lacks bloom . . ."; "the recorded quality of Pye's monaural disc is distinctly preferable to that of their stereo"). Much of the initial criticism, though, often stems from the fact that producers and engineers were unused to the techniques of producing stereo recordings. And similar questions still hang over the adequacies of digital sound, which many hold is abrasive and harsh, particularly when it is compared with that of the LP, whose acoustic qualities many hold to be unsurpassed and whose demise, for this reason, is much lamented.

The main concern of *Gramophone*, though—for which it is renowned— is judging the qualities of musical performance. If these are of a sufficiently high order, they can often override quibbles about a disc's auditory shortcomings. Much of the judgment in relation to a performance deals with its proficiency in terms of accurately rendering the score and interpreting a composer's intentions in a cogent and defensible way. Performances wildly at loggerheads with a score or otherwise in violation of its injunctions are identified and the nature of the violation specified ("in bars 29, 33, 301 and 305, Beethoven's dotted quaver-semiquaver degenerates into a slovenly near-triplet"). Equally, when music is executed in an inspired manner, reviewers will be unstinting in their praise ("the softly swirling strings after bar 120 are equally superb"). And in order to permit readers to assess the efficacy of those judgments, reviewers have resorted to various navigational measures to allow ill-distinguished passages to be played at home. For example, during the shellac era, reviewers would locate such passages in terms of their distance to the edge of a record ("The first subject comes at 2 in."). In the era of the CD player, minutes and seconds have superseded inches ("there was a curious patch of what sounded like faint interference beginning at 2'36" into track 4 . . .").

Reviewers also display strong preferences for recordings that defer to the keystone discourse. Those that are considered to deviate from it without any apparent musical justification are invariably criticized.[26] Such was the case with Karajan's later recordings ("whole sections are highlighted rather as if a television camera had been focused on them . . ."); as was noted in chapter 2, Karajan in his later years often favored recording techniques, on musical grounds, that transgressed the keystone. In a review that derides Decca's "Phase 4"—a label that made a specialty of violating the keystone—Robert Layton reveals a particular admiration for Karajan's recording of Prokofiev's Fifth Symphony, made in the days prior to his technophile proclivities. In this recording, unlike those of the much maligned Phase 4, the "orchestral colours speak for themselves without any highlighting of solo instruments" and serve to place the LP's "engineering on a level of artistry worthy of the performance itself" (Layton 1969: 259). Similar phonographic criteria extend to the evaluation of audio equipment. Loudspeakers, for example, that add color to the sound—a U.K. manufacturer even named one of its speakers "Achromat," which means "without color"—or otherwise deviate from the "closest approach to the original" principle are without exception derogated. Thus a degree of coalescence exists across the network of texts associated with classical recording: in matters of phonographic representation, the keystone discourse is a pervasive one.

Reviews also tend to individualize performances via the musical personalities of their performers, particularly when they involve well-known musicians with extensive discographies. This was not always the case but certainly coincides with the cult of the personality that has descended upon and in turn been fashioned by the recording industry. The cult began with Caruso and then was successfully applied to other classical artists in the 1930s such as Toscanini (Horowitz 1987). One aspect of the cult is that reviewers increasingly fingerprint interpretations in terms of the personality of the musicians involved. Now it is common to talk of Tennstedt's Mahler as distinct from Bernstein's, and to characterize performing styles in terms of their originators. This serves to give recordings a human face and a characteristic "personality." But this "personalizing" is also predicated on the fact—as was not the case in the past—that multiple performances now exist of most of the major works in the classical canon, enabling different interpretations of the same work to be compared with one another, and different interpretations of the same work from the same performers at different points in their careers as well. Thus it is now possible to compare Karajan-the-younger's Beethoven with that of Karajan-the-older. This was not always the case. In 1934, for instance, the public was still waiting for a recording of Brahms's Third Symphony: now there are at least eighty in the current catalog. This has led to another narrative strand in the review genre that compares performances of the same work with one another, not just those of the same conductor and performer(s) but also those of different conductors and performers.

Influencing the Invisible Hand: Reviews and the Marketplace

Although *The Gramophone*'s reviews in the 1920s paid heed to other recordings of the same work, the practice of listing such recordings as a formal part of their pre-text or post-text regions (see table 7.1) only commenced, as was noted earlier in the chapter, in late 1954. From then onward there has been a steady growth in more comparative approaches to reviewing, involving much sifting and sorting as well as the adoption of ranking processes designed to identify recordings of outstanding merit that exhibit superlative technical and interpretive distinction. For example, an annual feature of the magazine is "Critics' Choice," which involves reviewers nominating their six most outstanding releases of the year. In May 1993 the same processes of selection were extended to the identification of ten "recordings of the month," excerpts from which then appeared on the cover-mounted CD; many record retailers in turn spotlight this distinction in their advertising. Arguably the ultimate manifestations, at least to date, of this phonographic meritocracy are *Gramophone's* annual awards, the record industry's equivalent of the Booker Prize.[27] These were inaugurated in 1978, largely at the behest of the record industry. The actual awards night is now a major event in the phonographic calendar and has been televised since 1997 (Pollard 1998a: 137). To celebrate the twenty-fifth anniversary of these awards in 2003, Hyperion and Universal reissued a special limited edition series of the recipients of the Record of the Year award.

These developments accord with those occurring elsewhere in consumer culture, where similar approaches to appraising commodities are deployed. Their emergence in the record industry reflects the aforementioned economy of repetition, a market in which there is a surfeit of recordings. The number of listings in *Gramophone's* "New Releases" for July 2002 is over four hundred, a significant expansion that began three decades ago. Even though *Gramophone's* reviews have tripled between the years 1968 and 2002, there are still many more CDs released than there are reviewed, at least in that magazine.[28] It has been calculated that there are now 65,000 recordings by more than 13,000 composers from 1,300 recording companies (Walker 1998b: 93)—and this does not count those circulating in the secondhand market. And although there has been a considerable expansion of the classical canon, particularly as a result of the initiatives of adventurous independents, there has, at the same time, been a dramatic increase in the recordings of mainstream repertoire. In the two-volume edition of the *Red Classical Catalogue* (2002), which lists all classical releases in the U.K., there are so many recordings of the "warhorses" that it is easier to express their number in terms of centimeters of column space that they occupy (a centimeter corresponds to about six CDs). Max Bruch's G-minor Violin Concerto (a longtime favorite on the U.K.'s radio station, Classic FM) occupies 21.5 centimeters, Vivaldi's *Four Seasons* 34, Beethoven's "Moonlight" Sonata 31, Grieg's Piano Concerto 23, and so on. And the introduction to a 2002 guide to compact discs that is already of voluminous dimensions warns that it has reached the limit of its capacity and that future editions of the guide will have to be issued in separate volumes (March, Greenfield, and Layton 2002: xiii).

The simple conclusion to be drawn from these statistics is that the record market is more than adequately supplied with recordings of certain works, far in excess of demand. In this climate, the function of the review has become more exigent than ever and has a considerable potential to shape the invisible hand of the market and add an important textual factor to its dynamics. How much so, however, is a matter of contention. It seems that reviewers cannot override the public appetite for certain records irrespective of their brickbats and bouquets: "Fanfare is no guarantee against failure" (Marek 1955: 37). Criticism, even of the most vitriolic kind, need not of itself hobble sales, which are often boosted by nonmusical factors. But bouquets are equally unreliable. For example, even recordings considered to be inspired, whose merits attract laudatory notices in the phonographic press, can be greeted by complete consumer insouciance (Grubb 1986: 118; 142). On the other hand, severe censure is unlikely to boost sales (Pollard 1956: 1). And it does seem that record retailers take cognizance of sympathetic reviews when ordering stock. So what factors are critical in consumer decision making about discs? George Marek (1955: 37), a member of RCA's marketing division, suggested in the 1950s that Hollywood and music of the "sound for sound's sake variety" would appeal to record collectors who wanted to show off their high fidelity systems. This favored composers such as Rimsky-Korsakov rather than Handel. And certainly if one compares the bestselling recordings from those lists supplied by retailers with those recordings identified by the critics as outstanding, there is often a hiatus between the two. For example, an examination of the lists of bestselling discs published in *Gramophone* from April 2002 (when such lists first appeared in its pages) to July 2002, which are compiled by retailers from around the world, indicates that not one of the magazine's "Records of the Month" appeared in these lists.[29]

Nevertheless, reviewers do take seriously their role as consumer "consultants," and will frequently conclude their deliberations by identifying a recording that stands out among its peers as clearly the one to purchase ("I'd sooner have the Irving"). Occasionally a reviewer will suggest that a CD is the yardstick of performance whose merits will not be surpassed ("It is hard to imagine . . . [the work] being better performed or more faithfully recorded"). Indeed, a chronological overview of *Gramophone*'s reviews suggests that the matter of economic endorsement is a relatively recent addition to the review's rhetoric. Most reviewers in the early volumes of the magazine were primarily concerned with evaluating the musical merits of discs and eschewed matters to do with whether or not they constituted sound investments. In many instances consumers only had the one disc from which to choose, and labels would be congratulated for adding a work formerly absent from the catalog. It is only since the mid-1950s that the matter of a best choice, in terms of price and performance, has become a matter of real contesting. In the last few years, for example, the price range of records has acquired a much wider amplitude than it possessed in the past, when the 78 was, compared to the CD of today, relatively expensive. Collectors can now obtain recordings of classical works in the so-called "super-budget" category that exhibit qualities superior to many of their full-price rivals. Budget no longer signifies inferiority, if it ever did. Reviewers are not taciturn at pointing this out ("with no obvious alternative and at a super-bargain price, it earns the strongest recommendation").

Reviews thus serve a pecuniary function and attempt to play a role in the marketplace in terms of influencing the choices of consumers through actively deterring them from making unadvised purchases. The rhetoric of economic endorsement is distinctive: it is usually placed at the end of the review, following an extended encomium, and its phrasing adopts a regular array of rhetorical idioms that have strong enactive components focusing on self-indulgence ("So go on: treat yourself!") and seasonal imperatives ("This is surely the perfect Christmas present"). A new reprise is that of "limited availability": CDs from the smaller labels, with short production runs, might become hard to acquire, which enhances their desirability ("Acquire this while you can, would be my advice; it could well become a collectors' item"). However, for the most part the rhetoric of endorsement draws on a conventional register of superlatives and idioms ("the best recording available"; "sensational"; "an excellent choice"; "a splendid record"), utilizing a range of synonyms for and inflections of the word "recommended" ("Recommended from all points of view"). The use of modifiers such as "much," "strongly," "highly," or "warmly" further extends this register and produces an even larger range of linguistic combinations and permutations. Often the recommendation is concisely expressed, enhancing its trenchancy ("Do hear it").

At the brickbat end of the appraisal spectrum is another well-rehearsed set of idioms ("This issue is a great disappointment"; "this miserable record can scarcely be recommended"; "this concerto, her op. 241, arouses in me absolutely no desire to hear the other 240"). Sometimes the rhetoric errs on the side of caution ("these are not the most exciting performances available"; "there are better buys elsewhere") and cautions the reader to be careful. Such caveats are issued in other ways and are framed through "be that as it may" phrasing that mutes the overtness of the criticism, even suggesting that the reviewer might be at fault and that the record might appeal to some listeners ("those who enjoy lots of pounding rhythm may be satisfied by this"; "if you like this coupling, you may think the record worth acquiring").

The growth in recordings of more esoteric repertoire has produced another element in the review genre that pertains to discs of works that are new to the catalog. In these instances the focus of the review is on whether or not the music possesses sufficient intrinsic merit to warrant its acquisition by adventurous listeners. Indeed, reviewers often reserve most of their plaudits for when it does, therefore placing a disc before the public of a work long overlooked by other labels ("some inexplicably neglected Scottish music—it's even more extraordinary that this disc should be the first commercial recording"). The review will often even intimate that if the work were to be included in a concert it would surely win the applause of audiences. Sometimes this strategy extends to suggesting works for underendowed areas of the classical repertoire, such as cello concertos. A review of one such concerto, an arrangement of Grieg's Cello Sonata, suggested that its arrangers, Joseph Horowitz and Benjamin Wallfisch, consider arranging similar works: "Top of list (would be) the magnificent Rachmaninov."[30] Indeed, reviewers often indulge in a soupçon of self-congratulation when they have been percipient enough to anticipate recordings of a work that they had long yearned to see represented in the catalogue.[31]

One obligation that reviewers have when dealing with unfamiliar repertoire is to provide a thumbnail sketch of the composer and his or her compositions. Such reviews must locate the recorded work in its musical context and characterize its qualities in terms of better-known compositions, a strategy also often employed by writers of liner notes. For example, the reviewer of Reinhold Glière's Third Symphony in *The Gramophone* (October 1950), writing at a time when the composer was hardly a household name, notes that Glière's symphonic personality is an eclectic and derivative one that reminds him of Tchaikovsky and Myaskovsky "with a side-glance at Liszt"— composers with whose works most *Gramophone* readers would have had an acquaintance. Elsewhere Liadov's name is mentioned. The reviewer suggests that though Glière is not much of an individual voice, he is, nonetheless, worth hearing, and elsewhere the reviewer defuses any doubts about Glière's claims as a composer. He mentions his role in the "new Russian life" as President of the Union of Soviet Composers and teacher of the better-known Prokofiev and Khachaturian.

In these respects, the review is often an extension of the liner notes and sometimes draws much of its contents from them. Occasionally, though, a reviewer will challenge the claims made in these notes. Claims once made about Miklós Rózsa's Violin Concerto, to the effect that it was a masterpiece ranking with those of Prokofiev and Bartók, were said to be exaggerated.[32] In fact, over decades reviews can provide telling indices of a composer's career as it proceeds from obscurity to wider public recognition. For example, once the discography of a composer extends beyond a certain point, the need to provide biographical background diminishes. *Gramophone* readers would by now be familiar with Glière and the style of his compositions, thus allowing scope for reflection on other facets of his career and standing in the history of contemporary music, and indeed a 1992 review of the Third Symphony omits any references to his life and times. Instead, it places the symphony in a more historical and global context, suggesting that it ranks with those of other nationalistic composers—Elgar, for instance—and in fact could be favorably compared with the late symphonies of Tchaikovsky or the early ones of Shostakovich.[33]

The Glière review from the 1950s manifests another rhetorical tactic in the review genre, which is to situate its narrative within other narratives. In order to make a recording "come alive" and to reduce the distance between the music and the reader, reviewers often resort to personal anecdotes ("When an American friend played bits of this symphony . . . I couldn't name its composer"). Thus reviews are "multistoried," fluid rather than linear or monolithic; they provide several ways—some private, some public—of evaluating a recording and its music, and there is no single way of compiling one.

The other advantage of seeing reviews in a diachronic perspective is that they provide a temporal trace of the musical tradition as it moves onward and outward, being built around certain compositions that are continually reassessed and rearticulated while others fall by the wayside. Although they do not operate alone in this regard, reviews also play an important gatekeeping role, influencing the circulation of new works and new composers and assisting in determining their legitimacy and capacity to be admitted into the canon. Reviews are far from being always adulatory and take the task of alerting collectors to ill-performed and uninteresting discs very seriously. The lack of an individual compositional voice or highly derivative music of the crossover or wantonly commercial sort frequently attract invective and derision. One recent review, for example, which began by implying that corporate nepotism was responsible for the existence of the particular disc in the first place, heaps scorn on the pastiche effects of the music and its failure to reveal an "individual voice." Its reviewer speculates that it will be his "worst record of the year" and wonders whether he has been the subject of some premature April Fools' Day prank.

The exploration of new musical traditions is another conspicuous theme running through the review narrative that manifests itself in regular injunctions to record companies to be more adventurous in their recording philosophies. The accusation that record magazines are sycophantic mouthpieces of the majors because their economic viability depends, in large measure, upon their advertising seems unfair (Lebrecht 1992: 300). Particularly since the war, as much of the classical repertoire has been recorded *ad nauseam,* especially by the majors, reviewers have never shrunk from being critical of their alleged paymasters and have often drawn attention to the fact that some composers have been subject to undeserved neglect by record companies or have been deleted from the catalogue with too much celerity.[34] A review from 1949 devoted to the music of Constant Lambert thus suggests that Lambert's admirable compositional abilities have been unjustifiably underappreciated. Accusing record companies of being too European in their orientation, the review suggests that had Lambert been a "foreign composer," they would "have been falling over themselves to perform his works." In fact, using the review as a means of lobbying record companies was part of the inaugural issue of *The Gramophone.* The very first review to appear in its pages, of an HMV album of the *Brandenburg Concertos*—and a very perceptive one given the passion for instrumental authenticity that emerged in the 1970s— suggests that it would "be an interesting experiment to record one of these concerti with the very small chamber orchestra of the period at which they were written."

Although the sound-for-sound's-sake discourse is not a dominant one in *Gramophone,* its reviews nonetheless pay heed to the engineering qualities of recordings. Those held to be in the so-called demonstration category are regularly singled out for praise ("A record to show off the new gramophone"; "sounds magnificent") along with those displaying high standards of engineering ("beautifully recorded"; "especially vivid"; "awesome dynamic range"; "radiant"). Likewise, less than impressive recordings are singled out for rebuke ("the recording is frankly poor").

In the early days of 78s surface noise was a persistent problem and attracted widespread attention, especially when some new recording material promised its reduction or elimination. In the 1920s, when Columbia began to use a type of wax that reduced noise and made the record less prone to scratching, this claim was immediately challenged in the columns of *The Gramophone* (Mackenzie 1955). Likewise, when the LP arrived and was asserted to be a far more robust medium than shellac, this claim was assayed. The reviewer of one of the first LPs to be issued in the U.K., a Decca recording of Beethoven's "Emperor" Concerto, marveled at both its capacity to hold a whole concerto on one disc and the fact that it was possible to throw it down the stairs without any apparent damage.[35]

In the end, though, the sheer profusion of record reviews has produced its own textual response in the shape of compendium collections that are outside of the magazine format but abstract much of their copy from magazine reviews. Though magazines date their individual reviews, even with the assistance of annual indexes and other forms of textual navigation they can become difficult to locate, let alone compare one against another. Hence, more accessible review texts began to appear in the 1950s, comprised of anthologies of reviews, usually abridged, of the best LPs released during a calendar year (Orga and Orga 1978).

I have argued in this chapter that the record review is an important textual gatekeeper, differentiating recordings of merit from those whose standards are mediocre or even inferior; it enables some to be heard in advance as good recordings and others as bad. As such, the review is a standard-bearing discourse that acts as a vehicle for the value system underpinning records and the reproduction of classical music. Much of the importance of the review thus derives from its function as a mediating device, one that specifically evaluates the qualities of new releases and re-releases and determines whether they can be purchased with confidence and enthusiasm. In this respect, reviews have the power to influence a record's profile in the marketplace and to enlist consumer support for certain recordings while thwarting that for others. They function as powerful lenses that filter the "unreflected" light of advertising and other forms of promotional hype associated with the record industry.

I have also argued that *Gramophone* reviews have always followed principles and guidelines that were standardized early on in the magazine's history. The review has a distinctive narrative morphology that was invented to accommodate the particular demands of evaluating records, and it utilizes a range of rhetorical tactics and devices. As an important genre of musical criticism, the record review displays distinctive patterns and regularities, rules and conventions. By tracing these, much can be revealed about the nature of the record industry and its development throughout the twentieth century. Importantly, reviewers have been among the first groups to offer candid and uncompromising assessments of these developments. In spite of the symbiotic relationship that record magazines must, of necessity, have with the recording industry, it has never been sycophantic, at least in the case of *Gramophone*; from its earliest days, the magazine adopted the position of being the conscience of the recording industry, encouraging it to explore new repertoire and be less conservative in its recording policies.

At a more general level, reviews are significant texts in helping to spread the epistemology of recording and its basic values, and the reviews of *Gramophone* attest to the dominance of the keystone discourse. This is manifested not just in the way LPs and CDs have been reviewed but also in the reviews of high fidelity equipment and components. Thus reviews provide compact versions of the discourse of classical music in action, as well as the way the discourse is preserved even in the face of technological changes in the record industry. Thus the review, far from being a trivial form of music criticism, is an important life form in the textual habitat of recorded music, helping to sustain and manage the practices and values associated with recording. As such, its power as "an organ of candid opinion" should not be discounted.

CHAPTER EIGHT

Keeping Records in Their Place
Collections, Catalogs, Libraries, and Societies

There is in the life of a collector a dialectical tension between
the poles of disorder and order.
—Walter Benjamin, "Unpacking My Library," 60

Though many arguments have been presented in the preceding chapters, one is dominant: the idea that the act of playing records encompasses more than their auditory dimensions. The not unnatural tendency to regard the record as primarily a phenomenon of sound has typically detracted from the significance of this idea in the phonographic realm. I have argued, however, that the cultural "circumference" of the record extends well beyond its playing area, and many other kinds of text enter into it whenever listeners play records. These overlooked textual dimensions of the phonographic phenomenon are most obvious in the various types of narrative architecture that envelope the record, in cover notes, magazines, brochures, advertisements, and high fidelity manuals. They constitute a documentary reality consisting of a complex web of texts in which the discourses and practices of recording are articulated. These are an integral part of the lives of those who make records their *business*. It is thus possible to visualize this architecture as forming an ever-extending ring of concentric circles generated by the record's centrifugal forces whose overall impact has been to transform the consumption and production of music.

I have suggested that the physics of the phonograph produces an apposite metaphor in this regard: the transducer. Musical information is converted from one energy to another—sound waves into electrical charges into mechanical energy and back into sound waves—via the chain of transducers associated with the reproduction of sound: discs, record players, amplifiers, and loudspeakers. But there is another link in this chain of transducers that shunt musical signals back and forth, converting them into different forms of modality, and it is "linguistic" rather than electronic. The texts that extend the phonograph beyond its mechanical and electronic elements are also transducers, converting the musical energy generated by the technology of reproduction into their own signal system using the loudspeaker of the page as their principal vehicle of amplification and transmission. And these signals are in turn converted into other forms of modality by the last transducer in the chain of reproduction: the acquirer of records, the human record player. To use an example drawn from the previous chapter, record reviews have the capacity to transform consumption patterns associated with discs in powerful ways that are acted out in a range of contexts. A cartoon from the satirical magazine *Private Eye* spoofs the way in which reviews provide performing scripts for record collectors in the theater of the record shop. It shows one of the "Great Bores" of English society with a copy of *Gramophone* bulging from one of his pockets engaged in a one-sided conversation with the shop's proprietor, bombarding him with a monologue of made-up "reviewese": "Of course the 1969 Koussevitsky Brahms Two has been deleted so for that matter has the Leinsdorf Vienna Volkspopper Bruckner Five which was to my mind the definitive recording and I suppose the only thing to touch Leinsdorf at his peak were those 1938 Furtwängler Berlin Radio Transcriptions . . ."[1]

This chapter deals with a range of other forms of enactment associated with phonographic culture, particularly at the level of the "Great Bore," the record collector to whom a range of apposite books and magazines has always ministered. Such texts contain the conducts associated with the culture of the phonograph, mostly relating to the amassing and organizing of record collections, to the maintaining of one's records in a pristine and orderly state.

"Dark Leisure": Hobbies and Self-recreation

In a broader cultural context, the emergence of collecting across many domains of artifacts, not just records, is related to the more generalized regimentation of leisure that occurred toward the end of the nineteenth century. During this period, collecting was encouraged as a rational and self-improving activity that represented a constructive use of the increasing leisure time available to individuals (Gelber 1999). However, as with other aspects of phonographic culture, the forms of "collectivity" associated with recording were linked to textual prescription, which was, in its turn, embedded in a regulating moral discourse. This was and still is manifested in the many published guides to the recorded repertoire. These guides have exerted influence over the actions of collectors in manifold areas of listening practice, not just in obvious ways, through the recommendations of particular recordings, but also in less obvious ways, through advice on how to domesticate modes of phonographic listening or organize programs of recorded music in the home. These were rehearsed in the activities pioneered by the gramophone societies that emerged around the world in the early parts of the twentieth century, organizations that advanced the interests of amateur gramophiles.

In reflecting on the nature of the everyday objects with which individuals elect to surround themselves, it is useful to think in a biological sense: these objects have a distinct life and death cycle (Kopytoff 1988). After all, objects are produced, circulated through various spheres of exchange, and ultimately, as is the case with the majority of quotidian objects, discarded. In some instances, though, they are "reincarnated" as antiques, or collectors' items. During the interim, depending upon where they are located in their life cycle, they are variously constituted and reconstituted as having market and symbolic values. Objects, and records are no exception, have different values in different contexts of proprietorship, according to who owns or has owned them. As was noted in chapter 5, these contexts can be symbolically manifested in various palimpsests, either institutional ("Washed 6/83"; "Donated by the British Council") or personal ("from Nina, August 1983"), that are impressed on their various surfaces. The value and meaning of discs is thus polyvalent and varies according to their particular "biographical" history, eventually transcending their initial value as traded commodities.

Some objects, such as those acquired as gifts, are not eventually discarded but instead come to be regarded, because of the sentimental value attached to them, as priceless. They are thus retained irrespective of their material condition, which in some instances might be very decrepit. In the light of their special status they are sometimes even "enshrined"; that is, they are withdrawn from circulation and framed in some way, such as being housed in special cabinets (Csikszentmihalyi and Rochberg-Halton 1981: 96). This protects the objects but also differentiates them from the more run-of-the-mill objects of the quotidian environment; they become objects of contemplation and esteem. This happened to the Aeolian Vocalion recording of Schumann's E-Flat Piano Quintet, played by the London String Quartet and Mrs. Ethel Hobday, that was owned by Compton Mackenzie, for it was this particular record that produced the "road-to-Damascus experience" that converted Mackenzie to the religion of the gramophone. As befits its "spiritual" importance in the history of *Gramophone* magazine, a framed copy of this record, complete with an explanatory holograph from Mackenzie, now hangs in its London offices. At a more general level, the framing of the record in this way exemplifies the manner in which the meanings of objects are subjected to constant redefinition, and the capacity for apparently mundane artifacts to acquire broader cultural significance via their particular histories. The act of framing can confer special distinction on an object that might otherwise have been rendered obsolete by technological change. The frame thus acts to provide a narrative context for Mackenzie's record that is distinct from a phonographic and musical one and singles out its significance as a *record* among records. The appended holograph assists this process; it sets this particular record straight, drawing the Vocalion disc into another penumbra of meaning associated with its role in the birth of an important record magazine.

Unlike forms of collecting that focus on artifacts that have outlived their usefulness (Baudrillard 1994; Martin 1999), records are manufactured to be collected and are purchased either to extend or rejuvenate the contents of an existing collection. There is of course a secondhand market in discs, as there is with books, that attracts collectors, but this is secondary to the main phonographic market. Indeed, collecting new records was from its outset an indispensable requirement for participating in the phonographic culture, particularly in the days when records offered only limited playing time and could not be played *ad nauseam* without undergoing severe sonic degradation. Although this particular failing of the early disc has been redressed and the modern CD is virtually indestructible and has enough playing time that even a modest collection of CDs offers an almost unceasing variety of musical programs, two ongoing imperatives ensure that the political economy of the record industry continues to remain ebullient. First, the regular paradigm shifts that have beset the industry have continually coerced collectors into replacing discs that have become technologically, though not necessarily musically, obsolete.[2] Second, the strong imperative to assemble collections, which takes a multitude of forms in contemporary culture, constitutes one of the archetypal activities of modern leisure (Gelber 1999).

The zeal for acquiring and preserving myriad artifacts, including some of the most disposable and least wanted items of contemporary life, is a curious development in a culture where obsolescence is a vital dynamic of contemporary consumer capitalism.[3] Collecting is seemingly at odds with the throwaway ethic pervading modern culture. Interestingly, its most extreme forms have emerged in an era of economic neoliberalism, when the value of the market has supplanted the civic virtues associated with social capital and democratic participation. Collecting has offered citizens a sense of community lacking in the *real* community and a refuge from the hollow spectacle of unfettered capitalism (Martin 1999).

Yet the passion for collecting has its origins much earlier than the advent of CDs in the 1980s, in the radical reworking of lives that occurred during the latter part of the nineteenth century. As was noted in chapter 6, changes to the patterns of work at this time caused a significant expansion of leisure time, about which there was some ambivalence. Many people feared that unless individuals occupied their leisure time in approved and improving pursuits, they would be lured into activities beyond the boundaries of acceptable moral and sexual conduct, into the realm of so-called "dark leisure" (Rojek 1999). Governments were eager to avoid this and favored patterns and forms of leisure that encouraged self-cultivation and ethical development. In large measure this desire sprang from prudential concerns about the risks associated with dark leisure, that the citizens of contemporary society needed to be protected from themselves and encouraged to pursue activities devoid of dire psychological or physical consequences. Thus the objectives of leisure policy, propounded in a number of sites, including schools, intersected with other forms of population "control" in the cultural sphere.

In terms of their capacity to assist self-formation, hobbies were thus held to be ideal leisure pursuits. Although the range of interests involved was diverse, everything from collecting to handicrafts, playing sports to engaging in self-education, hobbies made common demands upon hobbyists. Chief among these demands were the acquisition of knowledge and training, which was seen to result in a number of lasting benefits, such as self-enrichment, fitness, and health (Stebbins 2001: 6–7). Prior to the twentieth century, hobbies had been disparaged as the avocations of eccentrics. With the rise of leisure time, however, they came to be regarded as valuable ways of engendering sober habits of mind and providing individuals with a sense of purpose outside of work. Indeed, it was the special virtue of hobbies that they not only provided a prophylaxis against feared promiscuous activities but also imposed a regimen of work on the domain of free time, infusing leisure pursuits with the work ethic: an antipathy toward frittering away one's time and a zeal to be constructively engaged. In fact, they were "the Trojan horse that bought the ideology of the factory and office into the parlor" (Gelber 1999: 30). In the end hobbies, albeit without any remuneration and at some financial and temporal cost, constitute the *work* from which individuals derive most satisfaction and to which they would most like to devote more time and energy (Stebbins 1992). Hobbies can thus compensate for the deep alienation often experienced in contemporary workplaces, and the ideological circuit between work and leisure becomes a continuous one. In effect, hobbies have acted as a safety valve, providing an escape from work yet at the same time reinforcing and refueling its ethical regimen.[4]

This helpful escape can be seen in collecting. From the outset, however, the act of collecting needs to be differentiated from that of mere accumulation, which produces holdings of objects amassed in an indiscriminate way and stored willy-nilly in a disordered fashion. Accumulation is very different from the scientific forms of collecting exemplified by libraries and museums, which provide institutional settings for the collection of culturally significant artifacts. They in fact occupy the top echelon of the collecting hierarchy

(Martin 1999: 54) and employ professional collectors: the librarian and the archivist, qualified in the "sciences" of classification and curatorial practice. Then there is the form of collecting practiced by hobbyists, whose habits are often derived from those of librarians and archivists. This is the case with record collecting, which in terms of leisure theorist Stebbins's categories falls into that of a "liberal arts hobby," one that is intrinsically worthwhile and satisfies the desire to become culturally enriched (2001: 29–30).[5] As distinct from the accumulation of discs for their own sake, irrespective of their merits,[6] records of classical music are typically acquired for the purposes of musical edification and enlightenment as well as for simple pleasure.

The idea of using records as an adjunct to education emerged on both sides of the Atlantic in the 1920s as central to the gramophone's mission. Up until this period, it was claimed, music teachers had been guilty of sitting on the sidelines and watching the "baneful influence" of mechanical music, the "noise" and "St. Vitus" of jazz, destroy the benefits of a music education.[7] Yet this was not fault of the "best makers of records," who had been committed to extending their catalogs of "classical compositions" and using the phonograph as an engine of liberal education (Symes 2004). Moreover, there was also broad support for this mission in the embryonic record criticism of the time. Part of the mission of *The Gramophone* included the belief that records had the capacity to transform the musical lives of the masses by making so-called "good" music more accessible. In fact Compton Mackenzie had drawn his inspiration from the Medici Society, which had made good paintings and good books more widely available.[8]

One much-heralded benefit of mechanical reproduction was said to be its capacity to engender a more egalitarian aesthetic and provide access to domains of art that had not hitherto existed for the majority of the population (Benjamin 1970a). Prior to the advent of the camera and the phonograph, many homes, particularly those of the working classes, were artistically "impoverished" environments devoid of "fine" music and paintings (Anderson 1991: 19). Thus the technology of cultural reproduction had the potential to popularize a liberal education in the arts, particularly once its rudiments had been instilled at school, which in the early twentieth century was regarded as an ideal site for cultivating esteem for aesthetic pursuits and values (Symes 1996: 98). Certainly the educational discourses appertaining to the gramophone emphasized its potential to awaken in children an enduring appreciation of good music, one of robustness sufficient to protect them from the seductions of jazz. The musical appreciation movement—prevalent in the 1920s and 1930s—condemned jazz and held that its specific moral hazards needed containment. An adequate grounding in music education via records, it was hoped, would armor-plate children against the "degrading sounds" encountered through (jazz) records (Hadow 1928: 270). In effect, the educational gramophone was designed to inoculate children against its own ill effects and discourage them from entering into a pact with the dark leisure of jazz. This proved to be a forlorn hope.

Record Organizations: The Gramophone Society Movement

But outside of the traffic in these broad cultural and educational objectives, the most ardent record collectors soon joined other kinds of collectors in forming their own "social world," akin to a learned society, which oversaw an arcane body of understanding—the object knowledge pertaining to records. This knowledge was published in newsletters and magazines, publications that promulgated the practices associated with collecting records and provided embryonic reflections on phonographic phenomena. These publications enabled collectors to gain more power over their collections but, in so doing, the collection came to exert a certain power over the collector as well, fashioning his life and giving him a purpose, duties, and goals—in other words, "serious leisure" incarnate (Stebbins 1992).

In fact, much of the initial collective action associated with records at the level of the hobbyist was sponsored through that phonographic form of the priesthood known as the "gramophone society movement," which had its origins prior to World War I and whose main focus of musical interest was popular music. It was not until the 1920s that a classical version of this movement emerged, first in the United Kingdom and then in other countries including the United States. However, it did not have the lasting power in the latter that it had in other parts of the world (Katz 1998).

The Gramophone helped to spearhead the gramophone movement in the United Kingdom and promulgate the activities of its constituent clubs and societies. Its inaugural issue carried an article on how to organize a gramophone society and stressed how important such societies were in raising the esteem of the gramophone in the public eye and awarding "to it its rightful place amongst musical instruments" (Rogers 1923: 10). It also carried a number of reports on the activities of gramophone societies across the U.K. These reports were a regular feature of *The Gramophone* and other British-based record magazines until the early 1970s.[9] A significant feature of the gramophone society was the monthly or fortnightly "recital" based on a program of recordings selected by one of its members. These recitals, according to a survey of gramophone societies conducted in the 1930s, were organized as if they were proper concerts (Johnson 1936a: 85; Johnson 1954: 153). They lasted from 7:30 to 11:00 PM and came with printed programs and intermissions and even featured applause, a habit that was only dropped in the 1960s (Frow 1994:

151). These recitals, in other words, invoked concert hall etiquette—another manifestation of the pervasiveness of the keystone discourse.

However, there were obviously notable differences between record recitals and real concerts. One was the nature of their programs, which were developed around themes, for example, "Music to Shakespeare," "Building a Record Library," "Gramophone Brains Trust," "Creatures, Great and Small," and so on.[10] In addition, record society recitals provided opportunities for the gramophone industry to promote its latest products and gadgetry. And if there was sometimes a measure of levity in their programs—one seemingly incompatible with the gravity of classical music in other contexts—it was clear, nonetheless, where the bounds of musical propriety lay: dance music was excluded from the agendas of the gramophone society, for it properly belonged to such venues of dark leisure as the "Hot Rhythm Club" (Rogers 1931: 86).

As the gramophone society movement evolved and its interests intersected with the more classically oriented gramophone, its cultural politics underwent a shift. In consolidating the schism between popular and serious music, it began to promote itself as dedicated to musical education and, to this end, contemplated undertaking a name change to that of a "Recorded Music Study Circle" (Johnson 1936b: 86). In harmony with these educational aspirations were the facts that record societies mostly met in libraries and lecture theatres, amassed collections of miniature scores and musical reference books, and kept extensive records of their recitals (Ridout 1944a; 1944b), which kept their members occupied as recording angels! Their members also published extensively, which was indicative of the important role amateurs played in the development of phonographic culture, particularly during the 1920s and 1930s when the mechanics of recording were still "primitive" and left scope for the amateurs to make substantial improvements in the euphony of the gramophone (Maisonneuve 2001: 15).

Another facet of the gramophone society movement was the annual conference held for the benefit of "gramophiles," which attracted a broad range of interest groups, including record companies. The first of these, the so-called "High Leigh" conference held in 1938, set the pattern for similar series of annual conferences convened under the aegis of various gramophone organizations in the postwar period. The proceedings of the 1938 conference included a number of important addresses (Lovegrove 1938). One was from Percy Scholes, who, as was his wont, used the occasion to aver the cause of the longer-playing record. The activities of these phonographic conferences, which were important forums for amateurs and professionals alike, should not be trivialized, for they provided the foundations of phonographic scholarship.[11]

Records of Records: The Science and Art
of Phonographic Cataloging

Turning now to another sense of collective action, the record catalog is the most primitive form of text associated with *recording* recordings in all their manifold types and forms. It utilizes the list as its narrative "grammar" and comprises a literal collection of records on paper, for, collectively speaking, recordings form a vast order of information, a "universe" of artifacts that did not exist prior to Edison's invention. Though recordings constant shifting to new reproducing formats has discouraged the record's preservation and millions upon millions of them have been destroyed, there are nonetheless still huge collections of records, both private and public, around the world.

Record catalogs in fact form a class of "inventory" or "enlisted" texts of which the discography, the record equivalent of the bibliography, and the advisory guide, a more "judgmental" form of discography listing esteemed recordings, are the main examples. Whereas the discography is comprehensive, the advisory guide is more selective. And here it is important to distinguish scholarly discographies, which aim to provide a complete listing of the recordings associated with a particular composer, performer, or type of music, and the more trade-oriented discographies that are the subjects of this chapter. The forerunners of the latter, in terms of their organization and function, were the primitive bibliographies and catalogs that began to appear during the early parts of the sixteenth century and played an important role in disseminating information about new and forthcoming books (Febvre and Martin 1997: 230, 235). The trade catalogs issued by the record companies played a similar role: they provided "traces" or "inscriptions" of the music available on record. As such, they assumed particular importance in record shops. However, prior to the development of global catalogs providing comprehensive listings of records, the only ones that were available were trade versions issued by record companies. Some dealers expected their assistants to memorize them; at HMV's Oxford Street shop, it was deemed very unprofessional to be caught consulting a record catalog (Walker 1998b: 92).

William Schwann, then a proprietor of a record shop in Cambridge and a regular record reviewer for the *Boston Herald,* issued the first global record catalog in 1949. The idea followed an enquiry from a customer in search of a particular recording that could not be traced in the trade catalogs Schwann had at hand. He decided to develop his own, which was, in fact, a concatenation of the existing trade catalogs. Its twenty-six pages listed 674 works by ninety-eight composers. By 1956, the original eleven cited labels had grown to 281 and the number of recordings listed had risen to 20,000 (Berger 1957). At the time of the silver anniversary edition, the number of discs had climbed to 45,000 and the catalog, which was now being prepared on a computer, had begun to appear in two volumes (Pfeiffer 1974). At this point the Schwann catalog had come to be accepted as the Bible of what was available on disc, at least in the United States, and, importantly, it provided a free entry and a market profile of sorts to the smaller, independent record companies lacking the financial means to place advertisements in mass-circulation record magazines (Berger 1957).

The underlying narrative architecture of Schwann, though, had been developed decades earlier. In 1912, Samuel Holland Rouse had compiled a self-indexing catalog of the Victor Talking Machine Company's holdings (Moran 1977: 677). This combined a disc inventory with sundry musical information and also contained numerous portraits of "noted singers, musicians and composers." (See Figure 8.1.) But it is R. D. Darrell's *Encyclopedia of Recorded Music,* first published in 1932, that is generally acknowledged to establish the modern "principles and procedures of discography." Certainly it influenced another pioneering discography, the *World Encyclopaedia of Recorded Music* (Clough and Cumming 1952: v). The main difference between Schwann and these incunabula catalogs, though, was the fact that its entries *only* included those records that were actually available.[12] Another of its valued features was the "black diamond," which identified a record listed for deletion and whose appearance alongside a valued recording sometimes induced enough consumer backlash to prevent that fate (Berger 1957: 128). This is an instance of the enabling power of information—texts are never inert but are frequently taken up by their readers to advance their own interests. Thus, those on the edge of the record industry, the consumers, can influence those at its center, the record industry executives.

Schwann thus represented an important landmark in the development of the narrative architecture of recording. It aggregated into one volume information that had been previously decentered and distributed in diverse sources, published at different times and places, and often out-dated. Schwann "rationalized" this disparate information, subjecting the universe of classical records to taxonomical classification by arranging it alphabetically according to composer and to the main categories of composition: orchestral, chamber, instrumental, and so on. The distillations of such information into a single volume helped to order and regulate the ever-expanding universe of discs. It provided a convenient epistemological tool—an "immutable mobile"—for inquiring into the state of the recorded repertoire at a particular point in time. Its pages provided documentary evidence of which

Figure 8.1 Record catalogues have a long tradition. One of the first is shown in the above advertisement, which appeared in *McClure's* (January 1915). The catalog is an early example of "infotainment," combining promotion with instruction. It is designed to help listeners become acquainted with "the works of the great composers" and lists over five thousand Victor Records to facilitate that acquaintance. The two pages displayed above have entries on Enrico Caruso and English contralto Clara Butt. Arguably, the advent of sleeve notes obviated the need for such informative catalogs, which nevertheless continued to be published until the end of the 1940s.

compositions were over-recorded and which had yet to be recorded. Thumbing through its pages in 1955, one record critic observed that there was still a dearth of recordings of music from the pre-Bach and post-Strauss eras. He lamented the fact that there was, as yet, little Josquin in the catalog, no John Ireland Piano Concerto, no Arnold Bax symphonies. What existed on record from these parts of the repertoire was mainly produced by the in-dependents, and he hoped that the more "adventurous record public," like those thousands of people who had begun to discover the delights of foreign travel, would want to explore these "hitherto undiscovered regions of music and find new joys therein" (Robertson 1955: 86). For others, though, the prospect revealed by Schwann was much less promising, as the catalogue seemed to show that there was a glut of recordings, more than any one listener could ever hope to digest, let alone determine the best from (Weinstock 1956).

Although catalogs such as Schwann have provided a systematic listing of the recorded repertoire, they have not displaced the old trade catalogues, which continue to be produced by the majors and the independents. Like everything else about the record industry, these works continue to march with the times, and many now include a bar code alongside each CD entry that dealers can use to automatically refurbish their stock. This is just one of the ways in which the various forms of narrative architecture associated with the phonograph have appropriated information technology, and it reflects the degree to which digital technology now permeates not just recording but also the supply and demand of information about discs. Nevertheless, Schwann and its European equivalents[13] remain important texts in the epis-temological formation of the record industry and provide dramatic indices, if any were needed, of the growth in recorded repertoire that began with the LP and has continued apace into the era of the CD. Until the early 1970s, cat-alogs of Schwann were the size of medium-sized paperbacks. One of its twenty-first-century descendents, the *RED Classical Catalogue* (2002), is a gargantuan tome, hard to handle, let along pocket, whose individual entries are printed in a microscopic font.[14]

Such catalogs, though, need to be differentiated from the more selective forms of inventory text whose purposes relate to evaluating recordings in terms of performance and technical criteria. Such texts belong to an emerging body of "literature" in consumer culture: the guide surveying and assessing the artifacts belonging to a particular commodity regime. These have become *vade-mecums* for consumers seeking advice and information about contem-porary commodities, assisting them in singling out their qualities and iden-tifying those among them most worthy of being acquired on the grounds that they possess durable and reliable qualities (Featherstone 1991: 18–19).[15]

The guides associated with CDs and LPs fulfill a number of advisory functions, the main one being to provide a series of recommendations to their readers regarding what records they *should* own rather than what they *could* own, the latter being more the function of the Schwann-style of catalog.

In fact, there are two forms of record guide. The first is the general guide to recordings modeled on Baedeker. It achieves what the disgruntled reader of *Schwann* said was impossible, namely to identify in a market overcrowded with choices an overall best recording and/or performance and thereby proscribe the acquisition of inferior discs. The second form is the more prescriptive guide. It identifies the contents of a basic library of recordings and provides a representative "sounding" of Western classical music. The prescriptive guide is usually written for the novice who is perplexed by classical music, but wants to make it part of his or her "serious leisure." Such guides are "brokerage" texts providing informed prejudgments for those who desire to buy "by the book" rather than "blind." Yet they also act as manuals of practice, providing advice on how to maintain, play, and organize record collections. These texts will be examined later in the chapter.

For guides to exist, a critical mass of recordings needs to exist from which to select. Notwithstanding the relative dearth of classical recordings available at the time, such guides began to be published in the 1920s, when the mania for collecting records was in its ascendancy. Interestingly, while there are modern guides to building book collections, they are far fewer in number than those pertaining to records. Part of the explanation for this discrepancy resides in the technologies of reproduction involved. Cervantes's *Don Quixote* is, word for word, still *Don Quixote* whether in a first or a modern paperback edition; this is not the case, however, with a recording of Richard Strauss's *Don Quixote*.[16] Each recording will offer a different, and more or less beguiling, version of the score. Guides—examples of the record review writ large—identify from among several recordings of the same work the version that is the *most* definitive and provides, note for note, the most persuasive of interpretations. For, from the 1960s onward, the catalog has become "super-saturated" with recordings in both the over-explored and "hitherto undiscovered" regions of the repertoire.[17] Moreover, there are CDs in all price categories: super-budget, budget, medium, and full. In this context of bewildering choice, the *caveat* obligation of *caveat emptor* discourse has assumed more urgency than ever. The "preselections" of recommended discs in record guides reduce many of the dilemmas consumers confront in purchasing classical records.

One of the pioneers of the modern record guide was David Hall. His original guide appeared at the beginning of World War II, and underwent annual updates until 1944, when it ceased publication. Hall's guide acknowledged that choice was increasingly difficult in a market, even then, oversupplied with its commodity—there were already fifteen versions of Beethoven's Fifth Symphony. It also provided an introduction to the world of music and offered recommendations, unusually, across the whole musical spectrum, not just classical but also jazz and folk (Hall 1940). These recommendations were intended to allow the "serious music lover" of the book's subtitle to acquire a "library of recorded masterpieces that will be of a permanent value" (Hall 1940: 1). Note the presence of caveat vocabulary ("of a *permanent* value"), which harks back to Mackenzie's observation that far too many record collections contain music whose pleasures prove ephemeral and soon pale. Yet although Hall's book provided suggestions for specific recordings, it stopped short of utilizing the type of "dividing practices" identifying good and bad recordings. It was thus not a guide in the Baedeker tradition, in which recordings of the same composition are compared to one another and symbols of merit used to rank recordings.

Although many such adjudication guides have appeared since the 1950s, most can trace their genealogy to Edward Sackville-West and Desmond Shawe-Taylor's pioneering *Record Guide*. This first appeared in 1951 and, to ensure the currency of its contents in a market of frequent additions and deletions, it was updated annually.[18] The contents of such guides are often drawn from the record magazines with which their compilers are associated. This is the case with *The Good CD Guide*, which is aptly named given the genealogy of its genre; it belongs to the stable of publications associated with *Gramophone* magazine and derives its "copy," albeit in a more distilled form, from its reviews. It was first published in a modest format in what was described as "the year of the compact disc," when the CD was making inroads on the LP market and its qualities were beginning to impress themselves on the public (Pollard 1987: v). Since then it has appeared annually, becoming more compendious and comprehensive with each new edition. It also re-presents many of the evaluation "tables" that are features of *Gramophone*, such as "Record of the Year," "Sounds in Retrospect," "Editor's Choice," "100 Great Recordings," "A Suggested Basic Library," and so on. *The Good CD Guide* also ranks recordings: three discs to denote "recordings that have acquired legendary status," one for recordings that lack that status but are still recommendable. This helps to expedite the selection of a choice recording and to fulfill the main function of the guide, which is to eliminate the "confusion of record-buying" and uniting the reader "quickly and painlessly with the best in classical music" (Bettley 2001: i). In fact, there are now so many such markers of merit (historic recording, value for money, *Gramophone* Award Winner, and so on) that the 2001 edition of the guide includes a bookmark on which the various markers are decoded. As it is with record magazines, much of the justification for possessing such guides is pecuniary. The outlay for them—they usually cost as much as two full-priced CDs—is more than recompensed if they stop consumers from acquiring inferior records. But they can also have the effect of introducing consumers to recordings whose costs will be repaid by hours of priceless pleasure (Osborne 1973: 8)

Of much the same textual pedigree as *The Good CD Guide* are the numerous record guides published by Penguin since the 1970s. These also recall the Long Playing Record Library's (LPRL) Treasury Guides, which were originally devised to list more recherché works that were absent from mainstream catalogs. The first of the LPRL Penguin guides was published in 1975 and was soon followed by a number of more specialist guides. Their covers sported a "dog-eared" version of the HMV trademark, whose twin heads spin in confusion, unable to cope with a market surfeited with choice (Figure 8.2).

The narrative architecture of the Penguin guides was more or less identical to that of *The Record Guide:* a preface, an introduction, and an editorial on the state of the recording industry, followed by an alphabetical listing of composers and their works. These were divided into further categories such as "Chamber and instrumental music," "Piano music," and "Opera." "Even allowing for its omissions"—inevitable in a market surfeited with LPs—the guide claimed "to be the most comprehensive coverage of the recorded repertoire ever attempted" (Greenfield, Layton, and March 1975: xiii). A particular feature of the Penguin guides is the "rosette" awarded to the record exhibiting "a magic, or spiritual quality that places it in a special category," a quality said to become immediately apparent upon first playing.[19]

The award of three stars in the *Penguin Guide* carries considerable prestige, which the record companies often use to promote their recordings. In the 1970s, for example, the U.K. distributor Conifer used the fact that a large number of its recordings received three stars as the theme of one of its advertisements. The advertisement features the relevant Penguin guide, which is described—thereby giving it a "plug" also—as providing "the definitive critical listing of classical recordings" (see Figure 8.2). The 2003 catalog of the Naxos label—perhaps conscious of the need to allay any view that its super-budget CDs have been produced at the expense of their quality—cites their "star ratings" not only in the Penguin guides but also in a range of other magazines and guides whose rating criteria are explained in the catalog. The Naxos catalog employs a consensus rhetoric using every accolade to reinforce the quality of its discs. The impact is somewhat akin to the coherence theory of truth applied to the domain of judgment: one accolade might be exceptional, but three cannot be and so must be grounded in truth.

Figure 8.2 This advertisement, first published in *Gramophone* (March 1983), shows the way companies, in this instance Conifer Records, have used the authority of the *Penguin Guides* to underwrite their performance. It also illustrates the complex circuitry that exists between the guides, record covers, and advertising copy, which comprise the intertextual nature of phonographic culture. This is also manifested by the dog motif—another allusion to HMV— on the cover of the *Penguin Guide,* and the use of the Penguin sticker, an example of palimpsest, on Lyrita's Malcolm Arnold LP. (Reproduced by permission of the editor of *Gramophone.*)

Sometimes the Penguin's stamp of approval has been deployed as an integral element of the cover design (see Figure 4.13), which is a twin "plug," for the disc also appears under the Penguin label. The web of evaluative texts in record magazines is thus given succinct expression in record guides, which, while they have currency, are used to promote superlative recordings and affirm their status as performances without compare. For record guides are the principal sources of an authoritative voice in the phonographic world. In turn, because of their standing and wide circulation in this world, guides are also used to promote other sectors of the recording industry. *The Good CD Guide,* for example, has attracted sponsorship from various arms of the audio industry, most recently from loudspeaker manufacturer Bowes and Wilkins, whose nautilus designs grace its "pre-text" (Bettley 2001).

As the audiences for recorded music have become more specialized, record guides have followed suit. Guides now exist that focus on the merits of recordings in a variety of disc categories, from their price—guides to bargain records (e.g. Greenfield, Layton and March 1980)—to their particular area of the repertoire. In due recognition of the audience for audiophile recordings, there is at least one guide listing so-called "demonstration recordings" as well, those exhibiting superior sound. There are no best buys in this case for any of the recordings listed, as they are all seen as worthy of acquisition; it is just that some excel more than others in terms of an absolute sound performance. Nonetheless, even this guide recognizes that, for classical music, at least, "a convincing sound stage" is the benchmark of excellence (Ferstler 1994: 3).

In the guides evaluating recordings of contemporary music, there is less focus on determining the ultimate choice among a range of recordings, for such music is one of the few realms of the repertoire that remains under-recorded. Instead, it is more a matter of identifying those works in the contemporary repertoire that repay repeated listening. And because such music often requires more explanation, these guides adopt a more expository approach that departs from the alphabetical form of listing typical of the standard record guide. This alphabetical form has the effect of separating composers from one another in terms of their times and their placement in particular musical communities, be they national or stylistic. It also tends to encourage selective forms of reading. But then, as is the case with most references books, cover-to-cover reading is unusual: readers read instead in terms of their immediate phonographic quandaries. By contrast, guides to contemporary music are often organized around explanatory chapters that place compositions in their geographical and chronological contexts. One of the most recent guides of this type—part of a series dealing with all of the dominant genres of contemporary music, including country and western, for example—adopts such a contextual approach. *The Blackwell Guide to Recorded Contemporary Music* provides a discursive "traversal" of music composed between 1940 and 1990, identifying, year by year, seminal compositions beginning with Olivier Messiaen's *Quatuor pour la fin du temps,* together with their relevant recordings (Morton 1996). Instead of evaluating these recordings as recordings—other guides do that, it is suggested—its approach is more "musical." Thus it overlaps with the functions of liner notes, but it also alerts curious listeners to other works that they might enjoy listening to. Its narrative organization, in fact, follows that articulated in a relatively modest guide to modern music on record that was edited by the noted English composer Robert Simpson and Oliver Prenn (1958). Its individual chapters dealt with particular forms of modern music, including Soviet, Scandinavian, serial, and neoclassical, and listed relevant recordings at the end of each. But, in addition, this guide performed other rhetorical maneuvers such as those deployed in record magazines, enjoining companies to be more adventurous and to record such absentees from the catalog as Ireland's Piano Concerto, a particular hobbyhorse among critics of the 1950s. Of more import, though, is the fact that the author of the foreword to the guide—and forewords always lend authority to a text (Genette 1997)—was another noted English composer of the time, Edmund Rubbra. In his piece, he endorses the view that the gramophone had become an important instrument of musical diffusion, especially for the circulation of modern works. The opportunity afforded by the gramophone to "savour again and again works that at a first hearing yield little but perplexity" helps reduce the hostility to the "new and strange" (Rubbra 1958: ix).

In the beginning, though, guides were justified by the dearth rather than the surplus of recordings, particularly of complete works, especially operas, for which the guides acted as a supplement, completing the work on paper and providing notes in lieu of the musical notes missing on the disc. Take, for example, *The Victor Book of the Opera,* which first appeared in 1912 and was reprinted many times: it was 375 pages long, extensively illustrated, and replete with stories of seventy operas—many more than were available on record at the time—and translations of their major arias. It thus served to overcome the problems of abridged recordings, providing a textual substitute for the missing music. But more importantly, it helped promote Victor's recordings through frequent references to them. It was soon followed by a host of kindred publications that ostensibly encouraged musical appreciation yet doubled as showcases for RCA's other products (Horowitz 1987: 206). These included everything from *A Musical Galaxy,* which described the most celebrated moments in music (see Figure 4.7), to a quiz book designed for parties, whose musical excerpts could be played, if they were available, using Victor records, thereby tapping the contestants' memories through "the ear rather than the eye" (Cott 1945: vi).

The coalescence of a mercantile imperative with cultural edification that was exhibited in RCA's publishing endeavors has been emulated by other labels. HMV, for example, published its own book on opera called *Opera at Home*. While still working in the Education Department of the Gramophone Company, Alec Robertson oversaw the publication of *The Golden Treasury of Recorded Sound*, a series of pamphlets issued at the end of the 1920s that explained the works of Bach and Wagner to the novice. These edificatory practices were, at one stage, extended to Decca's advertising, which for a time in the early 1950s provided short introductions to the music on its LPs.[20] Arguably, the era of sleeves and liner notes eventually rendered the need for such "off-the-record" explanations unnecessary.

The Rise of Record Libraries: From Books to Discs and Discs to Books

Libraries of records were, like much else associated with the phonograph, anticipated decades before they eventuated in the textual imagination, specifically the writings of Edison and Berliner. Another of the record library's early advocates was Compton Mackenzie. In one of his first articles on the gramophone, he entertained the hope that the record companies would eventually "build up for the public a library of good music" (Mackenzie and Marshall 1923: 8). Whether the word "library" in connection with recordings is ultimately appropriate or not has been a matter for debate. Given its "bookish" overtones, other alternatives such as "discothéque" have been championed (Lade 1979), but that one, of course, acquired more hedonistic connotations during the 1970s. On one hand, the use of the word "library" to describe large collections of recordings could be seen as entirely consistent with the way the vocabulary of the phonograph has always exhibited a degree of etymological latitude. But on the other hand, it also reflects at least three phonographic realities: first, record libraries are hardly ever independent institutions but are instead embedded in conventional libraries; second, records rarely stand alone as "texts" in their own right but are instead always supplemented by other texts such as magazines and guides; and third, the narrative architecture of the record has often drawn on the book, a fact reflected in the use of terms such as "cover" and "jacket." Moreover, many records label have exploited the record/book analogy. EMI's U.S.-based

Angel, for example, created a "Library Series" of chamber music recordings whose jackets were described as "simple, elegant and . . . *durable*" and "which will wear well no matter how often you take the record off the *library* shelf" (my emphasis).[21]

The first record libraries, in fact, were called "sound archives" and were assembled by ethnologists, who valued the phonograph as a scientific instrument that could preserve the languages and music of endangered cultures. Indeed, the first such archive, established in Vienna in 1899, did not collect "modern Western music" at all but specimens of dialect and language, voices of famous people, and so on. The only forms of music represented were indigenous ones such as "New Guinea natives amusing themselves with bamboo flutes and mouth drums" or "the plaintiff sounds of the 'bombarde' and 'cornemuse' of Brittany." The recordings were preserved on specially constructed metal matrixes that were fireproof and designed, in keeping with their scientific functions, to last for millennia (Pollak 1925: 415). In a *Gramophone* editorial applauding the Vienna initiative, it was observed, with the hope that the situation would soon be redressed, that no equivalent collection, outside of a small number of unplayable matrices and royal records in the British Museum, existed in the United Kingdom. The editorial thus helped generate the idea of a national library of recordings, an idea that was reiterated at a number of key forums in subsequent decades, including the High Leigh Conference (Lovegrove 1938). In fact, it was another twenty-three years before the idea became a reality with the establishment of the British Institute of Recorded Sound (BIRS), now the British Sound Archive at the British Library. For although records are, in theory, immutable, that is only the case if they are preserved. Many record companies at the time, for reasons of cost, were not avid preservers of their products (Saul 1961: 13). The existence of record libraries would guarantee that at least some records would be preserved, thereby enabling future musicologists to have a powerful resource for inquiring into the performing styles of the past (Philip 1992); Edison had always hoped that this would be one of the main cultural dividends of his invention. When, in the 1930s, one of the architects of the BIRS, Patrick Saul, had been seeking a recording of Ernö Dohnányi's Violin Sonata, he was singularly unimpressed with the British Museum's small collection of records. This prompted him to develop the idea of a national sound archive. Indeed, he even harangued the museum's director about the matter, who though sympathetic managed to placate Saul's enthusiasm and enjoined him to return when he was "older" (Day 1981: 120).

In the meanwhile, records had, by the late 1940s, been admitted into public libraries, where they were available for borrowing.[22] Yet librarians of the time were keen to keep records in their place and insisted that their acquisition should not compromise their commitment to the printed word, which was their principal priority. Records were often seen as second-class citizens, and their presence troubled librarians on a number of accounts (Stevenson 1949), including concerns about their upkeep and security in the lending arena. Collecting and borrowing policies were developed that were designed to placate these fears and were strongly biased toward those borrowers who appreciated "good music." Underlying these policies, at least during the 1950s and 1960s, was a hostile attitude toward popular music that in effect constituted an institutional echo of the great musical schism. Many librarians openly detested "songs for crooners and honky tonk" and saw themselves as safeguarding musical taste from its degradation by such music (Bryant 1985: 285; McColvin 1961: 22). They determined that public money should not be expended on inferior music and only begrudgingly made allowance for its popularity by including a few of the best recordings in their collections. A degree of terminological elasticity made this possible: although good music should have invariably meant "serious" music, it did not; there was a category of music that was not necessarily serious but had enduring value nevertheless. Libraries were enjoined to collect recordings of this more "permanent music" as well (March 1965: 28)—that word "permanent" again. Some of the ambivalence toward popular music stemmed not from its ephemeral character but from the sociological anxiety that its presence in libraries would attract "riff-raff," the sort of borrower who at best is likely to treat records unkindly and at worst "naturally indulges in petty larceny" (March 1965: 55). It was therefore seen as prudent to keep the record collections highbrow. In effect, these policies, even though governed by the desire to democratize the appreciation of "permanent music," affected to indulge certain patrons and dissuade others and illustrates the way librarians used their record collections as social gatekeepers. This was affected through other means as well, such as the monitoring, in the microgroove era, of borrowers' styluses and the insistence upon carrying cases to transport records, or at least a plastic bag with a zip-fastener to protect sleeves from the ravages of rain (Bryant 1985: 399).

The collections of records in public libraries need to be distinguished from their home equivalents. Although the majority of homes contain collections of records, some of which can be very large, they are not necessarily planned like those in public libraries, which are supposed to be representative and transcend the predilections of librarians (Bryant 1985: 314). Most home collections reflect only the predilections of their owners. They are often acquired in a haphazard rather than a planned way and frequently incline, in terms of Benjamin's epigraph, toward the pole of disorder rather than order.

There are reasons for this. Many records in home collections are inherited, given as presents, or acquired impulsively; as such, they are aggregates rather than collections. Nor is size relevant. Evan Eisenberg's Clarence, who was reported to own seventy-five thousand records jammed higgledy-piggledy into his Long Island apartment, and who acquired them five hundred at a time, owned huge numbers of records but *not* a collection (Eisenberg 1988: 17). For a "genuine" collection is an aggregate of objects displaying order, whose elements have been acquired rationally, following an overarching principle.

Building a Record Collection: Some Guiding Principles

One of the commonest of the collection principles involves covering the basics in a library of classical records, and at various times record companies have provided forms of assistance in this regard. For example, in the mid-1950s Decca issued its "Decca 50," a collection of representative LPs drawn from its back catalogue and given a new livery, which for an outlay of just under one hundred pounds, so it was claimed, would "supply, ready-made, a basic classical record library"—albeit one, according to one reviewer, that would be deficient in certain areas of the repertoire (Porter 1957: 283). Decca's initiative, as often happens in the recording industry, prompted other labels to follow suit. Fontana launched its own series in 1959, the so-called "Evergreen Treasury of Music," which traversed musical territory similar to that of the "Decca 50." These organized sets of issues aimed at the novice have continued into the CD era. Sony, EMI, Polygram, and Naxos have all produced, at various times, "ready-made" collections of classical music. Such collections are designed to limit the choices one faces in acquiring classical records. Would-be collectors do not have to exercise much thought; they just follow a list. In the guides accompanying such lists, the observation is often made that while classical music is heard everywhere and by everybody, few outside of a cultural elite have much knowledge about it. In a context, then, where the classical parts of the industry are in decline, there is a desire to nurture new audiences for classical music. One way of doing this is to intimate along with one of Polygram's brochures that it is, after all, "cool" to listen to classical music (Symes 1997: 88).

But the idea of assembling a basic library of recordings began in the 1920s with Percy Scholes (1924; 1925), who thought people were crying out for books that dealt with building such a library and that would specify a "canon" of recordings without which the library would be incomplete. The main difference between the canonical suggestions of the 1920s and those of more recent provenance is that the preselections of the latter draw on a much larger "vault" of recordings and specify not just particular compositions but definitive recordings of them. Thereby these library texts are somewhat more prescriptive than the aforementioned "good CD guides" and, in the words of one of them, "assist connoisseurs" in adding the "best versions" to their collections (E.M.G. 1964: 1). The accent is thus primarily on building a collection of recordings drawn from the best possible recordings of a certain type of music. A notable feature of these more prescriptive guides (including those produced by record companies) is that they also perform an educational function. As was noted earlier, liberal arts hobbies typically require from their participants levels of understanding and knowledge that are usually absent from more casual pursuits. The knowledge associated with classical music is not easy to acquire in a context where the opportunities to engage such music in a meaningful way have become fewer. The opportunities that do exist—attending concerts, for example—often alienate many listeners, who feel embarrassed about lacking the requisite "cultural capital" and fear exposure as ignoramuses. To overcome such fears, many guides include sections on basic music theory and history. Thus they set out to compensate for their readers' attenuated musical "capital" and provide them with the wherewithal to be more informed about music. To this end, many record guides, even quite early ones (Downes 1918), have included glossaries of musical terms and dictionaries on how to pronounce correctly the titles of works (*Rouët d'Omphale*—"rwe dom-fal") and the names of composers ("Rayfe," not Ralph, Vaughan Williams), an area of particular vulnerability.[23]

But the majority of these canonical texts are devoted to listing core musical works, the undisputed *classics* among the classics, to which new works, as record exploration has opened up "hitherto undiscovered regions" of music, have been gradually added. This is particularly true of the pre-Bach and post-Strauss repertoire. Compare the musical contents of Olin Downe's 1918 guide with that of Jonathan Buckley's published seventy-five years later. The former, despite having only a limited catalog of music on which to draw, had a very narrow compass and contained no Bach or Handel and little Beethoven (Downes 1918). Buckley's, by contrast, encompasses music from the Middle Ages to the present. It also includes, as no other equivalent guide had to date, representative women composers, not just the chic Hildegard of Bingen but also the lesser-known Elizabeth Lutyens and Ethel Smyth (Buckley 1994).

Another notable feature of Downes's guide is that it embedded its musical annotations in anecdotes about great composers, a frequent discourse strategy of the time that stemmed from the musical appreciation movement, which held that classical music would be made more palatable to the musical laity if it was brought to life and given a human face. Thus the more abstract and analytical approaches favored by the musical cognoscenti were eschewed. Although contemporary guides are less prone to lighten their approach to classical music than those of the 1920s, they do nonetheless continue to embed their records in a biographical and musical context. Indeed, the pre-text regions of the most recent edition of *The Good CD Guide* (Bettley 2001) now include a series of explanatory essays on the major eras of music, complete with a list of representative works and their recordings.

Such guides—which are almost akin to study guides—need to be differentiated from those created more democratically, on the basis of a popular vote, such as Keith Shadwick's *The Classic FM Hall of Fame Collection* (2000). This is compiled on an annual basis according to audience responses to the programming content of the U.K. commercial radio station Classic FM, which has adopted a sound bite approach to classical music.[24] Intended to provide a number of "entry points" for those starting in the "classical music field," Shadwick only includes music that has the assured appeal reflected in its position atop the Classic FM's request charts, the so-called "Hall of Fame" with which his guide is eponymous. Generally, though, like its radio incarnation, this guide is long on *shorter* works of music, arias and overtures that are statistically proven to be popular and that are drawn from a relatively restricted canon commencing in the 1770s and ending in the 1900s, more or less the compass of Downes's guide as well.

From the epoch of the LP, Martyn Goff's guides (1957; 1958; 1974) were also intended to make classical music more palatable and were pledged to repair the damage visited upon their readers as a result of an execrable music education. Bored silly and insensate by classical music, as they had been by Shakespeare and poetry, the people's desire for music had been captured by popular records, by "skiffle" and light music that Goff, like many gramophiles, pronounced tasteless and odious (1958: 100). Indeed, it is clear from the parenthetical asides pervading Goff's guides that he feared the threat posed by popular music, which he argued had led to lazy musical habits and an appetite for anodyne music, that he hoped in turn to dampen. His approach to classical music, which he had first pioneered in courses for the U.K.'s Workers' Education Association (WEA), was designed to instill an interest in higher quality music. This involved re-engineering the musical tastes of his readers via a ground plan of listening based on historical principles, one that recognized, for example, the foolishness of attempting to listen to Sibelius's Fifth Symphony before Beethoven's (Goff 1957: 4). It would further discourage, in the early stages of building a record collection, the acquisition of the more advanced symphonies of Mahler, Bruckner, and Walton. In fact, Goff counseled his readers against buying customized collections such as the "Decca 50" not because of the expense involved but because it might "have the effect of preventing you becoming *familiar* with the works" (my emphasis). Goff saw familiarity as the key principle upon which the appreciation of classical music depended and felt that listeners should endeavor to listen to one record and become fully acquainted with its contents before moving on to others. Furthermore, Goff argued that records, particularly complete operas, are relatively expensive and suggested that the sacrifice of certain vices could help subsidize their purchase; besides, *Don Pasquale* could be more of a tonic than "champagne or mescalin" (Goff 1958: 29). Serious leisure can thereby mimic "dark leisure" but without its associated risks.

Of particular significance in Goff's guides—though by no means exclusive to them—is the frequent observation that "serious music" requires "serious attention." This, he suggested, entailed a certain amount of self-pandering, including a comfortable chair and the presence of listening companions free of "musical allergies" (Goff 1957: 16). In fact, such additional sets of prescriptions are a regular feature of record guides and relate to the adoption of sound practices, both on and off the record, that permit the highest levels of edification to be elicited from listening. The conclusion to be drawn, then, is that the aesthetic benefits flowing from serious music are not yielded instantly but require tenacious listening habits—sentiments echoing those of Stravinsky cited in chapter 2. For example, at one point Goff suggests playing the exposition section of a symphony several times, taking care not to scratch its surface, in order to become fully accustomed to its "tunes" (1957: 43).

Thus, such guides—acoustic librettos, as it were—function as transducers creating bridges between recordings and their listeners by transforming the sound of one into the disciplined regimen of the other. This includes not just sitting comfortably but also organizing records into a playing order somewhat akin to a concert program: an overture to set the evening's mood, followed by a major work of a more contemplative and demanding nature—at least that is Goff's recommendation (1957: 28). One of his antecedents in the 1930s was even more specific: this guide advocated a two-hour program consisting of about twenty 78s of not too complex music, held between 7 and 9 PM and written out in advance and displayed. In order to "hear the best performance," the audience was to be kept at a distance from the gramophone, and if they started talking over the records or showing other signs of "flagging interest," the proceedings were to be stopped and coffee served. This break was supposed to revive the energies for listening and ensure that the rest of the recital proceeded uninterrupted (Rogers 1931: 91). In effect, these recital etiquettes exemplified the idea of a domesticated concert, which did not incur the expense of buying tickets or traveling to a concert (though one did sacrifice the concert's moral benefits). This sort of concert was promoted in other textual environments as well, such as a Decca advertisement from the 1950s. It depicts a man, and the gender is not without significance—women by this stage had been driven out of the phonographic picture—planning a home concert. It also describes the plan of such a concert: "Just four" Decca LPs and an "hour between the second and third for something to eat and drink" will provide the makings of a "really delightful evening of music from six-thirty to ten-thirty or seven to eleven"—more or less the time span of an actual concert. The central idea of the advertisement, then, is that a "take nine" LP can be transmuted into a "take one" concert and that the man of the house can play the role of concert impresario and bring into the home "some of the world's finest artists" (Figure 8.3).

In other words, guides, like Decca's advertisements, act as manuals of practice, prescribing not just records but sets of listening protocols and etiquettes. These have the effect of regulating listeners and choreographing their auditory habits, which includes making the conditions of the so-called "record recital" somewhat akin to those encountered at a real recital—a further reflection of the keystone discourse. For as was observed in the first chapter, this record recital could include such off-the-record practices as dressing for the part and attending it as one might a concert; with the advent of stereo, speakers were also supposed to be configured in such a way that they came to replicate the acoustic of a real concert hall, even at the risk of resisting the wife's desire to hide them (Goff 1974: 2).

Listening to Records and Keeping Them on File

In fact, while there is a surfeit of prescription in record guides about how and under what conditions records ought to be played as well as several studies about what types of music are played in the home (Bennett, Emmison and Frow 1999; Bourdieu 1989; Peterson and Kern 1996), there are very few studies of how records are actually played. The rare accounts suggest that evenings in which records are played in a formal way, followed by discussions on a range of musical and phonographic matters, have indeed been conducted. Alfred Kinsey, author of the Kinsey Report, was one who held such evenings, which benefited, apparently, from the insights of the professional musicians present (1956: 28). A letter published in *Gramophone* (March 1982), that prompted a whole chain of responses suggested that listening to classical records, in spite of the randomized approaches favored by the initial correspondent, by and large tended toward Benjamin's pole of order. Two of

CONCERT PLANNER!

With the Decca L.P. catalogue and supplements for the sixth and seventh releases (two shillings and threepence from your local dealer or two shillings and sixpence direct from us) it's easy to plan a concert to take place in your own home of just those things that both you and the family like. Four L.P. records, with an hour between the second and third for something to eat and drink, will give you a really delightful evening of music from six-thirty to ten-thirty or seven to eleven . . . and so to bed . . . a happy, memorable evening with some of the world's finest artists and *just four Decca L.P. records.*

The Long Playing Catalogue

THE DECCA RECORD COMPANY LTD., 1-3 BRIXTON ROAD, LONDON, S.W.9

Figure 8.3 Originally published in *The Gramophone* (September 1951), this Decca advertisement shows a "concert planner" at work. The man of the house is organizing a home concert from a Decca LP catalogue "of just those things that both you and the family like." It is suggested that an interval be included, just as in an actual concert, between the second and third LPs "for something to eat and drink." This advertisement is a statement of the keystone discourse. Through the italicization of "just four," it also stresses the temporal and spatial economy of the LP relative to the 78. (Reproduced by permission of the editor of *Gramophone*.)

the correspondents, for example, mention organizing concerts lasting a minimum of one and a half hours involving particular ensembles: orchestras one night, chamber groups another, and so on. Anniversaries of composers' birthdays also prompted "concerts" that were recorded in a "Concert Record Book" logging the use of the record collection and the amount of "life" left in the stylus. In these respects, there is a continuity of sorts between guides and home phonographic practices. In fact, one guide goes to considerable lengths to devise possible concerts that are timed and structured with contents calibrated with a five-point scale in terms of their aesthetic value and accessibility. In the latter case, this ranges from music that is austere and esoteric to that which "makes immediate connection" (Halsey 1976: 19).

The aforementioned chain of letters also contained observations on how record collections are organized and classified, which is another issue about which guides often comment. For once a collection surpasses a certain size, it requires organization so that its constituent elements can be retrieved with expedition. Collections of 400 to 500 CDs or many more are not uncommon among collectors. Indeed, it has been a matter of speculation as to whether once a collection surpasses a certain size its individual items can be played with sufficient regularity and frequency to justify being there.[25] Although some people such as the previously cited correspondent have argued that the pleasant surprise encountered each time a record is played justifies leaving a collection in a random state, most collectors and their doyens advocate more methodical modes of organization and collecting. Indeed, the writers of record guides tend to inveigh against indiscriminate collecting, arguing that it can produce unbalanced collections. There is a need to keep tabs on one's collection in order to ensure that it does not evolve haphazardly, and its systematic organization on shelves can help to pinpoint hiatuses (Bryant 1962: 26).

In his novel *High Fidelity*, Nick Hornby identified a number of possible ways of "filing" a collection of rock LPs, including ordering them according to their association with his various relationships with women (2000: 42–43). Capricious though it might sound, Hornby's organizing principle contains a cogent insight: individuals acquire records not just for the purposes of musical edification. Sometimes they acquire them for their ability to arouse nonmusical associations, "delineated meanings" (Green 1988) such as those of a love affair. Records are also *records* of peoples' lives: musical mnemonics that evoke fond memories and happy events. However, such idiosyncratic forms of organization as Hornby's are, in the end, self-defeating: they are too recondite, only permitting their owners and their intimates to navigate the collection.

Most record collections follow more conventional forms of organization echoing those used to organize books, that is, alphabetical by author, subject matter, publisher, price, time of publication or acquisition, size, or even color (Petroski 1999). But unlike most books, which are wide enough to carry identifying information on their spines, the width of a CD or LP's spine does not permit much information about its program to be recorded, let alone easily seen. As it was recommended that LPs and 78s—it is less important for CDs—were stored in an upright position, the need to organize them in a systematic way was therefore more exigent than for books. In most guides, the main principle of organization suggests that after grouping records of the same size together, the home record collection ought to follow shops and libraries in employing an alphabetical order by composer's name, with concerts comprising miscellaneous programs in which no one composer's works are dominant and recital discs filed separately (Bryant 1962: 70). In order to enhance accessibility, more discrete modes of organization are adopted in larger collections—and these can also be observed in record shops, where the impetus for expeditious access is even stronger. Thus all of Beethoven's symphonies might be kept together in numerical sequence, and the same for his piano concertos, string quartets, and so on. Although other forms of organization are possible, such as chronological or epochal ones— keeping all the records of Baroque music together, for example—alphabetical organization, since it is the least prone to fuzzy forms of categorization, is by and large favored. Nonetheless, in large record shops where the classical section is quarantined from the popular section, there is still scope for categorical fuzziness, particularly when the elasticity of musical divisions is insufficiently appreciated. The then director of Archiv records drew attention to this problem in the early 1960s and suggested that the mention of the word "dance" in many record shops invariably meant pop music, and "modern" meant Louis Armstrong. There was no recognition that classical composers also wrote dances, such as the Romanian ones of Bartók he sought, and could also be modern (Hickmann 1961: 14). Quite subtle forms of classification are, in fact, needed to avoid confusion. Recent developments in contemporary music that blur the distinctions between rock and classical, jazz and popular and appeal to a more "omnivorous" taste in music (Peterson and Kern 1996) pose special difficulties for retailers (Frith 1996: 77–78).[26]

In addition to being urged to sequentially order their collections, collectors are also urged to develop their own catalogs, textual records of their records. This is yet another practice that developed in the 1920s and again manifests the regulatory climate associated with phonograph practices. One early article on the subject, for example, expressed astonishment that collectors stacked their records in heaps and then wasted inordinate amounts of time searching for a particular record (Wyndham 1926). Various systems for tracking records were suggested that involved recording every one as fully as possible and with relevant cross-referencing, in a loose-leaf notebook or on system cards that could be alphabetically or numerically rearranged as a collection was expanded. When a commercial record index system was produced in the 1960s it was suggested that its compiling would be a "happy way" of spending "winter evenings."[27] Collectors are also exhorted, since the labels on records cannot always be trusted, to check any musical information noted against an authoritative source such as *The Grove Dictionary of Music and Musicians* (Bryant 1962: 85). They are also enjoined to develop an in-house system for numbering their records and to record other items of information such as when and from where they were acquired. These self-made discographies, which give "account" of a collection and render it more transparent, also enable a collection to be acted upon at a distance. Would-be listeners can review its contents without any need for physical contact with the actual record collection, thereby minimizing the risk of disturbing its careful organization (Wyndham 1926). Another early writer describing home discographies suggested that they should have pasted into them reviews and advertisements of one's records. Though making such a catalog involved considerable time and energy, the author suggested that the results would nonetheless add "one more joy to the pleasures of gramophony" (Chapman 1925: 23)—in effect an expression of where this chapter commenced, with the thought that one mark of serious leisure is that it is an extension of work, an occasion of the work ethic being applied to the sphere of leisure. In another sense, though, these various forms of "work on paper"—another manifestation of the recording angel at work—allow records to be tracked down in the home and, if they are lent, beyond it. But in keeping track of a home collection of records, they more importantly also contained its owner, keeping him or her preoccupied with a regimen of activities paralleling those of the professional workplace.

Of course, the containment of records and their subjection to various regimens of order and classification also involves their literal containment. This is at its most manifest in the specialized furniture designed to house records, which has undergone redesign as one format of recording has superseded another. As with books and shelving systems that have developed to contain them, the ways in which records are stored and accommodated influences behavior toward them (Petroski 1999: 4), either by keeping their users at a distance, as with a closed cabinet, or encouraging closer inspection, as in more open forms of storage. They also reflect the changing technologies of reproduction, from cylinders to CDs. For although cylinders were soon superseded by discs, this was not before furniture was developed to house them.[28] Record storage compartments were also built into phonographs as part of their transformation into "handsome" pieces of furniture (see Figure 1.2). As collections became more voluminous and outgrew the capacity of these compartments to accommodate them, freestanding shelving systems and cabinets were designed, into which colored dividers could be incorporated that would facilitate the division of recordings into their various categories and allow any gaps in the collection to be identified (Bryant 1962: 26). In order to prevent warping, 78s and LPs are supposed to be stored vertically, ideally with partitions or especially designed wedges between them (Wilson 1957: 108). Moreover, they are supposed to be regularly inverted to prevent the vinyl from sinking to the base of the disc (Wittleloostuyn 1997: 59).

The appropriate "shelving" of records, along with their physical coverage, was a way of ensuring their long-term playability and avoiding the effects of dust. Indeed, the latter, starting with Mackenzie and Marshall (1923: 14), led to its own catechism, including not smoking when playing a gramophone and dusting every record after it was played. And in light of these hazards imperiling the sound performance of records, collectors were exhorted to regularly employ a variety phonographic unguents designed to maintain records in a pristine state and protect them against the "pop and crackle" effects of dust and grease (Wilson 1972: 30). Such practices are less important with CDs, and position is a less critical element in their storage. This had led to the emergence of furnishing systems permitting CDs to be stored horizontally, in towers with special ejecting devices similar to those developed in the days of 78s (see Figure 1.2) or in chests-of-drawers (Humphreys 1998). The latter also serve to hide a collection of CDs, which makes them more attractive to women, who according to one recent advertisement continue to abhor the material expressions of CDs and LPs (Figure 8.4). But in addition to acting as a mechanism of gender appeasement in the home, such storage devices have the effect of separating record collections from the more quotidian environment around them. As was noted earlier in the chapter, collections, including those of CDs and LPs, are often accorded shelves and cabinets to themselves—in some instances, even whole rooms— which serves to underwrite their status as objects of cultural contemplation and esteem.

Among the diverse effects of record culture are those that impact upon individuals as they build collections of records as part and parcel of their leisure activities. It has been argued that such activities, far from being free and uncontrolled, as one might expect from spheres of activity outside of

Figure 8.4 This advertisement, published in the 1998 "Awards Issue" of *Gramophone*, provides an example of the chest-of-drawers approach to CD storage. It hides the collection, which many women generally find "unsightly." The advertisement also encapsulates the continuing antipathy that women feel toward "Hi-Fi, CDs & LPs," which "Ian's Furniture" redresses. The only acknowledgement to the changed context of sexual politics is that it has become women in general, not just wives, that are the problem. (Reproduced by permission of *Gramophone* and Ian Edwards.)

work, are characterized by discipline and regimen, by orderliness and temporal controls. They are, in fact, extensions of, not breaks from, the regulated conditions of work. This is true of record collecting, the particular focus of this chapter, as it is of other domains of collecting. It has also been argued that the discipline and regimen associated with record collecting, as with other aspects of record culture, has a significant textual component that is at its most manifest in discographies, catalogs, and guides to collecting and maintaining records. In effect, these comprise another form of transducer, extending the influence of the loudspeaker beyond mere listening to other, more constructive forms of engagement with records, such as collecting and cataloging. For the various epistemologies and information codes that are inherent parts of these collecting texts help to produce the novice and experienced collector, overseeing the graduation of one to the other, assisting them to navigate the cosmos that is the record industry, to name its important stars and its various constellations. But, at the same time, they also provide directions on how their readers can, in some more methodical way, keep tabs on themselves as collectors and on the collections they curate and are cajoled to maintain, develop, and house. All of this activity takes considerable time and energy, but that is the point: energy spent on organizing records is energy that cannot be spent in "dark leisure." In this respect, the pole of order has a political and cultural significance that extends beyond regulating a collection of records.

CHAPTER NINE

Coda

The End of the Record

We have a strong belief that the scientific ingenuities of our day, acting under the imperious guidance of our sensibilities . . . will contrive to fill the world we leave behind us much too full of us for the free growth of posterity; and that a time will come when it will be necessary to preach a sort of iconoclasm towards the pieties of ancestry in order to clear the way to anything like independent growth.
—From an anonymous editorial in *The Spectator* (1888), 881

The principal theme explored in this book is the degree to which the record has never been a medium sufficient unto itself but has always been extended and mediated by a number of "off-the-record" practices, both material and discursive. In the main these have taken textual forms ranging from those texts having some kind of direct contact with the record, such as covers and liner notes, to more indirect texts such as magazines and catalogues; their distinctive forms of narrative architecture have interlocked with recordings in manifold ways. These architectures are generally interpretive in the case of cover notes, ostensive in the case of catalogues, and normative in the case of record guides. Thus, the supplementing texts extend the envelope of the phonograph beyond its mechanical manifestations and represent the domains where the conceptual *invention* associated with the phonograph takes place. This process is epitomized in the idea of the listener as a transducer, extending the processes begun in the phonograph, in the amplifier, and in the loudspeaker into other modes of cultural practice, such as writing magazine articles about records and books such as this one.

At the same time, these textual contacts have provided a discursive site in which to situate the discourses that have helped to sell, and to tell the truth about, the phonograph. These discourses, so to speak, discovered the disc: they brought its nature out into the open and highlighted the musical opportunities—both good and ill—that its existence afforded. Thereby, they helped to offset the considerable disquiet that the phonograph first engendered. These discourses were circulated throughout the record community, and there are traces of them in a range of phonographic forms, from the mundane trademarks of record labels to philosophical speculations on the metaphysics of recording. They are as much a part of the material universe of the phonograph as records and the equipment on which to play them.

Once the battle as to whether records offered a cogent musical experience or not was won, the focus of the discourse conflict shifted to articulating an appropriate phonographic "aesthetic." This aesthetic centered on identifying the degree to which the recording of classical music—once the technology made it feasible to do so—should defer to the concert versus answer to its own needs as a medium sufficient unto itself. More or less at the same time, there emerged a campaign to win the hearts and minds of an audience not enamored of classical music, whose tastes had drawn them toward the popular end of the musical spectrum and about whom there was, at least in the 1920s and 1930s, some associated moral panic. The gramophone was seen as a weapon in the war on Tin Pan Alley that could be used, by way of musical example, to nurture enthusiasm for classical music. Some of this textual "coming to terms" with the gramophone extended beyond technical and musical contexts to poetry and literature and sought to demystify what many found to be an intimidating machine, one of the archetypal manifestations of technological modernity.

Nonetheless, through all of these threats and fears emerged a record culture administered by communities of professionals and amateurs across the world. It was manifested in various ways, from forms of "collective action" relating to building libraries of classical music to developing superior forms of reproduction. This, in its turn, generated a significant magazine literature that acted as a context in which the epistemology of the record culture—the object knowledge associated with the phonograph—was produced and reproduced, including the micropractices associated with playing records. An important function of this literature, which began to appear the moment the phonograph was invented, was that it provided discourses that mediated the way classical records were perceived and apprehended and set about positioning attitudes toward the phonograph. Often these discourses took the form of summary expression, an aphoristic string of words that crystallized the way recording was understood. One such string of words was the "best seat in the house." It has been argued that this has constituted a keystone discourse underpinning both the engineering of classical recordings and their evaluation that has subverted contesting discourses, such as Gould's idea of recording as an indigenous phenomenon. It has also served to mitigate the power of Celibidache's insistence that recording and music are contradictions in terms, that the very essence of music was in the fact that it transcended reproduction, which, had it been espoused as a keystone discourse, would have spelled the end of the recording industry. In light of the endemic "inscriptions" relating to the phonograph and its attendant culture, the "Recording Angel" represents a prescient and enduring icon: listeners have been consistently choreographed through the angel's chirography, which for a century or more has influenced their attitudes toward records and the way they listen to them. Its many manifestations have added new planes of meaning to the phonographic experience.

But concert hall discourse reveals itself in other ways, such as the ubiquitous seriousness and tastefulness that pervades classical recording and its various forms of presentation. This seriousness is evident in the design of covers, unique textual constructs crossing the modes of music, language, and image that have always provoked perturbation when they have deviated from the standards of taste held to be commensurate with classical music. In general, the discourses of classical recording have deferred to the concert and inveighed against manifestations of musical presentation—in all senses of the word—that have threatened to undermine these conditions. Hence, because their traditions are radically different and have taken dissimilar musical trajectories, classical recording has quarantined itself from the practices and discourses of popular recording—though there are signs that these differences are slowly being eroded. The advent of the phonograph, then, began to consolidate the "great musical schism" that existed between classical and popular music. This happened in spite of the concerted efforts of phonographic evangelists in the 1920s and 1930s on the classical side of the schism, who saw in the record a contrivance that might triumph over the popular once and for all. Their evangelism proved forlorn, for the phonograph helped to harness a groundswell of interest in popular music that has only grown in magnitude with the passage of the phonographic decades.

As a result of 130 years of phonographic development, there have been dramatic and radical changes to the culture of music: examples of virtually every domain of music from every phase of its history have now been recorded, and most households own a collection of records of some form or another. This has enabled individuals to privatize their musical experiences and circumvent the need to participate in their public form at concerts. Music culture has been "decentered"; the transporting effects of the phonograph have enabled the ordinates of time and space that once limited music to the here and now to be transcended, and for music to be placed in a state of suspended animation that can be unsuspended at will. The invention of the phonograph also transcended the need for music to be embodied, taking music, quite literally, out of the hands of its performers. In doing so, recording has transformed the entire political economy of music's production and consumption. And although the subject of this book has been music, specifically classical music, the territory of recording has been an extensive one, encompassing, as Thomas Edison and Emile Berliner always imagined it would, cultural realms including not only forms of music outside the Western tradition but also the spoken word, poetry, and drama.

The advent of recording has allowed a massive archive of sound to be amassed, providing a map of the diverse and varying acoustic landscape that exists on the planet and that prior to the advent of the phonograph had been impossible to preserve, diffusing into nothingness the moment it was created.[1] The "echo with a memory" that is the phonograph has led to a dramatic expansion of the nature of the musical and acoustic experience, adding copious new forms to its compass and diversity. For the advent of the phonograph led to a massive cultural undertaking—much of it generated by business and entrepreneurial interests—to preserve the most distinctive forms of music and sound that cultures had to offer; the earliest record entrepreneurs were also musical explorers who visited the remotest regions of the planet to record its sounds and songs.[2] While this effort was proceeding, the technology of recording was undergoing progressive development, undergoing compression and extension and becoming more robust and enduring. The two or so minutes of playing time of the fragile cylinder eventually gave way, by the end of the twentieth century, to the almost indestructible medium of the CD, which can hold eighty minutes of music and is small and light enough to be accommodated on one's person. The Discman, the digital descendant of Sony's Walkman, is one of a series of wireless artifacts that individuals have begun to "surround" themselves with and mount on their clothing, an incarnation, as it were, of the march of technology incorporated![3]

Yet with the conclusion of this book nearing, it is clear that the current technologies of information preservation and distribution that are now commonplace might render the recording obsolete, as many of its functions and facilities are "colonized" by the personal computer. The material reality of the record has been defined up until this point in its history as "paper plus disc." There also have been complex linkages between the written word and recordings, more sophisticated than the primary subjects of this book, that is, covers and liner notes. For example, in the 1930s Percy Scholes presided over the compilation of the *Columbia History of Music through Eye and Ear,* which consisted of "six albums of records" and a "lavishly illustrated booklet" chronicling the development of Western music (Scholes 1930). This significant form of intermodal architecture was very innovative for the times, with the gramophone incorporating the architecture of the book in an extended way, but also a way that Scholes considered subsidiary to the accompanying records (1930: 12). Such developments have continued through to the present, and many books, especially those devoted to musical subjects, now include CDs—usually inserted into a pocket located on the book's endpapers—as part and parcel of their narrative architecture (see Waugh 1995). Just as the architecture of the book imprinted itself onto the record, so the record has imprinted itself onto the book.

However, the bibliographic and phonographic extensions that are a marked feature of disc architecture are undergoing transition and becoming increasingly *immaterial*. Part of this change reflects the likewise changing nature of recording. Periodic technological change has been a cornerstone of the discursive environment of phonographic culture, for though there have always been cadres of traditionalists who have long resisted the digital age and looked back longingly on such formats of reproduction as the LP, which they avidly collect, such "phonoquarians" are the exceptions rather than the rule. The recording industry itself has never been hesitant in terms of embracing the latest technology or finding ways of establishing synergies between records and other up-and-coming media. The first such move occurred in the 1920s, when radio broadcasting was launched and many assumed it would cause the demise of the record. In fact, this was not the case, and records and radio soon began to enjoy a symbiotic relationship that has continued to this day. For although at first records were banned from the airwaves—at least those over which the BBC had control—radio programs soon developed for which records were the primary source materials. Indeed, the record program was one of the earliest genres of broadcasting. This genre has included a variety of request programs, such as the BBC's long-running *Desert Island Discs*, in which listeners and celebrities have the opportunity to play their favorite records and explain why they enjoy this status—itself a reflection of the degree to which records have become significant cultural reference points in our lives.[4]

Thus the envelope of the record's utility has always been a difficult one to contain, and it has always overlapped into other media, which have then threatened to supplant or incorporate it. In the 1960s, when record producer John Culshaw left Decca for BBC Television, he did so believing that the interface between film and recording afforded by the advent of video provided new opportunities for recording classical music that would eventually supersede sound-only approaches to musical representation (Culshaw 1967: 264–65). Exploiting the affinities that recording might have with other media technologies has thus always been a discursive impulse of the phonograph, one that CD technology is currently exploring through its appropriation of information technology. Indeed, the compact disc was itself an offshoot of this technology and like its antecedent, the phonograph, sprang from tele-communications research—specifically, that concerned with digitally repre-senting telephone signals.

Yet even before the CD eventuated from this research, the computer had been used as a technology in the phonograph's textual environment. *Schwann,* shortly to be followed by *Gramophone,* commenced using informa-tion technology to produce its monthly catalog in 1978. And a contributor to *High Fidelity* in the 1980s described how he was employing a mainframe com-puter to compile a catalog of his record collection (Kozinn 1984). During the interim a number of commercially available software packages have come on the market for this purpose. In addition, there are also a number of new digi-tal formats that are extending the capacity and quality of the original CD, such as DVD and SACD, and have led to a revival of multichannel sound.

But it is the advent of the World Wide Web that, more than anything else, is transforming the nature of the record culture, particularly its textual dimen-sions. Most of the companies associated with the record industry now own websites. The single most important characteristic of information technology lies in its capacity to access information at an enormous velocity and reduce the temporal hiatus between the demand for information and its supply. In ef-fect, digital technologies are producing a culture increasingly characterized by instantaneity, in which previous mediating forces such as the time required for production and the distance from the site of production are insignificant fac-tors in the acquisition of musical commodities. Such technologies are further-ing the annihilation of time and space, which, it was noted at the beginning of this book, were central components of the postmodern condition.

The appearance of record labels on the World Wide Web first became ap-parent at the end of 1995, when a handful of companies—Sony and Hyper-ion were among the first—began to include their e-mail and website ad-dresses in their advertisements. Their websites eventually allowed "sound clips" of CDs to be sampled and pioneered many of the options that are now normal parts of web architecture. By the end of 1998, most record companies and audio manufacturers had followed their example, as did retailers and dis-tributors, who began to offer on-line purchase facilities for obtaining com-pact discs. Forms of computer interaction and presentation are thus fast be-coming the norm in the record industry. In due recognition of the gathering significance of website technology there, *Gramophone* launched its own web-site in December 1997. Interestingly, though, it did not establish its own monthly column on the website until the new millennium (it is now discon-tinued). And there are now a number of freestanding on-line magazines de-voted to record coverage that have followed the narrative templates of their page-based equivalents.[5]

Some record labels have begun to explore the potential for more interactive forms of disc architecture and issued a number of such CDs. Three examples will suffice. The first is from British label Chandos. In 2001, it launched its "Cultural Heritage Series," the first volume of which was devoted to the music of Dmitri Shostakovich. It comprises a multimedia DVD-ROM containing eighty-seven musical excerpts, 800 photographs, 350 pages of text, and video files that provide an extensive musical and biographical profile of the composer.[6] The second is from the Black Box label, which specializes in contemporary classical and jazz music and has a strong commitment to adopting new modes of distributing and reticulating music (Denton 2000: 51). Its so-called "iClassics" offer, alongside the normal CD's music "channel," the option of being played through a personal computer, which provides a number of hot-links to relevant websites.[7] These links thus extend the spatial-temporal frames of the CD well beyond their normal "sound" parameters. The third is from the French independent Montaigne Naïve: their CD of the music of Franco-Finnish composer Kaija Saariaho includes a supplementary CD–ROM that provides around fifteen hours of extramusical entertainment and information, including an interactive game enabling its "players" to compose their own music from the samples of Saariaho's provided.

Such CDs, then, adopt new forms of paratext and new ways of interfacing with music. They constitute electronic versions of cover architecture that are screen- rather than page-based and that increase the options available to the "reader" and listener. But the real significance of these textual innovations derives from the fact that they make the disc increasingly autonomous, less dependent on an envelope of textual interfaces that to date have "enclosed" discs. They potentially have the capacity to make the compact disc an entirely self-sufficient and independent textual system—a device that offers, via the web, many more channels and vehicles of musical exposition and explanation.

A central argument of this book has been that records have always been interfaced with other facets of musical culture. This begins with the cover notes but does not cease there. Thus, once upon a time collectors were encouraged to amass a collection of musical reference books that would augment their record collections, take out a subscription to a reputable record magazine, usually *Gramophone*, that would place them in touch with the latest developments in the recording industry (Bryant 1962),[8] and generally immerse themselves in the phonographic universe, almost all of which was *off* the record. The newer forms of CD are equipped with more extensive and complex forms of paratext, most of which are *on* the record. Moreover, this paratext is seemingly without boundaries, temporal or spatial, and it provides portals to a superabundance of sound and music, to an almost infinitely extended *record* of records. Moreover, this superabundance can be accessed almost without effort, instantaneously, and for an infinitesimal cost.

But therein the users of contemporary CDs confront a different variety of tyranny: there is not enough time to experience this abundance of musical possibility in and among options and diversions that are all encompassing and provide an ever-expanding source of musical allures and opportunities. It might be that the "echo with the memory" has acquired too much memory for its own good, and that phonographic culture—and it is not alone in this regard—is beginning to suffer from the chronic after-effects of not using the delete button frequently enough.

In writing his "life and opinions"—a process he likened to taking a journey—Laurence Sterne, in the guise of his eponymous hero, Tristram Shandy, observed that he had confronted "fifty deviations from the straight line" (1970: 42), innumerable views and prospects that solicited his eye and demanded his attention and whose compound impact slowed his writing to an almost stationary state—an eighteenth-century expression of information overload. The listener to the new, more interactive CD confronts similar "deviations from the straight line" whose aggregate impact invokes the epigraph to this chapter, written at the beginning of the age of the phonograph, which questions the soundness of a culture that records everything and in which nothing, apparently, is unforgettable! If that was the case in 1888, how much more true it has become in 2004. There might be a need to subject the "pieties of ancestry" to some form of concerted iconoclasm and to a clear path "for anything like independent growth."

Yet these trends show no signs of abating. As the technology becomes more accessible and individuals are able to express their musical preferences to an even greater degree of specificity, the universe of musical options has expanded accordingly. Symptomatic of the "greater eclecticism" that digital technologies have facilitated are so-called "Musical Points" where consumers can compile their own CD programs (Taylor 2001: 19). The most dramatic of these trends is the downloading of music from the web through various processing devices such as the notorious MP3 and Apple's iPod, a device not much larger than a compact disc that can store upwards of 10,000 songs—a more than modest library of music. Though more of a threat to popular than classical music, these devices have seen the majors' market share of the music dollar fall quite dramatically. However, as the majors have traditionally used profits from popular music to underwrite their classical endeavors, this is likely to have consequences for classical music as well. Moreover, the majors also face fierce competition from other forms of electronic *divertissement* such as computer games and mobile phones, which are also eating into their profits (Needham 2003: 32). It could be that these are the first signs of a retreat from music, akin to that from the word, which, it has been said, was prompted by the existence of recordings.

Although the results of the web provision of music to date, at least for those demanding the highest form of high fidelity, are inferior to the sound quality of most contemporary CDs, the prospects of a dematerialized record culture in which items of music can be instantaneously accessed from a "globalized" library of music along with all of the information about it is an alluring and seductive one, particularly if one merely wishes to sample music. Such developments are likely to further disrupt the social and civic dimensions that have been, to date, perennial parts of the musical experience, and lead to further, more extreme forms of musical privatization.

If this prospect becomes a reality, then it will spell the end of the record and recordings, at least as they have been known for the last 130 years, along with their supporting narrative architecture. In this case much of what has been described in this book will be destined for libraries and archives and will be seen as a mere transitional point on the way to a wholly digitalized and dematerialized culture—the complete subjugation of music to the hegemony of numbers. It would seem therefore appropriate to conclude this book with an oxymoron—that most postmodern of tropes—and suggests that the record's imminent end might foreshadow the beginning of a new type of "record"—one without the need for any complementary narrative architecture such as covers and liner notes, catalogues and records, guides and magazines, shelves and shops. When this point in the dematerialization of the record is reached—as it may well be—then the need to *set the record straight* will be at an end.

Notes

1. Playing by the Book

1. "Classical" is a value-laden term. In this book it is used, with some circumspection, in its vernacular sense to refer to that music—sometimes called "art" or "serious" music, terms that are also value laden—remaining outside the traditions of "popular" music. Historically speaking, "classical" refers to music composed between 1770 and 1820. It was first used in this way during the nineteenth century, but it has now come to refer routinely to certain forms of music composed between the fourteenth and the twenty-first centuries, e.g., symphonies, chamber music, opera, etc. (Blake 1997: 26). The advent of recording has, if anything, consolidated the abuse of the term, which is widely deployed in the record industry (where the word "classics" is also gaining currency) and in record journalism to describe music of a non-popular variety. The subtitle of *Gramophone,* one of the largest-selling record magazines in the world, is "The Classical Music Magazine." Yet it reviews discs of music much older than 1770 and much younger than 1820.

2. Two of the more famous reactions are those of the conductor Hans von Bülow, who reportedly fainted on first hearing the phonograph (Gelatt 1977: 39), and the soprano Adelina Patti, who on hearing her singing voice exclaimed "Ah! Mon Dieu! Maintenant je comprends pourquoi je suis Patti! Oh, oui! Quelle voix. Quelle artiste! Je comprends tout!" (Moore 1999: 136).

3. In book 5 of *Pantagruel,* Rabelais's eponymous hero visits a region where words are frozen in ice and then heard as speech when it melts (Rabelais 1955). In Bacon's utopian *New Atlantis* there are "sound houses" that synthesize sounds and songs, including those of birds (Bacon 1974). For more examples, see Marcus 1977 and Marty 1979: 9.

4. Indeed there has been some speculation on the part of his son, Guy-Charles Cros, about whether Edison might have, through his Parisian contacts, known of his father's deposition (Cros 1951: 17).

5. The period 1870 to 1930 was one in which sound was overwhelmingly "in the air." It saw the invention of not only the phonograph but also the telephone, microphone, amplifier, valve, loudspeaker, and radio (Wile 1977b: 10).

6. The development of the light bulb had consequences for recording, too; it led to the development of the "thermionic valve" used in electrical amplification (Ford 1962b).

7. The cover of *The "Review of Reviews"* (May 1892) has a telling illustration. Captioned "A Voice from the Dead," it shows a group listening to a record of one

such voice, that of the poet Robert Browning. The event is described as "a notable moment in the history of science and literature."

8. More revealing are the actual demographics of this percentage, which suggest that the main market for classical music is literally a dying one, restricted to the "over-fifties."

9. Though there was by no means a lexicographical consensus about these terms; for a long time the word "needle" was used instead of "stylus." Indeed, if a proper stylus were not available, sewing needles with rounded points were often used instead (Wile 1977a: 10). And even though the CD does not use a stylus as such, it is common to talk of the laser "reading" the CD.

10. In the Lynds' study of Middletown, one of the families interviewed talked of putting the "Victrola in the back seat with the little girl," which suggests that the word enjoyed some currency in the United States during the 1920s (Lynd and Lynd 1929: 242). With the exception of the word "Tannoy," which is widely used in Australia and Britain as a term for a public address system, not many words from the audio industry have passed into the vernacular, nor has the gramophone generated many idioms. One of the few is "sounds like a broken record," which is actually erroneous—it is impossible to sound like a broken record; it should be a "scratched" record.

11. The French anthropologist Michel Leiris's autobiography, which is also notable for its reflections on the language of the phonograph, provides an account of home recording in the early part of the twentieth century, including the way his father recorded "specimens of the vocal or instrumental talents" of his family (1997: 80).

12. Edison was also personally lukewarm toward music, possibly due to his partial deafness. He had a particular antipathy toward jazz and classical music. Famously, he thought that contemporary composers such as Debussy had lost the ability to write the "heartfelt" melodies he thought the general public craved (Edison and Sousa 1923: 663).

13. Scholes's selection of articles from the *Musical Times* notes how the reviewers of concerts frequently complained about the conduct of audiences, especially their tendency to break into applause at inappropriate points in a performance. Indeed, the critic Ernest Newman even hoped that one day it would be common practice for audiences to mark their respect for a great performance by not applauding at all (Scholes 1947: 218–19).

14. This schism became more pronounced in the twentieth century and has been expressed in the record industry in a variety of ways, such as the hierarchy that once operated at EMI's Abbey Road Studios, where classical producers were regarded as "field marshals" and the pop producers as "sergeants" (Southall 1982: 46), or in the musical demarcation evident in the retailing sector where specialized shops for popular and classical music exist.

15. Herman Klein, the well-known opera critic who was for a time adviser to Victor, had recognized that Caruso's voice would be admirably suited to the gramophone but was beaten to the punch by Gaisberg in persuading Caruso to record (Klein 1990a: 64). Gaisberg's initiative was not unprecedented; Columbia had already made a number of operatic recordings before stopping because of the costs involved (Smart and Newsom 1977: 14), as had Gianni Bettini, though his were only available by special order (Gelatt 1977: 78).

16. The status of opera relative to the other branches of classical music has been questioned and it has been suggested that Caruso's success was not necessarily a sign that the phonograph had achieved overall classical legitimacy. Opera was very popular at the time, however, particularly in Italy and among Italian immigrant communities in the United States (Chanan 1995: 5).

17. In order to appease local sensitivities, sometimes other animals were used instead, such as the cobra in India, where the dog is considered impure (Lowe, Miller, and Boar 1982: 36; Martland 1997: 46). It is also worth noting that the slogan "His

Master's Voice" preceded the development of the trademark and that there had been several attempts to portray the gramophone with a range of animals, including parrots and monkeys prior to the adoption of Nipper (Wilson 1964: 401).

2. Disconcerting Music

1. Interestingly, questions that range beyond the ambit of a mere note could be posed regarding whether recording is an art or a science, certainly in relation to the classifications of the arts prevalent during the Middle Ages and the Renaissance. During this period, when the contemporary demarcation between the arts and the sciences was far less pronounced, recording would have almost certainly been classed, like painting, as belonging to the category of "imitative arts" (Kristeller 1951).

2. In 1913, for example, it cost two pounds to purchase Nikisch's recording of Beethoven's Fifth Symphony, and the weekly average wage for males at the time was only one pound six shillings and eight pence (Day 2000: 7). In Australia, the cost of the same symphony on a super-budget CD is around ten Australian dollars in 2003, which is about 1.15 percent of average weekly earnings (Australian Bureau of Statistics, 2003).

3. The gender practice was reversed in the public sphere, where the majority of piano virtuosos were men. The same is true of the phonograph, which was and remains dominated by men, who purchase the majority of records and control the equipment used to play them. Indeed it has been argued that men use hi-fi systems as a way to colonize the domestic space, making a masculine incursion into an area over which women traditionally exerted the most authority (Ehrenreich 1984: 44). There was one notable exception to this pervasive phonographic patriarchy; when record sections opened in department stores during the 1920s it was women who, because they were often more knowledgeable about music than men, staffed them (Kenney 1999: 97).

4. Whilst Berliner's company opened its first record shop in the United States in 1895, such shops took longer to establish in other parts of the world. HMV did not open its Oxford Street shop until 1921. In fact, Edward Lewis, the director of Decca, was irked to discover that many of his company's discs were still being sold in bicycle shops in the 1930s (Lewis 1956: 28). One exception in this regard was London's House of Imhof which began as a music shop before devoting itself exclusively to the sale of records and record players (Mackenzie, F. 1929: 257).

5. Indeed, the meaning of "phoney," which might well have been a corruption of the word "phonograph," exemplifies its vernacular adoption and possibly reflects the low standing of the phonograph during this period.

6. Even histories of contemporary classical music written in the last decade or so rarely if ever mention the contribution that recording has made to its development. This is not true, however, of histories of popular music; Russell Sanjek's (1988), for example, contains a comprehensive examination of the phonograph's contribution to the development of popular music in the United States.

7. This idea accorded with the widespread interest in the occult in the early twentieth century, which the wireless and electricity also helped to catalyze. The notion that there were electric-magnetic waves circulating through the ether on which voices could ride was a powerful one, lending support to the idea that there might be as yet undiscovered waves that carried the voices of the dead. For an examination of the literary explorations of this idea, see Thurschwell 2001.

8. Sinclair Lewis and Virginia Woolf also utilized the phonograph as a leitmotif of modernity. In Lewis's novel *Babbit* (Lewis 1922/1998) the phonograph is the ultimate modern gadget, the mechanical symbol of the jazz age and a metaphor for the moral torpor that eventually overwhelms the main character. In Woolf's last novel,

Between the Acts (Woolf 1941/1992), a gramophone plays an integral part in Miss La Trobe's pageant, where its constant "chuff, chuff" has a haunting presence (Scott 2000). For more on the phonograph's other literary connections, see Kittler 1999.

9. Some of the opposition to mechanized music was possibly an extension of the antipathy toward industrialization in general that had its first stirrings in Victorian England. Thinkers such as John Ruskin and William Morris were vehemently opposed to the destruction of the craft traditions wrought by the Industrial Revolution (Weiner 1981).

10. They were not unlike the villagers of Corkadoragha in Flann O'Brien's satire *The Poor Mouth*, who were silenced by the anthropologist's phonograph and were unable to be their normal, voluble selves. Not that the anthropologist went home empty handed; at the end of the evening of silence a pig appeared and set about regaling the tavern with grunts that the anthropologist took as Gaelic at its most authentic (O'Brien 1973: 43–45).

11. Among the wealthy classes, at least, the burden might not have been too great, for a servant was always on hand to change the records and insert a new needle, at least if Pierre Benoît's novel is at all representative (1929: 212–13). It might be, for Compton Mackenzie, who used gramophone music to stimulate his concentration, asked his secretary to change the records (Mackenzie 1967: 15).

12. His desires in this respect, much to the chagrin of the purists (Gerke 2001: 9), have been posthumously disregarded, and various sets of his recordings, many pirated from radio broadcasts, have been issued.

13. And they do not necessary have to be benchmark recordings. In readying himself to conduct a new work, Roger Norrington uses CDs, which he plays while driving, as a way of getting the work into his mind. The standard of their performances, apparently, is irrelevant (Wagar 1991: 201).

14. In one of its advertisements, Acoustic Research (*Gramophone*, March 1976) suggests that some of the "great musicians of the past," e.g. Handel, Mendelssohn, and Beethoven, would have been audiophiles and used, naturally, Acoustic Research speakers to listen to their music.

15. This quotation is taken from the LSO Live CD packaging. Many radio stations, including the BBC, are beginning to release onto CD many live recordings originally made for broadcasting. This trend is not without precedent, though. One of the most famous recordings of all time and, incidentally, probably one of the most execrable, is a live recording originally made for radio of Sviatoslav Richter's March 1958 Sofia recital, which includes a riveting performance of *Pictures at an Exhibition*. As an influenza epidemic was sweeping through Sofia at the time, the recording is notorious for its coughs and sneezes. There were forty minutes of encores but no tape left to record them (Mazlowski 1960).

16. On Channel 9's (Australia) *Wide World of Sports*, the "Dies irae" section of Verdi's *Requiem* has been used as background music to accompany moments of sporting triumph, when loss would have been, surely, more appropriate!

17. Sentiments shared with music critic Ernest Newman, who in writing about the BBC's radio program *Desert Island Discs* remarked that proper musicians would only have need of scores on their desert islands (Plomley 1975: 40).

18. In fact, this parallels what occurred in the first century of printing, when many of the post-Gutenberg titles published were classical Roman and Greek works (Febvre and Martin 1997: 255).

19. One composer who championed the idea that factories could be a source of musical inspiration was Maurice Ravel (Day 1984: 64), and they actually were for Sergey Prokofiev (*Le Pas d'acier*) and Alexandr Mosolov (*Iron Foundry*).

20. Antheil's interest in technology was not restricted to music; he even helped codesign a torpedo. But unlike some of his artistic contemporaries, e.g. the Vorticists,

Antheil was critical of technology and thought society should be warned of its possible dangers (Antheil 1981: 140).

21. In fact, the phonograph was widely used by ethnographers from the 1890s through the 1930s as a way of preserving aspects of indigenous cultures, e.g. the Australian Aborigines, who it was thought were being driven into extinction by civilization (Brady 1999; Laird 1999: 12). The phonograph was also taken on expeditions to regions considered to be dangerous as an instrument of pacification. Local populations were often entranced by its seemingly magical powers, something captured in one of the classic films of cinematic ethnography, *Nanook of the North*. In it, an Eskimo is shown mesmerized by a phonograph, and at one stage—though one anthropologist has questioned the authenticity of the incident (Taussig 1993: 200)—tries to eat the phonograph. Captain Robert E. Scott also took a phonograph on his expedition to the Antarctica. The local penguin population was, apparently, quite bemused by the voice of Dame Nellie Melba (Fowler 1961: 16).

22. Mosco Carner, Puccini's biographer, suggests another possible source: manuscripts of Japanese music held in Leipzig that Puccini consulted (1992).

23. It was even suggested that by playing records backwards, composers might "arrive" at popular tunes (Sanjek 1988: 364). At any rate, these sound experiments with the gramophone predate by some seventy or eighty years the scratching of LPs now widely used in hip-hop and techno music. Interestingly, that is one of the last domains of recording where LPs remain the preferred format.

24. Frederic Delius was another composer who enjoyed cordial relations with the record industry. He was happy, for example, to have his name appear in EMG's advertising, as he was quite complimentary about their gramophones (James 1998: 33).

25. Late in his career, for example, he was a strong advocate of CD-video and made certain that all of his recording sessions were also videotaped. In fact, Karajan believed that the conjunction of video (or film) and music was an ideal one, and he allowed instruments to be brought into the picture in such a way as to illustrate the musical argument the composer was making (Osborne 1989: 132).

26. The rationale for doing so was outlined in an advertisement appearing at the time of the set's release (*The Gramophone*, February 1975). Extracts from this advertisement appear in the liner notes (from which the quotation is taken) of the rerelease of the recording on CD, though it is suggested there that they are from an article in the magazine, not an advertisement. Incidentally, the set of recordings in which Schoenberg's work is included alongside the works of his fellow composers Alban Berg and Anton von Webern was one that none of the majors would take on, so Karajan funded it himself. He later told Richard Osborne that the market vindicated his decision, for the number of sets eventually sold was sufficient to "reach the top of the Eiffel Tower" (Osborne 1989: 120).

27. These annotations are, unfortunately, omitted from the version of the essay in Tim Page's collection of Gould's writings (1987c).

28. See his letter to Augustus Perry of 17 April 1970 (Gould 1992: 123).

29. These types of "acoustic orchestration" were pioneered in such film scores as Eisenstein's *Alexander Nevsky*, for which Prokofiev was responsible. As a director, Eisenstein had been interested in developing the "contrapuntal use of sound" to complement the montage effects of cinema or sharpen the sense of discord between sound and image (Eisenstein, Pudovkin, and Alexandrov 1988: 114). In *Nevsky*, for example, the "disagreeable" effects of sudden and violent blasts of sound through the microphones are used to represent the Russian hatred for the Teutonic peoples (Samuel 1971: 136–37). These techniques were not transferred to the "cantata" arrangement of *Nevsky*.

30. This is similar to Otto Klemperer's oft-cited aphorism, that listening to a record is equivalent to sleeping with a photograph of Marilyn Monroe (cited in Lebrecht 1991: 305).

3. The Best Seat in the House

1. The "divine music" is Handel's F-major Concerto Grosso.

2. Latour examined "textual" activities in an endocrinology laboratory. However, such activities are by no means restricted to laboratories; they are also apparent in homes and in workplaces, where specialized forms of paper work and inscription have evolved to facilitate the collection, storage, and circulation of information.

3. An advertisement describing the "Tone Tests" appeared in *The Etude* (April 1920).

4. At the time of writing there are two formats that might come to supersede the CD: the Super Compact Audio Disc (SACD) and the audio version of the Digital Video Disc (DVD).

5. See advertisement in *The Gramophone* (July 1947).

6. Shellac was imported from India and Malaysia, which was impossible during World War II. In order to overcome the shellac shortage, the owners of unwanted 78s were encouraged to hand them in for recycling. See letter headed "NEW RECORDS DEPEND ON YOU!" signed by a consortium of companies (*The Gramophone*, February 1943: 134).

7. The Danish engineer Vlademar Paulsen developed wire recording in 1894, which was used in the telephone industry. However, it did not achieve the same quality of sound as magnetic tape, which German National Radio began using in the 1930s along with other innovative recording practices such as mixing and stereo. Most of the recordings and the machines used to make them were destroyed during World War II. The first company outside Germany to manufacture tape was the U.S. firm Ampex (McWilliams 1979: 15–16).

8. Pre-tape examples of such editing included a speech of Winston Churchill—an omitted "Dominion" was inserted—and a performance of Caruso's to which an orchestral backing was later added (Batten 1956: 128).

9. There is some question about the authenticity of Gaisberg's story. Another circulating at EMI held that it was Franck's Symphony that was ruined, which as a result came to be known as the "stocking" symphony (Meadmore 1935: 478; Moore and Rust 1972: 669). Sometimes such offstage whispers do find their way onto a disc. On a 78 of Koussevitsky conducting *Lieutenant Kijé*, it is just possible to hear someone, perhaps the conductor, asking the orchestra to repeat the music's opening bars (Blanks 1968: 102).

10. Advertisement for a Beauhorn loudspeaker (*Gramophone*, September 1999).

11. Advertisement for a Bowes and Wilkins speaker (*The Gramophone*, December 1970).

12. These experiments also took place in the cinema, most famously in the Disney film *Fantasia*, which also pioneered a form of surround sound: three speakers in front of the auditorium and more around it, which reduced cross-modulation and gave priority to the sound of the instruments (Stokowski 1943: 228).

13. Actually, such novelty recordings had been issued as early as 1901. Called "puzzle recordings," they had three interleaved grooves and played, depending upon where the stylus was set down, three different tunes (Adamson 1977: 82).

14. Edward Greenfield's review of Schubert's Ninth Symphony is a case in point (*Gramophone*, June 1975).

15. This was not always the case. The labels HMV, Decca, RCA Victor, and Pye, to name but a few, all manufactured reproducing equipment. The separation became pronounced in the 1960s, however, when specialized component manufacturers began to dominate the industry. Some of these manufacturers, for example Quad, Linn, and Naim, have occasionally issued LPs and CDs. Some equipment manufacturers have also sponsored recordings, for example Bowes and Wilkins for Black Box.

16. One such event, in Lisbon, involved Debussy's *Claire de Lune* played first on a piano and then from a recording. The change from one to the other "was unnoticeable to the majority of the people" (Briggs, G 1961: 65).

17. Some manufacturers have included lists of such recordings—usually classical—in the manuals accompanying loudspeakers, for example, Spendor's manual for its BC1 model. And articles listing recordings that reveal a loudspeaker's ability in particular areas of the audio spectrum have appeared in high fidelity magazines (see Lanier 1972).

18. The U.S.-based Telarc and Swedish BIS are two labels that in the past claimed to preserve the "staggering dynamics of the original" on their discs.

19. Interestingly, digital sound was anticipated in record magazines several years prior to its launch. An Isaac Asimov short story in *High Fidelity* does so (1976), and at least one composer, Alvin Lucier, wrote an experimental work, *North American Time Capsule,* using the Vocoder developed by Sylvania Electronics System in 1967.

20. The refurbishment of early recordings began in the 1960s, when producer Suvi Raj Grubb began "renovating" some of EMI's important recordings, including Furtwängler's *Tristan.* In this case, the original recording was reconfigured to remove a "risible turn-over," and the balance favoring the voices over the orchestra was put right (Grubb 1986: 112–13). More or less at the same time, John Pfeiffer of RCA renovated their Jascha Heifetz recordings, made from 1917 to 1955. This involved using the original metal masters or mint condition shellacs, optimizing the stylus used to play them, and so on (Pfeiffer 1976: 8).

21. See the advertisement for such audiophile recordings of EMI LPs in the *International Classical Record Collector* (February 1996), which claims that the LPs are "hand pressed on 180 gm virgin vinyl" and "reproduced from the original EMI mastertape."

22. Studio One at EMI's Abbey Road Studio complex, which opened in 1931, is generally reckoned to be an exemplary recording environment, notable for its capacity to reveal the "anatomy" of an orchestra.

23. For example, sometimes composers write passages for instruments for other reasons than to be heard. In one of Elgar's symphonies there is a passage for clarinet that is impossible to hear against the sound of the full orchestra, the sole function of which is to warm the instrument up so that it sounds sweeter when it actually comes to be heard (Blanks 1968: 78).

24. Some of the techniques were already evident in Culshaw's production of an *Aida* recording with Karajan conducting; the reviewer Andrew Porter described it as "a sound realization of the score" rather than a "theatre performance" (*The Gramophone,* December 1959). This was consistent with Culshaw's view that a "record is a record, not a theatre performance" (1967: 113).

25. When Culshaw left Decca he joined BBC Television, where he produced a number of programs that "visualized" music, including projected collaborations—they were never fulfilled—with Gould that involved "devising scripts primarily in visual terms" (see Gould's letter to Culshaw of 22 June 1968; Gould 1992: 106–108). In fact, Culshaw had always been interested in the conjunction of film and music and argued that the most effective film music was that which did not detract from the visual action it supported (Culshaw 1952: 189). However, when confronted with the reality of the video disc as a new musical carrier, Culshaw expressed some reservations. He felt that the television screen of the time was too small to provide an adequate "picture" for music. Once this had been redressed, he had no doubt that video was where the future of music lay (Culshaw 1969: 60).

26. This advertisement, entitled "Serious about Stereo," appeared in the *Saturday Review* (31 January 1959).

27. But as Michael Flanders and Donald Swan pointed out in the introduction to their "Song of Reproduction" from their live recording of *At the Drop of a Hat*, why would anyone really want to have a "symphony orchestra" playing at full tilt in their sitting room? (*At the Drop of the Hat*).

28. A number of apartment blocks in Sydney now contain "media rooms" for this purpose.

4. Creating the Right Impression

1. Whether the advent of the digital video disc (DVD) will change this, at least in terms of adding a visual dimension to listening, is debatable. Many regard the audio merits of DVD as unimpressive and hold that it will gain its foothold in the domestic market only as a home theater format.

2. Of course it is possible to know from the position of the stylus how close a record is to its beginning or end, and from the density of the grooves on an LP's surface whether passages of music are likely to be loud or soft. It is not possible to observe a CD's progress directly, though the information panel—other than when it is, as is recommended in many CD player manuals, e.g. Marantz CD 10, dimmed—on a CD player provides much temporal and tracking data about its progress.

3. During the LP era there were some irregular formats, such as the long-playing 45s (Nimbus's Super Analogue Master, or Quarante-Cinq) that were said to offer improved sound quality, and Vox's Extended Long Play 16 2/3 rpm, which had an hour of music per side (Weber 1995: 28).

4. Other advertisements of the time were designed to persuade equivocating consumers who still needed convincing that LPs were not flashes in the phonographic pan (see Decca's advertisement in *The Gramophone*, December 1950).

5. See Rob Cowan's review in *Gramophone* (April 1998).

6. Because of the frictional effects of the stylus against the groove, 78s and LPs undergo slow degradation from the moment they are played, a fact that led some dealers, e.g. Henry Stave, to guarantee that their LPs had never been touched by a stylus. Because CD surfaces are read by a laser with no contact involved, CDs are free from attrition effects and, in theory, never wear out. Even so, some early CDs were subject to so-called "rusting," which eventually impaired their sound. That problem has now been remedied.

7. The market price for mint copies of LPs, particularly for rock albums, has begun to skyrocket, and not only because many of LP aficionados insist that vinyl sounds better than CD—the LP presentation is also superior. In due recognition of this demand, annual fairs devoted to vinyl and related merchandise are held in London and Sydney. A recent book listing the prices of discs reveals that a secondhand copy of the Who's *Tommy* is worth six times that of the Columbia 78 album of Mahler's song cycle *Das Lied von der Erde* (Stanley 2002: 6).

8. In fact, Digipak pioneered the move to recycled cardboard containment; see the story in *Gramophone* (November 1991: 9).

9. Occasionally phonographic formats have influenced magazine design. Since the majority of its contents dealt with records, the late 1960s Australian magazine *Sound* was presented in a jacket about the size of a 45.

10. However, EMI record producer Suvi Raj Grubb noted the impact of a fetching cover for Weber's *Invitation to the Dance*, which featured "a picture of a lady and gentleman, elegantly and decorously poised for the dance, advertising HMV D1285" (1986: 35).

11. Epitexts also accompany films and other "products" emerging from the cultural industries. In fact, the promotional endeavor of cultural commodities now embraces a number of media forms, including the appearances of their main protagonists at

launchings and signings on television and radio programs, as well as an ever-increasing presence on the World Wide Web.

12. Another material similarity between the record and the book is the lampblack used in printer's ink and to color shellac and vinyl (McWilliams 1979: 24). Some LPs have used colors other than black; those from the Record Society came in a range of colors (Patmore 2002).

13. Not that information on the label was infallible. This was particularly true in the days of 78s, when the quality of labeling left much to be desired. Frederic Delius, for one, did not appreciate the fact that *On Hearing the First Cuckoo in Spring* was labeled as Moritz Moszkowski's *Scherzo Capriccioso* (Batten 1956: 79). Such labeling errors are not unheard of even today; a Hyperion recording of the Mendelssohn string symphonies issued in 1986 attributed one of its movements to the wrong symphony. In fact, one of the regular concerns of correspondents to record magazines is identifying such sleeve howlers as *The Wonderful Tangerine* for *The Miraculous Mandarin*.

14. Not all labels have "classical" names. Some pay heed to the country of their origin (Finlandia, Deutsche Grammophon, Columbia), or to the label's philosophy, e.g. Marco Polo, a label dedicated to the exploration of unfamiliar musical regions. Others have more idiosyncratic origins. Nimbus was named after a henpecked academic featured in a French cartoon (Griffiths 1995: 76).

15. Other forms of iconographical intervention have been utilized. For example, L'Oiseau-lyre added a second lyrebird to its trademark for stereo LPs (Davidson 1994: 430). Incidentally, similar forms of typographical figuration were used for advances in film such as cinemascope. The advent of stereo was marked by other gimmicks, too, such as the inclusion of the French and English flags, one for each speaker, in Mercury's LP of *Wellington's Victory* (Rooney 2001: 16).

16. Not infrequently exhibitions are held of CD and LP covers. In 1994 London's Design Museum hosted an exhibition of covers from EMI's British Composer's series (*Gramophone*, February 1994). Covers are also prominent in exhibitions dealing with the recording industry, especially those dedicated to popular music, for example, *Festival Records* at the Power House Museum in Sydney in 2001.

17. See the Decca advertisement, one of several related to the launch of the LP, in *The Gramophone* (June 1950). In addition to listing its first LP releases, the advertisement shows a picture of an LP being removed from its container—though incorrectly, as the playing surface should never be touched.

18. Sometimes the notes even include explanations about the sponsor. The Australian Chamber Orchestra's recordings for Chandos are sponsored by LogicaCMG and assure listeners that though the ACO and LogicaCMG might be worlds apart in their businesses, they "share the same dynamic culture and energy and enthusiasm." But usually the sponsor's presence is merely symbolic, taking the form of a logo or a discreet phrase in a corner of the liner notes ("Recorded in association with John West Fast Foods").

19. In fact, the press had already commissioned Laurencin, whom Louise Hanson-Dyer had befriended through her Les Six contacts, to design a set of lithographs to illustrate its edition of Blow's opera. This set was published in 1939 (Davidson 1994: 325).

20. The Art label's "Art and Music" series, which is devoted to contemporary music, has commissioned a number of artists for its CD packaging, including Michelangelo Pistoletto, Jean-Michel Folon, and Sol Le Witt. Le Witt's designs were included in an exhibition at the Museum of Modern Art in New York. Some of its CDs are available in limited editions and feature original serigraphs from their designers, including a release of Luciano Berio's *Folksongs,* which came in a metal container with graphics designed by Pistoletto (see the advertisement in *Gramophone*, November 1998).

21. An anonymous illustrated article entitled "Musicians as Artists" in *High Fidelity* (October 1977) identifies a number of musicians who have dabbled in the visual arts, e.g. Stokowski and Schoenberg.

22. There are several contemporary artists who have used recordings in their work, e.g. Jean Debuffet and Joseph Beuys (Celant 1976).

23. One exception is David Hockney, who has produced designs for a number of operas, including Stravinsky's *The Rake's Progress.*

24. To cite but one example, the cover of Soft Machine's *Soft Machine* contains actual moving parts. There are several anthologies of rock and jazz covers that contain examples from the notable cover artists, e.g. Hipgnosis, Neon Park, and Richard Dean. With the notable exception of Thorgenson and Powell (1999), these are not much better than picture books and they fail to examine the links between the sleeve and the music (see Gilroy 1993; Taylor 2001).

25. Two other exceptions were the English publishers Collins and Paul Hamlyn, which developed the budget label "Music for Pleasure." Schott, the German music publisher, also controls Wergo, the contemporary music label.

26. Ligeti's opera takes place in "Breughelland," and accordingly Wergo uses Breughel's *Triumph of Death* for its cover.

27. This has now changed, and the cartouche on recent CDs from this label is the size of a logo.

28. The exception was Deutsche Grammophon's "scholarly" label, Archiv, which maintained the "abecedarian" principle for much longer.

29. William S. Harvey, who worked for Nonesuch, was determined to undermine this impression (Webb 1966: 86–87). LP jackets have also been subject to parody; see those of "Rodrigues" in *High Fidelity* (February 1955).

30. See the advertisement in *Saturday Review* (27 April 1955: 53) describing this series of recordings. Incidentally, in another series of this type, Fontana's "Masters of Art," which promised "enchantment for the ear and eye!" the paintings, mostly impressionist, had only an indirect connection to the music, which was mostly Beethoven and Mozart (see the advertisement in *Records and Recording,* June 1961).

31. This symphonic work is drawn from Hindemith's opera of the same title, which deals with the *life* of Mathis Grünewald, not his paintings.

32. The practice of giving precedence to performer over composer upset some collectors from the earliest days of the LP. See the letter in *High Fidelity* (March 1954) complaining about Toscanini's presence on the cover of a Beethoven recording. The correspondent points out that Toscanini is only the "re-creator" of Beethoven, and therefore he does not deserve his face on the sleeve.

33. The uproars about the covers of "nymphet" violinists Vanessa-Mae Nicholson and Lara St. John are cases in point (Taylor 2002: 106).

34. These evaluations are drawn from *Records and Recordings* (April 1966) and *Gramophone* (April 2002) respectively.

5. Off the Record

1. Examples from the acoustic era are included on *A Voice to Remember: The Sounds of 75 Years on EMI Records,* compiled by Roland Gelatt and Alistair Cook. One recent example of the practice is Leonard Bernstein's reflections on Charles Ives's Second Symphony, which are included on a 7" 33⅓ rpm accompanying its LP. Another is a Classic Production Osnabrück (CPO) recording of Benjamin Frankel's Second and Third Symphonies that includes the composer's introductions to the symphonies, which were originally broadcast on the BBC.

2. An Australian company for the manufacture of such LPs was established in Hong Kong; see "Musicolor Records" in the *Australian Record Review* (October

1962). As with other types of phonographic innovation, the so-called "Pictorial Records" released by Trusound in the 1930s anticipated this later idea; see the advertisement in *The Gramophone* (December 1931).

3. See Lionel Salter's review in *The Gramophone* (July 1950) of Ansermet's Decca recording of *Petrouchka*.

4. See advertisement for this LP in *The Gramophone* (September 1979). The sleeve design was based on the four stamps in the series, portraits of the conductors Thomas Beecham, Malcolm Sargent, John Barbarolli, and Henry Wood.

5. Crossover groups such as the Kronos Quartet have been noted for "classicizing" rock music. For an interesting discussion of the ways in which rock music has appropriated the "classics," see Timothy Taylor's discussion of space-age music in the 1960s (2001).

6. The appearance of such sets often coincides with important musical anniversaries; in 1927, for example, Columbia used the centenary of Beethoven's death to issue the first complete recording of Beethoven symphonies.

7. See the advertisement in *The Gramophone* (September 1969). Such hybrid texts were pioneered in the late 1930s—a set of bird recordings produced by Ludwig Koch and E. M. Nicholson, for example, had an accompanying book. See *The Gramophone* (December 1937). For an examination of such "record books," see Brook 1977.

8. See David Gutman's "Leonard Bernstein Conducts" (*Gramophone* "Awards Issue," 2002).

9. By virtue of the so-called "Gruve Gard," the surface of microgroove discs is raised at the beginning and end of the record to reduce the number of scuff marks on the playing surface as discs were handled (Dearling and Dearling 1984: 198).

10. When a changeover occurred in the "middle of the second movement," as happened in a recording of Kabalevsky's Second Symphony, reviewers such as Lionel Salter often complained (see *The Gramophone*, October 1950). But such breaks were the exception rather than the rule, and producers would endeavor to accommodate a work within the boundaries of the LP, even at the risk of inducing end-of-record distortion, for which the sleeve note of Decca's recording of Britten's Symphony for Cello tendered an apology.

11. One classical recording to have a dedication is Neeme Järvi's CD of Shostakovich's "Leningrad" Symphony, which is dedicated to the memory of the Russian conductor Yevgeny Alexandrovich Mravinsky.

12. According to Joe Laredo, Pianissimo's proprietor, this was because the pianist on the recording, Richard McMahon, was not as well known as Auger. Unfortunately, the strategy backfired, and many thought that Auger owned Pianissimo. I am grateful to Laredo for providing this information.

13. The inclusion of lyrics on rock albums appears to have commenced with *Sergeant Pepper* (Inglis 2001: 87).

14. Others in the series included Culshaw/Karajan's recording of *Carmen* and Verdi's *Requiem* from Fritz Reiner and the Vienna Philharmonic. These recordings were all also issued in "paperback" without the Soria extras. Angel had a similar series also issued in "thrifty" and deluxe versions. The "perfectionist package" of Poulenc's *Les Mamelles de Tirésias* included drawings by Picasso and Cocteau, photographs of the Opéra-Comique production of the opera, and Erté sketches (see advertisement in the *Saturday Review*, 24 April 1954).

15. According to the notes, this was at the insistence of Milhaud, who was adamant that only paintings of artists *born* in Provence were to be used; he was fearful that the work of Van Gogh, who sojourned in Provence but only for a short time, might be chosen instead.

16. For some of its LPs of early music Harmonia Mundi also used such inserts.

17. See the letters pages of *Gramophone* (February 1991), whose editorial also

deals with a related issued, i.e., the parlous documentation of CDs of lieder, which were often being issued without texts or translations.

18. DG's budget label "Resonance"—no longer issued—was guilty of such lamentable documentation. But this was the exception rather than the rule, for most budget labels have extensive documentation, rivaling and in some cases actually surpassing that available on many full-price CDs.

19. Take EMI Classic's CD of Grieg's *Lyric Pieces:* the notes are printed on sea-green pages and inset with orange and dark blue panels and photographs of the performer, Lief Ove Andsnes, and Grieg's piano and villa.

20. The *British Music Yearbook* lists "scholars" specializing in cover notes.

21. See the advertisement in *The Gramophone* (February 1953) promoting the idea that such guides are part of a "comprehensive musical and technical service" offered by Decca. A complete set of the guides—twelve in all—was made available in a presentation box.

22. Although this recording postdates Karajan's death and therefore escaped his direct intervention, the conductor did have more than a passing interest in his recordings and attempted to ensure that they accounted for a large proportion of classical sales (Lebrecht 1992: 306). Constructing a playboy image for Karajan was, at one stage, one of the ploys Deutsche Grammophon used to market his LPs—a ploy revived in 2003 for the re-release of these LPs on CDs. A sleeve note from the 1960s of Beethoven's Eighth Symphony and Schubert's "Unfinished" Symphony dealt entirely with Karajan's lifestyle, including the fact that he piloted his own jet—moreover, as one aggrieved letter writer to *The Gramophone* (May 1966) pointed out, in several European languages.

6. *Just for the Record*

1. One sociological study observed that by the 1920s a decline in music making had occurred and the Victrola had become the main source of music. This confirmed Sousa's worst fear: phonographs turning music into "a passive matter of listening to others" (Lynd and Lynd 1929: 248).

2. An issue of *McClure's Magazine* contained a rather racy 1903 short story from O. Henry (William Porter) about the phonograph and its "transporting" effects in Mexico. The articles were not always sycophantic to their advertisers; an article on the "Dynaphone" criticized the "scrapping sounds common to the phonograph" (Baker 1906: 205).

3. The exceptions are those categories of sports and male interest magazines that fulfill similar functions to those of women's, concentrating on the cultivation of male identity (Prendergast 2000).

4. The only two that I have been able to identify are *Recorded Sound* (now defunct) and the *Association of Recorded Sound Collections,* a journal devoted to analysing archival aspects of discs. To these could be added the technical journal, e.g. *Journal of Audio Engineering.*

5. This editorial coincided with the appearance of the first record reviews. Interestingly, even though the journal now has an enlightened policy toward musical technology, articles dealing with its analysis have a separate department and editor from the "mainstream" parts of the journal.

6. The industry was shut down by the Russian Revolution in 1917, because its ideologues saw recording, at least until the 1930s, as a manifestation of capitalist excess (Kerridge 1934). Incidentally, similar views pertained in capitalist New Zealand, whose prewar government banned the import of 78s from the United Kingdom on the grounds that they were luxury goods (Blanks 1968: 241).

7. A pioneer in this respect was the London-based *Musical Times,* which from January 1920 onward carried a monthly feature called "Gramophone Notes" that contained "frank discussions" of new recordings (Discus 1920: 40).

8. Eventually Mackenzie became disillusioned with the piano rolls. He thought they provided too much latitude for their "players," who felt compelled to outperform Chopin, which was "dangerous for art" (Mackenzie 1923b: 358).

9. Many of the discussions about the projected magazine took place in London's Saville Club, to which two other prominent "gramophiles," Robin Legge and Percy Scholes, also belonged (Mackenzie 1966: 232).

10. These circulation figures are drawn from the *British Phonographic Industry Statistical Handbook* (1998) and indicate that the readership per month of the magazine has been on the decline from the 1960s, when it peaked at 80,000. This was from a starting point of around 8,000 (Mackenzie 1967: 23). Much of this decline can be attributed to the fact that the magazine now faces fierce competition; in addition, these figures omit *Gramophone*'s "secondary" readership, comprised of those readers who consult it in libraries or record shops.

11. This strategy is also apparent in the field of scholarly inquiry, particularly at their own times of paradigm shift, and the development of new academic journals are one manifestation of the shift (Kuhn 1962: 177).

12. Not all record magazines review record equipment. Two that do not are *Fanfare* and *International Record Review.*

13. During the early 1960s, *The Gramophone* provided the "Audio Notes" for the magazine, and some of its reviewers, e.g. Charles Cudworth and Edward Greenfield, also wrote for the magazine.

14. The Paris-based magazine *Sonarama* pioneered a type of "recorded" text. Along with its standard pages, it contained sheets of plastic into which five centimeters of microgroove were pressed. The magazine was spiral-bound and holed in such a way that its pages were actually playable (see note in *Records and Recording,* January 1959).

15. Such magazine specialization occurred in the past as well. The U.K.-based *Record Collector* dealt exclusively with opera and vocal recordings. However, such specialization became more pronounced in the 1990s with the appearance of such magazines as *Classic Record Collector* (formerly *International Classical Record*), *International Opera Collector,* and *International Piano Quarterly.* Many of these publications were or are part of the *Gramophone* folio of publications.

16. In fact, the U.S. record industry was adversely affected by radio, and several companies, e.g. Victor, were incorporated into radio corporations, such as RCA (Kenney 1999: 163).

17. See Mackenzie's "Prologue" to the first issue of *Gramophone* (1923a) and his entry "Gramophone" in Dent's *Dictionary of Modern Music and Musicians.* In this entry, he compares the impact of the gramophone on musical education with that of the printing press on the spread of knowledge generally (Mackenzie 1924: 196).

18. Mackenzie was not alone in being fanatically anti-jazz. His magazine regularly published anti-jazz articles from Terpander, a nom de plume of a contributor to the magazine in the 1920s, thought to be M.K. Jacobs, and letters such as the one from the composer Kaikhosru Sorabji (*The Gramophone,* February 1932) suggesting that jazz was not rhythmically complex, certainly when compared with the "classic Ragas of India." It needs to be born in mind, however, that the word "jazz" in the 1920s was used as a catch-all term, covering a range of popular music, much of which would not now be called jazz.

19. Mackenzie was particularly gratified when he saw evidence of his mission bearing fruit. In one of his editorials he quoted at length from a letter from "A Working

Lad" explaining the impact that Schubert's *Unfinished* had on his life (Mackenzie 1931a: 73).

20. This shibboleth has been questioned, because they are likely to stay in the catalogue far longer, classical records may actually prove more profitable over the long term than popular records, which diminish in sales once they disappear from the hit parade (Culshaw 1981).

21. Loyal readers are often hostile to any radical changes made to a magazine's layout. Having become familiar with it, they resent having to renavigate a magazine to find their favorite features.

22. This is not wholly new. A Canadian magazine invited Glenn Gould to name his favorite restaurant. It produced a predictably ascetic response: the only restaurant that would ever gain his patronage would be one offering his nutritional needs in the form of tablets. See his letter to Susan Edwards of 27 March 1971 (Gould 1992: 137).

23. The first issue of the volume for 1975, consisting of 146 pages, contained eighty-seven pages of advertisements including the classifieds—a staggering 59 percent, more advertising than articles. The issue for the same month in 2001, June, which was about the same length as that for 1975, has 33 percent of its pages devoted to advertising. By comparison, the July/August 2001 issue of *Fanfare* has 13 percent of its pages devoted to advertising, and for *International Record Review,* also published bimonthly, the figure is 29 percent.

24. A letter from the Antipodes praising conductor Adrian Boult's recording of Elgar's Second Symphony produced an invitation from a Trinity College examiner to meet its writer on a forthcoming visit to Australia and New Zealand, which he did, bringing with him a recording of the *Dream of Gerontius* (Blanks 1968: 75).

25. See the advertisement in *Gramophone* (February 1980).

26. Early on in the magazine's history a series of letters—mainly from women—proffered reasons for this. One published in December 1925 suggested that women had no need of the gramophone, because they had been taught to play musical instruments as girls and would naturally turn to their instruments to satisfy their musical appetites.

27. One of the few was a series of "Epigramophones" written by Hilaire Belloc (1929: 289). *High Fidelity* was generally more adventurous in its contents. In 1955 it introduced a regular feature called "Living with Music" that provided a forum for well-known writers to discuss recording. Among those who appeared were William Saroyan, Jacques Barzun, and Alfred Kinsey. "My Music," a recent feature in *Gramophone,* performs a similar function and has invited a range of celebrities, e.g. actor Simon Callow and Jon Lord (a founder of rock group Deep Purple), to discuss the significance of records in their lives.

28. Sometimes these games offer an opportunity to snipe at the industry. Following the débâcle of four-channel sound, *High Fidelity* (November 1973) published a board game entitled "Quadopoly" that drew attention to the difficulties of obtaining an RCA quad recording of Rachmaninov's Second Piano Concerto.

29. There are some notable exceptions. Faith Compton Mackenzie (1940), who used the nom de plume "F Sharp," seems to have singlehandedly produced the early issues of *The Gramophone.* And there have been several notable women record journalists, e.g. Joan Chissell, and magazine editors: beginning in 1976, *Records and Recording* had Edna Pottersman and the *International Record Review* currently has Harriet Smith.

30. The equipment required by stereo encroached even more on domestic space, and at a time when houses were becoming smaller this led to the development of bookshelf speakers. Advertisements for them, e.g. the Leak Mini-Sandwich, showed women in euphoric states (*The Gramophone,* December 1966).

7. Compact Discourse

1. John Conly, who was later associated with *High Fidelity,* began his career in 1949 as a record journalist for *Atlantic Monthly.* His articles generated much interest and led the magazine to appoint him as their regular columnist on "music, records, and sound gear"(Conly 1961: 86).

2. See the advertisement in *Records and Recording* (September 1960).

3. Though not, so as far I have been able to discover, on television. Rock music has always been different in this respect, and there have been many TV shows, beginning with the BBC's *Juke Box Jury,* that have evaluated rock records.

4. Glenn Gould (1987h) also penned pseudo-reviews under various nom de plumes, e.g. Sir Humphrey Price Davis, for fictional magazines such as the English *Phonograph.* These appeared on his CBS LP—now transferred to CD—of Liszt's arrangement of Beethoven's Fifth Symphony.

5. Though this generally means only the film music of those composers, e.g. Malcolm Arnold and Nino Rota, who also composed "real" classical music.

6. See the advertisement in *Records and Recording* (December 1970).

7. *Hi-Fi News and Record Review* contained about thirty record reviews per month. However, the balance between these two types of review can shift in magazines according to the predilections of their editors or to increase a magazine's share of the market.

8. A reviewer of *The Gramophone Jubilee Book, 1923–73* noted that their absence gave a false impression of the magazine (Crankshaw 1973: 6).

9. Examples include the claim that Ravel composed a harpsichord concerto, as the notes in a Poulenc CD put forth (*Gramophone,* June 1999), or the case of the LP of Prokofiev's *Ugly Duckling* that also included, but failed to identify, Debussy's *Children's Corner Suite* (*High Fidelity,* September 1963).

10. In order to do justice to the number of CDs submitted for review, *Gramophone* began to give what it called "brief reviews" in the late 1990s. These have since been dropped in favor of "group reviews"—the review of two or more discs at once that are usually in the same area of the repertoire or by the same composer.

11. A letter from the director of Nimbus defending its recording philosophy was published in *Gramophone* (May 1990).

12. This is not just true of *Gramophone.* Similar positional hierarchies are evident in other magazines, e.g. *Fanfare* and *Hi-Fi News and Record Review.*

13. *The Musical Times* in the 1920s also ordered reviews by label, though not on a regular basis.

14. See the advertisement in *The Gramophone* (November 1959) for an RCA LP called *Conduct-'em-yourself,* designed for the frustrated conductor, which came complete with "baton and do-it-yourself leaflet."

15. See *The Gramophone* (October 1972).

16. See P. Wilson's letter to *The Gramophone* (October 1925), which asks reviewers to concentrate on evaluating "the playing, singing and recording."

17. See the review of Stokowski's recording of *L'Arlésienne* in *The Gramophone* (May 1930).

18. See the review in *The Gramophone* (July 1930).

19. Many early CDs contained as little as thirty-five minutes of music. See the review of Mozart's *Eine kleine Nachtmusik* (*Gramophone,* April 1983), which complains about the meager fare on CDs.

20. It was a practice followed in *Records and Recording.*

21. This is an extract from Andrew Porter's review of a London Ducretet Thomson LP of Debussy's *La Mer* (*The Gramophone,* December 1954).

22. See Alan Sanders's review of Dvořák's Works for Cello and Orchestra (*Gramophone*, September 1987).

23. Every so often the magazine provides brief portraits of its reviewers. One set of portraits from the mid-1960s includes details of education and musical expertise. Felix Aprahamian was a trained organist; Lionel Salter founded the Cambridge Gramophone Society and played harpsichord; Jeremy Noble was an expert on Renaissance music; Roger Fiske produced music programs for BBC Schools. Only two of the reviewers had any experience as journalists: Edward Greenfield had worked at the *Manchester Guardian*, and Roger Wimbush, after graduating from Oxford, managed *Music Weekly*.

24. The views of leading musicians about reviews have been seldom sought. When they have, as in the case of Yehudi Menuhin, the response is generally positive; he said that he appreciated reviews that guided listeners to "less obvious beauties and less known literature" (Jacobs 1960: 6).

25. *Gramophone*, for example, rarely reviews "novelty" albums, the musical equivalents of theme parks. Most notorious was the magazine's dismissive attitude to the crossover violinist Vanessa-Mae Nicholson, whose CDs it refused to review on principle, a principle it then abandoned in the case of her later CD *The Classic Album*. Its review, though, was rather lukewarm (see *Gramophone*, January 1997). Similar critical treatment has been meted out to other media "constructs" such as the Australian pianist David Helfgott, who came to public prominence after the Oscar-winning film *Shine* and whose recordings are described as an "abomination of marketing" (*Gramophone*, September 1997).

26. Reviewers will occasionally countenance such deviance if they think the music justifies it, as in the case of Michael Tilson Thomas's *Tangazo*, a program of music from Latin America, which is described as "multi-microphone, definitely hi-fi, certainly sonically thrilling"(Borwick 1993).

27. Similar awards exist elsewhere as well, such as *Les Grand Prix du Disc*, which was first awarded in 1931 as part of *L'Academie du disque Française*, on whose jury sat, among others, the novelist Colette and the composer Arthur Honegger; they also had the patronage of the French gramophone magazine *Disques* (Quiévreux 1931: 63; Sarnette 1951).

28. And there remains the suspicion that, in spite of editorial claims to the contrary, the magazine is not beholden to the majority of them, instead favoring those labels that are regular advertisers.

29. The only one to feature in any of these lists in the first six months of 2002 was André Previn's CD for Deutsche Grammophon of Erich Korngold's *Film Music*, and it only made it to number three, and then only at the one record dealer.

30. See the review in *Gramophone* (November 2001).

31. One reviewer in *Gramophone* (August 2002) points out that in March 2000 he had lamented the absence of outstanding recordings of Ignaz Moscheles, and he suggests that his prayers had been answered with the release of Moscheles's piano concertos on Hyperion.

32. See the review in *Records and Recording* (April 1965)—a sentiment, incidentally, echoed by *The Gramophone*'s reviewer of the same LP (April 1965).

33. This review appeared in May 1992 and was written by David J. Fanning.

34. Sometimes this extends to books. A laudatory review (in the *Gramophone*, June 1982) of a Pearl LP of John Fould's works for string quartet also urges that the composer's *Music Today* be republished.

35. The review, written by W. R. Anderson, appears in *The Gramophone* (September 1950).

8. Keeping Records in Their Place

1. This cartoon first appeared in the *Private Eye* for 30 May 1975 and was subsequently reprinted, with no apparent animosity, in the August *Gramophone*.

2. For unlike the publishing industry, whose economic health depends on an unceasing flow of new titles, the public has never expressed much interest in contemporary classical music—it is the opposite with popular music—and has remained loyal, with some notable exceptions, e.g. Henryk Górecki's Third Symphony, to classical music at its most *classical*.

3. Collections know no bounds in terms of the trivialness of the objects collected, e.g. plastic bags or toilet paper. The dream of turning detritus into gold seems to be the main motive here (Gelber 1999: 64).

4. The hobbies that individuals follow are often consonant with their occupations: professionals invariably follow more cultural hobbies, manual workers more practical ones (McKibbin 1983: 129). In line with the changing profile of the labor market, collecting appears to have overtaken crafts as the dominant category of hobbies, and the readymade, not the handmade, has become their main focus (Martin 1999).

5. An advertisement from Cramer in *The Gramophone* (May 1928) suggested that "EVERYONE should have a hobby—Let the GRAMOPHONE be yours."

6. In a slightly tongue-in-cheek but nonetheless insightful article, critic Peter Munves argued that the "X-ray efficiency era of the LP" had led some collectors with a nostalgia for 78s and a passion for completeness to want to own every record issued by a particular label (1956: 35).

7. This new plea for a more enlightened view towards mechanized music was included in an article entitled "A Great Force Needs Your Guidance" (*The Musician*, May 1920). Victor had established, almost a decade earlier, an education department headed by U.S. music educator Francis Clarke. HMV established a similar department after World War I, through which Alec Robertson began his long association with the gramophone.

8. Indeed, for a short period the magazine combined musical with visual edification in the guise of an art supplement, mostly consisting of prints of paintings. Readers thought portraits of great composers might be more apt ("London Office Notes," *The Gramophone*, June 1925).

9. Whereupon they were, perhaps to save space, confined to the magazine's classified pages. This move also reflected the diminishing popularity of such societies, of course. Although they continue to meet, their membership numbers are dwindling and are mainly drawn from the older generation (Sanders 1996: 1).

10. This is a selection of programs drawn from gramophone society reports published in *The Gramophone* (November 1943).

11. One thinks of the rise of the subject of geology in the latter part of the eighteenth and the nineteenth centuries, which benefited from the work of amateurs, that is, liberally educated antiquarians and clerics, whose fieldwork helped to establish its scientific principles (Porter 1977).

12. In this respect, it served a similar function to *Books in Print*. I am grateful to Claire O'Conor for this observation.

13. These include Sam Goody's *The Long Player*, the *Gramophone Long Playing Record Catalogue* (U.K.), *Diapason-Harmonie* (France), *Catalogue generale dischi microsoli* (Italy), and *Bielefelder Katalogue* (Germany) (Walker 1998b: 93).

14. In order to read the indescribably small print of this catalogue, my own record dealer in Sydney employs a specially designed magnifying glass.

15. There are very few domains of consumer society that have not been the subject of some kind of guide. Cities, restaurants, shops, cameras, schools, and universities have all have been put through to the "Baedeker treatment."

16. This argument owes much to Nelson Goodman's notion of "autographic" and "allographic" forms of art (1968). It does not apply to translations, which are often dissimilar from one another and can be ranked as being more or less close to their originals.

17. The over-exploration of the standard repertoire results from the fact that record labels are obligated to the artists with whom they have contracts. Every major conductor wants to record the Beethoven symphonies, every tenor and soprano to sing in *La Bohème,* and their labels are reluctant to break faith with them by denying those opportunities to do so (Culshaw 1961: 10).

18. Though, as its compilers stressed, the rating of superlative recordings was not applied to the music itself (Sackville-West and Shawe-Taylor 1951: 17), the inclusion of music in the guide in the first place represents a judgment of value.

19. Other guides also use rosettes, e.g. the French version of the *Penguin Guide,* which awards them for "disques" considered "particulièrement remarquables" (Damian 1988). Interestingly, *Diapason* uses five tuning forks, a semiotic echo of the *cinq fucheurs* used in the *Michelin Guide.*

20. The advertisement also includes notes on *The Planets* and Kodaly's *Psalmus Hungaricus* and came with an endorsement from the record critic Felix Aprahamian, who claimed that Decca's LPs had "revolutionised listening habits" (*The Gramophone,* April 1954).

21. See the advertisement for Angel Records in the *Saturday Review* (26 January 1957). A review by Irving Kolodon of one of the advertised LPs in the magazine's "March Record Supplement" notes the "library garb" of the LPs, which "conjures up slippers, easy chair and other adjuncts of contented listening," the *habiliments* of Decca's "listening man" (see figure 8.3).

22. Well in advance of the U.K., U.S. public libraries established record collections beginning in 1914. They also had more enlightened policies than their U.K. counterparts where popular music was concerned (Cooper 1970). This slowness in the U.K. was not for lack of demand; when it became known that the S. E. London Recorded Society possessed a library, the *Musical Times* had to publish a note to the effect that the society only loaned records to its bona fide members (Discus 1926: 143).

23. Dealers can be disdainful towards customers lacking the requisite musical knowledge (Tuttle 1999: 119). Such disdain is vividly depicted in the novel *High Fidelity;* Nick Hornby's Championship Vinyl, a secondhand record store, is managed by surly "phonophiles" who take pleasure in humiliating customers (2000: 42–3).

24. Moreover, its programs stress the diversionary aspects of music as well as its capacity to act as a psychological balm. Many of its programs also provide opportunities for its listeners to request their favorite music, including music with romantic associations. The accent is on bestselling records and on playing the most well-known parts from the classics. BBC Radio 3 produced a riposte to this approach that was encapsulated on a promotional bookmark included in the *Classical Good CD Guide* (Pollard, C. 1998). It implied that, as opposed to Classic FM, Radio 3 played "more than just the famous bits."

25. In response to a reader of *Gramophone* (August 1996) claiming to have over 15,000 CDs, it was suggested that it would be impossible to play each CD more than once, even if one played five CDs a day for twenty years!

26. Joanna MacGregor, pianist and founder of the label Sound Circus, found this ambiguity to particularly vex the programs of music she favored, those mixing contemporary and classical, e.g. Bach and Nancarrow. Retailers never knew where to locate them (Cullingford 2002).

27. Collectors do use card indexes to keep tabs on their collections (see letter in *Gramophone,* March 1993). Given that there is a strong demand for such items of stationery "technology" as address books, it is surprising that more technologies do not

exist to document record collections. Past means have included the *Record Plan Index Folder* (see advertisement in *The Gramophone*, December 1968) and a record index by a French company (see advertisement in *Gramophone*, December 1987). The latter was promoted as being an absolute must for the "well-run discotheque" (a word posing no difficulties for the French).

28. Cylinder Record Cabinets contained solid "record pins" in their drawers that had "spring attachments to prevent there coming out, except at the will of the operator" (see Moogk 1975: 412).

9. *Coda*

1. This ineffability led to its own cultural projects, such as R. Murray Schafer's "Soundscape," which involved acoustically documenting, before they vanished, representative examples of the late twentieth century's sound environment (1980). Not that the acoustic landscape of the past cannot be pieced together from other sources; from the evidence presented in poems and plays of the sixteenth century, for example, it is possible to recreate an impression of the sound of Tudor England (Smith, B. 1999).

2. In the 1930s Columbia's Australian branch conducted what it called a "Maori Recording Expedition," which collected examples of Maori music in context (see *Music in Australia*, 25 June 1930).

3. To this end, Levi-Strauss, the U.S.-based clothing company, has developed in conjunction with the Dutch-based electronics company Philips a jean jacket incorporating a mobile phone and MP3 device (Everard 2000).

4. According to the program's first compère, Roy Plomley, the idea for *Desert Island Discs* was not an original one but had been outlined first in the *Music Teacher* in 1921 and also described by the libertarian pedagogue A. S. Neill in his *Dominie* trilogy (Plomley 1975: 24). After Compton Mackenzie appeared as a guest on the program, he set a competition based on the program's idea. The winner, who received records to the value of ten guineas, was the one whose selection of eight discs "expresses most nearly the taste of the majority of competitors" (1952: 221–22). This represented an instance of a "reverse" synergy between records and radio, a radio program arising from the existence of the recordings that in turn influenced a gramophone text. Incidentally, the winning list of records, published in the issue of *The Gramophone* for June 1952, included Bach's Toccata and Fugue in D minor, the Overture to *Fingal's Cave*, and "Nimrod" from the *Enigma Variations*.

5. Two are *Classical Net* (*http://www.classsical.net*) and the *Flying Inkpot* (*http://inkpot.com/classical*), which at the time of writing has reached issue 114.7.

6. See Chandos's *The Complete Catalogue*.

7. For example, the links accompanying Steve Martland's *Horses of Instruction* are an extension of the CD's liner notes and include reviews, extensive details about the performers, an interview with the composer, and information about the Society for the Promotion of New Music (SPNM), which encourages music styled in the Martland mold. Such off-the-record facilities, however, can be inconvenient, particularly when listeners lack the technology to access the relevant web links. A song recital disc from the same label abandoned the normal practice of including the lyrics in the liner notes in favor of their online downloading, which disadvantaged those without the requisite technology (see the review in *Gramophone*, November 2001).

8. Two early correspondents to *The Gramophone* (June 1924) compiled "book lists" for this purpose.

Bibliography

Primary References

Adamson, Peter G. 1977. "Berliner Discs: From Toys to Celebrity Records." In Alistair G. Thomson, et al., *Phonographs & Gramophones: A Symposium Organised by The Royal Scottish Museum in Connection with the Exhibition "Phonographs and Gramophones" and the Centenary of the Phonograph by Thomas Alva Edison.* Edinburgh: Royal Scottish Museum, 73–93.

———. 1995. "The Committee for the Promotion of New Music: A 50th Birthday Look at an Early Recording Initiative." *Hillandale Music* 195: 355–61.

Adorno, Theodor W. 1978. "On the Fetish Character in Music and the Regression of Listening." In *The Essential Franfurt School Reader,* ed. by Andrew Arato and Eike Gebhardt. Oxford: Blackwell, 270–99.

———. [1969] 1990. "Opera and the Long-Playing Record." *October* 55: 62–66.

Amis, John. 1985. *Amiscellany: My Life, My Music.* London: Faber and Faber.

Anderson, John. 1964. "A Portfolio of Stereo Décor." *High Fidelity* 14(1): 39–45.

Anderson, Martin. 2000. "That Special Quality: An Interview with Stefan Winter, Founder of Winter & Winter." *Fanfare* 23(3): 179–84.

Anderson, Patricia. 1991. *The Printed Image and the Transformation of Popular Culture 1790–1860.* Oxford: Clarendon Press.

Angus, Robert. 1973. "75 Years of Magnetic Recording." *High Fidelity* 23(1): 42–50.

Antheil, George. [1945] 1981. *Bad Boy of Music.* New York: Da Capo Press.

Asimov, Isaac. 1976. "Marchin' In." *High Fidelity* 26(5): 60–64.

Attali, Jacques. 1985. *Noise: The Political Economy of Music,* transl. by Brian Massumi. Manchester: Manchester University Press.

Babbitt, Milton. 1958. "Who Cares If You Listen." *High Fidelity* 8(2): 38–40, 126.

Bacon, Francis. [1626] 1974. *The Advancement of Learning and New Atlantis,* ed. by A. Johnson. Oxford: Clarendon Press.

Badal, James. 1996. *Recording the Classics: Maestros, Music, and Technology.* Kent, Ohio: Kent State University Press.

Baker, Ray Stannard. 1906. "New Music for an Old World." *McClure's* 27(3): 291–301.

Banfield, Edward C. 1984. *The Democratic Muse: Visual Arts and the Public Interest.* New York: Basic Books.

Banfield, Stephen. 1998. *Gerald Finzi: An English Composer.* London: Faber and Faber.

Barker, Frank Granville. 1958a. "Planning the Sleeves." *Records and Recording* 1(9): 12–13.

———. 1958b. "Programme Notes for Discs." *Records and Recording* 1(12): 11–12.

Barzun, Jacques. 1955. "Living with Music." *High Fidelity* 5(5): 32–33, 82, 84.

———. 1969. *Music in American Life.* Bloomington: Indiana University Press.

Batten, Joe. 1956. *Joe Batten's Book: The Story of Sound Recording.* London: Rockcliff.

Baudrillard, Jean. 1994. "The System of Collecting." In *The Cultures of Collecting,* ed. by John Elsner and Roger Cardinal. Carlton, Victoria: Melbourne University Press, 7–24.

Bauman, Zygmunt. 1998. *Work, Consumerism, and the New Poor.* Buckingham: Open University Press.

Becker, Howard S. 1984. *Art Worlds.* Berkeley: University of California Press.

Bellamy, Edward. 1889. "With the Eyes Shut." *Harper's Monthly Magazine* 79: 736–45.

Belloc, Hilaire. 1929. "Epigramophones." *The Gramophone,* 7(79): 289.

Benjamin, Walter. [1936] 1970a. "The Work of Art in an Age of Mechanical Reproduction." In *Illuminations,* ed. by Hannah Arendt and transl. by Harry Zohn. London: Fontana, 219–53.

———. [1931] 1970b. "Unpacking My Library." In *Illuminations,* ed. by Hannah Arendt and transl. by Harry Zohn. London: Fontana, 59–67.

Bennett, Tony, Michael Emmison, and John Frow. 1999. *Accounting for Tastes: Australian Everyday Culture.* Cambridge: Cambridge University Press.

Benoît, Pierre. 1929. *Erromango: Roman.* Paris: Albin Michael.

Berger, Arthur. 1957. "A Census Every Month." *High Fidelity* 7(2): 38–40, 125, 127.

Berliner, Emile. 1888. "The Gramophone: Etching the Human Voice." *Journal of the Franklin Institute* (June): 425–47.

Berliner, Oliver. 1977. "Ways and Tales that Started a Revolution." *Audio* 61(12): 36–46.

Bernard, Albert. 1951. "L'Épopée Française du phonographe." In *Almanach du disque.* N.p.: Pierre Horay Éditions de Flore et La Gazette des Lettres, 12.

Bettley, Kate. 2001. *Gramophone Classical Good CD Guide* 2002. Teddington: Haymarket Magazines.

BFPI (British Federation of Phonographic Industries). 1998. *British Federation of Phonographic Industry Statistical Handbook.* London: BFPI.

———. 2001. *British Federation of Phonographic Industry Statistical Handbook.* London: BFPI.

Biocca, Frank A. 1988. "The Pursuit of Sound: Radio, Perception, and Utopia in the Early Twentieth Century." *Media Culture and Society* 10: 61–79.

Blake, Andrew. 1996. "Replacing British Music." In *Modern Times: Reflections on a Century of English Modernity,* ed. by Mica Niva and Alec O'Shea. London: Routledge, 208–238.

———. 1997. *The Land without Music: Music, Culture, and Society in Twentieth-Century Britain.* Manchester: Manchester University Press.

Blanks, Harvey. 1968. *The Golden Road: A Record Collector's Guide to Music Appreciation.* Adelaide, South Australia: Rigby.

Bliss, Arthur. 1991. "A Musical Pilgrimage of Britain (1935)." In *Bliss on Music: Selected Writings of Arthur Bliss, 1920–1975,* ed. by G. Roscow. Oxford: Oxford University Press, 107–155.

Bloch, Susi R. 1987. "The Book Stripped Bare." In *Artists' Books: A Critical Anthology and Sourcebook,* ed. by Joan Lyons. New York: Visual Studies Workshop Press, 133–47.

Blyth, Alan. 1968. "Georg Solti talks to Alan Blyth." *The Gramophone* 45(539): 527–28.

———. 1972. "Sir Georg Solti Talks to Alan Blyth." *The Gramophone* 50(593): 659–60.

———. 1973a. "Edo de Waart Talks to Alan Blyth." *The Gramophone* 50(596): 1303.

———. 1973b. "Alicia de Larrocha Talks to Alan Blyth." *Gramophone* 51(605): 654.

———. 1974. "Record Resolutions for 1974." *Gramophone* 51(608): 1349–50.

Boorstin, Daniel. 1974. *The Americans: The Democratic Experience*. New York: Vintage Books.

Borwick, John. 1974. *Quadraphony Now*. Harrow: Gramophone.

———. 1975. "Grumbles about Gramophone Records." *Gramophone* 52(621): 1575.

———. 1978. "Record Quality—Results of Our Enquiry." *Gramophone* 56(662): 269–70.

———. 1981. "The Gramophone Interview: Ivor Tiefenbrun of Linn Sondek." *Gramophone* 59(703): 957–58.

———. 1982. *The Gramophone Guide to Hi-Fi*. Newton Abbot: David and Charles.

———. 1983. "Recording and Reproduction." In *The New Oxford Companion to Music, Volume 2, K–Z*, ed. by Denis Arnold. Oxford: Oxford University Press, 1535–46.

———. 1993. "Sounds in Retrospect." *Gramophone* 71(844): 139–41.

———. 2000. "Surrounded by Sound." *International Classical Record Collector* 6(20): 56–60.

Boulez, Pierre. 1986. "Technology and the Composer." In *Orientations: Collected Writings*, transl. by Martin Cooper and ed. by Jean-Jacques Nattiez. Cambridge, Mass.: Harvard University Press, 486–94.

Boult, Adrian. 1934. "Depression Means Better Music." *The Gramophone* 11(131): 432.

Bourdieu, Pierre. 1989. *Distinction: A Social Critique of the Judgement of Taste*, transl. by Richard Nice. London: Routledge.

Bourdieu, Pierre, and Jean-Claude Passerson. 1977. *Reproduction in Education, Society, and Culture*, transl. by Richard Nice. London: Sage.

Bourdieu, Pierre, with Luc Boltanski, Roger Castel, Jean-Claude Chamboredon, Dominique Schnapper. 1990. *Photography: A Middle-brow Art*, transl. by Shaun Whiteside. Cambridge: Polity.

Bowes, Q. David. 1972. *Encyclopaedia of Automatic Musical Instruments*. New York: Vestal Press.

Brady, Erika. 1999. *A Spiral Way: How the Phonograph Changed Ethnography*. Jackson, Miss.: University of Mississippi Press.

Brendel, Alfred. 1976. *Musical Thoughts and Afterthoughts*. Princeton, N.J.: Princeton University Press.

———. 1984. "A Word in Favour of Live Recordings." *Gramophone* 61(731): 1157–58.

Briggs, Asa. 1961. *The History of Broadcasting in the United Kingdom, Volume I: The Birth of Broadcasting*. London: Oxford University Press.

———. 1965. *The History of Broadcasting in the United Kingdom, Volume II: The Golden Age of Wireless*. London: Oxford University Press.

———. 1988. *Victorian Things*. London: B. T. Batsford.

Briggs, G. A. 1950. *Sound Reproduction*. Idle, Bradford: Wharfedale Wireless Works.

———. 1956. *High Fidelity: The Why and How for Amateurs*. Idle, Bradford: Wharfedale Wireless Works.

———. 1961. "Looking Back Again." In *Audio-biographies*, G. A. Briggs and Sixty-Four Collaborators. Idle, Bradford: Wharfedale Wireless Works, 11–22.

Britten, Benjamin. 1964. *On Receiving the First Aspen Award*. London: Faber and Faber.

Brook, Claire. 1977. "The Book Publisher and Recordings." In *The Phonograph and Our Musical Life: Proceedings of a Centennial Conference, 7–10 December 1977*, ed. by H. Wiley Hitchcock. New York: Institute for Studies in American Music, 72–77.

Brown, Clement. 1963. "Hearts on Sleeves." *Records and Recording* 6(12): 63.

Brown, Royal S. 1993. "Telarc and the Atlanta Symphony Orchestra: Happy Fifteen." *Fanfare* 17(1): 38–46.

Brunner, Lance W. 1986. "The Orchestra and Recorded Sound." In *The Orchestra: Origins and Transformations,* ed. by Joan Peyser. New York: Charles Scribner, 479–532.

Bryant, E. T. 1962. *Collecting Gramophone Records.* London: Focal Press.

———. 1985. *Music Librarianship: A Practical Guide.* Metuchen, N.J.: Scarecrow Press.

Buckley, Johnathan. 1994. *Classical Music on CD: The Rough Guide.* London: Rough Guides/Penguin.

Cage, John. 1976. "Interviewed by Jeff Goldberg." *Transatlantic Review* 55/56: 103–110.

Canby, Edward Tatnall, C. G. Burke, and Irving Kolodin. 1956. *The Saturday Review Home Book of Recorded Music and Sound Reproduction.* Englewood Cliffs, N.J.: Prentice Hall.

Carey, John. 1992. *The Intellectuals and the Masses: Pride and Prejudice among the Literary Intelligentsia, 1880–1939.* London: Faber and Faber.

Carlyle, Thomas. [1841] 1897. *Hero as Man of Letters (Johnson, Rousseau, Burns).* London: George Bell.

Carner, Mosco. 1992. *Puccini: A Critical Biography.* London: Duckworth.

Celant, Germano. 1976. "Record as Artwork." *Studio International* 192(984): 267–73.

Celibidache, Serge Ioan. 2001. "Chosen Pieces." In *Celibidache!* ed. by Klaus Gerke and transl. by Tania Calingaert. Chicago: Facets Multi-media, 51–83.

Chanan, Michael. 1994. *Musica Practica: The Social Practice of Western Music from Gregorian Chant to Postmodernism.* London: Verso.

———. 1995. *Repeated Takes: A Short History of Recording and Its Effects on Music.* London: Verso.

Chapman, John C. W. 1925. "Of Catalogues and Scrapbooks." *The Gramophone* 3(1): 22–23.

Chavez, Carlos. 1937. *Towards a New Music: Music and Electricity.* New York: Norton.

Charry, Michael. 1999. "Szell: Champion of the Contemporary?" Introduction to brochure notes for Béla Bartók, Concerto for Orchestra, and Sergei Prokofiev, Symphony No. 5, Cleveland Orchestra, George Szell. Sony MHK 63124.

Chislett, W. A. 1925. "The Gramophone as a Member of the Orchestra." *The Gramophone* 3(6): 277.

———. 1960. "Both Sides of the Counter." *The Gramophone* 38(445): 6–7.

Clarke, Robert S., ed. 1976. *High Fidelity's Silver Anniversary Treasure.* Great Barrington, Mass.: Wyeth Press.

Clough, Francis F., and G. J. Cumming. 1952. *World's Encylopaedia of Recorded Music.* London: Sidgwick and Jackson.

Codrington, Andrea. 1996. "Making Masterworks." *Eye* 21: 42–51.

Conly, J. M. 1961. "J. M. Conly." In *Audio-biographies,* G. A. Briggs and Sixty-Four Collaborators. Idle, Bradford: Wharfedale Wireless Works, 84–86.

Cooper, Eric. 1970. "Gramophone Record Libraries in the United States of America." In *Gramophone Record Libraries: Their Organisation and Practice,* ed. Henry F. J. Currall. London: Crosby Lockwood and Son, 247–58.

Cooper, Matt. 1978. "American Record Guide in Retrospect: The First Year." *American Record Guide* 41(6): 6–7.

Copland, Aaron. 1941. "The World of the Phonograph." In *Our New Music: Leading Composers in Europe and America.* New York: McGraw-Hill, 243–59.

Cott, Jonathan. 1984. *Conversations with Glenn Gould.* Boston: Little, Brown.

Cott, Ted. 1945. *The Victor Book of Musical Fun*. New York: Simon and Schuster.

Crankshaw, Geoffrey. 1973. "*The Gramophone* Jubilee Book, 1923–73, edited by Roger Wimbush." *Records and Recording* 16(9): 6.

Craft, Robert. 1957. "The Composer and the Phonograph." *High Fidelity* 7(6): 34–35, 99–102.

Cros, Guy-Charles. 1951. "L'Invention." In *Almanach du disque*. N.p.: Pierre Horay Éditions de Flore et La Gazette des Lettres, 13–17.

Cross, G. 1993. *Time and Money: The Making of Consumer Culture*. London: Routledge Kegan and Paul.

Csikszentmihalyi, Mihaly, and Eugene Rochberg-Halton. 1981. *The Meaning of Things: Domestic Symbols and the Self*. Cambridge: Cambridge University Press.

Cudworth, Charles. 1962. "Watch Your Jacket." *High Fidelity* 12(3): 58–9, 112, 113.

Cullingford, Martin. 2002. "From Where I Sit: Joanna MacGregor." *Gramophone* 80(959): 19.

Culshaw, John. 1952. *A Century of Music*. London: Dennis Dobson.

———. 1961. "What to Record and Who to Record It?" *Records and Recording* 4(5): 10–12, 47.

———. 1966. "The Mellow Knob, or the Rise of Records and the Decline of the Concert Hall as Foreseen by Glenn Gould." *Records and Recording* 10(2): 26–28.

———. 1967. *The Ring Resounding: The Recording in Stereo of Der Ring des Nibelung*. London: Secker and Warburg.

———. 1969. "The Coming Revolution in Home Recordings, or Where Do We Go From Hear?" *High Fidelity* 19(11): 56–60.

———. 1981. *Putting the Record Straight*. London: Secker and Warburg.

Cunningham, Mark. 1998. *Good Vibrations: A History of Record Production*. London: Sanctuary Publication.

Damian, Jean-Michel. 1988. *Dictionnaire des disques et des compacts: Guide critique de la musique classique enregistrée*. Paris: Robert Laffont.

Danto, Arthur. 1981. *The Transfiguration of the Commonplace*. Cambridge: Cambridge University Press.

Daubeny, Ulric. 1920. "Gramophone 'Why Nots?'" *The Musical Times* 61: 486–87.

Davidson, Jim. 1994. *Lyrebird Rising: Louise Hanson-Dyer of L'Oiseau-lyre, 1884–1962*. Carlton, Victoria: Melbourne University Press/Miegunyah Press.

Dawson, Peter. 1933. "Thirty Years of Record Making." *The Gramophone* 10(116): 315.

Day, Timothy. 1981. "Sound Archives and the Development of the BIRS." *Recorded Sound* 80: 119–27.

———. 1984. "The Organised Sound of Edgard Varèse (1883–1965)." *Recorded Sound* 85: 63–70.

———. 2000. *A Century of Recorded Music: Listening to Musical History*. New Haven: Yale University Press.

Dearling, Robert, and Celia Dearling with Brian Rust. 1984. *The Guinness Book of Recorded Sound*. Enfield, Middlesex, U.K.: Guinness Superlatives.

Demény, János. 1971. *Béla Bartók Letters*, ed. by János Demény and transl. by Péter Balabán and István Farkas, and rev. by Elizabeth West and Colin Mason. Budapest: Corvina Press.

Denton, David. 2000. "The Black Box Story: An Interview with Chris Craker, Founder of a New Independent Label." *Fanfare* 24(1): 49–52.

DiMaggio, Paul. 1987. "Classification in Art." *American Sociological Review* 52: 440–55.

DiMaggio, Paul, and Michael Useem. 1982. "The Arts in Class Reproduction." In *Cultural and Economic Reproduction in Education: Essays on Class, Ideology, and the State*, ed. by Michael Apple. London: Routledge and Kegan Paul, 181–201.

Discus. 1920. "Gramophone Notes." *The Musical Times* 61: 40–42.

———. 1926. "Gramophone Notes." *The Musical Times* 67: 143.

Doctor, Jennifer. 1999. *The BBC and Ultra-Modern Music, 1922–1936: The Shaping of a Nation's Taste*. Cambridge: Cambridge University Press.

Dorati, Anton. 1979. *Notes of Seven Decades*. London: Hodder and Stoughton.

Downes, Olin. 1918. *The Lure of Music: Depicting the Human Side of Composers, with Stories of Their Inspired Compositions*. New York: Harper and Brothers.

Doyle, Arthur Conan. 1929. "The Japanned Box." *The Conan Doyle Stories*. London: John Murray, 609–623.

Duckenfield, Bridget. 1990. "Sir Landon Ronald and the Gramophone." *Hillandale News* 117: 139–41.

Du Gay, Paul, and Keith Negus. 1994. "The Changing Sites of Sound: Music Retailing and the Composition of Consumers." *Media, Culture, and Society* 16(3): 394–413.

Dunn, David. 1996. "A History of Electronic Music Pioneers." In *Classic Essays on Twentieth-Century Music: A Continuing Symposium*, ed. by Richard Kostelanetz and Joseph Darby. New York: Schirmer Books, 87–123.

Duro, Paul. 1996. "Introduction." In *The Rhetoric of the Frame: Essays on the Boundaries of the Artwork*, ed. by P. Duro. Cambridge: Cambridge University Press, 1–10.

Dyson, George. 1935. "The Future of Music." *The Musical Times* 78 (February): 115–121.

Edison, Thomas. 1878. "The Phonograph and Its Future." *North America Review* 136: 527–36.

———. 1888. "The Perfected Phonograph." *North America Review* 146: 641–50.

Edison, Thomas, and John Philip Sousa. 1923. "A Momentous Musical Meeting." *The Etude* (October): 663–64.

Editorial. 1888. "What Will Come of the Phonograph?" *The Spectator* 3131: 881.

Ehrenreich, Barbara. 1984. *The Hearts of Men: American Dreams and the Flight from Commitment*. New York: Anchor.

Eisenberg, Evan. 1988. *The Recording Angel: Music, Records, and Culture from Aristotle to Zappa*. London: Picador.

Eisenstein, Elizabeth. 1980. *The Printing Press as an Agent of Change: Communications and Cultural Transformations in Early-Modern Europe*. Cambridge: Cambridge University Press.

Eisenstein, Sergei, Vsevolod Pudovkin, and Alexandrov Grigori. [1928] 1988. "Statement on Sound." In S. M. Eisenstein, *Selected Works, Volume 1: Writings 1922–34*, ed. and transl. by Richard Taylor. London: BFI, 113–114.

Elias, Norbert. 1994. *The Civilising Process: The History of Manners and State Formation and Civilisation*, transl. by Edmund Jophett. Oxford: Blackwell.

E.M.G. (Expert Made Gramophones). 1964. *The Art of Record Buying: A List of Recommended Microgroove Records*. London: EMG.

Everard, Andrew. 2000. "Philips Tune into the Future." *Gramophone* 78(935): 152.

Featherstone, Mike. 1991. *Consumer Culture and Postmodernism*. London: Sage.

Febvre, Lucien, and Henri-Jean Martin. [1958] 1997. *The Coming of the Book: The Impact of Printing 1450–1800*, transl. by David Gerard. London: Verso.

Ferstler, Howard. 1994. *High Definition Compact Disc Recordings*. Jefferson, N.C.: McFarland.

Fielden, Thomas. 1932. *Music and Character*. London: Ivor Nicholson and Watston.

Finch, Hilary. 2002. "A Practical Visionary." *Gramophone* 79(949): 8–11.

Fine, Wilma Cozart. 1997. "You Are There!" *Mercury Living Presence: You Are There: The True Story of a Legendary Label*. Baarn, Netherlands: Philips Classics Production, 2.

Flichy, Patrice. 1995. *The Dynamics of Modern Communication: The Shaping and Impact of New Communication Technologies.* London: Sage.

Ford, Peter. 1962a. "History of Sound Recording I: The Age of Empiricism (1877–1924)." *Recorded Sound* 1(7): 221–29.

———. 1962b. "History of Sound Recording II: The Evolution of the Microphone and Electrical Disc Recording." *Recorded Sound* 1(8): 266–76.

———. 1964. "History of Sound Recording IV: The Evolution of Stereophonic Sound Techniques." *Recorded Sound* 13: 181–88.

Foucault, Michel. 1972. *The Archaeology of Knowledge and the Discourse on Language,* transl. by Alan Sheridan. New York: Harper Colophon.

———. 1974. *The Order of Things: An Archaeology of the Human Sciences.* London: Tavistock.

———. 1979. *Discipline and Punish: The Birth of the Prison,* transl. by Alan Sheridan. Harmondsworth: Penguin.

———. 1980. *The History of Sexuality, Volume 1: An Introduction.* New York: Vintage Books.

———. 1983. *This Is Not a Pipe,* transl. by James Harkness. Berkeley, Calif.: University of California Press.

Fowler, Edward. 1961. "Milestones in Recording." *Records and Recording* 4(7): 15–17, 50–51.

Fox, Sue. 2002. "After Hours: Leif Ove Andsnes." *Classic FM* (May): 54–57.

Foy, Jessica H. 1994. "The Home Set to Music." In *The Arts and the American Home, 1890–1930,* ed. by Jessica Foy and Karal Anne Marling. Knoxville: University of Tennessee Press.

Frank, Mortimer. 2000. "Turning the Tables: A Review of the Record Reviewer." *International Classical Record Collector* 6(20): 50–55.

Frankenstein, Alfred. 1954. "The Other Side of the Sleeve . . ." *High Fidelity* 4(8): 59, 117, 119.

Fraser, Patrick. 2001. "ATC SCM7/Dynaudio Audience 52." *Gramophone* 79(946): 111, 113.

Friedrich, Otto. 1990. *Glenn Gould: A Life and Variations.* London: Lime Tree.

Frith, Simon. 1978. *Sociology of Rock.* London: Routledge and Kegan Paul.

———. 1996. *Performing Rites: Evaluating Popular Music.* Oxford: Oxford University Press.

Frost, Thomas. 1987. "Interview." In *Edison, Musicians, and the Phonograph: A Century in Retrospect,* ed. by John Harvith and Susan Edwards Harvith. New York: Greenwood Press, 351–78.

Frow, George. 1994. "Musical Circles: The Evolution of Talking Machine Societies in Great Britain." *Hillandale News* 200: 147–53.

Frow, George, and Albert F. Sefl. 1978. *The Edison Cylinder Phonographs: A Detailed Account of the Entertainment Models until 1929.* Sevenoaks, Kent: George L. Frow.

Gaisberg, Fred. 1943. *The Music Goes Round.* New York: Macmillan.

Gardner, Douglas. 1959. *Stereo and Hi-fi as a Pastime.* London: Souvenir.

Garlick, Lewis. 1977. "The Graphic Arts and the Record Industry." *Journal of Audio Engineering Society* 25(10/11): 779–84.

Gay, Peter. 1995. *The Naked Heart: The Bourgeois Experience: Victoria to Freud, Vol. IV.* New York: W. W. Norton.

Gaydon, Harry A. 1928. *The Art and Science of the Gramophone and Electrical Recording Up to Date.* London: Dunlop.

Gelatt, Roland. 1961. "Editorial." *High Fidelity* 10(4): 35, 40.

———. 1977. *The Fabulous Gramophone, 1877–1977.* London: Cassell.

Gelber, Steven M. 1999. *Hobbies: Leisure and the Culture of Work in America*. New York: Columbia University Press.

Genette, Gerald. 1997. *Paratexts: Thresholds of Interpretation*, transl. by Jane E. Lewin. Cambridge: Cambridge University Press.

———. 1999. *Work of Art*, transl. by G. M. Goshgarian. Ithaca, N.Y.: Cornell University Press.

Gergely, Vilmos. 1955. "Zoltán Kodály Meets High Fidelity." *High Fidelity* 5(12): 58–59, 137.

Gerke, Klaus. 2001. "Preface." In *Celibidache!* ed. by Serge Ioan Celibidache and Klaus Gerke and transl. by Tania Calingaert. Chicago: Facets Multi-media, 9.

Giddens, Anthony. 1990. *The Consequences of Modernity*. Cambridge: Polity.

Gilbert, John. 1983. "60 Years of Gramophone, Part Two: Towards Electrical Recording." *Gramophone* 61(721): 96–98.

Gilroy, P. 1993. "Wearing Your Heart on Your Sleeve." *Small Acts: Thoughts on the Politics of Black Culture*. London: Serpent's Tail, 237–57.

Gitelman, Lisa. 1999. *Scripts, Grooves, and Writing Machines: Representing Technology in the Edison Era*. Stanford, Calif.: Stanford University Press.

Goff, Martyn. 1957. *A Short Guide to Long Play*. London: Museum Press.

———. 1958. *A Further Guide to Long Play: Or How to Buy and Enjoy Records of Opera, Chamber Music, Oratorio and Lieder, and Modern Music*. London: Museum Press.

———. 1974. *Record Choice: A Guide to a Basic Classical Record Collection*. London: Cassell.

Goffman, Erving. 1986. *Frame Analysis: An Essay on the Organization of Experience*. Boston: Northeastern University Press.

Gombrich, E. H. 1960. *Art and Illusion*. London: Phaidon.

Goodchild, R. 1924. "Stick to the Score!" *The Gramophone* 2(1): 15.

Goodman, Nelson. 1968. *Languages of Art: An Approach to a Theory of Symbols*. Indianapolis, Ind.: Bobbs-Merrill.

Gottdiener, M. 1995. *Postmodern Semiotics: Material Culture and the Forms of Postmodern Life*. Oxford: Blackwell.

Gould, Glenn. 1966. "The Prospects of Recording." *High Fidelity* 16(4): 46–63.

———. 1987a. "Stokowski in Six Scenes." In *The Glenn Gould Reader*, ed. by Tim Page. London: Faber and Faber, 258–82.

———. 1987b. "Music and Technology." In *The Glenn Gould Reader*, ed. by Tim Page. London: Faber and Faber, 353–57.

———. 1987c. "The Prospects of Recording." In *The Glenn Gould Reader*, ed. by Tim Page. London: Faber and Faber, 331–53.

———. 1987d. "The Grass Is Always Greener in the Outtakes: An Experiment in Listening." In *The Glenn Gould Reader*, ed. by Tim Page. London: Faber and Faber, 357–68.

———. 1987e. "A *Festschrift* for 'Ernst Who???'" In *The Glenn Gould Reader*, ed. by Tim Page. London: Faber and Faber, 189–94.

———. 1987f. "Glenn Gould in Conversation with Tim Page." In *The Glenn Gould Reader*, ed. by Tim Page. London: Faber and Faber, 456–61.

———. 1987g. "Strauss and the Electronic Future." In *The Glenn Gould Reader*, ed. by Tim Page. London: Faber and Faber, 92–93.

———. 1987h. "Beethoven's Fifth Symphony on the Piano: Four Imaginary Reviews." In *The Glenn Gould Reader*, ed. by Tim Page. London: Faber and Faber, 57–61.

———. 1992. *Selected Letters*, ed. by John P. L. Roberts and Ghyslaine Guertin. Toronto: Oxford University Press.

Gracyk, Theodore. 1997. "Listening to Music: Performances and Recordings." *The Journal of Aesthetics and Art Criticism* 55(2): 139–50.

Grainger, Percy Aldridge. [1908] 1997. "Collecting with the Phonograph." In *A Musical Genius from Australia: Selected Writings By and About Percy Grainger*, ed. by Teresa Balough. Perth: University of Western Australia Press/Soundscapes, 19–64.

Gray, Michael. 1996. "Hearing with Both Ears: A Brief History of Stereo Sound in the 1930s and 1940s." *International Classical Record Collector* 2(5): 69–75.

Green, Lucy. 1988. *Music on Deaf Ears: Musical Meaning, Ideology, and Education.* Manchester: Manchester University Press.

Greenfield, Edward, Robert Layton, and Ivan March. 1975. *The Penguin Stereo Record Guide.* Harmondsworth: Penguin.

———. 1980. *The New Penguin Guide to Bargain Records.* Harmondsworth: Penguin.

Griffiths, John. 1995. *Nimbus: Technology Serving the Arts.* London: Nimbus with Andre Deutsch.

Griffiths, Paul. 1997. "Interview with the Composer." In *György Ligeti.* London: Robson Books, 3–18.

Gronow, Pekka. 1983. "The Record Industry: The Growth of a Mass Medium." *Popular Music* 3: 53–75.

Gronow, Pekka, and Ilpo Saunio. 1998. *An International History of the Recording Industry*, transl. by Christopher Moseley. London: Cassell.

Grubb, Suvi Raj. 1986. *Music Makers on Record.* London: Hamish Hamilton.

Gutman, David. 1999. "Prokofiev's Symphony No. 5." *Gramophone* 77(919): 24–28.

Hadow, W. H. 1928. "Music and Education." In *Collected Essays.* London: Oxford University Press, 27–289.

Haddy, Arthur. 1960. "The Inside Story of Decca Sound." *Records and Recording* 3(6): 14–15, 19, 51.

———. 1968. "A. C. Haddy." In *Audio-biographies*, G. A. Briggs and Sixty-Four Collaborators. Idle, Bradford: Wharfedale Wireless Works, 157–63.

Hall, David. 1940. *The Record Book: A Music Lover's Guide to the World of the Phonograph.* New York: Smith and Durrell.

Halsey, Richard Sweeney. 1976. *Classical Music Recordings for Home and Library.* Chicago: American Library Association.

Hamm, Charles. 1975. "Technology and Music: The Effect of the Phonograph." In Charles Hamm, Bruno Nettl, and Ronald Byrnside, *Contemporary Music and Music Cultures.* Englewood Cliffs: Prentice Hall, 253–70.

Harlow, Lewis A. 1964. "Bad Sound from Great Composers: Sometimes the Composer Is to Blame." *Audio* 48(2): 21–22, 58–59.

Harvey, David. 1990. *The Condition of Postmodernity: An Enquiry into the Origins of Cultural Change.* Oxford: Blackwell.

Harvith, John, and Susan Edwards Harvith. 1987. "Introduction." In *Edison, Musicians, and the Phonograph: A Century in Retrospect.* New York: Greenwood Press, 1–23.

Hayden, Eleanor. 1923. "Phonographs as Art Furniture." *International Studio* 78: 249–57.

Heinitz, Thomas. 1965. "Betrayal in Phase-4." *Records and Recording* 8(6): 83, 92.

Heller, Steven. 1994/1995. "Incomparable Alex Steinweiss." *Affiche* 12: 69–75.

———. 2000. "Introduction." In Jennifer McKnight-Tontz and Alex Steinweiss, *For the Record: The Life and Work of Alex Steinweiss.* New York: Princeton Architectural Press, 1–13.

Helots, The. 1940. "Things Remembered." *The Gramophone* 17(200): 284–86.

Hennion, Antoine. 2001. "Taste as Performance." *Theory, Culture, and Society* 18(5): 1–22.

Henry, O. 1903. "The Phonograph and the Graft." *McClure's* 20(4): 428–34.

Herdeg, Walter. 1974. *Record Covers: The Evolution of Graphics Reflected in Record Packaging*. Zurich: Graphis Press.

Hesse, Hermann. [1927] 1965. *Steppenwolf*, transl. by Basil Creighton. Harmondsworth: Penguin.

Heyworth, Peter. 1973. *Conversations with Klemperer*. London: Victor Gollancz.

Hibbs, Leonard. 1960. "Editorial." *Gramophone Record Review* (May): 381–82.

Hickmann, Hans. 1961. "Recording the Past, Present, and Future." *Records and Recording* 4(8): 14–16, 49.

Hirsch, P. M. 1990. "Processing Fads and Fashions: An Organization Set-analysis of Cultural Industry Systems." In *On Record: Rock, Pop, and the Written Word*, ed. by Simon Frith and Andrew Goodwin. London: Routledge, 126–39.

Holst, Imogen. 1974. *Holst*. London: Faber and Faber.

Hobsbawn, Eric. 1984. "Introduction: Inventing Traditions." In *The Invention of Tradition*, ed. by Eric Hobsbawn and Terence Ranger. Cambridge: Cambridge University Press, 1–14.

Honegger, Arthur. 1966. *I Am a Composer*, transl. by William O. Clough and A. A. Williams. London: Faber and Faber.

Horn, Geoffrey. 1978. "The Electrostatic Comes of Age." *Gramophone* 55(658): 1642–43.

———. 1997. "Audio Alchemy ACD-Pro Compact Disc Player." *Gramophone* 74(886): 128–31.

Hornby, Nick. 2000. *High Fidelity*. London: Penguin.

Horowitz, Joseph. 1987. *Understanding Toscanini: How He Became an American Culture-God and Helped Create a New Audience for Old Music*. New York: Alfred A. Knopf.

Humphery, Kim. 1998. *Shelf Life: Supermarkets and the Changing Cultures of Consumption*. Cambridge: Cambridge University Press.

Humphreys, Ivor. 1998. "Shelving—the Whole Idea." *Gramophone* 76(907): 132, 134, 137.

Huyssen, Andreas. 1986. *After the Great Divide: Modernism, Mass Culture, Postmodernism: Theories of Representation and Difference*. Bloomington, Ind.: University of Indiana Press.

Inglis, Ian. 2001. "'Nothing You Can See That Isn't Shown': The Album Covers of the Beatles." *Popular Music* 20(1): 83–97.

Ivashkin, Alexander. 1996. *Alfred Schnittke*. London: Phaidon.

Jackson, Edgar. 1933. "Music Is a Progressive Art." *The Gramophone* 10(117): 367.

Jacobs, Arthur. 1960. "Six Artists View the Decade." *The Gramophone* 38(445): 5–6.

———. 1984. *Arthur Sullivan: A Victorian Musician*. Oxford: Oxford University Press.

James, Francis. 1998. *The E.M.G. Story*. Arbertillery: Old Bakehouse Publications.

Jewell, Brian. 1977. *Veteran Talking Machines*. Tunbridge-Wells: Mida.

Johns, Graeme. 1958. "The First Disc Jockey." *The Gramophone* 36(421): 3–4.

Johnson, David. 1994. "Claves Records: The First Quarter-Century." *Fanfare* 17(3): 20–56.

Johnson, E. R. Finemore. 1974. *His Master's Voice Was Eldridge R. Johnson: A Biography*. Milford, Del.: State Media, Inc.

Johnson, Edward H. 1877. "Wonderful Invention—Speech Capable of Infinite Repetition from Automatic Records." *Scientific American* 37(20): 304.

Johnson, William H. 1936a. *The Gramophone in Education: An Introduction to Its Use in School and the Home*. London: Sir Isaac Pitman.

———. 1936b. "The Gramophone Society Movement: A Survey of Its Present Activities." *The Gramophone* 14(158): 85–86.

———. 1954. *The Gramophone Book: A Complete Guide to All Lovers of Recorded Music*. London: Hinrichsen.

Jolly, James. 1994. "Editorial." *Gramophone* 72(853): 1.
———. 1998. "*Gramophone* Reviews." In *Gramophone: The First 75 Years,* ed. by Anthony Pollard. Harrow: Gramophone Publications, 202–203.
Jones, Geoffrey. 1985. "The Gramophone Company: An Anglo-American Multinational, 1898–1931." *Business History Review* 59: 76–100.
Kahn, Douglas. 1999. *Noise, Water, Meat: A History of Sound in the Arts.* Cambridge, Mass.: MIT Press.
Kaplan, Louis. 1995. *László Moholy-Nagy: Biographical Writings.* Durham, N.C.: Duke University Press.
Katz, Mark. 1998. "Making America More Musical through the Phonograph, 1900–1930." *American Music* 16(4): 448–76.
Karwalky, Wolf-Dieter. N.d. "Recording Grieg with Gilels." Introduction to brochure notes for Edvard Grieg, *Lyric Pieces,* Emil Gilels (piano). Deutsche Grammophon DG 449 721–2.
Keightley, Keir. 1996. "'Turn It Down!' She Shrieked: Gender, Domestic Space, and High Fidelity, 1948–59." *Popular Music* 15(2): 149–77.
Kemp, Ian. 1984. *Tippett: The Composer and His Music.* London: Eulenburg.
Kemper, Peter. 1996. "Along the Margins of Murmuring." In *ECM: Sleeves of Desire: A Cover Story.* Baden: Lars Müller, 7–14.
Kenney, William Howland. 1999. *Recorded Music in American Life: The Phonograph and Popular Memory, 1890–1945.* Oxford: Oxford University Press.
Kern, Stephen. 1983. *The Culture of Time and Space, 1880–1918.* Cambridge, Mass.: Harvard University Press.
Kerridge, W. H. 1934. "The Gramophone in the Soviet Union." *The Gramophone* 12(133): 5–6.
Kinsey, Alfred C. 1956. "Living with Music." *High Fidelity* 6(7): 27–28.
Kittler, Friedrich A. 1999. *Gramophone, Film, Typewriter,* transl. by Geoffrey Winthrop-Young and Michale Wutz. Stanford, Calif.: Stanford University Press.
Klein, Herman. [1924] 1990a. "The Gramophone and the Singer." In *Herman Klein and the Gramophone,* ed. by William R. Moran. Portland, Ore.: Amadeus Press.
———. [1929] 1990b. "Columbia Album of Madame Butterfly." In *Herman Klein and the Gramophone,* ed. by William R. Moran. Portland, Ore.: Amadeus Press.
———. [1930] 1990c. "The Distortions of Over-Amplification." In *Herman Klein and the Gramophone,* ed. by William R. Moran. Portland, Ore.: Amadeus Press.
Knussen, Oliver. 1990. "The Prince of the Pagodas: A Personal Note." Introduction to the brochure notes for Benjamin Britten, *The Prince of the Pagodas.* Virgin VCD 791103–2.
Kopytoff, Igor. 1988. "The Cultural Biography of Things: Commoditisation as Process." In *The Social Life of Things: Commodities in Cultural Perspective,* ed. by Arjun Appadurai. Cambridge: Cambridge University Press, 64–91.
Kozinn, Allan. 1984. "Setting Up a Super Catalog." *High Fidelity* 34(2): 41–45.
Kristeller, Paul Oskar. 1951. "The Modern System of the Arts: A Study in the History of Aesthetics (1)." *Journal of the History of Ideas* 11: 496–527.
Kuhn, Thomas. 1962. *The Structure of Scientific Revolutions.* Chicago: University of Chicago Press.
Kupferberg, Hubert. 1957. "Markevitch in Transit." *High Fidelity* 7(5): 42–44, 116.
Lade, John. 1958. "Reviewing Records on Air." *Records and Recording* 1(4): 12.
———. 1979. *Building a Library: A Listener's Guide to Record Collecting.* London: Oxford University Press.
Laird, Ross. 1999. *Sound Beginnings: The Early Record Industry in Australia.* Sydney: Currency Press.
Lake, Stephen. 1996. "Looking at the Cover." In *ECM: Sleeves of Desire: A Cover Story.* Baden: Lars Müller, 45–48.

Lambert, Constant. 1934. *Music Ho! A Study in the Decline of Music.* London: Faber and Faber.

Lang, Paul Henry. 1952. "Editorial." *The Musical Quarterly* 38(3): 426–34.

Lanier, Robin. 1972. "Ten Records to Test Speakers By." *High Fidelity* 22(6): 60–63.

Latour, Bruno. 1987. *Science in Action: How to Follow Scientists and Engineers through Society.* Milton Keynes: Open University Press.

———. 1990. "Drawing Things Together." In *Representation in Scientific Practice,* ed. by Michael Lynch and Steve Woolgar. Cambridge, Mass.: MIT Press, 19–68.

Layton, Robert. 1967. "The Orchestral Repertoire (including Concertos)." In *The Great Records,* ed. by Ivan March. Blackpool: The Long Playing Record Library, 5.

———. 1969. "A Quarterly Retrospect." *The Gramophone* 47(555): 259–60.

Lebrecht, Norman. 1991. *The Maestro Myth: Great Conductors in Pursuit of Power.* London: Simon and Schuster.

———. 1992. *When the Music Stops . . . Managers, Maestros, and the Corporate Murder of Classical Music.* London: Simon and Schuster.

Lees, G. 1974. "The Vinyl Shortage: Does It Mean Poorer and Fewer Records?" *High Fidelity* 27(7): 69–72.

Legge, Walter. 1982. "Autobiography." In Elizabeth Schwarzkopf, *On and Off the Record: A Memoir of Walter Legge.* London: Faber and Faber, 15–89.

Lehmann, Bernice. 1966. "The Mind of a Pianist." *Records and Recording* 9(11): 16–17, 80.

Leiris, Michel. [1948] 1997. *Rules of the Game, Volume 1: Scratches,* transl. by Lydia Davis. Baltimore, Md.: The Johns Hopkins University Press.

LeMahieu, D. L. 1982. "*The Gramophone:* Recorded Music and the Cultivated Mind Between the Wars." *Technology and Culture* 23(2): 372–91.

———. 1988. *A Culture of Democracy: Mass Communication and the Cultivated Mind between the Wars.* Oxford: Oxford University Press.

Levine, Lawrence W. 1988. *Highbrow/Lowbrow: The Emergence of Cultural Hierarchy in America.* Cambridge, Mass.: Harvard University Press.

Lewis, E. R. 1956. *No C. I. C.* London: Universal Royalties.

Lewis, Sinclair. [1922] 1998. *Babbitt.* New York: Bantam.

Lieberson, Goddard. 1947. "Editor's Preface." In *The Columbia Book of Musical Masterworks,* ed. by Goddard Lieberson. New York: Allen, Towne and Heath, v–vii.

Ligeti, György. 2001. "From Where I Sit: An Interview with Paul Cutts." *Gramophone* 78(940): 27.

Long, Robert. 1971. "The Story of an Idea." *High Fidelity* 20(4): 46–56.

Lotz, Rainer F. 1983. "Early Gramophone Periodicals in Russia." *Talking Machine Review* 12(67): 1831.

Lovegrove, V. 1938. "The 'High Leigh' Conference." *The Gramophone* 16(187): 277–79.

Lowe, Jacques, Russell Miller, and Roger Boar. 1982. *The Incredible Music Machine.* London: Quartet.

Luke, Carmen. 1989. *Pedagogy, Printing, and Protestantism: The Discourse on Childhood.* Albany, N.Y.: State University of New York Press.

Lynd, Robert S., and Helen Merrell Lynd. 1929. *Middletown: A Study in American Culture.* New York: Harcourt, Brace.

Lyons, James, and Jess T. Casey. 1990. Introduction to brochure notes for Ottorino Respighi, *Orchestra Works: Dorati Conducts Respighi.* Mercury CD 432 007–2.

Mackenzie, Compton. 1922. "The Gramophone." *The Daily Telegraph* 22 (September): 5.

———. 1923a. "Prologue." *The Gramophone* 1(1): 1

———. 1923b. "In Praise of the Gramophone." *John O'London's Weekly* 8: 358.

——. 1924. "Gramophone in Musical Culture." In *A Dictionary of Modern Music and Musicians,* ed. by A. Eaglefield-Hull. London: Dent, 196–97.

——. 1929. "The Gramophone and Chamber Music." In *Cobbett's Cyclopedic Survey of Chamber Music,* ed. by Walter Wilson Cobbett. London: Oxford University Press, 488–95.

——. 1931a. "Editorial." *The Gramophone* 9(99): 73–75.

——. 1931b. "Editorial." *The Gramophone* 9(100): 109–112.

——. 1939. *A Musical Chair.* London: Chatto and Windus.

——. 1940. "Editorial." *The Gramophone* 17(200): 279–83.

——. 1952. "Editorial." *The Gramophone* 29(346): 221–22.

——. 1955. *My Record of Music.* London: Hutchinson.

——. 1966. *My Life and Times, Octave Five: 1915–1923.* London: Chatto and Windus.

——. 1967. *My Life and Times, Octave Six: 1923–1930.* London: Chatto and Windus.

——. 1973. "Introduction". In *The Gramophone Jubilee Book 1923–1973,* ed. by Roger Wimbush. Harrow: Gramophone Publications.

Mackenzie, Compton, and Archibald Marshall. 1923. *Gramophone Nights.* London: William Heineman.

Mackenzie, Faith. 1929. "The House of Imhof," *The Gramophone,* 7(78): 257.

Mackenzie, Faith. 1940. *More Than I Should.* London: Collins.

Maisonneuve, Sophie. 2001. "De la 'machine parlante' à l'auditeur: Le disque et la naissance d'une nouvelle culture musicale dans les années 1920–1930." *Terrain* 37: 11–28.

Maitland, J. A. Fuller, Ernest Newman, Joseph Holbrooke, Norman O'Neill, Edward German, Eugène Goosens, Arnold Bax, Julius Harrison, Landon Ronald, and Cyril Scott. 1921. "Musical Taste in England and the Influence of the Gramophone." *The Bookman* (April): 31–41.

Mann, Thomas. 1968. *Doctor Faustus: The Life of the German Composer Adrian Leverkühn as Told by a Friend,* transl. by H. T. Lowe. Porter, Harmondsworth: Penguin/Secker and Warburg.

Mann, William. 1960. "The Artistic Achievement." *The Gramophone* 38(445): 2–5.

March, Ivan. 1965. *Running a Record Library.* Blackpool: Long Playing Record Library.

March, Ivan, Edward Greenfield, and Robert Layton. 1994. *The Penguin Guide to Compact Discs and Cassettes.* Harmondsworth: Penguin.

——. 2002. *The Penguin Guide to Compact Discs.* Harmondsworth: Penguin.

Marco, Gary A., with F. Andrews. 1993. *Encyclopaedia of Recorded Sound in the United States.* New York: Garland Publishing.

Marcowicz, Pali Meller. 1995. "A Yellow Story." *Gramophone* 72(864): 26–29.

Marcus, Leonard. 1977. "Recordings before Edison." *High Fidelity* 27(1): 58–67.

Marek, George R. 1955. "Do Critics Influence Record Sales?" *Saturday Review* (10 December): 36–37.

Marsh, Robert C. 1961. "Conversations with Stokowski." *High Fidelity* 10(3): 44–47, 162.

——. 1973. "Bartók in the Round." *High Fidelity* 23(8): 65–66.

Martin, Paul. 1999. *Popular Collecting and the Everyday Self: The Reinvention of Museums.* London: Leicester University Press.

Martland, Peter. 1997. *Since Records Began: EMI: The First 100 Years.* London: Batsford.

Marty, Daniel. 1979. *The Illustrated History of Talking Machines.* Lausanne: Edita.

Marvin, Carolyn. 1988. *When Old Technologies Were New: Thinking about Electric Communication in the Late Nineteenth Century.* New York: Oxford University Press.

Mattick Jr., Paul. 1993. "Mechanical Reproduction in the Age of Art." *Theory, Culture, and Society* 10: 127–47.

Mayer, Martin. 1961. "The Claude Hummel Diary: Being the Melancholy Chronicle of a Dedicated Record Reviewer Who Found Life Too Overwhelming." *High Fidelity* 10(4): 41–43, 152–53.

Mazlowski, Igor. 1960. "Recording Richter in Sofia." *Records and Recording* 3(6): 9, 50.

McColvin, L. R. 1961. "Gramophone Records in Public Libraries." *Recorded Sound* 1(1): 22–27.

McCracken, Edna. 1993. *Decoding Women's Magazines: From Madamoiselle to Ms.* Basingstoke: Macmillan.

McGinn, Robert E. 1983. "Stokowski and the Bell Telephone Laboratories: Collaboration in the Development of High-Fidelity Sound Reproduction." *Technology and Culture* 24: 38–75.

McKibbin, Ross. 1983. "Work and Hobbies in Britain, 1880–1950." In *The Working Class in Modern British History: Essays in Honour of Henry Pelling,* ed. by Jay Winter. Cambridge: Cambridge University Press, 127–46.

McIntyre, Edward F. 1969. "Use Your Room to Enhance Your Stereo." *High Fidelity* 19(9): 50–55.

McKnight-Tontz, Jennifer, and Alex Steinweiss. 2000. *For the Record: The Life and Work of Alex Steinweiss.* New York: Princeton Architectural Press.

McLuhan, Marshall. 2001. *Understanding Media: The Extensions of Man.* London: Routledge.

McWilliams, Jerry. 1979. *The Preservation and Restoration of Sound Recordings.* Nashville, Tenn.: American Association for State and Local History.

Meadmore, W. S. 1935. "Twenty-five Years of the Gramophone." *The Gramophone* 12 (144): 471–80.

Melville-Mason, Graham. 1996. "Esta, Ultraphon, and Supraphon: A Short History of the Czech Recording Industry." *International Classical Record Collector* 2(5): 38–43.

Middleton, Richard. 1990. *Studying Popular Music.* Milton Keynes: Open University Press.

Milhaud, Darius. 1952. *Notes without Music. An Autobiography,* transl. by Donald Evans. London: Dennis Dobson.

Millard, Andre. 1995. *America on Record: A History of Recorded Sound.* Cambridge: Cambridge University Press.

Moogk, Edward B. 1975. *Roll Back the Years: History of Canadian Recorded Sound and Its Legacy (Genesis to 1930).* Ottawa: National Library of Canada.

Moor, Peter. 1976. "The Conductor Who Refuses to Conduct." *High Fidelity* 26(3): 12, 14.

Moore, Gerald. 1962. *Am I Too Loud? Memoirs of an Accompanist.* London: Andre Deutsch.

Moore, Jerrold N. 1974. *Elgar on Record: The Composer and the Gramophone.* London: EMI Records/Oxford University Press.

———. 1976. *A Voice in Time: The Gramophone of Fred Gaisberg, 1873–1951.* London: Hamish Hamilton.

———. 1999. *Sound Revolutions: A Biography of Fred Gaisberg, Founding Father of Commercial Sound Recording.* London: Sanctuary.

Moore, Jerrold N., and Brian Rust. 1972. "Collectors' Corner." *The Gramophone* 50(593): 669–70.

Moore, Ray. 1987. "Interview." In *Edison, Musicians, and the Phonograph: A Century in Retrospect,* ed. by John Harvith and Susan Edwards Harvith. New York: Greenwood Press, 317–40.

Moorhouse, H. F. 1987. "The Work Ethic and the Hot Rod." In *The Historical Meanings of Work,* ed. by P. Joyce. Cambridge: Cambridge University Press, 237–57.

Moran, W. R. 1977. "Discography: Rules and Goals." *Recorded Sound* 66–67: 677–81.

Morgan, Kenneth. 2001. "Mercury Still Rising." *Classic Record Collector* 26: 22–28.

Morton, Brian. 1996. *The Blackwell Guide to Recorded Contemporary Music.* Oxford: Blackwell.

Morton, David. 2000. *Off the Record: The Technology and Culture of Sound Recording in America.* New Brunswick, N.J.: Rutgers University Press.

Moser, Sir Claus, Peter Andrey, John Denison, Edward Greenfield, and Manoug Parikan. 1978. "The Influence of the Record Industry on Musical Life Today." A Symposium Organized by BIRS, 22 February 1977. *Recorded Sound* 69: 746–54.

Munves, Peter R. 1956. "The Spirit of 78." *Saturday Review* (January 30): 35.

Myers, Paul. 1972. "Quad: Musical Progress." *Records and Recording* 15(10): 22–24.

Needham, Kirsty. 2003. "Last Blast for Music Moguls." *The Sydney Morning Herald* (September 13–14): 25, 32.

Negus, Keith. 1999. *Music Genres and Corporate Cultures.* London: Routledge.

O'Brien, Flann. [1941] 1973. *The Poor Mouth: A Bad Story about the Hard Life.* London: Grafton Books.

O'Connell, Charles. 1947. *The Other Side of the Record.* Sydney: Invincible Press.

O'Connell, Joseph. 1992. "The Fine-Tuning of a Golden Ear: High-End Audio and the Evolutionary Model of Technology." *History of Technology* 33(1): 1–37.

Ohmann, Richard M. 1996. *Selling Culture: Magazines, Markets, and Class at the Turn of the Century.* London: Verso.

Olson, David R. 1994. *The World on Paper: The Conceptual and Cognitive Implications of Writing and Reading.* Cambridge: Cambridge University Press.

Ong, Walter J. 1982. *Orality and Literacy: The Technologizing of the Word.* London: Methuen.

Opperby, Preben. 1982. *Leopold Stokowksi.* New York: Hippocrene Press.

O'Reilly, John. 1999. "The Graphic Codes of Late-1990s Commercial Music Packaging Design." *Eye* 33: 49–61.

Orga, Ates, and Josephine Orga. 1978. *Records and Recording: Classical Guide 78.* Tunbridge-Wells: Mida.

Ormandy, Eugene. 1987. "Interview." In *Edison, Musicians, and the Phonograph: A Century in Retrospect,* ed. by John Harvith and Susan Edwards Harvith. New York: Greenwood Press, 143–51.

Orwell, George. [1939] 1990. *Coming Up for Air.* Harmondsworth: Penguin.

——. [1939] 1962. "Boys' Weeklies." In *Inside the Whale and Other Essays.* Harmondsworth: Penguin, 175–203.

Osborne, Conrad L. 1976. "Elektra: A Stage Work Violated? Or a New Sonic Miracle?" In *High Fidelity's Silver Anniversary Treasure,* ed. by Robert S. Clarke. Great Barrington, Mass.: Wyeth Press, 307–10.

Osborne, Richard. 1973. "The Stereo Record Guide Volume 7 (A–Ma) and Volume 8 (Me–Z), by Edward Greenfield, Robert Layton, and Ivan March (Editor)." *Records and Recording* 16(5): 6–8.

——. 1989. *Conversations with Karajan.* Oxford: Oxford University Press.

Packer, Steve. 2003. "You Ain't Read Nothing Yet." *The Sydney Morning Herald* (May 3–4): 11.

Panel Review (A). 1971. "Sounds in Retrospect—1971." *The Gramophone* 49(583): 1007–1008.

Parrott, Jasper, with Vladimir Ashkenazy. 1985. *Beyond Frontiers.* New York: Atheneum.

Patmore, David. 2000. "Clubs Were Trumps." *International Classical Record Collector* 6(20): 42–47.

———. 2002. "High Society." *Classic Record Collector* 28: 22–31.

Peterson, Richard A., and Roger M. Kern. 1996. "Changing Highbrow Taste: From Snob to Omnivore." *American Sociological Review* 61: 900–907.

Peterson, Theodore. 1964. *Magazines in the Twentieth Century.* Urbana, Ill.: University of Illinois Press.

Petroski, Henry. 1999. *The Book on the Bookshelf.* New York: Alfred Knopf.

Petts, Leonard. 1983. *The Story of "Nipper" and "His Master's Voice" Picture Painted by Francis Barraud.* Bournemouth: Talking Machine Review.

Pfeiffer, Ellen. 1974. "Schwann at 25." *High Fidelity* 24(10): 45–47.

Pfeiffer, John. 1976. "Record Reissues—An American Perspective; an Interview with John Pfeiffer, RCA Records." *Association for Recorded Sound Collections—Journal* 8(2–3): 6–18.

———. 1987. "Interview." In *Edison, Musicians, and the Phonograph: A Century in Retrospect,* ed. by John Harvith and Susan Edwards Harvith. New York: Greenwood Press, 341–50.

Philip, Robert. 1992. *Early Recordings and Musical Style: Changing Tastes in Instrumental Performance, 1900–1950.* New York: Cambridge University Press.

"Phonograph and Microphone." 1878. *The Illustrated London News* (August 3): 114.

Piore, M. J., and C. F. Sabel. 1984. *The Second Industrial Divide.* New York: Basic Books.

Plasketes, George. 1992. "Romancing the Record: The Vinyl De-Evolution and Subcultural Evolution." *Journal of Popular Culture* 21(1): 109–122.

Plomley, Roy. 1975. *Desert Island Discs.* London: William Kimber.

Pollak, Hans. 1925. "Archives in Sound: An Account of the Work of the 'Phonogram-Archives' in Vienna." *The Gramophone* 2(11): 415–18.

Pollard, Anthony. 1998a. "Gramophone: A Reminiscence." In *Gramophone: The First 75 Years,* ed. by Anthony Pollard. Harrow: Gramophone Publications, 14–184.

Pollard, Anthony, ed. 1998b. *Gramophone. The First 75 Years.* Harrow: Gramophone Publications.

Pollard, Christopher. 1956. "Editorial." *The Gramophone* 33(393): 340.

———. 1994. "Passing Notes Through Yellow Tinted Spectacles." *Gramophone* 71(849): 18–20.

Pollard, Christopher, ed. 1987. *The Good CD Guide.* Harrow: Gramophone Publications.

———. ed. 1998. *The Gramophone Classical Good CD Guide 1999.* Harrow: Gramophone Publications.

Porter, Andrew. 1957. "The Decca Fifty." *The Gramophone* 34(415): 283.

Porter, Roy. 1977. *The Making of Geology: Earth Science in Britain, 1660–1815.* Cambridge: Cambridge University Press.

Prendergast, Tom. 2000. *Creating the Modern Man: American Magazines and Consumer Culture, 1900–1950.* Columbia, Mo.: University of Missouri Press.

Quiévreux, Louis. 1931. "Grand Prix du Disque." *The Gramophone* 9(98): 63.

Rabelais, François. [1532–1534] 1955. *The Histories of Gargantuan and Pantagruel,* transl. by J. M. Cohen. Harmondsworth: Penguin.

Rabinowitz, Peter J., and Jay Reise. 1994. "The Phonograph behind the Door: Some Thoughts on Musical Literacy." In *Reading World Literature: Theory, History, Practice,* ed. by Sarah Lawall. Austin: University of Texas Press, 286–308.

Rachmaninov, Sergei. 1973. "The Artist and the Gramophone." In *The Gramophone Jubilee Book, 1923–1973,* ed. by Roger Wimbush. Harrow: Gramophone Publications, 99–102.

Ranada, David. 1983. "How to Judge a Record Without Playing It." *Stereo Review* 48(5): 56–59.

Raynaud, H. B. 1978. "Sound Reflections and Echoes VII." *Hillandale News* 104: 132–35.

Read, Oliver, and Walter L. Welch. 1976. *From Tinfoil to Stereo: Evolution of the Phonograph*. Indianapolis, Ind.: Howard W. Sams.

RED. 2002. *RED Classical Catalogue: Master Edition 1*. London: RED/Gramophone.

Redfern, Walter. 1984. *Puns.* Oxford: Blackwell.

Revill, Adrian. 1987. "Classical Music." In *Sound Recording Practice*, ed. by John Borwick. Oxford: Oxford University Press, 315–26.

Ridout, Herbert C. 1942. "Behind the Needle–XX: Looking Back Over the Gramophone." *The Gramophone* 19(209): 145–46.

———. 1944a. "The Gramophone Society Movement." *The Gramophone* 21(251): 172.

———. 1944b. "The Gramophone Society Movement." *The Gramophone* 22(253): 13.

Robertson, Alec. 1946. "The Record Collector." In *The Penguin Music Magazine, No. 1*, ed. by Ralph Hill. Harmondsworth: Penguin.

———. 1950. "Decca Issues L.P. Records." *The Gramophone* 27(325): 4.

———. 1955. "Record Repertoire." *The Gramophone* 33(386): 85–86.

———. 1956. "Editorial." *The Gramophone* 33(393): 341–42.

———. 1961. *More Than Music*. London: Collins.

———. 1973. "Reviewing the Records" In *The Gramophone Jubilee Book*, ed. by Roger Wimbush. Harrow: Gramophone Publications, 17–23.

Roell, Craig. 1994. "The Piano in the American Home." In *The Arts and the American Home, 1890–1930*, ed. by Jessica Foy and Karal Anne Marling. Knoxville: University of Tennessee Press, 85–110.

Rogers, W. S. 1931. *The Gramophone Handbook: A Practical Guide for Gramophone Owners on All Matters Connected with Their Instrument*. London: Sir Isaac Pitman.

Rogers, William J. 1923. "How to Start a Gramophone Society." *The Gramophone* 1(1): 10–11.

Rohan, Michael Scott. 2002. "CD Deterioration and Conservation." *Gramophone* 80(956): 105.

Rojek, Chris. 1995. *Decentering Leisure: Rethinking Leisure Theory*. London: Sage.

———. 1999. *Leisure and Culture*. Basingstoke: Palgrave.

Rooney, D. 2001. "A Fine Way to Go Stereo." *Classic Record Collector* 8(26): 14–20.

Rössing, Helmut. 1984. "Listening Behaviour and Musical Performance in the Age of 'Transmitted Music.'" *Popular Music* 4: 119–49.

Rubbra, Edmund. 1958. "Foreword." In *Guide to Modern Music on Records*, ed. by Robert Simpson and Oliver Prenn. London: Anthony Blond.

Sackville-West, Edward, and Desmond Shawe-Taylor. 1951. *The Record Guide*. London: Collins.

Said, Edward W. 2000. "Glenn Gould, the Virtuoso as Intellectual." *Raritan* 20(1): 1–16.

Samuel, Claude. 1971. *Prokofiev,* transl. by Miriam John. New York: Grossman.

Sanders, Alan. 1996. "Editorial." *International Classical Record Collector* 2(5).

———. 1998. *Walter Legge: Words and Music*. London: Duckworth.

Sanjek, Russell. 1988. *American Popular Music and Its Business: The First Four Hundred Years, Vol. II, from 1790 to 1909*. Oxford: Oxford University Press.

Sarnette, Eric. 1951. "Les Grand Prix du Disque." In *Almanach du Disque*. N.p.: Pierre Horay Éditions de Flore et La Gazette des Lettres, 26–29.

Saul, Patrick. 1961. "A Sound-Museum for the Future." *Records and Recording* 4(4): 13, 15.

———. 1962. "Busoniana." *Recorded Sound* 1(7): 256–59.

Scanlon, Jennifer. 1995. *Inarticulate Longings: The Ladies' Home Journal, Gender, and the Promises of Consumer Culture*. New York: Routledge.

Schafer, R. Murray. 1980. *The Tuning of the World: Toward a Theory of Soundscape Design*. Philadelphia: University of Pennsylvania Press.

Schebera, Jürgen. 1995. *Kurt Weill: An Illustrated Life*, transl. by Caroline Murphy. New Haven: Yale University Press.

Schicke, C. A. 1974. *Revolution in Sound: A Biography of the Recording Industry.* Boston: Little Brown.

Schneirov, Matthew. 1994. *The Dream of a New Social Order: Popular Magazines in America, 1893–1914.* New York: Columbia University Press.

Schoenberg, Arnold. [1926] 1975. "Mechanical Musical Instruments." In *Style and Idea: Selected Writings of Arnold Schoenberg,* ed. by Leonard Stein and transl. by Leo Black. London: Faber and Faber, 226–30.

Scholes, Percy. 1921. *Learning to Listen.* London: Gramophone Company.

———. 1924. *The First Book of the Gramophone: Giving Advice Upon the Selection of Fifty Good Records from Byrd to Beethoven, a Listener's Description of Their Music and a Glossary of Technical Terms.* London: Oxford University Press.

———. 1925. *The First Book of the Gramophone: Giving Advice Upon the Selection of Fifty Good Records from Schubert to Stravinsky, a Listener's Description of Their Music, Translations of the Words of Any Songs Included.* London: Oxford University Press.

———. 1930. *The Columbia History of Music through Ear and Eye: Period I to the Opening of the Seventeenth Century.* London: Oxford University Press.

———. 1933. "'Cuts' Have Gone—'Breaks' Must Go!" *The Gramophone* 10(117): 345–46.

———. 1935. *Music, the Child, and the Masterpiece: A Comprehensive Handbook of Aims and Methods in All That Is Usually Called "Musical Appreciation."* London: Oxford University Press.

———. 1947. *The Mirror of Music, 1844–1944: A Century of Musical Life in Britain As Reflected in the Pages of the Musical Times, Volume 1.* London: Novello and Oxford University Press.

Schuller, Gunter. 1987. "Gunter Schuller." In *Edison, Musicians, and the Phonograph: A Century in Retrospect,* ed. by John Harvith and Susan Edwards Harvith. New York: Greenwood Press, 397–408.

Schwartzman, Arnold. 1993. *Phono-Graphics: The Visual Paraphernalia of the Talking Machine.* San Francisco: Chronicle Books.

Scott, Bonnie K. 2000. "The Subversive Mechanics of Woolf's Gramophone in 'Between the Acts.'" In *Virginia Woolf in the Age of Mechanical Reproduction,* ed. by Pamela L. Caughie. New York: Garland Publishing, 97–113.

Scott, Derek B. 1990. "Music and Sociology for the 1990s: A Changing Critical Perspective." *The Musical Quarterly* 74(3): 385–410.

Scott, Howard H. 1998. "The Beginnings of the LP." *Gramophone* 76(903): 112–13.

Seibert, Don C. 1985. "An Interview with Brian Couzens, the Producer of Chandos Records." *Fanfare* 9(1): 96–105.

Senior, Evan. 1957. "What WE Think." *Records and Recording* 1(1): 5.

Sessions, Roger. 1970. *Questions about Music.* Cambridge: Cambridge University Press.

Shadwick, Keith. 2000. *The Classic FM Hall of Fame of Collection.* London: Virgin.

Shaughnessy, Adrian. 1996. "Reinterpreting the Classics." *Eye* 21: 42–51.

Shawe-Taylor, Desmond. 1960. "The Gramophone and the Voice." *The Gramophone* 37(440): 341–43.

Siefert, Marsha. 1994. "The Audience at Home: The Early Recording Industry and the Marketing of Musical Taste." In *Audiencemaking: How the Media Create the Audience,* Sage Annual Review of Communication Research, Vol. 22, ed. by James S. Ettema and D. Charles Whitney. Thousand Oaks, Calif.: Sage, 186–214.

———. 1995. "Aesthetics, Technology, and the Capitalization of Culture: How the Talking Machine Became a Musical Instrument." *Science in Context* 8(2): 417–49.

Simpson, Robert, and Oliver Prenn, eds. 1958. *Guide to Modern Music on Records.* London: Anthony Blond.

Smart, James R., and Jon W. Newsom. 1977. *"A Wonderful Invention": A Brief History of the Phonograph from Tinfoil to LP.* Washington, D.C.: Library of Congress.

Smith, Bruce R. 1999. *The Acoustic World of Early Modern England: Attending to the O-factor.* Chicago: Chicago University Press.

Smith, Dorothy. 1999. *Writing the Social: Critique, Theory, and Investigations.* Toronto: University of Toronto Press.

Soames, Nicolas. 1990. "Paradise and the Perry." *Gramophone* 68(808): 504–505.

Sousa, John Philip. 1906. "The Menace of Mechanical Music." *Appleton's Magazine* 8(3): 278–84.

Southall, Brian. 1982. *Abbey Road: The Story of the World's Most Famous Recording Studios.* Cambridge: Patrick Stephens.

Stanley, John. 2002. *Collecting Vinyl.* London: Octopus.

Starker, Janos. 1987. "Interview." In *Edison, Musicians, and the Phonograph: A Century in Retrospect,* ed. by John Harvith and Susan Edwards Harvith. New York: Greenwood Press, 182–91.

Stauffer, George B. 1986. "The Modern Orchestra: A Creation of the Late Eighteenth Century." In *The Orchestra: Origins and Transformations,* ed. by Joan Peyser. New York: Charles Scribner, 37–68.

Steane, John. 2002. "Singertalk." *Gramophone* 80(957): 22.

Stebbins, Robert. 1992. *Amateurs, Professionals, and Serious Leisure.* Montreal: McGill-Queen's University Press.

———. 2001. *New Directions in the Theory and Research of Serious Leisure.* Lewiston, N.Y.: Edward Mellen.

Stegermann, Michael. N.d. "Elective Affinities." Introduction to brochure notes for *The Glenn Gould Edition: Edvard Grieg, Piano Sonata; Georges Bizet, Premier Nocturne, Variations Chromatiques; Jean Sibelius, Sonatines, Kylliki—3 Lyric Pieces,* Glenn Gould, piano. Sony SM2K 52654.

Steinberg, S. H. 1974. *Five Hundred Years of Printing.* Harmondsworth: Penguin.

Steiner, Georges. 1967. *Language and Silence: Essays 1958–1966.* London: Faber and Faber.

Sterling, Louis. 1975. "The Music Industries of Today and Tomorrow." Speech delivered before the British Music Trades Convention (1926). In Edward Moogk, *Roll Back the Years: History of Canadian Recorded Sound and Its Legacy (Genesis to 1930).* Ottawa: National Library of Canada, 389–90.

Sterne, Laurence. [1760] 1970. *The Life and Opinions of Tristram Shandy Gentleman.* London: Folio Society.

Stevens, Denis. 1966. "Music in Its Proper Acoustic." *Records and Recording* 10(3): 25–27.

Stevenson, W. B. 1949. "Discophily." *The Library Association Record* 51(7): 203.

Stock, Garry. 1978. "Tuning Up Your Stereo." *Schwann—1, Record and Tape Guide* 30(4): A1–7.

Stoker, Bram. [1897] 1997. *Dracula,* ed. by Maurice Hindle. Harmondsworth: Penguin.

Stokowski, Leopold. 1943. *Music for All of Us.* New York: Simon and Schuster.

Stone, Christopher. 1933. *Christopher Stone Speaking.* London: Elkin Mathews and Marrot.

———. 1935. "Introduction." In Courtney Bryson, *The Gramophone Record.* London: Ernest Benn.

Stravinsky, Igor. 1936. *Chronicle of My Life.* London: Victor Gollancz.

Strevens, Patrick. 1961. "From the Other Side of the Fence." *Records and Recording* 4(12): 16.

Struthers, Stephen. 1987. "Recording Music: Technology in the Art of Recording." In *Lost in Music: Culture, Style, and the Musical Event,* ed. by A. L. White. London: Routledge.

Stuckenschmidt, H. H. 1970. *Ferruccio Busoni: Chronicle of a European.* London: Calder and Boyars.

Swinnerton, Frank. 1923. "A Defence of the Gramophone." *The Gramophone* 1(4): 52–53.

Symes, Colin. 1996. "Building the Queenslander: The Contribution of School Architecture to the Formation of the Child." In *Young in a Warm Climate: Essays in Queensland Childhood,* ed. by Lynette Finch. St Lucia: University of Queensland Press, 86–99.

———. 1997. "Beating Up the Classics: Aspects of Compact Discourse." *Popular Music* 16(1): 80–95.

———. 2004. "A Sound Education: The Gramophone and the Classroom," *British Journal of Music Education* 21(2): 163–78.

Taussig, M. 1993. *Mimesis and Alterity: A Particular History of the Senses.* New York: Routledge.

Taylor, Timothy D. 2001. *Strange Sounds: Music, Technology, and Culture.* London: Routledge.

———. 2002. "Music and Musical Practices in Postmodernity." In *Postmodern Music/Postmodern Thought,* ed. by Judy Lochhead and Joseph Auner. New York: Routledge, 93–118.

Théberge, Paul. 1997. *Any Sound You Can Imagine: Making Music/Consuming Technology.* Hanover, N.H.: Wesleyan University Press.

Thompson, Emily. 1995. "Machines, Music, and the Quest for Fidelity: Marketing and the Edison Phonograph in America, 1877–1925." *The Musical Quarterly* 79: 131–71.

Thompson, John B. 1995. *The Media and Modernity: A Social Theory of the Media.* Stanford, Calif.: Stanford University Press.

Thorgerson, S., and Audrey Powell. 1999. *100 Best Albums: The Stories behind the Sleeves.* London: Dorling Kindersley.

Thurschwell, Pamela. 2001. *Literature, Technology, and Magical Thinking, 1880–1920.* Cambridge: Cambridge University Press.

Turner, W. J. 1933. *Facing the Music: The Reflections of a Music Critic.* London: G. Bell.

Tuttle, Raymond. 1999. "Read Any Good CDs Lately? Penguin Classic's 'Flight to Quality.'" *Fanfare* 22(4): 119–24.

Unruh, D. R. 1980. "The Nature of Social Worlds." *Pacific Sociological Review* 23: 271–96.

Van der Merwe, P. 1989. *Origins of the Popular Style: The Antecedents of Twentieth-Century Popular Music.* Oxford: Clarendon Press.

Velez, Sandra. 1993. "Sound Recording Periodicals." *Encyclopedia of Recorded Sound in the United States,* ed. by Guy A. Marco with Frank Andrew. New York: Garland, 646–73.

Verne, Jules. [1879] 1963. *The Tribulations of a Chinese Gentleman.* London: Arco.

Wagar, Jennifer. 1991. *Conductors in Conversation: Fifteen Contemporary Conductors Discuss Their Lives and Professions.* Boston: G. K. Hall.

Walford, A. J. 1986. "The Art of Reviewing." In *Reviews and Reviewing: A Guide,* ed. by A. J. Walford. London: Maxwell.

Walker, John A. 1987. *Cross-Overs: Art into Pop/Pop into Art.* London: Comedia.

Walker, Malcolm. 1998a. "Pseudonyms." *Gramophone: The First 75 Years,* ed. by Anthony Pollard. Harrow: Gramophone, 195.

———. 1998b. "Record Catalogues." *Gramophone: The First 75 Years,* ed. by Anthony Pollard. Harrow: Gramophone, 92–93.

Wallerstein, Edward, and Ward Botsford. 1976. "Creating the LP Record." *High Fidelity* 26(4): 56–61.

Waugh, Alexander. 1995. *Classical Music: A New Way of Listening*. London: De Agostini.

Weber, Jerome. 1995. "Vox Productions—A Short History." *International Classical Record Collector* 1(3): 15–32.

Weber, William. 1975. *Music and the Middle Class: The Social Structure of Concert Life in London, Paris, and Vienna*. London: Croom Helm.

Webb, Carolyn. 1966. "Turntable." *Records and Recording* 9(4): 84–87.

Weidemann, Kurt. 1969. *Book Jackets and Record Sleeves*. London: Thames and Hudson.

Weiner, M. J. 1981. *English Culture and the Decline of the English Industrial Spirit, 1850–1950*. Harmondsworth: Penguin.

Weinstock, Herbert. 1956. "Three-and-a-Half Years of Uninterrupted Listening." *Saturday Review* (September 29): 31, 33, 65.

Welch, Walter L., and Leah Brodbeck Stenzel Burt. 1994. *From Tinfoil to Stereo: The Acoustic Years of the Recording Industry from 1877–1929*. Gainesville, Fla.: University of Florida Press.

Whiteley, Nigel. 1994. "High Art and the High Street: The "Commerce-and-Culture Debate." In *The Authority of the Consumer*, ed. by Russell Keat, Nigel Whiteley, and Nicholas Abercrombie. London: Routledge, 119–37.

Wile, Raymond. 1977a. "At the Creation." *American Record Guide* 40(3): 6–10.

———. 1977b. "The Wonder of the Age—the Edison Invention of the Phonograph." In Alistair Thomson, et al., *Phonographs & Gramophones: A Symposium Organised by The Royal Scottish Museum in Connection with the Exhibition "Phonographs and Gramophones" and the Centenary of the Phonograph by Thomas Alva Edison*. Edinburgh: Royal Scottish Museum, 9–41.

Williams, Raymond. 1962. *Communications*. Harmondsworth: Penguin.

Williamson, Judith. 1978. *Decoding Advertisements: Ideology and Meaning in Advertising*. London: Marion Boyars.

Wilson, Christopher P. 1983. "The Rhetoric of Consumption: Mass-Market Magazines and the Demise of the Gentle Reader, 1880–1950." In *The Culture of Consumption: Critical Essays in American History, 1880–1980*, ed. by Richard Wrightman Fox and T. J. Jackson Lears. New York: Pantheon Books.

Wilson, Conrad. 1997. *Giacomo Puccini*. London: Phaidon.

Wilson, H. L. 1926. *Music and the Gramophone and Some Masterpiece Recordings: A Collection of Historical, Biographical, and Analytical Notes, and Data of Generally Interesting Nature, Concerning Musical Works of Importance Completely Recorded for the Gramophone*. London: Gramophone/George Allen and Unwin.

Wilson, Percy. 1957. *The Gramophone Handbook*. London: Methuen.

———. 1964. "Fourth USA Audio Report." *The Gramophone* 41(488): 401–402.

———. 1972. "Care of Records." *Audio* 56(12): 30–32.

———. 1973a. "Reproducing Records." In *The Gramophone Jubilee Book*, ed. by Roger Wimbush. Harrow: Gramophone, 24–36.

———. 1973b. "My Fifty Years with Gramophone Records." *Gramophone* 50(600): 2137–38.

Wimbush, Roger (RW). 1964. "Portrait of a Reviewer, No. 1., A. R. (Alec Robertson)." *The Gramophone* 41(488): 321–22.

Wimbush, Roger, ed. 1973. *The Gramophone Jubilee Book*. Harrow: Gramophone.

Windreich, Leland. 1956. "Album Antics." *High Fidelity* 6(8): 28–29, 91.

Winston, Brian. 1998. *Media, Technology, and Society, a History: From the Telegraph to the Internet*. London: Routledge.

Wittleloostuyn, Jaco van. 1997. *The Classical Long Playing Record: Design, Production, Reproduction: A Comprehensive Survey*, transl. by Antoon Hurksmans, Evelyn Kort-van Kaam, and Shawm Kreitzman. Rotterdam: A. A. Balkema.

Woolf, Virginia. [1941] 1992. *Between the Acts.* Harmondsworth: Penguin.

Wyndham, O. H. 1926. "Filing Your Records." *The Australasian Phonograph Monthly* (July 20): 13.

Young, Michael. 1988. *The Metronomic Society: Natural Rhythms and Human Timetables.* London: Thames and Hudson.

Young, Percy M. 1965. *The Concert Tradition: From the Middle Ages to the Twentieth Century.* New York: Roy Publishers.

Zolberg, Vera L. 1990. *Constructing a Sociology of the Arts.* Cambridge: Cambridge University Press.

Main Periodicals Consulted

American Record Guide
Audio
Australian Record Review
Australasian Phonograph Monthly
BBC Music Magazine
British Phonographic Industry Year Book
British Phonographic Industry Statistical Handbook
Classic FM
The Etude
Fanfare
(The) Gramophone
Gramophone Record Review
High Fidelity
International Record Review
McClure's Magazine
Music in Australia
Musician
The Music Student
The Musical Times
The Phonogram: A Monthly Journal Devoted to the Science of Sound and Recording of Speech
Records and Recording
Saturday Review
Scientific American
Soundscapes
Talking Machine Review

Discography

Alwyn, William. *Symphony no. 1; Piano Concerto,* Howard Shelley (piano), London Symphony Orchestra, Richard Hickox. Chandos, 9155.

Bach, Johann Sebastian. *Goldberg Variations,* András Schiff (piano). London, 289 460-611-2.

Bach, Johann Sebastian, and Uri Caine. *The Goldberg Variations,* Uri Caine Ensemble. Winter and Winter, 910 054-2

Bantock, Sir Granville. *Hebridean Symphony; Celtic Symphony; The Witch of Atlas; The Sea Reivers,* Royal Philharmonic Orchestra, Vernon Handley. Hyperion, CDA20450.

Bartók, Béla. *Concerto for Orchestra* / Prokofiev, Sergei. *Symphony no. 5,* Cleveland Orchestra, George Szell. Sony, MHK 63124.

Barber, Samuel. *Excursions; Nocturne; Ballade; Piano Sonata,* Angela Brownridge (piano). Helios, CDH88016.

*Beethoven, Ludwig van. *Symphony no. 8* / Schubert, Franz. *Unfinished Symphony,* Berlin Philharmonic Orchestra, Herbert von Karajan, Deutsche Grammophon, SLPM 193 001.

Beethoven, Ludwig van, and Franz Liszt. *Piano Transcriptions, Symphony no. 5; Symphony no. 6 ("Pastoral"),* Glenn Gould (piano). Sony SMK 52 636.

Bernstein, Leonard. *Symphony no. 2 for Piano and Orchestra ("The Age of Anxiety")* / Bolcolm, William. *Concerto for Piano and Large Orchestra,* Marc-André Hamelin (piano), The Ulster Orchestra, Dmitry Sitkovetsky. Hyperion, CDA 67170.

Bridge, Frank. *Cherry Ripe; Enter Spring; Lament; Summer; The Sea,* Royal Liverpool Philharmonic Orchestra, Sir Charles Groves. EMI, CDM 5 66855 2.

*Britten, Benjamin. *Symphony for Cello and Orchetra* / Haydn, Josef. *Cello Concerto in C major,* Mstislav Rostropovich (cello), English Chamber Orchestra, Benjamin Britten. Decca SXL 6138.

———. *Overture, The Building of the House* / Bridge, Frank. *The Sea, Enter Spring* / Holst, Gustav. *A Fugal Overture; Egdon Heath,* English Chamber Orchestra, Benjamin Britten; Imogen Holst; New Philharmonia, Benjamin Britten. BBC Legends, B 8007-2.

* ———. *Three Canticles,* John Hahessey (alto), Peter Pears (tenor), Barry Tuckwell (horn), Benjamin Britten (piano). Argo, ZRG 5377.

*Bush, Alan. *Violin Concerto; Dialectic; Six Short Pieces,* Manoug Parikian (violin), BBC Symphony Orchestra, Norman del Mar; Medici Quartet; Alan Bush (piano). Hyperion, A66138.

Chabrier, Emmanuel. *Impromptu; Dix pièces pittoresques, Bourrée fantasque,* Richard McMahon (piano). Pianissimo, PP10792.

*Chopin, Frederic. *Les Sylphides—Ballet* / Ibert, Jacques. *Divertissement for Chamber Orchestra,* L'Orchestre de la Société des Concerts du Conservatoire de Paris, Roger Desormière. London, J-LLA 14.

Dvořák, Antonin. *Slavonic Dances, Op. 46 and 72,* Bavarian Radio Symphony Orchestra, Rafael Kubelík. Deutsche Grammophon, DG 457 712-2.

Frankel, Benjamin. *Symphony no. 2; Symphony no. 3,* Queensland Symphony Orchestra, Werner Andrea Albert. CPO, 999 214-2.

Grieg, Edvard. *Lyric Pieces,* Leif Ove Andsnes (piano). EMI 7243 5 57296 2 0

Hindemith, Paul. *Mathis de Maler—Symphonie; Noblissima Visione—Suite; Symphonic Metamorphosis on Themes of Carl Maria von Weber,* Berliner Philharmonic Orchestra, Claudio Abbado. Deutsche Grammophon, 447 389-2.

*Holst, Gustav. *The Planets,* London Symphony Orchestra, Sir Malcolm Sargent. Decca, LXT 2871.

* ———. *Suite no.1 in E-flat; Suite no. 2 in F* / Handel, Georg Frideric, *Music for the Royal Fireworks* / Bach, J. S., *Fantasia in G,* The Cleveland Symphonic Winds, Frederick Fennell. Telarc, Dig DG 5038.

*Ives, Charles. *Second Symphony,* New York Philharmonic Orchestra, Leonard Bernstein. CBS, 72451.

*Kagel, Maurizio. *'1898',* Children's Voices and Instruments, Silvio Foretic and Maurizio Kagel. Deutsche Grammophon, DG 2543 007.

———. *Solo Works for Accordion and Piano,* Teodore Anzellotti (accordion) and Lus Vaes (piano). Winter and Winter New Edition, W & W 910 035-2.

Korngold, Erich Wolfgang. *String Trio; Suite for 2 Violins, Cello, and Piano (Left Hand),* Czech Trio. Supraphon SU 3347-2131.

*Denotes long-playing record. All other discs listed are compact discs.

Ligeti, György. *Le Grand Macabre*, Das ORF Symphonie Orchester, Elgar Howarth. Wergo 286 170-2.

*Lucier, Alvin. *North American Time Capsule (1967); Extended Voices*, New Pieces for Chorus and for Voices Altered Electronically by Sound Synthesizers and Vocoder, The Brandeis University Chamber Chorus, Alvin Lucier. Odyssey, 32 160156.

Martland, Steve. *Horses of Instruction*, The Steve Martland Band. Black Box, BBM1033.

*Martin, Frank. *6 Monologes from Jedermann; 3 Fragmente from Der Sturm*, Dietrich Fischer-Dieskau (baritone), Berlin Philharmonic Orchestra, Frank Martin. Deutsche Grammophon, 138 871 SLPM.

*Mendelssohn, Felix. *Symphony no. 5 ("Scotch"); Hebrides Overture*, Philharmonic Orchestra, Otto Klemperer. Angel, S 35880.

*Milhaud, Darius. *La Création du monde; Suite Provençale*, Boston Symphony Orchestra, Charles Munch. RCA Victor Soria, LDS 2625.

Mozart, Wolfgang Amadeus. *Piano Concerto no. 11 (K413); Piano Concerto no. 12 (K414)*, Robert Levin (piano), The Academy of Ancient Music, Christopher Hogwood. L'Oiseau-lyre, CD 443 328-2.

———. *Symphony no. 36 in C Major ("Linz"; K425)*, Columbia Symphony Orchestra, Bruno Walter. Coronet, KLC 512-513.

*Mussorgsky, Modest / Arthur Willis (arranger) *Pictures at an Exhibition*, Arthur Willis (organ). Hyperion, AS66006.

Penderecki, Krzysztof. *St. Luke Passion*, Wotowicz, Stefania, Hillski, Andrzej, Ladysa, Bernard, Cracow, Philharmonic Choir and Orchestra, Henryk Czyz. Philips, SAL 3163-4.

*Pijper, Willem. *Piano Concerto; Six Symphonic Epigrams; Six Adagios* / Badings, Henrik. *Concerto for Two Violins and Orchestra*, Herman Krebbers and Theo Olof (violins), The Concertgebouw Orchestra, Eduard van Beinum; Hague Philharmonic Orchestra, Eduard Flipse; Hague Philharmonic Orchestra, Willem van Otterloo. Philips, A 02242 1.

Poulenc, Francis. *Les Soirées de Nazelles; Trois Novelettes; Pastourelle; Trois mouvements perpétuels; Improvisations; Valse; Trois pièces*, Pascal Rogé (piano), Decca 417 438-2.

*———. *Quatre cycles de mélodies*, Gérard Souzay (baritone) and Dalton Baldwin (piano). Philips, SAL 3635.

*Prokofiev, Sergey. *Piano Concerto no. 1* / Ravel, Maurice. *Piano Concerto for the Left Hand*, Andre Gavrilov (piano), London Symphony Orchestra, Simon Rattle. HMV, ASD 3571.

———. *Symphony no. 5*, Orchestra of the Bolshoi Theatre, Yuri Simonov. Melodiya, CM 03879-80.

———. *Symphony no. 5; Symphony no. 1 ("Classical")*, Orchestre Symphonique de Montréal, Charles Dutoit. Decca, 421 813-2.

———. *Symphony no. 1 ("Classical"); Symphony no. 5*, Atlanta Symphony Orchestra, Yoel Levi. Telarc, CD-80289.

———. *Symphony no. 5*; Stravinsky, Igor. *Le Sacre du Printemps*, Berlin Philharmonic Orchestra, Herbert von Karajan. Deutsche Grammophon, 463 613-2.

*———. *Symphony no. 5*, Philadelphia Orchestra, Eugene Ormandy. RCA Victor, ARL1-1869.

———. *Symphony no. 5; Dreams*, Concertgebouw Orchestra, Vladimir Ashkenazy. Decca, 417 314 2DH.

Rachmaninoff, Serge. *Piano Concerto no. 3* / Tchaikovsky, Peter Ilyich. *Piano Concerto no. 1*, Martha Argerich (pianist), RSO Berlin, Riccardo Chailly; Symphonie-Orchester des Bayerischen Rundfunks, Kirill Kondrashin. Philips, 446 673-2.

*Resphigi, Ottorino. *The Birds; Brazilian Impressions*, London Symphony Orchestra, Antal Dorati. Mercury, SR 90153.

*Rósza, Miklós. *Concerto for Violin and Orchestra* / Benjamin, Arthur. *Romantic Fantasy for Violin and Viola*, Jaschia Heifetz (violin) and William Primrose (viola), RCA Victor Orchestra, Izler Solomon. RCA Victor, LSC 2767.

Saariaho, Kaija. *Prisma*. Montaigne Naïve, MO782087.

Saint-Saëns, Camille. *Le Carnaval des animaux; Piano Trio; Septet*, The Nash Ensemble. Virgin Classics, VC 7 90751-2.

*Sauguet, Henri. *Les Forains; Piano Concerto no. 1*, Vasso Devetzi (piano) Orchestre des Concerts Lamoureux, Henri Sauguet; USSR Radio Symphony Orchestra, Gennady Rozhdestvesky. Philips, A 02298 L.

*Scarlatti, Alessandro. *La Dama spagnola eil Cavaliere romano* / Confalonieri, Giuli. *Gala*, Complesso Strumentale di Milano, Giuli Confalonieri. Decca, SET 230.

Schoenberg, Arnold. *Five Pieces for Orchestra* / Webern, Anton von. *Five Pieces for Orchestra* / Berg, Alban. *Three Pieces for Orchestra*, London Symphony Orchestra, Antal Dorati. Mercury, 90316.

Shostakovich, Dmitry. *Hypothetically Murdered; Four Romances on Poems by Pushkin; Five Fragments; Suite no. 1 for Jazz Band*, Dimitri Kharitonov (bass), City of Birmingham Symphony Orchestra, Mark Elder. United, 88001.

———. *Symphony no. 7 ("The Leningrad")*, Scottish National Orchestra, Neemi Järvi. Chandos CHAN 8623.

*———. *Symphony no. 10, Op. 93*, National Philharmonic Orchestra, Dmitri Shostakovich. Coliseum, CRLP 173.

*———. *Symphony no. 13 ("Babi-Yar")*, Philadelphia Orchestra, Eugene Ormandy. RCA Victor, LSC-3162.

Sibelius, Jean. *Violin Concerto in D minor*, Leonidas Kaakos (violin), Lahiti Symphony Orchestra, Osma Vänskä. BIS, BIS-CD-500.

*———. *Violin Concerto in D Minor*, Ginette Niveu (violin), Philharmonia Orchestra, Walter Susskind. HMV ALP 1479

*Stockhausen, Karlheinz. *Klavierstücke I-IX*, Aloys Kontarsky (piano). CBS, 7291-2.

Strauss, Richard. *Don Quixote* / Schumann, Robert. *Cello Concerto in A minor*, Mistislav Rostropovich (cello), Berliner Philharmonic Orchestra, Herbert von Karajan; Orchestre National de France, Leonard Bernstein. EMI 7243 5 66913 2 2.

———. *Symphonia Domestica; Parergon on Symphonia Domestica*, Gary Graffman (piano), Vienna Philharmonic Orchestra, André Previn. Deutsche Grammophon, 449 188-2.

Stravinsky, Igor. *Apropos of "Le Sacre,"* A Recorded Commentary by the Composer, *The Rite of Spring*, Columbia Symphony Orchestra, Igor Stravinsky. CBS, 72054.

*———. *Noces, Renard, Ragtime for 11 instruments*, Ensemble Instrumental and Grand Choeur de l'Université de Lausanne, Charles Dutoit. Erato, STU 70737.

*Tippett, Michael. *Second Symphony*, London Symphony Orchestra, Colin Davis. Argo, ZRG 535.

Vivaldi, Antonio. *Violin Concertos, "The Four Seasons,"* Concerto Italiano, Rinaldo Alessandrini. Opus 111, OP30363.

Walton, William. *Sinfonia Concertante* / Ireland, John. *Piano Concerto* / Bridge, Frank. *Phantasm for Piano and Orchestra*, Kathryn Stott (piano), Royal Philharmonic Orchestra, Vernon Handley. Conifer, CDCF 175.

Collections

At the Drop of the Hat, Donald Flanders and Michael Swan. Parlophone, PCSO 3001.

Contemporary Ballets from France, Orchestre de la Société Concerts du Conservatoire, Georges Prêtre. HMV ASD 496.

From My Home, Deutsch Kammerphilharmonie, Gidon Kramer. Teldec 0630-14654-2

Enjoyment of Stereo (and How to Get the Best Out of Your Record Playing Equipment), introduced by John Borwick. HMV SEOM 26.

A Voice to Remember: The Sounds of 75 Years on EMI Records, compiled by Roland Gellatt and Alistair Cook. EMI EMSP 75.

Ephemera

The brochures and advertising materials are from a number of recording labels including BBC/IMG, Polygram, EMI, Decca, Hyperion, Nimbus, Chandos, Phillips, Da Capa, Naxos, and CPO.

Index

Page numbers in *italics* indicate illustrations.

Audiences for music *(cont'd)*
    culture, 60–62, 84–86; maintenance in-
    structions for records, 137–39; textual dis-
    course role for, 9–10, 18; and visual cues in
    listening, 83, 193. *See also* Collectors/col-
    lecting of recorded music; Consumers
Audio equipment: and concert hall norm,
    77–78; and dynamic frequency range issue,
    80, 81; recording company manufacture of,
    260n15; reviews of, 188, 203
Auger, Bob, 136

Babbitt, Milton, 56, 57
Bahr, Robert von, 144
Ballet mécanique (Antheil), 50
Barber, Samuel, 119
Barbirolli, Sir John, 70
Barenboim, Daniel, 70
Barraud, Francis, 29
Bartók, Béla, 50, 139–40
BBC Radio, 164, 184–85
BBC record label, *106*, 112
BBC Record Magazine, 186–87
Beckmann, Max, 116
Bell, Chichester, 11
Bellamy, Edward, 37
Bell Telephone Laboratories, 41, 54
Bentham, Jeremy, 6
Berliner, Emile, 14, 19, 20, 24, 63, 248
Berlioz, Hector, 115
Les Biches (Poulenc), 115
Birnbaum, Theodore, 27
BIRS (British Institute of Recorded Sound),
    231
*The Blackwell Guide to Recorded Contempo-
    rary Music,* 229
Bliss, Arthur, 48
Blumlein, Alan, 75
Book vs. phonograph: cataloging considera-
    tions, 224; digital merging of, 249–50; and
    liner notes, 126, 133–34, 143; material simi-
    larities, 263n12; musical adoption of book
    features, 92, 93, 95–96, 99, 105, 108, 110;
    and organization of music collections,
    239; printing developments, 3–5, 107–8,
    110; and public record libraries, 230; and
    review architecture, 184; technological
    mediation issues, 18; and texts for deluxe
    editions, 141–42; and texts for omnibus
    editions, 129
Bottomley, Gordon, 188
Boulez, Pierre, 44–45, 47, 48
Boult, Adrian, 48

Bourgeois lifestyle, phonograph as essential
    to, 25, 27, 64
Boxed sets, booklets for, 129, 141–42
Brendel, Alfred, 43, 45, 70
Bridge, Frank, 103, 105
Briggs, Gilbert, 77–78
British Institute of Recorded Sound (BIRS),
    231
British Sound Archive, 231
Britten, Benjamin, 46, 47, 105
Buckley, Jonathan, 234
Bülow, Hans von, 255n2
Burghardt, Ursula, 149
Bush, Alan, 116, 144
Busoni, Ferruccio, 39, 50

Cage, John, 49, 52
Cahill, Thaddeus, 50
Caine, Uri, 149
Calligraphy: in cover designs, 101, *102*, 110–
    11; and liner notes, 135, 142, 143
Canticles (Britten), 105
Capitalism and rise of mass-circulation maga-
    zines, 153–59. *See also* Consumers
Cardboard materials in packaging, 92, 93
Le Carnaval des animaux (Saint-Saëns), 113
Caruso, Enrico, 25, 27, 256nn15–16
Cassette tapes, 69
Catalogues of recordings, 25, 220–30, 240–
    41, 250
Categorization of subjects in record maga-
    zines, 188, 189–91
CBS record label, 105
Celibidache, Sergiu, 42, 43
Cerebral culture of classical music. *See* Seri-
    ousness discourse in classical music
Chandos record label, 105, *106*
Channeling of auditory signals. *See* Quad-
    raphony; Stereo recording phase
Chislett, W. A., 192
Chopin, Frédéric, 101
Circulation of records, 149–50
Class, socioeconomic: middle class as target
    for phonograph, 25, 27, 35, 64;
    phonograph's equalizing role, 38, 46, 48,
    217. *See also* Elitism
Classical music: declining audience for re-
    corded, 18, 256n8; definitional issues, 255n1;
    elitism in, 38. *See also* Popular vs. classical
    music
Classic FM, 171
The Classic FM Hall of Fame Collection
    (Shadwick), 234–35

Classification issues in record organization, 240

Classified section of record magazines, 172

Claves record label, 143

Cobbett, Walter, 36

Collectors/collecting of recorded music: cataloging techniques, 220–30, 240–41; emotional motivations for collecting, 239, 272n24; guidance for home collections, 233–43; library collections, 230–32; and life history of possessed records, 149–50; magazines as advocates for, 159; moral dimension of, 213–18; and programming organization, 130–31; reviewer role for, 205–6; societies for, 218–19; as transducer of energy in recording, 212–13; vinylphiles, 82, 90, 262n7. *See also* Readers, record magazine

Columbia History of Music Through Eye and Ear (Scholes), 248–49

Columbia record label: advertising, 26; composer competitions, 54; cover designs, 93, 97, 99; and LP and tape developments, 68; support for *Gramophone,* 160

Coming Up for Air (Orwell), 37

Commercialism and loss of value in music, 38

Compact discs (CDs): advantages of, 66, 80, 81, 90, 262n2, 262n6; collection aspects of, 215, 225, 228, 234; computer-assisted design technology, 107; and cultural legitimacy issue, 134; and labeling conventions, 99, 133; liner notes for, 126, 140, 142–43; and live recordings, 45–46, 70, 258n15; maintenance of, 138–39, 242, 243; musician collaboration in development of, 55; and new record magazines, 162; packaging, 89, 90, 92; and programming trends, 130; punctuation issues, 132; and reviews, 194t, 195t, 197–98; as self-sufficient multimedia resource, 249–53; and super-realism, 80–83; technical overview, 65, 69

Comparative analysis of performances, 193, 198, 203

Compendium collections of reviews, 209

Competitions, magazine, 176, 177

Completists, catering to, 130–31

Composers: in cover designs, 109, 114, 118–19, 120; liner note treatment of, 140, 143–50; responses to recorded music, 38–42, 44, 46–47, 48–54; sponsorship of phonograph legitimacy, 52, 53; textual spotlighting of, 135; use of recorded folk music by, 50–51

Composers' Recordings, Inc. (CRI), 98–99

Compression of time and space by phonograph, 12–13, 61, 247

Computer-assisted design technology, 107

Computers and virtualization of recorded music, 248–53

Conan Doyle, Arthur, 37

Concept albums, 129

Concert hall vs. phonograph: and acoustic-to-digital progression, 62–66, 80–83; advertising debate, 173, 174–75, 176; and concert as intimidating for listeners, 234; and culture of listening, 60–62; and etiquette of music appreciation, 23–24; home replication of concert hall, 29, 55, 236, 237, 238; idealism vs. realism debate, 66–72, 86–87; as keystone discourse for classical music, 7, 34, 49, 246–47; and liner notes, 125; live recordings, 45–46, 70; local recording recitals, 218–19, 236, 237, 238; magazine reinforcement of concert hall norm, 153, 193, 196, 202–3, 210–11; and music program organization, 128–29; as problematic recording location, 82; pros and cons of, 42–59; and super-realism in recording, 72–86

Concert program booklets, 101, 125–31

Conductors: cover design highlighting of, 118; in liner notes, 139–40; response to recorded music, 40, 41, 42, 43, 44–45, 48

Conly, John, 269n1

Consensus, 184

Consumers: catalog value for, 221; collection and obsolescence factor, 215; magazines' role in supporting, 152–59, 163, 183; reviews as protective device for, 187, 188, 201, 205–10; as target for cultural transformations, 8

Containment of records, 89–95, 241, 242, 243

Contemporary classical music, 228–29, 271n2

Copland, Aaron, 54

Cover design: artistic partnerships, 105, 107, 109, 113–22, 263nn19–20; exhibitions for, 263n16; labeling conventions, 95–99; as mediating text for music, 88–89, 122–23; naming conventions, 139–43; packaging/containment, 89–95; purposes for, 99–108; styles and traditions, 108–12. *See also* Liner notes

La Création du monde (Milhaud), 51, 142

CRI (Composers' Recordings, Inc.), 98–99

Criticism, music. *See* Reviews/reviewers

Cros, Charles, 11, 19

Culshaw, John, 83–84, 103, 143, 249, 261n25

Cultural context: and discourses as realities, 6; and disembodiment of recorded music, 3, 83, 247–48, 253; and etymology of phonographic terms, 19–24; listening culture, 60–62, 84–86; mechanized reproduction effects, 1–5; paratexts' role in, 15–16, 95–96, 170–73, 251–52, 262–63n11; phonograph as exemplar of mass culture, 38; time/space compression role of phonograph, 12–13, 61, 247, 250; visual character of contemporary, 31–32, 197–98. *See also* Discourses for phonograph; Gendered nature of record culture; Moral dimension

Cultural legitimacy for phonograph: and composers as sponsors, 52, *53;* and cover design traditions, 97, 105; early opposition to recording, 6–8, 9, 257n6, 258n9; and lack of ISBNs for CDs, 134; Mackenzie's crusade for, 164; and magazine development, 159; overview of, 24–32; and public's preference for popular music, 22; and records' status in libraries, 231–32; and reviewers, 199, 201, 208; and scholarly tone of liner notes, 141

Cylinder vs. disc, 63, 89–90

Dali, Salvador, 105
La Dama spagnola e il Cavaliere romano (Scarlatti), 105
Dark leisure, music appreciation as escape from, 155, 216, 235–36
Darrell, R. D., 221
Dawson, Peter, 39
Dbx technology, 81
Debussy, Claude, 38, 49, 116
Decca record label: cover designs, 97–98, 99, 101, 103; full-frequency range recording, 68, *91,* 196; home library recommendations, 233; humor in advertising, 177; liner note styles, 143, 144; rejection of concert hall norm, 76, 202–3; verisimilitude claim for recorded music, 173, *174,* 176
Delius, Frederic, 259n24
Dematerialization of culture in digital era, 253
Demuth, Charles, 119
Department structure of record magazines, 170–71
Dependency texts, reviews as, 185
Deutsche Grammophon record label: commemorative sleeve, 54; cover designs, 110, 111, *114;* insert slips, 142; label designs, 99; marketing tactics, 266n22
Dictionary and encyclopedia treatment of recorded music terms, 36

Digital technology: ambivalence about, 78, 202; and designations for digital and analog sources, 133; and discography forms, 223; future directions, 249–53, 262n1; Karajan on, 259n25. *See also* Compact discs (CDs)
Direct-to-disc recording, 81
Disc, gramophone: vs. cylinder, 63, 89–90; etymology of, 19–20. *See also specific recording formats*
Discographies, cataloging of, 220–30
Discourses for phonograph: audience role in, 9–10, 18; and cultural legitimacy campaign, 24–25; fictional, 36–37, 48, 257–58n8; vs. film industry norms, 79, 259n29; and musicians' views, 34–35; overview, 5–10, 245–47; reviewers' role in, 182–84, 201, 210–11. *See also* Concert hall vs. phonograph; Seriousness discourse in classical music
Disembodiment of recorded music: cultural consequences of, 3, 83, 247–48, 253; liner notes as recovery of concert hall, 125; and loss of audience inspiration, 45; need for visual cues in cover design, 88; reviewer use of visualizing vocabularies, 193
Diversion vs. abstract focused form of listening, 140–41
Divertissement (Ibert), 101
Divine art, music as, 22–24, 44
Doctor Faustus (Mann), 48
Documentary reality, definition, 5
Domestic space: advertising campaign for phonograph in, 25, *26,* 63–64; consumer economy's transformation of, 154; control of musical experience in, 58; guidance for home collections, 233–43; loss of instrument playing activity in, 35–36, 257n3, 268n26; and realism goal for recorded music, 73; recording invasion of, 2–3, 179, 268n30; replication of concert hall performance, 29, 55, 236, 237, 238; and training of music listeners, 84–86
Donialoff, Hans, 110
Dorati, Antal, 41, 144
Downe, Olin, 234
Doyle, Arthur Conan, 37
Dracula (Stoker), 37
Dvořák, Antonín, 192
Dynamic frequency range and audio equipment limitations, 80, 81
Dynaphone, 50

ECM (Editions Contemporary Music), 116, 118

Edison, Thomas Alva: and development of phonograph, 3, 4, 11–12; and etymology of phonographic terms, 19; non-musical focus of, 3, 20–21, 24, 256n12; opposition to phonograph as toy, 22; and phonograph as time capsule, 13–14

Editing of recorded music: advantages of, 56; development of, 41–42; and live vs. recording debate, 43, 69–71, 72; pre-tape, 260n8

Editions Contemporary Music (ECM), 116, 118

Educational motivations for phonograph, 63, 217, 219, 233–38

Egalitarian society, phonograph's contribution to, 38, 46, 48, 217

Electric recording phase, 24, 39, 65, 194t, 195t, 196

Electronic instrumentation, 50

Elgar, Edward, 44, 54, 70

Elitism: in classical music, 3, 22–24, 38, 163–67; and education of novice collectors, 233; and librarians' record borrower biases, 231–32; vs. recorded music's egalitarianism, 48

EMG Hand-Made Gramophones, Ltd., 17, 29

EMI record label: Abbey Road Studios, 256n14; cover designs, 103, 106, 112; and lack of full credits list, 136; Recording Angel trademark, 29, 30; rejection of concert hall norm, 76; studio environment, 261n22

Emotional motivations for music collection, 239, 272n24

Encyclopedia of Recorded Music (Darrell), 221

Endorsement, rhetoric of, 52, 53, 54, 206

Engineering of recordings: and rejection of concert hall norm, 76, 202–3; reviewer analysis of, 193, 201–2, 209; super-realism of, 72–86; textual support for, 183. *See also* Gould, Glenn; Karajan, Herbert von

Engineers, recording: at Abbey Road Studios, 256n14; and illusion of live concert standard, 62, 66–67, 71, 72–80; as major contributors to art, 56; manipulation of musical performance, 44; recognition in liner notes, 135–36; and super-realism, 82

Entertainment, public preference for phonograph as, 21–22

EP (extended play) records, 100

Epistemology of recording: and guidance on home collections, 233–34; magazines as source of, 16, 152–53, 154; and magisterial discourse consequences, 201; and value of catalogs, 221, 223; as work of leisure time, 216

Ethnomusicology, 13, 50–51, 230–31, 259n21

Etiquette of music appreciation: home concert guidance, 29, 55, 236, 237, 238; and liner note purposes, 125, 148; magazines as sources for, 178–80; need for training in, 84–86, 256n13; and punctuation of music, 131; record guide role in, 213–14, 224, 238–43; Romantic-era transformation of, 22–24. *See also* Seriousness discourse in classical music

The Etude, 103, 104

Etymology of phonographic terms, 19–22

Exosomatic form, phonograph as, 10–11

Experimentation in music, recording as restriction on, 48–49. *See also* Engineering of recordings

Extended play (EP) records, 100

Fanfare, 162

Farrar, Geraldine, 27, 28

Ffrr ear icon, 91, 97

Fictional discourses on phonograph, 36–37, 48, 257–58n8

Film vs. recording industries' norms, 79, 259n29

Flagstad, Kirsten, 70

Folk music, classical composers' adoption of, 50–51

Fontana record label, 233

Formats, recording, accommodating in reviews, 197. *See also specific formats*

45 rpm (single play) records, 100

Foucault, Michel, 5–6

Four-channel sound (quad), 55, 65, 76–77, 194t, 195t

Framing devices, textual adjuncts as, 124–25, 214–15

French inventors and phonographic developments, 11

Frequency range, expansion of phonographic, 63, 65, 80, 81, 97

Full-frequency range recording (ffrr), 68, 97, 196

Gabrieli, Giovanni, 58

Gaisberg, Fred, 24, 25, 256n15

Gamelan music, 49

Gatefold packaging for LPs, 92

Gayenah (Khachaturian), 119

Gelatt, Roland, 169

Gendered nature of record culture: and cultural hegemony struggle, 8; men as primary phonograph hobbyists, 176, 177, 236;

Gendered nature of record culture *(cont'd)*
men's vs. women's musical activities, 35–36, 257n3, 268n26; women's objection to phonographic home invasion, 86, 268n30; women's vs. men's magazine content, 157

Genette, Gerald, 18, 95–96

Geographical links to music on cover designs, 111, *114*

Geography of music, recording's effect on, 3, 12–13, 61, 247, 250

Gilels, Emil, 76

Glass, Louis, 21

Glass, Philip, 201

Glière, Reinhold, 207, 208

Goff, Martyn, 235

Goldberg Variations (arr. Caine), 149

The Golden Treasury of Recorded Sound (Robertson), 230

Goldmark, Peter, 68

The Good CD Guide, 225, 228, 234

Gould, Glenn, 42, 56–58, 59, 72, 129–30, 179–80, 261n25

Grainger, Percy, 50

Gramophone, definitional issues, 19–20, 36. *See also* Phonograph

Gramophone (The Gramophone): aesthetic crusade of, 163–67; catalog of, 250; establishment of, 159–63; moral motivations for creation of, 217; narrative architecture of, 171–72, 176–77, 178–79; punctuality and topicality of, 167, 168–70; record guides, 225; reviews in, 186, 187–88, 189–98; and spread of live concert norm, 66–68; support for local clubs/societies, 218

Gramophone Record Review, 187

Graphic designers, recognition in liner notes, 135–36

Graphic design processes, 101, 105, 161. *See also* Cover design

Graphophone, 11–12, 19, 21

Grubb, Suvi Raj, 261n20

Guides for record collecting, 220, 223–30, 234–43

Hall, David, 224

Hanson-Dyer, Louise, 110

Harmonia Mundi record label, 93, *94*

Hegemonic historicism and stagnation of music, 48–49

Heifetz, Jascha, 139

Henry Stave (retail outlet), 184

High Fidelity: as appreciation etiquette manual, 179–80; content philosophy of, 268n27; corporate progress of, 162; humor in, 177; reviews' function in, 188, 197; timely orientation of, 167–68, 169

High Fidelity (Hornby), 239

High fidelity concept, 49, 73, 97–98, 162

Hillandale News, 158

Hindemith, Paul, 51–52, 115

His Master's Voice (HMV) trademark: background of, 27, 29, 256–57n17; cover designs, 100, 112, *120;* in record guides, 229–30

Historical imagery on cover designs, *109,* 111

HMV (His Master's Voice) trademark. *See* His Master's Voice (HMV) trademark

Hobby, recorded music as, 157, 176, 177, 213–18, 236. *See also* Collectors/collecting of recorded music

Hogwood, Christopher, 43

Holst, Gustav, 40, 101, 196

Home environment. *See* Domestic space

Homogenous programming on records, 128–29

Hopper, Edward, 119

Hornby, Nick, 239

Human voice, initial focus on reproduction of, 11, 12, 13–14

Humor in classical music recordings, 112, 177

Hyperion record label, *106,* 116, 118, 131, 144–45

Hypothetically Murdered (Shostakovich), 112, *120*

Ibert, Jacques, 101

Idealism vs. realism debate, 22, 66–87

Imaginary Landscapes (Cage), 52

Immortality of sound recording, 10–14, 29, 37, 43, 63

Immutable mobiles, 13, 61

Independent vs. major record labels, 143, 221, 223

Indigenous phenomenon, record as, 83–84, 87

Information protocol in record reviews, 196–98

Insert slips, 142

Institutional collecting, 216–17, 230–32

Instrument, musical, phonograph as, 10, 48–54

Intellectualization of music appreciation. *See* Seriousness discourse in classical music

Interactivity and digital recording formats, 251, 252

International Association of Sound Archives, 133

International Record Review, 162–63

Lowry, L. S., 116
LSO Live, 46

Machaut, Guillaume de, 44
Mackenzie, Compton: and care of records, 243; and early reviewing process, 191–92; enshrinement of record by, 214; and establishment of *Gramophone*, 66, 159–60; and etymology of gramophone terms, 19; musical crusade of, 163–67, 267–68n19; on nicknaming of classical compositions, 139; pedantic language of, 179; support for public record libraries, 230
Mackenzie, Faith Compton, 268n29
Magazines, record: and discourse on recorded music, 9–10; *Gramophone's* battle against jazz, 163–67; history and functions of, 16, 152–63, 180–81; narrative architecture of, 170–79, 184–88, 189–91, 194t, 195t; overview of discourse role, 246; relationship with readers, 178–80; as time machines, 167–70. See also *Gramophone; High Fidelity;* Reviews/reviewers
Magisterial discourse and alienation of readers, 201
Major vs. independent record labels, 143, 221, 223
Malevich, Kasimir, 116
Mandeville, Edouard-Léon Scott de, 11
Mann, Thomas, 48
Marek, George, 205
Marketing of recorded music. *See* Advertising
Markevitch, Igor, 44
Marshall, Arthur, 163, 243
Mass-circulation magazines and consumer capitalism, 153–59. *See also* Magazines, record
Mass culture. *See* Cultural context
Materials, record: packaging, 89, 90, 92–93; shellac for 78s, 68–69, 90, 260n6; vinyl for LPs, 68–69, 135, 173
Medium play (EP) records, 100
Melba, Dame Nellie, 97
Memory: and advantages of recorded music for musicians, 44; and information overload of digital era, 252; phonograph as preserver of, 10–11, 29, 37, 43, 63, 248
Mercury record label, 73, 83
Metaphysics of music, 9, 12–13, 56, 69–70. *See also* Audiences for music; Concert hall vs. phonograph
Microphones, improvements in, 54–55

Middle classes as target for phonograph, 25, 27, 35, 64
Milhaud, Darius, 51–52, 142
Moholy-Nagy, Lázló, 52
Monophony and philosophy of recorded sound, 58
Moral dimension: classical music as elevator of society, 22–24, 163–67; and constructive leisure, 154–55, 166, 213–18, 235–36, 240–41, 244, 246; and cultural legitimization of phonograph, 24; and inferior quality of recorded sound, 39; loss of domestic instrument playing, 35–36; and phonograph as corrupt, 3, 7, 22, 46–47. *See also* Popular vs. classical music
Morita, Akio, 55
Multilingual liner notes, 142–43
Musical establishment: live performance vs. recording control, 42–48, 54–59; overview of response to recorded music, 33–38; and phonograph as musical instrument, 10, 48–54; recording industry's campaign to convert, 25, 27; response to recording process, 38–42. *See also* Composers; Conductors; Performers
Musical instrument, phonograph as, 48–54
Music and Musicians, 162
Musical Quarterly, 184
Mussorgsky, Modest, 115

Narrative architecture of recorded music: cover design, 99–112; and discourse development, 9–10; and etymology of phonographic terms, 19–22, 33; labeling conventions, 95–99; liner notes, 136–43; live performance vs. edited recording, 43; overview, 4–5, 7–8, 14–18, 31–32; record magazines, 170–79, 184–88, 189–91, 194t, 195t, 208; and trademark symbols, 29, 30
Nash, John, 113
Needles for 78s and LPs, 41, 54, 64–65, 137, 256n9
Needless duplication of recorded works, 129–30
Newman, Ernest, 52, 141
Nighthawks (Hopper), 119
Nimbus record label, 190, 263n14
Nipper the dog, 29
Niveau, Ginette, 121
Noise, signal. *See* Signal-to-noise ratio
Non-musical sounds in composition, 49–50
Norms, cultural. *See* Cultural context; Discourses for phonograph; Moral dimension

Notation, musical. *See* Scores, musical
Number 5 (Demuth), 119

O'Connell, Charles, 55
Office applications for early phonograph, 20–21
Offset printing, introduction of, 107–8, 110
Omnibus recording sets, 129, 144
Opera: cover designs, *104*, 111; and cultural legitimacy for phonograph, 25, 27, *28;* early difficulties with recording, 256nn15–16; libretto booklets for, 141; maximum recording engineering of, 84; record guides for, 229
Ormandy, Eugene, 40, 147
Orwell, George, 37
Osborne, Conrad, 84

Packaging for records, 89–95, 241, *242, 243*
Paintings in cover designs, 105, *106,* 107, *109,* 113–22, *117,* 263nn19–20
Palimpsests, cover designs as, 122
Palmer, Christopher, 147, 148
Parade (Satie), 50
Paratextuality: and CD/computer impact on recording, 251–52; conceptual overview, 15–16; in magazine architecture, 170–73; in other cultural products, 262–63n11; and record cover role, 95–96
Parerga, textual portions of recorded music as, 124
Participation in music, phonographic effects on, 35–36, 47–48, 155, 257n3, 268n26
Patti, Adelina, 255n2
Paulsen, Vlademar, 260n7
Penguin Guide, 226–29, *227*
Penguin Music Classics, 108, *109,* 148
Performance, reviewer analysis of, 193, 202. *See also* Concert hall vs. phonograph
Performers: cover design highlighting of, 118; and homogenous programming on records, 128–29; liner note focus on, 127, 135, 139–40; magazines' focus on, 170, 203; recording focus on, 264n32
Permanence of sound recording, 10–14, 29, 37, 43, 63, 248
Pétrouchka (Stravinsky), 192
Pfeiffer, John, 261n20
Phonautograph machine, 11
Phonogenic sound, definition of, 61–62
Phonograph: compression of time/space by, 12–13, 61, 247; and cultural elevation of music, 22–24; dictionary neglect of, 36;

etymology of term, 19–22; overview of cultural impact, 1–4; and permanence of sound recording, 10–14, 29, 37, 43, 63, 248; printing press as antecedent of, 4–5; writing as integral to, 14–18. *See also* Cultural legitimacy for phonograph; Discourses for phonograph
Phonographische Zeitschrift, 158–59
Photography as precursor to phonograph, 11
Piano tuners, recognition in liner notes, 136
Piano vs. phonograph: cost issue, 35; as home furnishings, 25; player pianos, 10, 31, 62, 127, 187
Pictures at an Exhibition (Mussorgsky), 115
Pines of Rome (Respighi), 52
Piper, John, 105
Pires, Maria João, 170
Pitman, Isaac, 19
The Planets (Holst), 101, 196
Plastic packaging materials, 90, 92
Player pianos, 10, 31, 62, 127, 187
Playing of music, phonographic effects on, 35–36, 47–48, 155, 257n3, 268n26
Popular-choice music collection guides, 234–35
Popular vs. classical music: and artistic design partnerships, 107; cover design traditions, 110, 118; freedoms of popular music, 48–49, 72, 87; keystone discourse as classical survival, 247; lack of combined programs, 129; librarians' disdain for popular music, 232; and liner notes, 133, 140; Mackenzie's crusade for quality music, 163–67; origins of schism, 7, 23–24, 256n14; public preferences for popular music, 21–22; record guides as gateway to classical level, 235; and reviewing traditions, 183, 187–88. *See also* Jazz music
Populations, phonographic listening. *See* Audiences for music
Portraiture in cover designs, *106,* 111, *114,* 118–19, *120*
Poulenc, Francis, 115–16
Prenn, Oliver, 229
Preservation of music: ethnomusicology, 13, 50–51, 230–31, 259n21; phonograph as medium of, 63; record labels' neglect of, 231
Price range of records, changes in, 206
Printing developments, 3–5, 107–8, 110
Privatization of music: and audience control of musical experience, 58; digital era's impact on, 253; and perceived loss of cultural norms, 7; phonograph's transformative

Privatization of music *(cont'd)*
  role, 1, 3; and triumph of recorded sound,
  56. *See also* Domestic space
Producers, recording, recognition in liner
  notes, 135–36
Prokofiev, Sergey, 116, 145–46, 147–48
The Prospects of Recording (Gould), 57, 179–
  80
Public activity, advent of music as, 127
Public record libraries, 230–32
Punctuation of music on disc, 131–36
Pye High Fidelity Systems, 73, 74

Quad (Acoustical Manufacturing Company),
  73, 80, 173, *175*, 176
Quadraphony, 55, *65*, 76–77, 194t, 195t

Rachmaninov, Sergei, 39
Racism and hatred of jazz, 192–93
Radio: adoption of records by, 164, 249; and
  aesthetic dangers of popular music, 163–
  64; consolidation of U.S. record industry,
  267n116; establishment of classical recordings, 165; and popular vote-basis for record
  collection guide, 234–35; and record reviews, 184–85
Rankings of music by reviewers, 186–87, 204,
  225
Ravel, Maurice, 116
RCA Victor record label, 41, 52, 103, *104*
Readers, record magazine: attachments of,
  169–70; feedback options, 172–73, 176; and
  magazines as etiquette manuals, 178–80;
  reactions to narrative architecture changes,
  171; and record reviews, 185, 186, 189, 201
Realism vs. idealism debate, 22, 66–87
Recitals, local recording, 218–19, 236, *237*,
  238
Record, dictionary neglect of, 36
Record clubs and competition for record labels, 98
Record Guide (Sackville-West and Shawe-
  Taylor), 225
Record guides for collecting, 220, 223–30,
  234–43
Recording Angel trademark, 27, 29, *30*
Recording industry: cultural legitimacy for
  phonograph, 24–25, 27; and digital virtualization of music, 252–53; independent vs.
  major record labels, 143, 221, 223; lack of
  attention to preservation, 231; manufacture
  of audio equipment, 260–61n15; naming
  and trademarks, 96, 134, 136; profitability

of, 60; publishing by, 158, 220–21; rejection
  of concert hall norm, 76, 202–3; reviewer
  pressure to innovate, 209; support for
  gramophone societies, 219; technical col-
  laborations with musicians, 54–55. *See also*
  Advertising; *individual record labels*
Recording of music. *See* Phonograph
Record production. *See* Studios, recording
Records and Recording, 162, 168, 172
Record shops. *See* Retailing of records
Reel-to-reel tapes, 69
Regimes of truth in musical discourses, 5–6,
  7, 8. *See also* Discourses for phonograph
Reith, John, 164
Renovation of musical recordings, 81–82,
  261n20
Repetition function of records, 192, 228–29
Respighi, Ottorino, 52
Retailing of records: and classification ordering issues, 240; and cover designs, 100; development of, 36, 257n4; discography role
  in, 220; magazines as support material for,
  182; reviews from dealers, 184
Reviews/reviewers: advisory guides, 223–30;
  and CD introduction, 78; of cover designs,
  122; discourse function of, 182–84, 210–11;
  and establishment of record magazines,
  158–59; in *Gramophone,* 186, 187–88, 189–
  98; magazines as forum for, 160–61, 162–
  63, 166; marketing impact of, 203–10; overview of narrative architecture, 184–88; profile of reviewer responsibilities, 198–203,
  270n23; reader responses to, 172; on recorded sounds in compositions, 52; and
  spread of concert hall norm, 66–67, 72, 73,
  84; as writers of liner notes, 140
Rheingold (Wagner), 84, 141
Ridout, Herbert C., 127
Rimsky-Korsakov, Nikolai, 39
Ring cycle, Wagner's, 84
Robertson, Alec, 110, 196, 230
Romantic literary influence on music, 22–24
Ronald, Landon, 25
Rouse, Samuel Holland, 221
Rózsa, Miklós, 145, 207
Rubbra, Edmund, 229

SACD (super audio compact discs), 77
Sackville-West, Edward, 19, 225
Saint-Saëns, Camille, 113
Sales outlets for recorded music. *See* Retailing
  of records
Salter, Lionel, 199

Satie, Erik, 50
Saturday Review, 184
Saul, Patrick, 231
Scarlatti, Alessandro, 105
Schnittke, Alfred, 144
Schoenberg, Arnold, 38, 49, 55
Scholarly journals and music criticism, 184
Scholarly vs. trade-oriented discographies,
  220
Scholes, Percy, 36, 159, 233, 248–49
Schwann, William, 220
Schwann catalog, 220–21, 223, 250
Science vs. art, recording as, 75, 257n1
Scores, musical: in cover designs, 110–11; as
  precursor to mechanized recording, 10;
  reviewers' use of, 191–92, 196, 199, 202
The Sea (Bridge), 105
Second Viennese School, 116, 119
Self-service retailing and need for cover designs, 100
Sensuality as evil of popular music, 165
Seriousness discourse in classical music: and
  cover design traditions, 89, 110, 111, 118,
  123; and liner notes' scholarly tone, 140–41,
  148–49; magazine promotion of, 177; and
  moral crusade for classical music, 155, 165,
  216, 235–36
Sessions, Roger, 130
78 rpm records: and liner notes, 127–28;
  maintenance of, 137, 241; packaging, 92–
  93; punctuation issues, 132; recording re-
  strictions of, 40, 41, 64, *91;* reviewer analysis of, 191–92, 209; and shellac material,
  68–69, 90, 260n6
Shadwick, Keith, 234–35
Shahn, Ben, 105
Shawe-Taylor, Desmond, 19, 225
Sheet music, phonographic impact on, 35,
  101. *See also* Scores, musical
Shellac record material, 68–69, 90, 260n6
Shostakovich, Dmitry, 112, *120, 147*
Siefert, Marsha, 29
Signal-to-noise ratio, challenges of: and CD
  advantage, 80, 81; and musical verisimili-
  tude goal, 41; in technological progression,
  65, 66, 69
Simpson, Robert, 229
Single play (45 rpm) records, 100
Les Six, 115
Sleeves, record. *See* Cover design; Liner notes
Social context. *See* Cultural context
Social status of phonograph. *See* Cultural le-
  gitimacy for phonograph

Societies for record collectors, 214, 218–19
Solti, Georg, 44, 45
Sondek, Linn, 78
Sound archives, 230–31
Sound aspects of recording. *See* Engineering
  of recordings
Sousa, John Philip, 47
Souzay, Gérard, 105
Special Committee for the Promotion of
  New Music, 98–99
Spoken word collections, 130
Starker, Janos, 52
Steinweiss, Alex, 101
Stenographer, phonograph as, 20–21
Stephens, Denis, 82
Stereophile, 162
Stereo recording phase: cover advertising of,
  98; and editing issues, 71; need for listener
  training on, 84–86; overview of technical
  developments, *65;* and philosophy of re-
  corded sound, 58; and realism vs. idealism,
  65–66, 72–76; and reel-to-reel tape record-
  ing, 69; review architecture during, 194t,
  195t
Sterling, Louis, 27
Sterne, Laurence, 252
Stockhausen, Karlheinz, 144
Stoker, Bram, 37
Stokowski, Leopold, 40, 50, 54–55
Stone, Christopher, 66, 164
Storage of records, 89–95, 241, *242, 243*
The Strad, 184
Strauss, Richard, 115
Stravinsky, Igor: compositions designed for
  recording, 52; enthusiasm for jazz, 51; re-
  corded sound as too perfect, 46; sponsor-
  ship of audio equipment, *53, 54;* support
  for concert hall norm, 61–62
Stromberg-Carlson, *53*
Studios, recording: acoustic orchestration
  techniques, 58; conditions in, 39–40, 45–
  46, 261n22; and control of musical compo-
  sition, 49; and editing power, 41–42;
  musicians' response to early, 38–42
Styluses for 78s and LPs, 41, 54, 64–65, 137,
  256n9
Suite Provençal (Milhaud), 142
Sullivan, Sir Arthur, 39
Super audio compact discs (SACD), 77
Super-realism in recording, 72–86
Supply of works and need for reviewer analy-
  sis, 205, 272n17
Surround sound, 77, 260n12

Surveys, magazine, 177
Les Sylphides (Chopin), 101
Symphonia Domestica (Strauss), 115
Szell, George, 139–40

Tainter, Charles, 11
Talking machine and etymology of phonographic terms, 20
Tape, magnetic, recording with, 41–42, 56,
  68, 69–71
Tate, Alfred O., 22
Taubman, Howard, 73
Technological developments: and acoustic-
  to-digital progression, 62–66, 80–83; and
  active leisure time, 154–56; and continual
  rebirth of recorded music, 9; electronic instrumentation, 50; full-frequency range recording, 68, 196; in graphic design, 107–8;
  and liner notes, 125–31; and magazine development, 161, 162–63, 178; musicians' responses to, 38–42, 54–55; and punctuation
  in longer playing formats, 131–32; and recognition of recording creators, 136; recording societies' promotion of, 219; reviewer analysis of, 197, 201–2; textual
  support for, 15–16, 18, 137–39, 152–53. *See
  also* Digital technology; *specific recording
  formats*
Telarc record label, 136, 139, 190
Telegraph as precursor to phonograph, 11
Telharmonium, 50
Templates for record review sections, 194t,
  195t, 197–98
Temporal effects of phonograph: and digital
  annihilation of time/space, 250; perma-
  nence of sound recording, 10–14, 29, 37, 43,
  63, 248; time compression, 12–13, 61, 247
Textual context for recorded music. *See* Col-
  lectors/collecting of recorded music;
  Cover design; Liner notes; Magazines,
  record
Theater of mind philosophy of recording,
  83–86
Thematic titles, development of, 139–40
Theory of recording, lack of, 34
Theremin, 50
Timely orientation of magazines, 167–70, 185,
  208
Tippett, Michael, 118
Titling devices and record covers, 96, 139
Toscanini, Arturo, 40
Tracking of recorded music, 132–33
Trade catalogs, 220–21, 222, 223

Trademarks: development of, 17, 27, 28, 29,
  30; and naming conventions, 96, 134, 136.
  See also His Master's Voice (HMV)
  trademark
Transducer metaphor: cover design's role,
  89; and EMG trademark, 17, 29; listener's
  role, 245; magazine's role, 153; record guide
  role, 236, 243; textual role, 15–16, 17, 212–13
Trompe l'oeil cover designs, 112, 114
Turntables as musical instruments, 52

Ulysses (Joyce), 37
United record label, 112

Varèse, Edgard, 50
Variations for Orchestra (Schoenberg), 55
Venus and Adonis (Blow), 105
Verisimilitude, musical: advertising promotion of, 29, 64, 173, 174, 176; and live concert standard, 62; signal-to-noise ratio
  challenges to, 41; tests for, 67, 79
Verne, Jules, 37
The Victor Book of the Opera, 229
Victor record label: advertising in magazines,
  156; catalog of, 221, 222; color coding of labels, 97; cultural legitimacy campaign for
  phonograph, 24–25, 27, 28; and domestication of phonograph, 63–64; and Victrola
  as generic term, 19. *See also* His Master's
  Voice (HMV) trademark; RCA Victor
  record label
Victrola as generic term for phonograph, 19,
  256n10
Vinyl material for LPs, 68–69, 135, 173
Vinylphiles, 82, 90, 262n7
Visual character of contemporary culture, 31–
  32, 88, 193, 197–98
Visual cues in listening to music, compensation for, 83, 193

Waart, Edo de, 43
Wagner, Richard, 84
Walton, William, 51
Weill, Kurt, 52
Weitz, Antoine, 115
Wilson, Percy, 67
Winter, Stefan, 148–49
Winter and Winter record label, 90, 148–49
Wire recording, 260n7
Women in classical music recording culture,
  268n29. *See also* Gendered nature of record
  culture
Woolf, Virginia, 257–58n8

Music/Culture

A series from Wesleyan University Press
Edited by George Lipsitz, Susan McClary, and Robert Walser

Angora Matta: Fatal Acts of North-South Translation
by Marta Elena Savigliano

False Prophet: Fieldnotes from the Punk Underground
by Steven Taylor

Phat Beats, Dope Rhymes: Hip Hop Down Under Comin' Upper
by Ian Maxwell

Locating East Asia in Western Art Music
edited by Yayoi Uno Everett and Frederick Lau

Making Beats: The Art of Sample-Based Hip-Hop
by Joseph G. Schloss

Identity and Everyday Life: Essays in the Study of Folklore, Music and Popular Culture
by Harris M. Berger and Giovanna P. Del Negro

The Other Side of Nowhere: Jazz, Improvisation, and Communities in Dialogue
edited by Daniel Fischlin and Ajay Heble

Setting the Record Straight: A Material History of Classical Recording
by Colin Symes

ABOUT THE AUTHOR

Colin Symes is a lecturer in the School of Education, Australian Center for Educational Studies, Macquarie University. He is the author of several recent books, including *Working Knowledge: The New Vocationalism and Higher Education*, and his work has appeared in such journals as *Popular Music*, *Time and Society*, and *Mosaic*.